An Economic Analysis of the Family

An Economic Analysis
of the Family

John F. Ermisch

PRINCETON UNIVERSITY PRESS

PRINCETON AND OXFORD

Copyright © 2003 by Princeton University Press
Published by Princeton University Press, 41 William Street,
Princeton, New Jersey 08540
In the United Kingdom: Princeton University Press,
3 Market Place, Woodstock, Oxfordshire OX20 1SY

Library of Congress Cataloging-in-Publication Data
Ermisch, John.
  An economic analysis of the family / John F. Ermisch
    p. cm.
  Includes bibliographic references and index.
  ISBN 0-691-09667-8 (alk. paper)
    1. Family--Economic aspects. I. Title.
  HQ518 .E76 2003
  306.85--dc21
                          2002192462

British Library Cataloguing-in-Publication Data is available

This book has been composed in Sabon

Printed on acid-free paper ∞

www.pupress.princeton.edu

Printed in the United States of America

10 9 8 7 6 5 4 3 2 1

To Dianne

Contents

Preface

IN THE TWENTY YEARS since Nobel Laureate Gary Becker published his *Treatise on the Family* there has been a large amount of theoretical and applied research based on his original idea that the standard analytical methods of microeconomics can help us understand family behaviour. It is no longer necessary to offer a defence for using the tools of economic analysis in the study of the family. They have proved very fruitful. Many economists whose primary interests were not issues like marriage, fertility, household production and divorce have both drawn on and contributed to family economics because it helped them understand more mainstream economic issues. The purpose of this book is to present the main elements of the economic analysis of the family in an integrated way, providing examples of empirical studies from a variety of international contexts to help bring the theory to life. I am indebted to the many economists who have contributed to the economic analysis of the family, upon whose work this book is based. The main contributors will be evident from the references throughout the book, but there are many more who have made this field of study what it is today. I am grateful to Ken Burdett for his major contribution to the analysis of single mothers reported in Chapter 7 and for general discussions concerning the analysis of matching in marriage markets. I would like to thank Janice Webb for preparing the figures in the book and for the preparation of the final manuscript. I am also grateful to the Research Resources Unit of the Institute of Social and Economic Research at the University of Essex for their help in my review of the literature. Of course, I take full responsibility for the analysis and views reported in the book.

An Economic Analysis of the Family

CHAPTER ONE

Introduction

THE FAMILY has been undergoing dramatic changes during recent years. In richer countries, marriage and childbearing are occurring much later in people's lives, and they are having fewer children. There is more childbearing outside marriage, more divorce and more one parent families. In some poorer countries, fertility has fallen sharply, while in others there has been little change. Associated with these developments, there have been changes in the ways in which family members interact with one another, including support for elderly parents or children (e.g. payments after divorce), and with markets.

The analysis in this book aims to improve our understanding of how families and markets interact, why important aspects of families have been changing in recent decades and how public policy affects them. It is built on the idea that the standard analytical methods of microeconomics, including the techniques of constrained optimization, can help us to understand resource allocation and the distribution of welfare within the family, intergenerational transfers and transmission, family formation and dissolution and household formation. It also aims to show how economic theories of the family can help to guide and structure empirical analyses of demographic and related phenomena (e.g. labour supply and child support).

The book is intended for research students, social scientists and policy makers who wish to learn how economists analyse family issues. The analysis is relevant to family behaviour in rich and poor countries. Examples of studies that apply the theory are provided throughout the book. This chapter outlines the main arguments of the book.

1.1 INTRA-HOUSEHOLD ALLOCATION

Analysis of the impact of many public policies and technological developments on the welfare of *individuals* requires that we take seriously the view that individualism is the foundation of microeconomic theory. The family is an important institution in the determination of an individual's welfare, and so we must try to understand behaviour within the family in order to assess the welfare consequences of policies and social developments. The analysis allows for individuals within a family to have different preferences.

When putting a social institution like the family under analytical scrutiny, it is helpful to assume that individuals understand their environment and act rationally to maximize their own welfare. This does not mean that people are perfect in these respects, but to focus on analysis of the institution, we abstract from idiosyncratic aspects of individual behaviour. A fruitful starting point is to assume that people act to maximize their welfare as they evaluate it, given the predicted behaviour of others. It provides a foundation for modelling cooperative behaviour within a family. Family members must obtain welfare from cooperation that is at least as high as they would achieve from this non-cooperative outcome.

Chapter 2 focuses on the behaviour of couples with children. Decisions about when to have children and how many to have are considered later. Benefits from expenditure on children are assumed to be a "public good" for the parents, in the sense that an individual parent's welfare from total expenditures on children is not affected by the presence of the other parent. Suppose initially that the parents do not cooperate in making decisions in the sense that each parent chooses his(her) contribution to child expenditures to maximize his(her) welfare, taking the contribution of their partner as given. There are two types of outcome from this behaviour. When one parent's share of total income is not "sufficiently different" from the other's, both contribute to child expenditures, and only joint family income matters for expenditures on children and each parent's expenditure on him(her)self. How much is "sufficiently different" depends on each parent's preferences. If, however, one parent has a relatively small share of family income, then that parent will not contribute to child expenditures. In contrast to the first type of outcome, redistribution of income between parents affects expenditures on children, private expenditure and individual welfare.

The non-cooperative outcome is inefficient (i.e. one parent could be made better off while not making the other worse off), because it encourages "free riding" on the other parent. The best strategy for one parent is to reduce his(her) contribution to expenditure on children when the other parent increases hers(his), and this usually produces too little expenditure on children relative to the efficient level. This non-cooperative model can indicate what the "fallback position" would be if communication and bargaining within the family break down, and how individual preferences and incomes affect this fallback position.

Cooperation between parents is usually a better representation of family behaviour. It achieves an efficient allocation between parents' private consumption and child expenditure. For the types of individual preferences usually assumed in economic analysis, the outcome is equivalent to giving each parent a share of joint family income and letting each choose his(her) consumption and his(her) contribution to child expenditure according to his(her) own preferences. In other words, it is like there is an *income sharing rule*, which in general depends on individual incomes and prices and possibly other factors such as marriage market conditions and divorce laws. One interpretation of it is that it reflects bargaining within the family.

Each parent has the alternative of not cooperating, providing an alternative level of welfare, which is called their *threat point*. Corresponding to these threat points are minimum and maximum shares of income allocated to the mother in the cooperative outcome. Individual incomes can affect the cooperative outcome by affecting these threat points. One possible bargaining rule is to maximize the welfare of a "dominant partner". For example, if the husband were dominant, he would offer his wife just enough to accept this arrangement, which would be her threat point. Another rule is so-called "Nash bargaining", which maximizes the product of the parents' *gains from cooperation* (i.e. welfare in the cooperative outcome minus the threat point).

There are two prime candidates for the threat points: welfare if the parents divorce and welfare from a non-cooperative marriage, considered above. It is shown in Chapter 2 that divorce is often not a credible threat, even when welfare in the divorced state exceeds that from a non-cooperative marriage for both partners. This is because bargaining based on the threat points from a non-cooperative marriage produces a better welfare outcome for both parents than divorce. In this case, small changes in the welfare if divorced, say because of changes in welfare benefits to divorced mothers, have no impact on the cooperative outcome from bargaining. There are, however, situations when divorce is a credible threat, but then the outcome is not the one produced by Nash bargaining with the welfare if divorced as the threat points, but rather one partner is indifferent between divorce and marriage. In this case, the opportunities available to each parent if the relationship dissolved would affect allocation and distribution when the couple are together.

Bargaining within the family makes it possible that, for example, an increase in the mother's income has two effects. It increases family income, which increases expenditure on children and herself. It also may increase the bargaining power of the mother, which could reinforce or offset the income effects, depending on each parent's preferences for child expenditure. If, as many believe, mothers' preferences put more weight on children than fathers' preferences do, then an increase in her bargaining power would also increase expenditure on children. But note that if the threat points are determined by the outcome of a non-cooperative marriage in which both parents contribute to expenditure on children, then an increase in the mother's income would not affect her threat point or her bargaining power.

Traditional consumer theory usually assumes that the household behaves "as if" it is a single agent, allowing an application of the tools of consumer theory at the household level. This assumption, which is often called the "unitary model", or "consensus model", amounts to assuming that the income sharing rule does not vary with individual incomes. Thus, one important implication of it is that expenditure on children and each parent's private consumption depend only on total family income—the so-called "income pooling" hypothesis. Suppose, for example, that we were comparing two possible cash transfer policies, one which paid the transfer to the mother and the other which paid it to the father. Under the unitary model, expenditure patterns would be invariant to the policy chosen. When the sharing rule is affected by individual incomes, expenditures on children and private expenditure would depend on who received the transfer. An important real-world example of such a policy change in the United Kingdom during the late 1970s soundly rejects the unitary model, as do many other studies. This suggests that children do better when mothers control more of the family resources, that developments which improve women's earning opportunities affect the distribution of welfare within families and that it is possible to target policies on individuals within families.

1.2 ALTRUISM IN THE FAMILY

In economic analysis, a person is said to be *altruistic* toward someone if his(her) welfare depends on the welfare of that person. Altruism, or "caring", is usually defined such that the altruist's welfare depends on the "private utilities" of the altruist and his(her) beneficiary, each of which represents their "private preferences" defined over the person's private consumption and consumption of public goods, such as child expenditures. That is, the altruist's welfare does not depend on how the beneficiary's welfare is obtained. Chapter 3 focuses on the implications of a family decision making rule that maximizes an *effective* altruist's welfare. An altruist is *effective* if he(she) makes financial transfers to his(her) beneficiary, and this happens when he(she) is sufficiently rich relative to his(her) beneficiary.

Maximizing the welfare of an *effective* altruist has some important implications. First, redistribution of income between the altruist and his(her) beneficiary has no effect on outcomes, provided that he(she) remains an effective altruist. Shifting income from him(her) to his(her) beneficiary would produce an offsetting reduction in transfers to him(her). This means that the income sharing rule is independent of individual incomes.

Altruistic behaviour also provides partial insurance. Suppose that the beneficiary lost his(her) job, causing a fall in his(her) income. Both parties would suffer a decline in welfare, but part of his(her) welfare loss would be offset by higher transfers from the altruist. For the same reason, it also partially insulates them from targeted changes in taxes and benefits.

If private preferences take a particular form, effective altruism also has powerful effects on incentives. A selfish beneficiary has the incentive to choose the efficient level of a public good consumed by both, or alternatively is perfectly content to let the altruist choose it, even though their preferences differ. More generally, both parties would take actions that raise their *joint* income and avoid actions that lower it. This is what Gary Becker has called the "Rotten Kid Theorem". But the existence of altruistic preferences per se does not eliminate conflict and generate efficient outcomes. When individual incomes are similar, an *effective* altruist may not emerge.

Unfortunately, it is not difficult to find preferences for which even effective altruism does not automatically align the interest of the beneficiary with those of the altruist, in contrast to what the Rotten Kid Theorem would suggest. Except for a very special case of altruistic preferences, a *necessary* condition for such conflict to be avoided is that private preferences take a particular form analysed in Chapter 3.

The Rotten Kid Theorem suggests that parents should delay transfers to their children until late in their lifetime or indeed until after their death, because this provides children with a long-run incentive to consider the interests of the entire family and maximize joint family income. Thus, it suggests that altruistic parents should use bequests rather than gifts. But if beneficiaries suffer disutility of effort in earning their income, bequests discourage effort by the child, because effort is costly and parents compensate for exerting less effort through larger bequests. Because bequests are inefficient, the Rotten Kid Theorem does not hold. Gifts (pre-committed fixed transfers) are preferable in the sense that they are efficient for the family because they only have an income effect. The child is worse off than if he(she) received bequests, because he(she) could work less and obtain higher transfers with bequests, but the parents are better off.

This is an example of the general phenomenon called the "Samaritan's dilemma." It arises when a benefactor's generosity encourages beneficiaries to be less self-sufficient. In the context of saving decisions, parents' bequests to their child encourage him(her) to over-consume early in life in order to be more impoverished and receive larger bequests later. He(she) does, however, have an incentive to maximize joint family income with bequests. If the parents pre-commit to gifts, he(she) allocates his(her) lifetime income efficiently between periods, but once he(she) has received the gift, he(she) would wish to take actions that maximize his(her) own income, even if it reduced joint family income. Thus, bequests would produce an inefficient outcome because of the Samaritan's dilemma, while gifts would be inefficient because of the failure of the Rotten Kid Theorem. Even effective altruism fails to produce efficient outcomes in this situation, irrespective of whether transfers are given "early" or "late".

1.3 HOME PRODUCTION AND INVESTMENT

Many goods important to the family, such as investment in children, are "produced" by the family themselves through the combination of parents' time and purchased goods and services. To take a trivial example, the production of meals and the nutrition of family members require someone's time and food purchased on the market. The division of parents' labour and the implications for the costs of home-produced goods, such as the child's human capital, depend on these "home production" relationships. In many respects this is a straightforward application of production and cost analysis from the theory of the firm, but it is helpful to put it in the family context.

Parents can make investments in their own human capital that improve their earning power or their productivity in home production of goods such as their children's human capital. There is substantial evidence, for instance, that more experience in paid employment increases a person's wage. Suppose that this takes the form of simple learning-by-doing. The more a parent works in paid employment, the higher the wage and therefore the cost of his(her) time in home production. If learning-by-doing is sufficiently strong, it leads to complete specialization in market production by one parent. Small differences in wages could tip the balance in favour of complete specialization in paid work by one parent, even though both have exactly the same ability and each parent's time is equally productive in home production. If, for example, sex discrimination in the labour market makes men's wages higher than women's for a given level of human capital, then specialized human capital investments could result in women doing all of the home production and men specializing in market production.

Similar results emerge if home productivity increases with time spent in home production. If, for example, the woman's role in childbearing gives her a comparative advantage in home production, this could tip the balance toward her contributing all of the home production time when there is learning-by-doing in home production.

Household production theory is primarily used in the book to represent family investments in children's human capital that require parents' time and goods. But it also aids in estimating and interpreting relationships that summarize more specific family activities, such as those that promote the health of family members and those that control fertility. Chapter 4 considers the production of "healthy infants", as indicated by birth weight, the health of family members through nutritional intake, and the "reproduction function", which relates contraceptive use, natural fecundity and luck to the number of births.

1.4 INVESTMENTS IN AND FINANCIAL TRANSFERS TO CHILDREN

Generations are linked by parents' gifts and bequests to their children and by investment in their children's human capital, which affect their earnings and income when they become adults. Whether and how these two types of intergenerational transfer depend on parents' resources and other aspects of family background such as parents' education are studied in Chapter 5. It is assumed that parents care about their children's incomes as adults.

Suppose first that parents have only one child. If parents are rich enough to make financial transfers to their child, then investment in the child's human capital (e.g. his educational level) does not depend on parents' incomes. Parents invest in their child's human capital up to the point that its marginal return equals its marginal cost. Thus, parents make an efficient investment in their child's human capital and then make financial transfers to their child according to their incomes and preferences.

If parents are too poor to make transfers, in the sense that the marginal utility of their own consumption exceeds the marginal utility of transfers, then parents invest less than the efficient amount, and human capital investment depends on their incomes. This suggests three separate effects of, for example, a mother's education on the education of her child. First, there is an *income effect*, which is positive because more educated women earn more. Second, there is a *bargaining effect*, which is positive if mothers' preferences put more weight on the child's income than fathers' and higher education and income increases her bargaining power. Thirdly, there is a *substitution effect*, which depends on any impact of mother's education on the cost of human capital investment in children.

Investments in children may be riskier than many financial investments that the parents could make. Parents' preferences and incomes would then also matter for the human capital investment among parents who are rich enough to make financial transfers to their child, because of variation in parents' risk aversion with the child's income as an adult. For instance, parents would increase the level of (risky) human capital investment when their own income is larger if they are less averse to risk when their child's future income is larger.

With more than one child, how might parents treat their different children if they are equally concerned about each? Suppose parents' preferences are defined over the total income of each child as an adult. If the parents are sufficiently wealthy to make financial transfers to each of their children, then parents invest in the human capital of each child up to the point that the marginal return equals its marginal cost. Parents invest more in the human capital of a more able child, who then ends up with higher earnings, but a less able child is *fully* compensated by higher monetary transfers in the form of gifts and bequests. Financial transfers would generally differ substantially among children in the family.

Alternatively, parents' preferences may weight children's earnings differently from income derived from parents' gifts and bequests. In this case, financial transfers are the same for each child, and parents' human capital investments may *reinforce* or *compensate* for differences in children's "earnings endowments", depending upon their aversion to inequality between children's earnings. With reinforcement, the ratio of human capital investment (e.g. education levels) between children is larger than the ratio of endowments, and with compensation the opposite is the case. If parents are extremely averse to inequality between children, they invest in the human capital of their children so as to eliminate differences in earnings between children; that is, only equity considerations matter. When there is no inequality aversion, only efficiency matters. In general, both equity and efficiency considerations play a role in parents' human capital investment decisions. Chapter 5 considers the implications of these two models for estimating the returns from education, how we might choose between the two and how we can estimate whether parents compensate for or reinforce differences between their children in innate endowments.

1.5 ECONOMIC THEORIES OF FERTILITY

An important idea in the modern theory of fertility is that the psychic satisfaction parents receive from their children is likely to depend on the amount that parents spend on them as well as the number of children that they have. Gary Becker calls children who have more spent on them "higher quality" children, the basic idea being that if parents voluntarily spend more on a child, it is because they obtain additional satisfaction from the additional expenditure. It is this additional satisfaction that is called "higher quality". "Child quality" is now usually identified with the lifetime well-being of the child, which can be increased by investing more in the child's human capital or by the direct transfer of wealth to the child. An increase in parents' income may increase the amount spent on children substantially, but this would mainly take the form of higher quality rather than more children. In other words, the income elasticity of the number of children ("quantity") is probably small compared to the income elasticity of child quality.

It is often assumed that parents view child quantity and quality as substitutes and that they treat all their children equally, in the sense that child quality is the same for each of their children. In this case, their budget constraint contains the product between the number of children and child quality, which implies that the cost (or "shadow price") of an additional child is proportional to the level of child quality, and the cost ("shadow price") of raising child quality is proportional to the number of children the parents have. As a consequence, there is an important interaction between family size and child quality. Suppose, for example, that there is a decline in the cost of averting births, say because of the introduction of the oral contraceptive pill, which increases the net marginal cost of a birth without affecting the marginal cost of child quality, thereby reducing family size. This lowers the shadow price of child quality, which in turn raises child quality, which raises the shadow price of children, which lowers family size further, and so on. Lower contraception costs can, therefore, produce *large* increases in child quality and further large declines in fertility. Family size can be highly responsive to changes in prices and incomes, even though children have no close substitutes.

A higher return to human capital increases desired child quality, and through a similar cumulative process reduces fertility and raises human capital investment. Thus, the increases in the returns to human capital investment associated with technical change lead to simultaneous reductions in fertility and increases in human capital investment in children, thereby accounting for important stylized facts of economic development.

Now suppose that there is an increase in parents' income. If the quality income elasticity exceeds the one for quantity, then the ratio of quality to the number of children rises, thereby increasing the shadow price of an additional child relative to the shadow price of child quality. The substitution effect induced by this increase may be sufficiently large to produce a decline in fertility when income increases. It may, therefore, appear that the income elasticity of fertility is negative, even though children are "normal goods", in the sense that parents want more of them when parental income increases.

The factors affecting the cost of children are closely associated with the key role of parental time in the rearing of and investment in children. Parental time in the production of child quality is primarily the mother's time, and the rearing of children is assumed to be *time intensive* relative to other home production activities. Thus, the cost of children relative to the cost of the parents' living standard is directly related to the mother's cost of time. If she has ever been in paid employment, her cost of time is the wage she could earn in employment (i.e. her foregone earnings). The higher her wage, the higher the cost of an additional child and of additional quality per child relative to the cost of improving the parents' living standard. The relative cost of children also depends on the father's wage, but probably weakly.

Thus, there are two channels through which men's and women's wages affect fertility and child quality. Higher wages for either parent means higher family income, encouraging parents to have more children and to invest more in the human capital of each child or to make larger monetary transfers to them (i.e. higher quality). Higher women's wages also raise the opportunity cost of a child. If the opportunity cost effect on family size (child quality) dominates the income effect of women's wages, higher women's wages reduce family size (child quality). Higher men's wages mainly affect childbearing through their effect on the couple's income.

The possibility of purchasing child care, an imperfect substitute for the mother's time in child rearing, weakens the link between a woman's wage and the cost of an additional child. Mothers with high wages tend to purchase a much larger proportion of child care time. For them, higher wages have little effect on the cost of children, making it more likely that they increase fertility by raising family income. Similarly, in countries with heavily subsidized child care, mothers contribute much less to child care themselves, making it more likely that women earning higher pay have larger families. At low to moderate levels of wages, a higher mother's wage tends to reduce fertility, but its negative impact attenuates as her wage rises, or the price of child care falls, because mothers purchase a larger proportion of child care time. The impact of the price of child care on fertility displays a similar interaction, becoming more negative as the mother's wage rises.

Nevertheless, when examining changes over time, the cost of purchased child care and women's wages tend to move together, because women's labour is such an important input to the provision of child care services. Thus, over time we may still expect women's pay relative to men's and fertility to be negatively related, because higher women's pay raises the cost of children.

The ultimate manifestation of low child quality is a child not surviving to adulthood. In light of the *demographic transition* (i.e. the change from a high fertility–high child mortality environment to a low fertility–low mortality one), an interesting question is how fertility responds to changes in the "risk" of child mortality. An autonomous increase in the probability of child survival (e.g. from better water supply or public health) has conflicting impacts. On the one hand, it reduces the price of a surviving birth, thereby encouraging higher fertility. But if parents can influence the chances that their own children survive to become adults by spending more on each child, then it is *possible* that better chances of child survival reduce fertility, provided that exogenous factors affecting child survival substitute for parents' expenditure.

If we wish to consider decisions about the timing of births, imperfect fertility control, or the consequences of unexpected outcomes like birth control failure or child mortality, a dynamic model is needed. Chapter 6 surveys some of these.

1.6 MATCHING IN THE MARRIAGE MARKET

The process of finding a spouse is one in which information is scarce, and it takes time to gather it. These market frictions affect who marries whom, the gains from each marriage and the distribution of gains between spouses. From an individual woman's (or man's) point of view, higher welfare when single, faster arrival of marriage offers and a higher maximum attainable offer allow her to be choosier when selecting a husband. A higher discount rate makes her less choosy, and a higher divorce rate has the same effect because it reduces the perceived benefits from waiting for a better match by making it more likely that a woman will return to the single state.

The behaviour of both sexes is integrated in a marriage market equilibrium in Chapter 7. Suppose first that people's utility from a marriage depends on their "type" of partner, which can be characterized by various attributes associated with their "attractiveness" as a husband or wife, and that there is no way to "transfer utility" between spouses. The latter assumption means that an individual who would obtain large gains from a match with a particular partner cannot compensate that potential partner to ensure the match is made. Then if marriage market frictions are not too large, positive assortative mating by attractive attributes emerges.

Alternatively, if we assume away frictions, but allow "transferable utility", there is, in effect, a price mechanism that ensures that jointly efficient matches are made and that each match can be characterized by the "total utility" it generates. Suppose that each person is endowed with a single attribute (e.g. education), which has a positive effect on total utility from the marriage. Positive (negative) assortative mating with respect to the attribute occurs when attributes are complements (substitutes) in the production of total utility in the marriage, in the sense that the marginal product of one person's attribute is increasing (decreasing) in the attribute of the spouse. With frictions in searching for a partner, it is no longer the case that complementary inputs necessarily generate positive assortative mating.

In the absence of search frictions, the equilibrium outcome is socially efficient. But search frictions produce "sorting externalities", which lead to an inefficient equilibrium. When a man and woman meet, they only match if it is jointly efficient to do so, but by leaving the marriage market they change the composition of types in the market, which affects the expected returns to search for single persons in the market. Their failure to take into account the impact of their match on the welfare of singles in the market produces the inefficiency.

Marriage market frictions also open the possibility of childbearing outside marriage. When a man and women meet, the man can choose to marry the woman, or not, if she will have him. While a woman faces the same choice when she meets a man, she can also choose to have a child by the man and then raise it without the father. Depending on the social welfare system she faces, and whether the father is willing to contribute resources, a woman's welfare when raising a child by herself may be greater than what she obtains when single and childless. But there are also costs in terms of marriage market prospects associated with raising a child alone. A single woman with child may find it more difficult to contact potential husbands while looking after a child. A woman who contacts a man she does not wish to marry, or who will not marry her, would choose to have a child by the man if the short-run gain exceeds the long-term costs in terms of her marriage prospects. Those women who expect to obtain a significant increase in welfare when they marry suffer a greater long-term cost by having a child while single than women whose marriage prospects are such that they expect to gain little from marriage. Thus, women with poorer marriage prospects are more likely to have children outside marriage.

1.7 Divorce and Child Support

As mentioned earlier, expenditure on children, such as investment in their human capital, is considered to be a public good to the parents. When living together, they choose the efficient level of this public good. But after breaking up, the mother usually obtains custody of the children and she decides the level of expenditure on children. Her former husband can only influence it by making transfers to his former wife. This is plausible because the father cannot usually monitor the division of his transfer between expenditure on children and the mother's consumption, particularly expenditure on young children. The allocation of resources to child expenditure implied by this "contract" is not efficient, because the mother does not take into account the effect of her choices on the welfare of the father. The inefficiency can be interpreted as an *agency* problem— the father can only indirectly affect child expenditure through his ex-wife's choices.

Any such transfers from the father to the mother are voluntary on his part. He makes them because more expenditure on children increases his welfare. He will only make such transfers if his income is "high enough" relative to the mother's income, and this threshold depends on his preferences for child expenditure relative to hers. He will transfer more to the mother the higher his income and the lower is hers. A key feature of the relationship between transfers and child expenditure is that he must transfer more than $1 to obtain $1 more expenditure on children, because the mother spends part of the transfer on herself. In other words, he faces a higher effective price for child expenditure when divorced than when he was married, encouraging him to spend less on children after divorce (perhaps nothing), resulting in a lower level of expenditure on children overall.

The probability that a couple divorce is inversely related to the efficiency loss associated with divorce. It is smaller the higher is either spouse's income, because the efficiency loss is larger for a higher desired level of expenditure on children, which increases with income.

Courts or government agencies often stipulate a minimum level of child support payments. Enforcement is not, however, likely to be perfectly effective. A policy that provided better enforcement of child support orders would either increase child support transfers or have no effect on them (because the father already paid more than the ordered amount). Such a policy would also raise expenditure on children among families in which child support increased thereby improving some children's welfare and having no effect on others. But there is another view of the role of child support orders.

Divorced parents and their children could be better off if they could come to a cooperative agreement on resource allocation. There are, of course, an infinite number of such efficient allocations, each involving different amounts of transfers from the father to the mother and entailing different levels of expenditure on children. The court can resolve this indeterminacy by in effect "suggesting" a given cooperative allocation indirectly through the child support order. If the cooperative allocation implied by that order gives each of the parents higher welfare than they would obtain in the non-cooperative contract just described, then they cooperate. There is a maximum level of child support that the father would pay in the cooperative equilibrium, and a minimum transfer that the mother would accept. If the court sets an order in this range, the divorced couple cooperate and the father pays the ordered amount of child support, even though it may be above the transfer that he would pay in the non-cooperative equilibrium. This is because the efficiency gains from cooperation are sufficient for the father to agree to cooperate and transfer more. If the support order is below the bottom of this range, the mother would not agree to cooperate, despite the fact that the order exceeds what she receives from the father in the non-cooperative equilibrium.

This model has implications for the impact of better enforcement of child support orders. If some parents were induced by the child support order to cooperate when there was no enforcement, perfect enforcement would reduce expenditure on children among this group of parents. The reason is that perfect enforcement changes the order from being a suggested efficient outcome to being the starting point of a bargaining situation between the parents in which their income distribution shifts from the father to the mother by the amount of the child support order. The result is a non-cooperative outcome, which produces lower expenditures on children. In other words, with perfect enforcement, the court becomes an agent for income redistribution rather than an arbitrator who leads some couples to an efficient allocation.

Chapter 8 shows that there are more efficient marriage contracts that specify transfers if the couple divorce. The divorce settlement in these tends to prevent a large discrepancy in each party's welfare between marriage and divorce, thereby providing partial insurance. But these contracts are not likely to be enforceable.

In light of the efficiency losses associated with divorce, behaviour within marriage is likely to be affected by its possibility. If, for example, more participation in paid employment raises future wages, it is likely that the risk of divorce encourages more paid employment by the mother during marriage and, by raising the cost of child quality, lower expenditure on children and lower fertility. These "defensive investments" are undertaken to increase utility later, when utility outcomes are uncertain because of the possibility of divorce.

Divorce law confers certain rights concerning marital dissolution. They define, for each spouse, an *outside option*. For a law that allows unilateral divorce, the outside option is divorce. Either spouse can, without consent of the other, force the marriage to dissolve. With a law requiring mutual consent for divorce, the outside option is marriage. Either party can refuse to divorce, and without consent of the other, force the marriage to continue.

There are situations in which the law does not matter. Even if, for example, the husband would gain from divorce, his wife may be able to compensate him for staying in the marriage by some change in the way the marriage is conducted. Thus, even if there were unilateral divorce, he would not seek a divorce. In effect, he sells his right to divorce under a unilateral divorce law. A husband who gains from divorce may be able to compensate a wife who loses from divorce by a suitable divorce settlement so that she would also be better off from divorce. Thus, even under a mutual consent law, they would divorce. In effect, she sells her right to the marriage under a mutual consent law.

There are, however, also situations in which divorce would occur under a unilateral divorce law, but not with a divorce law requiring mutual consent, and vice versa. In these situations, a change in the law, including laws relating to marital property and divorce settlements, could affect whether couples divorce, and the outcome is efficient.

1.8 Non-Altruistic Family Transfers

Can inter vivos transfers between generations within a family be explained by pure self-interest? In the usual model of consumer theory resources are transferred through time by borrowing and lending in the capital market. But suppose there is no such market, or that the person does not have access to it, say because of difficulties in monitoring loans or very large transaction costs. An extended family network including three generations at different stages of life could substitute for a capital market by arranging "loans" to its young members from its middle-aged ones and enforcing repayment later when the young borrowers have become middle-aged and the middle-aged lenders have become old. In this situation, selfish people only have children because they are needed to transfer resources through time. Chapter 9 shows how such an intra-family transfer system can work.

The family transfer rules are set so that it is not possible to devise a different set of family rules that makes any generation better off without making another generation worse off. Once established, these rules would persist over generations until there is a change of circumstances outside the family. Each generation would, of course, prefer that transfers to it when a child be as large as possible and that its transfers to aged parents when middle-aged be as small as possible. But since everyone needs the family transfer rules to survive in old age, the prospect of receiving no support from the family in old age deters any member from disobeying the rules. These rules also determine fertility. Larger transfers to the elderly relative to those to children increase the fertility required to sustain the family system.

Now suppose that the family has access to a capital market, but that nobody outside the family would lend to a child. The middle-aged now have a choice between providing for their old age by lending in the capital market or by staying within the family system and "lending" to their children, awaiting transfers from them in old age. If the market interest rate is high enough, the middle-aged would be better off by lending to the market than remaining in the family system. A threat of no support from the family in old age is no longer a deterrent, because they can make their own provision for old age through the market.

The opening of a capital market offering a sufficiently high interest rate, or an unexpected rise in the interest rate to such a level in an existing market, toll the death knell for this family system of transfers. Childbearing would also cease in this model of selfish persons. In broad terms, the prediction of this model is consistent with the observation that the growth of the financial sector (or introduction of a state pension system) tends to coincide with a sharp fall in fertility and a decline in private transfers from the middle-aged to their elderly parents. The fact that fertility does not fall to zero, even for couples who make no contribution to the consumption of their own parents (and expect their children to do the same), suggests that the demand for children is not entirely derived from the need for transfers from them to finance consumption in old age.

Adult children can also provide "services" to their parents that do not have clear market substitutes, such as companionship, attention and conforming their behaviour to their parents' wishes. An increase in such services tends to reduce a selfish child's well-being because it undermines his(her) independence and may use scarce non-working time. Parents make transfers to their child in exchange for these services. Higher parents' income always increases their demand for services and therefore transfers. Higher child's income has an ambiguous effect on transfers. On the one hand, transfers tend to decrease because higher child's income increases joint family income, which increases the parents' consumption. On the other hand, the parents must compensate the child by more to achieve the same level of services because the welfare the child requires to participate in the service arrangement increases with his(her) income. If the latter effect dominates, then the positive impact of child's income on transfers from parents is the opposite to that when altruistic motives dominate parents' transfer decisions.

Parents' inter vivos transfers to their children could also reflect a situation in which parents have access to a capital market, but their adult children are not able to borrow against their future income. This can arise because young adults have not yet established their reputation with lenders. Even though many are a good credit risk, financial intermediaries may not lend to them because they do not know this. The parents of these young adults have an informational advantage on other lenders. They have better information about whether their child will repay a loan. Selfish parents would exploit their bargaining power and charge their child an interest rate in excess of the market rate.

Higher income for the child when he(she) is a young adult (for given future income) raises the family wealth. In this intra-family lending arrangement, the parents wish to share in this higher family wealth in terms of higher first period consumption, which encourages them to make smaller transfers. But higher child's income also increases the bargaining power of the child because his(her) welfare outside the family lending arrangement increases, and this improves the terms of the family loan from the child's point of view, leading to larger transfers. The net effect is unclear, but it is possible that a higher child's income could increase transfers to him(her), in contrast to what altruistic motives would suggest. Furthermore, higher parents' income does not affect transfers, because these are determined by the child's demand for loans. Also, the probability of receiving transfers is directly related to the child's income later in life, another prediction that contrasts with what altruistic motives would suggest (i.e. no relation).

Chapter 9 also considers the interaction between transfers from parents to their children and the labour market effort of children (e.g. their labour supply). A child's earnings are determined in part by the effort that he(she) expends, but also by luck. His(her) effort may not, however, be observed by his(her) parents (i.e. it is private information), and while parents want to help their children financially when they need it, they also want them to behave responsibly in the sense of expending sufficient effort to support themselves. Transfers from parents may decline or increase with higher child's income depending on the balance of altruistic motives and the aim to provide an incentive for high effort.

1.9 HOUSEHOLD FORMATION

Sharing housing and other consumer durable goods is an implicit transfer that can fully or partially substitute for financial transfers motivated by either exchange or altruistic motives. It is a key factor in household formation decisions (for reasons other than marriage). As a child who becomes an adult starts out in the parental home, there is likely to be asymmetry in bargaining power between them. If the parents are selfish, they could use their bargaining power to extract the child's gain from the joint consumption economies that arise when they live together. As the predictions of such a model, derived in Chapter 10, are opposite to most empirical evidence, the analysis focuses on parents with altruistic preferences.

It suggests that higher parental income should reduce the probability that the child lives apart from his(her) parents, while higher child's income should increase this probability. When parents do not make financial transfers, higher parental income increases the chances of co-residence because it increases the amount of (joint) housing consumption in the parental home relative to that when living apart. Without financial transfers, higher child's income means that he(she) can more easily afford to purchase his(her) own housing. If financial transfers are made when living apart, but not when living together, higher parental income increases the chances of co-residence because parents would like to provide more help to their child when their income is higher and it is cheaper to do so when living together because of the public good aspect of housing. Conversely, when the child's income is higher, parents choose to provide less help to their child, thereby reducing the need for co-residence to provide support.

The impact of the price of housing on the probability of living apart is intimately related to the price elasticity of parents' housing demand when parents do not make financial transfers to their child. When it is less than a critical value, a higher price of housing reduces the probability that the young adult lives apart from his(her) parents, but the opposite is true if it is above the critical value. These predictions reflect the fact that a higher housing price reduces the child's welfare in the parental home as well as when he(she) lives away from home. If parents did not adjust their housing consumption (zero price elasticity of housing demand), then a young adult's housing and welfare in the parental household would not change, while his(her) utility when living apart would fall; thus, the probability of living apart would fall. When the parents' housing response is relatively small (inelastic housing demand), this fall in the probability continues to hold. If, however, parents' housing response is relatively elastic, a higher housing price entails that the young adult's utility falls more in the parental household as a consequence of the large decline in the public good available when living with parents.

1.10 SOCIAL INTERACTION

An individual's preferences, and therefore behaviour, may depend on what others in society are perceived to be doing. This may take the form of "learning" or "social influence". Certain decisions, particularly concerning the use of new technology, such as modern contraception, are subject to substantial uncertainty. Learning about other people's experiences through social interaction may reduce this uncertainty and make it more likely that a person adopts a new technology. Social influence captures the possibility that a person's preferences may be altered by those with whom the person interacts. For instance, childbearing outside marriage may be discouraged by social stigma when non-marital births are rare, but this stigma may be eroded as more childbearing is outside marriage.

If this type of social influence is large enough, it is possible that there is more than one stable equilibrium: one in which the phenomenon (e.g. non-marital childbearing) is rare and another in which it is common. If so, "history matters" for the selection of the low-level or high-level equilibrium. Furthermore, *temporary* changes in the socio-economic environment that alter, for example, non-marital childbearing behaviour and/or expectations, can produce dramatic changes in the proportion who become single mothers.

If social influence is relatively strong, but not large enough to produce multiple equilibria, small changes in the socio-economic environment, such as higher state benefits for single mothers, can still produce large changes in the proportion becoming single mothers and other social phenomena. There is a "multiplier effect" of such changes in the "fundamental" determinants of differences in utility between two actions. In other words, each person's actions change not only because of the direct change in some fundamental determinant, but also because of the change in the behaviour of their peers. If this social multiplier is large, populations with slightly different distributions of attributes or preferences could, for example, exhibit very different proportions of women who become single mothers. Social influence or social learning may also explain large and rapid fertility decline in one country or region while there is little change in another, which is similar in terms of socio-economic conditions.

Chapter 11 explores how information on the density of social networks can be used to distinguish between the dominance of social influence or social learning on fertility behaviour. If learning dominates, then both dense and sparse networks containing a larger proportion of women using modern contraceptive methods should increase the chances that a woman will adopt these methods. Because sparse networks are more efficient sources of information, the impact of density on these chances is either zero or negative. By integrating a woman into a larger group, dense networks are more likely to constrain a woman's ability to deviate from prevailing behaviour; that is, they exert a stronger normative influence than sparse networks. A woman's only alternative to agreeing with other members of this group may be to leave the group. If social influence dominates, then the proportion of women in a woman's social network using modern methods would have a weak effect on her adoption of these methods in sparse networks, but a strong effect in dense networks. That is, the impact of the proportion increases with the density of the network.

Social multipliers and multiple equilibria can also arise through market interactions. For instance, the expected gain from divorce depends on the prospects of remarriage. These prospects depend on the decisions of others to divorce and remarry. If many couples are expected to divorce, then the prospects of remarriage are high because there are more people in the remarriage market. Divorce is then less costly and each particular couple is more likely to decide to divorce. If instead the divorce rate is expected to be low, then divorce is more costly and is less likely to occur. Either a high-divorce or a low-divorce equilibrium may be supported with the same set of fundamental factors affecting divorce decisions. Much of this book focuses on decisions at the individual level and the impacts of prices and resources on them, but chapter 11 indicates that there are often these important feedback effects of the choices of one's peers on one's own choices.

This introductory chapter has suggested how economic analysis can derive predictions about family behaviour, particularly its response to developments in markets, to technological developments and to public policy. The remaining chapters provide details of these analyses, which hopefully provide the foundation for readers to apply these methods to a range of issues related to family behaviour.

CHAPTER TWO

Conflict and Cooperation in the Family: Intra-Household Allocation

2.1 INTRODUCTION

There are a number of economic advantages to forming a household with another person. First, there are joint consumption economies associated with "local public goods", such as housing. These are goods in which "individual consumption services" decline less than proportionately with the number of consumers of the good. In the extreme, if the public good is "pure", individual consumption services do not fall at all as the number of consumers increase (i.e. there is no "congestion" in the consumption of the good). Second, division of labour between household and labour market activities can be practised. The person with the higher wage can spend more time in the labour market while the lower wage person takes on more household activities. These two advantages apply to any two (or more) people living together. If, in addition, a conjugal relationship exists between them, living together facilitates the raising of their children.

A fruitful starting point in studying the family is to assume that each person will act to maximize his(her) welfare as he(she) evaluates it, given the predicted behaviour of others. The concept of "Nash equilibrium" is, in its essence, the general formulation of this assumption. Nash (1950b) defined an equilibrium of a non-cooperative game to be a profile of *strategies*, one for each "player in the game", such that each player's strategy maximizes their expected utility payoff against the given strategies of the other players. If behaviour does not satisfy the conditions for such a "Nash equilibrium", then at least one person could improve his(her) welfare, which violates our assumption about individual rationality. This is a useful solution concept to begin the analysis of incentives in the family.

Thus, we start by assuming that the behaviour of members of a family can be described by a Nash equilibrium. As will be shown, this is not because families are likely to behave in this non-cooperative way in most instances, but because it provides a foundation for modelling cooperative behaviour within a family. Family members must obtain welfare from cooperation that is at least as high as they would achieve from a Nash equilibrium. We then consider what are the appropriate threat points for cooperation through bargaining. We start with a simple model in which there is no home production, nor labour supply decisions by parents, but which yields some of the main insights into intra-household allocation/ distribution and expenditures on children. In the penultimate section of the chapter, we consider the advantages of household formation when there is household production but not household public goods and how the cooperative allocation is achieved in this case. The chapter concludes with a discussion of some empirical implications and studies of how relative incomes of members of a couple affect intra-household allocation decisions.

2.2 BASIC MODEL

The analysis in this chapter focuses on the behaviour of couples with children. Decisions about when to have children and how many to have are considered in Chapter 6. Benefits from children are assumed to be a public good for the parents, but each parent has his(her) own preferences. The preferences of each parent j are represented by the utility function $U^j = U^j(x_j, G)$, where G is the amount of a "child good" ("child quality"), which is a pure public good to the parents. It may represent expenditures on children, including investment in children's future earning capacity. Private consumption by parent j is denoted by x_j.

2.2.1 Non-Cooperative Equilibrium

In this section, we assume that members of a family cannot cooperate because they cannot communicate with one another, and so the best that they can do is behave according to the definition of a Nash equilibrium.[1] In the context of our basic model, each parent may make voluntary contributions to child expenditures. These are given by g_j ($g_j \geq 0$), and so $x_j = y_j - g_j$ and $G = (g_1 + g_2)/p$, where y_j is the income of parent j and p is the price of the child good relative to that of the private good. Each parent chooses his(her) contribution to child expenditures, g_j, to maximize their utility, taking the contribution of their partner as given (i.e. we are considering a Nash equilibrium). Thus, parent j chooses g_j to maximize $U^j(y_j - g_j, (g_1 + g_2)/p)$, subject to $g_j \geq 0$, which implies

$$\frac{U_G^j(x_j^*, G^*)}{U_x^j(x_j^*, G^*)} \leq p, \qquad j = 1, 2 \tag{2.1}$$

where U_i^j is the partial derivative of $U^j(x_j, G)$ with respect to its ith argument and the * indicates the optimum value given the partner's contribution to child expenditures. The left-hand side is the marginal rate of substitution (MRS) between the public and private good (given the other parent's contribution) and the right-hand side is the relative cost of the public good.

If (2.1) holds with equality for both parents, it provides two equations in g_1 and g_2, which describe their strategies, and these can be solved for the Nash equilibrium contribution. Thus, this is the model of the private provision of public goods, introduced by Warr (1982) and Bergstrom et al. (1986), applied to a family context. If, however, the inequality in (2.1) holds for parent j, his(her) contribution is zero. In other words, when parent j is "too poor", in the sense that their MRS is less than the marginal cost of the public good, that parent does not contribute to the public good. To be more concrete, let us assume a particular utility function: $U^j = \alpha_j \ln(x_j) + (1 - \alpha_j)\ln(G)$, which has the advantage that each parent's preferences are represented by one parameter, α_j. Without loss of generality we can define the units of G so that $p = 1$. Then, when $g_1 > 0$ and $g_2 > 0$, (2.1) implies

$$g_1 = (1 - \alpha_1)y_1 - (\alpha_1 g_2) \tag{2.2a}$$

$$g_2 = (1 - \alpha_2)y_2 - (\alpha_2 g_1) \tag{2.2b}$$

Equations (2.2a) and (2.2b) represent the strategies of each parent, often called their "reaction functions", which are illustrated in Figure 2.1, with $\alpha_1 > \alpha_2$. They show that the best strategy for one parent is to reduce his(her) contribution to expenditure on children when the other parent increases hers(his), and the amount of this reduction depends on their preferences, captured in the parameter α_j. The intersection of these two reaction functions yields the Nash equilibrium.

Thus, solving (2.2a) and (2.2b), the Nash equilibrium is given by

$$g_1^N = \frac{(1 - \alpha_1)y_1 - \alpha_1(1 - \alpha_2)y_2}{1 - \alpha_1\alpha_2} \tag{2.3a}$$

$$g_2^N = \frac{(1 - \alpha_2)y_2 - \alpha_2(1 - \alpha_1)y_1}{1 - \alpha_1\alpha_2} \tag{2.3b}$$

The contribution of parent j is increasing in their income and decreasing in the other parent's. From (2.3),

$$G^N = \frac{(1 - \alpha_1)(1 - \alpha_2)(y_1 + y_2)}{1 - \alpha_1\alpha_2} \tag{2.4a}$$

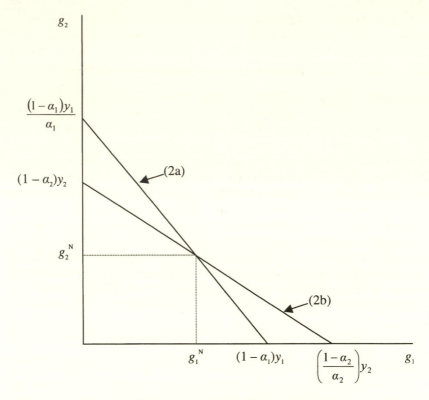

Figure 2.1 Reaction functions.

$$x_1^N = \frac{\alpha_1(1 - \alpha_2)(y_1 + y_2)}{1 - \alpha_1\alpha_2} \qquad (2.4b)$$

$$x_2^N = \frac{\alpha_2(1 - \alpha_1)(y_1 + y_2)}{1 - \alpha_1\alpha_2} \qquad (2.4c)$$

It is clear from (2.4) that when both parents contribute to child expenditures, only joint family income matters. Redistribution of income between parents has no effect on the choice of the level of child expenditures nor parents' private consumption.

This is not the case when only one parent makes contributions to child expenditure. Taking the father as parent 1, he will not contribute when

$$\frac{y_1}{y_1 + y_2} < \frac{\alpha_1(1 - \alpha_2)}{1 - \alpha_1\alpha_2} \qquad (2.5)$$

That is, when the father has a relatively small share of family income, $g_1 = 0$. It is clear from (2.5) that the dividing line of what is a "small

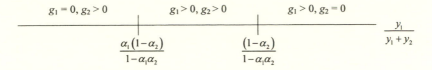

$g_1 = 0, g_2 > 0$ $g_1 > 0, g_2 > 0$ $g_1 > 0, g_2 = 0$

$$\dfrac{\alpha_1(1-\alpha_2)}{1-\alpha_1\alpha_2} \qquad \dfrac{(1-\alpha_2)}{1-\alpha_1\alpha_2} \qquad \dfrac{y_1}{y_1+y_2}$$

Figure 2.2   Contributions to child expenditure.

share" depends on the preferences of each parent. The inequality in (2.5) is more likely to hold if the father sufficiently favours private consumption over the public good (i.e. α_1 is "large") and/or the mother sufficiently favours child expenditure (i.e. α_2 is "small"). In this case, $G^N = (1 - \alpha_2)y_2$, $x_1^N = y_1$ and $x_2^N = \alpha_2 y_2$. Thus, redistribution from the mother to the father reduces G^N because the mother reduces her contribution, and x_2^N also declines. Conversely, redistribution in the other direction increases both G^N and x_2^N.

Using the analogous condition for no contribution by the mother, we see from Figure 2.2 that both parents contribute to child expenditure when the share of the father in family income ($y_1/(y_1 + y_2)$) is between $\alpha_1(1 - \alpha_2)/(1 - \alpha_1\alpha_2)$ and $(1 - \alpha_2)/(1 - \alpha_1\alpha_2)$. When the father's share exceeds $(1 - \alpha_2)/(1 - \alpha_1\alpha_2)$, only he contributes to child expenditure ($g_2 = 0$). Clearly the range over which both parents contribute depends on their preferences.

Again, it is not claimed that this model describes family behaviour. It can, however, indicate what the "fallback position" would be if communication and bargaining within the family break down, and how individual preferences and incomes affect this fallback position.

2.2.2 Cooperative Equilibrium

We now allow for communication and cooperation between parents to achieve an allocation between parents' private consumption and child expenditure such that one parent cannot be made better off without making the other worse off (i.e. a Pareto-efficient allocation). It must maximize the utility of one parent subject to the other achieving at least a given utility and to the resource constraint. That is, an efficient allocation must maximize $U^1(x_1, G)$ subject to: (a) $U^2(x_2, G) \geq U^{2^*}$ and (b) $y_1 + y_2 = x_1 + x_2 + pG$. Or equivalently, it must maximize $U^1(x_1, G) + \mu U^2(x_2, G)$ subject to constraint (b), where μ is the Lagrange multiplier associated with the "efficiency constraint" (a). This is what Chiappori (1992) calls the "collective" approach (model), and it is referred to as the cooperative model in the remainder of the book.

The solution to this problem implies that $U_x^1(x_1^e, G^e) = \mu U_x^2(x_2^e, G^e)$ and that

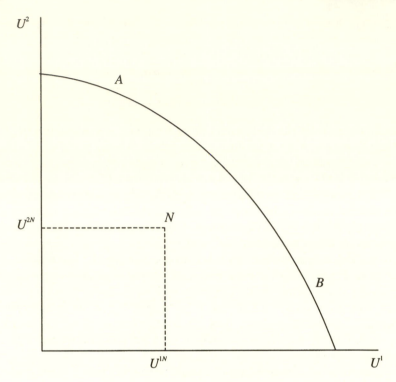

Figure 2.3   Utility possibility frontier.

$$p = \frac{U_G^1(x_1^e, G^e)}{U_x^1(x_1^e, G^e)} + \frac{U_G^2(x_2^e, G^e)}{U_x^2(x_2^e, G^e)} \qquad (2.6)$$

where the superscript e indicates an efficient solution. Condition (2.6) states that the marginal cost of providing the public good of child expenditure (p) equals the sum of the parents' marginal rates of substitution, which is the Samuelson (1954) condition for the efficient provision of public goods. Comparison of this condition with that given in (2.1) immediately suggests, as we would expect, that the non-cooperative equilibrium is inefficient.

By assuming different values of U^{2^*}, and substituting the solution into the father's utility function we trace out the *utility possibility frontier*, illustrated in Figure 2.3. This is the locus of Pareto optimal utility levels for the two parents corresponding to given values of y_1, y_2, p and the parameters of their utility functions. The non-cooperative Nash equilibrium of the previous section lies inside this frontier (e.g. point N). Cooperation between the parents would move them to the frontier, but there is clearly the potential for conflict, as higher welfare for one partner implies lower welfare for the other along the frontier.

The first- and second-order conditions for a maximum associated with the efficient allocation problem above imply (via the implicit function theorem) the following demand functions in terms of μ, joint parents' income and the price of the public good:

$$G = G^e(y_1 + y_2, p, \mu) \tag{2.7a}$$

$$x_j = x_j^e(y_1 + y_2, p, \mu), \qquad j = 1, 2 \tag{2.7b}$$

The implicit utility weighting factor μ indicates the location chosen on the utility possibility frontier. In general, μ is a function of individual incomes and the price of the public good (i.e. $\mu = \mu(y_1, y_2, p)$). Cooperation and efficiency are indicated by the presence of this common (unknown) function in all the demand functions. This common factor can be exploited to obtain cross-equation restrictions, which represent a test of intra-family efficiency in resource allocation. In particular, because $\partial G/\partial y_j = (\partial G^e/\partial \mu)(\partial \mu/\partial y_j)$, $j = 1, 2$, and similarly for x_j,

$$\frac{\partial G/\partial y_1}{\partial G/\partial y_2} = \frac{\partial \mu/\partial y_1}{\partial \mu/\partial y_2} = \frac{\partial x_1/\partial y_1}{\partial x_1/\partial y_2} = \frac{\partial x_2/\partial y_1}{\partial x_2/\partial y_2} \tag{2.8}$$

In other words, the marginal propensities to consume out of different sources of income must be proportional to each other across all of the goods. These proportionality conditions apply more generally, for all well-behaved preferences and when there are many goods (Bourguignon 1999). These include parents' preferences that are *interdependent* in the sense that their utility functions take the form $U^j(x_1, x_2, G)$, with $\partial U^j/\partial x_k \neq 0$, $j \neq k$, because these would produce the same general form of demand functions as those given in (2.7a) and (2.7b). Browning et al. (1994) call these "altruistic" preferences. Efficiency through cooperation restricts the impact of individual incomes because they only affect outcomes through the common factor μ.

With the particular utility function assumed above, we can solve explicitly for the demand functions in (2.7a) and (2.7b):

$$pG^e = [(1 - \alpha_1) + \mu(1 - \alpha_2)]\frac{y_1 + y_2}{1 + \mu} \tag{2.7a*}$$

$$x_1^e = \frac{\alpha_1(y_1 + y_2)}{1 + \mu} \quad \text{and} \quad x_2^e = \frac{\mu\alpha_2(y_1 + y_2)}{1 + \mu} \tag{2.7b*}$$

These equations indicate that the outcome for each parent's consumption and total child expenditure is equivalent to giving each a share of joint income, $1/(1 + \mu)$ and $\mu/(1 + \mu)$, respectively, and letting each choose their consumption and their contribution to child expenditure according to their own preferences. In other words, it is like there is an income "sharing rule" (Chiappori 1992), and then parents each make their own choices based on their share of income and their preferences.

Note that μ is the father's marginal utility from relaxing the constraint that $U^2(x_2, G) \geq U^{2^*}$, and μ increases with U^{2^*}. One possible interpretation of $\mu(y_1, y_2, p)$ is that it reflects bargaining in the family, with μ increasing in y_2 and decreasing in y_1. Define $\theta = \mu/(1 + \mu)$ as the share of family income allocated to the mother. Then, from (2.7a*),

$$\frac{\partial G^e}{\partial y_2} = \frac{[(1 - \theta)(1 - \alpha_1) + \theta(1 - \alpha_2)] + (y_1 + y_2)(\alpha_1 - \alpha_2)(\partial\theta/\partial y_2)}{p} \quad (2.9)$$

Equation (2.9) can be used to give the impact of differences in one parent's income on child expenditure a general bargaining interpretation. It indicates that higher mother's income has two effects. It increases family income, which increases expenditure on children. It also may increase the bargaining power of the mother (i.e. $\partial\theta/\partial y_2 > 0$), which could reinforce ($\alpha_1 > \alpha_2$) or offset ($\alpha_1 < \alpha_2$) the income effect, depending on each parent's preferences for child expenditure. It is also clear from (2.9) that if income is redistributed between parents ($dy_1 = -dy_2$), child expenditure would also change if preferences differ between parents and $\partial\theta/\partial y_2 \neq 0$. If, as many believe, mothers' preferences put more weight on children than fathers' preferences ($\alpha_1 > \alpha_2$), then redistribution from fathers to mothers would increase expenditure on children.

The factors affecting μ, and therefore θ, could also include what are called "extra-environmental parameters" (McElroy 1990), or "distribution factors" (Browning and Chiappori 1998). These are variables that affect the intra-family decision process without affecting individual preferences or resources. These may include marriage market attributes and divorce laws that, in some circumstances (see Section 2.4), affect bargaining between spouses within marriage. If there are at least two such distribution factors (D_k), then we obtain restrictions analogous to those in (2.8), with D_1 and D_2 replacing y_1 and y_2. Again, these restrictions arise because the distribution factors only affect outcomes through the common factor μ (equivalently, through the location on the utility possibility frontier). With more distribution factors there are more cross-equation restrictions, which provide a test of intra-family efficiency in resource allocation in a very general setting (Chiappori et al. 2002).

With the special preferences leading to (2.7a*), it is clear that if parents' preferences are the same ($\alpha_1 = \alpha_2$), child expenditure only depends on joint family income, namely $pG^e = (1 - \alpha_1)(y_1 + y_2)$. Comparing this with the non-cooperative Nash equilibrium when both parents contribute, given in (2.4a), $G^e/G^N = 1 + \alpha_1 > 1$. When only parent j

contributes to child expenditure, $G^e/G^N = (y_1 + y_2)/y_j$. Thus, in the special case of identical preferences, we can clearly conclude that the non-cooperative equilibrium produces too little expenditure on children relative to the efficient level. More generally, with different preferences, if we (reasonably) restrict ourselves to cooperative equilibria in which each parent receives a share of family income that ensures that their utility is higher than in the non-cooperative equilibrium, then expenditure on children is higher in the cooperative equilibrium. Analysis of how each parent's share may be determined follows in Section 2.4.

Another implication of the analysis so far is that in both the cooperative and non-cooperative models there are situations in which individual parents' incomes matter for expenditures on children and private consumption, and these depend on the preferences of the parents. In the non-cooperative model, this is the case when parents' incomes differ substantially (i.e. $y_j/(y_1 + y_2)$ is "high" or "low"). In a middle range of individual shares in family income, only joint family income matters and income redistribution between parents does not affect choices. In the cooperative model, individual incomes matter for choices when individual income affects the sharing rule, perhaps by affecting bargaining power. This is the case even if parents have the same preferences, because each parents' private consumption is affected. In both models, we expect heterogeneity in preferences to produce differences among families in whether only joint family income matters or not.

2.2.3 Sharing Rules

The sharing rule interpretation of demand equations (2.7a*) and (2.7b*) is not specific to the special preferences assumed there. Indeed, the selfish (or "egoistic") preferences assumed from the outset of the chapter are also not needed for the cooperative model to be equivalent to the existence of a sharing rule. Let preferences take the form $V^1 = V^1[U^1(x_1, G), U^2(x_2, G)]$, and similarly for parent 2, where the $U^j(\ )$ are "private" utility indices for each parent and $V^j[\ ]$ is "social utility" to parent j, which is a natural way to represent parents caring for each other (i.e. $\partial V^j/\partial U^k > 0$ for $j \neq k$). Chiappori (1992) and Browning et al. (1994) call these "caring" preferences. Clearly if $\partial V^j/\partial U^k = 0$ for $j \neq k$, or equivalently, $V^j = U^j(x_j, G)$, then these preferences collapse to selfish ones. The weak separability in each parent's preferences implicit in caring preferences means that each parent does not care how (in terms of x_j and G) a given level of utility is obtained by the other parent. It is straightforward to show that the solution to the efficient allocation problem with "caring" preferences implies the Samuelson efficiency condition in (2.6),[2] and of course demand functions of the same general form as those in (2.7a) and (2.7b).

In a more general context, assume that the private preferences are separable in private and public goods; that is, $U^j(x_j, G)$ takes the form $U^{j^*}(u^j(x_j), G)$, where x_j represents a vector of private goods, and G a vector of public goods. The existence of a sharing rule means that the solution to the efficient allocation problem for the private goods also maximizes $u^j(x_j)$ subject to $\sum_{k=1}^{n} q^k x_j^k = Z_j$, $j = 1, 2$, where q^k is the price of private good k, and $Z_1 + Z_2 = \sum_{k=1}^{n} q^k[x_1^k + x_2^k] = y_1 + y_2 - \sum_{k=1}^{m} p^k G^k$, where p^k is the price of public good k.

Efficiency in family resource allocation is equivalent to the existence of a "sharing rule" for caring preferences if the private preferences are separable in private and public goods. To show this, let x_1^c and x_2^c be the solution to the efficient allocation problem. If x_1^c and x_2^c did *not* also solve the maximization problem of the preceding paragraph, then there would exist another two consumption bundles x_1^a and x_2^a that cost no more and provide a higher private utility for one parent without making the other worse off. Because both V^1 and V^2 would increase in consequence, x_1^c and x_2^c could not be efficient, which produces a contradiction (see Browning et al. 1994). The sharing rule evident from demand equations (2.7a*) and (2.7b*) is a special case of this general proposition.

It is as if allocations within the family are made in two stages. First, joint income $(y_1 + y_2)$ is allocated among public good expenditure $(\sum_{k=1}^{m} p^k G^k)$ and each of the parents for private expenditure (Z_1 and Z_2). At the second stage, each parent chooses his(her) bundle of private goods with the money allocated to them (Z_j). Even in the absence of separability of public goods, a sharing rule exists, but it and the demand functions for private goods are conditional on expenditures on public goods (Browning et al. 1994). If there were no public goods and selfish preferences, the sharing rule would be an application of the Second Theorem of Welfare Economics: an efficient allocation can be decentralized using appropriate lump sum subsidies.

Any outcome that is efficient in the context of caring preferences would also be efficient if the parents were selfish. This is because any change that increases $U^1(x_1, G)$ without decreasing $U^2(x_2, G)$ would strictly increase both V^1 and V^2, but such a change is not possible if the starting point is efficient for the caring preferences given by V^1 and V^2. Among the outcomes that are efficient for selfish preferences, which are given by the utility possibility frontier in Figure 2.3, those that are also efficient for caring preferences form a continuous part of the frontier between the parents' respective best choices under caring (Chiappori 1992), such as between points A and B in Figure 2.3, at which the indifference curves associated with $V^2(U^1, U^2)$ and $V^1(U^1, U^2)$, respectively, are tangent to the utility possibility frontier (see Section 3.1 for further details). The efficient outcomes with caring preferences eliminate two segments at the extremes of the frontier because parents who care for one another do not want their partner's private (egoistic) utility to fall below some minimum level.

Efficiency is not, however, equivalent to the existence of an income sharing rule if the parents' preferences are inter-dependent ("altruistic" preferences). The distinction between private and public goods is blurred in this case because both x_1 and x_2 are in effect public goods.

The preferences that we have characterized as "caring" are equivalent to what Becker (1981) has called "altruism". Because the behaviour that such altruism may produce has been so important in the economic analysis of the family, the next chapter examines in some detail the implications of caring preferences when combined with a special assumption about family decision making. It should, however, already be clear that the implications of the general cooperative model, such as the existence of a sharing rule and the possible impact of individual incomes and distribution factors on outcomes, are the same for these preferences as for selfish ones. What is discussed in Chapter 3 is a special case of the cooperative model examined here, not an alternative. We return to the issue of how individual income may affect bargaining power after expanding the basic model to include home production.

2.3 MODEL WITH HOME PRODUCTION

Explicit treatment of household production is standard in family economics. Here we follow Konrad and Lommerud (1995) and specify a very simple home production technology in which each parent may contribute time to the raising of their children, and the resulting child "quality" is a pure public good to the parents:

$$G = h_1 t_1 + h_2 t_2 \qquad (2.10)$$

where t_j is the amount of time that parent j contributes to child care/raising and h_j is the productivity of parent j's time. Thus, we have replaced purchases of the child good in the basic model with home production.[3]

2.3.1 Non-Cooperative Equilibrium

Even if parents do not cooperate, it may be in the interest of one parent to make financial transfers to the other. Let us look at it from the father's point of view, with the mother being the potential recipient of transfers. Then private consumption of the mother is given by $x_2 = (T - t_2)w_2 + y_2 + s_1$, where T is the total time available, w_j is parent j's wage, y_j is j's non-labour income and s_1 is transfers from the father to the mother. The mother chooses her time allocation, t_2, to maximize her utility, taking the time allocation of her husband and the financial transfer from him as given (i.e. we are again considering a "Nash equilibrium"). Thus, the mother chooses t_2 to maximize $U^2((T - t_2)w_2 + y_2 + s_1, h_1 t_1 + h_2 t_2)$, which implies a condition analogous to (2.1):

$$\frac{U_G^2(x_2^*, G^*)}{U_x^2(x_2^*, G^*)} = \frac{w_2}{h_2} \tag{2.11}$$

where the * indicates the optimum value given the father's time allocation and transfer. The left-hand side is the marginal rate of substitution between the public and private good (given the father's time allocation and transfers) and the right-hand side is the marginal cost of her child rearing time relative to that of the private good. In the case of the utility function assumed above, this condition, along with the budget constraint and the home production technology (2.10), implies the following reaction function for the mother's time allocation:

$$t_2 = (1 - \alpha_2)\frac{w_2 T + y_2 + s_1}{w_2} - \frac{\alpha_2 h_1 t_1}{h_2} \tag{2.12}$$

Analogous to (2.2b), the mother's best strategy is to reduce her time in child-raising when the father increases his. How much she does so depends on her preferences and the productivity of his child time relative to hers (h_1/h_2).

The father chooses his time allocation and monetary transfers to his wife, s_1, so as to maximize his utility, $U^1((T - t_1)w_1 + y_1 - s_1, h_1 t_1 + h_2 t_2)$, subject to the way in which she will respond to the transfers from him, which is given by her reaction function (2.12), and the constraints that time allocation and transfers must be non-negative ($t_1 \geq 0$, $s_1 \geq 0$). The solution to this problem implies two conditions:

$$\frac{w_1}{(1 - \alpha_2)h_1} \geq \frac{U_G^1(x_1^*, G^*)}{U_x^1(x_1^*, G^*)} = \frac{(1 - \alpha_1)x_1}{\alpha_1 G} \tag{2.13a}$$

$$\frac{w_2}{(1 - \alpha_2)h_2} \geq \frac{U_G^1(x_1^*, G^*)}{U_x^1(x_1^*, G^*)} = \frac{(1 - \alpha_1)x_1}{\alpha_1 G} \tag{2.13b}$$

Clearly at most one of these can hold with equality if $w_2/h_2 \neq w_1/h_1$. If, for example, $w_2/h_2 < w_1/h_1$, only (2.13b) can hold with equality, and if it does so, then $t_1 = 0$ and $s_1 > 0$. In other words, there is full specialization in market work by the father and he effectively buys the time of the mother through voluntary transfers. The father has a comparative advantage in market work, and he contributes no time to child rearing.

If (2.13b) holds with equality, the amount of voluntary transfer from the father to his wife is given by

$$s_1 = (1 - \alpha_1)(w_1 T + y_1) - \alpha_1(w_2 T + y_2) \qquad (2.14)$$

Equation (2.14) shows that the amount of the transfer clearly rises with the father's "full income", which includes his earning capacity ($w_1 T$) and non-labour income (y_1), and falls with the mother's full income. The total amount of the child good in the Nash equilibrium, G^N, which is entirely provided by the time inputs of the mother (i.e. $G^N = t_2 h_2$), depends on the "full income" of the family, $Y_F = (w_1 + w_2)T + y_1 + y_2$, and the marginal cost of child rearing, w_2/h_2:

$$G^N = \frac{(1 - \alpha_1)(1 - \alpha_2)Y_F}{w_2/h_2} \qquad (2.15)$$

Private consumption of each parent only depends on family full income: $x_1 = \alpha_1 Y_F$ and $x_2 = \alpha_2(1 - \alpha_1)Y_F$. Involuntary transfers between the parents (e.g. through the tax and benefit system) will not affect outcomes, provided that they do not make the father so poor as to be unable to make transfers to his wife.

If the inequality in (2.13b) also holds, the father will neither devote time to child rearing, nor give transfers to the mother. He finds the child good too expensive. This occurs when $(w_2 T + y_2)/(w_1 T + y_1) > (1 - \alpha_1)/\alpha_1$; that is, when the father is "too poor" relative to his wife, with the threshold clearly depending on the father's preferences. In this case, $G^N = (1 - \alpha_2)(w_2 T + y_2)/(w_2/h_2)$. Redistribution from the father to the mother clearly raises provision of the child good and increases her private consumption while lowering the father's.

Of course, the mother is solving a similar problem, and conditions analogous to those in (2.13) are implied. When $w_2/h_2 < w_1/h_1$, the mother will never make financial transfers to her husband because she has the comparative advantage in child rearing. She would make transfers to him if $w_2/h_2 > w_1/h_1$ and $(w_2 T + y_2)/(w_1 T + y_1) > \alpha_2/(1 - \alpha_2)$. Thus, in this model with home production, who, if anyone, makes transfers depends on the relative cost of the child good as well as relative full incomes, because the cost of producing the child good usually differs between parents (i.e. $w_2/h_2 \neq w_1/h_1$).

We have shown that the parent with the comparative advantage in market work would specialize in such work and *may* make transfers to his(her) partner, who will do all of the child rearing. Whether or not the mother devotes all of her time to child rearing (i.e. $t_2 = T$), when $w_2/h_2 < w_1/h_1$ and she receives transfers from the father, depends on the wage component of her full income relative to family full income. From (2.15) and $G^N = t_2 h_2$, $t_2 < T$ requires that $w_2 T/Y_F > (1 - \alpha_1)(1 - \alpha_2)$. Thus, if the value of the mother's time ($w_2 T$) is sufficiently low relative to family full income, the mother will fully specialize in child rearing, making both partners fully specialized. It should be noted, however, that the tendencies for one or both parents to specialize fully is a reflection of the particular production technology assumed, and it may not hold with diminishing marginal productivity of each parent's time input. More general household production technologies are examined in Chapter 4.

When $w_2/h_2 < w_1/h_1$, increases in the mother's wage (w_2) give rise to both a substitution effect and an income effect on provision of the child good. With the particular utility function assumed here, the substitution effect always dominates. When $s_1 > 0$,

$$\frac{\partial G^N}{\partial w_2} = -\frac{(1 - \alpha_1)(1 - \alpha_2)h_2(w_1 T + y_1 + y_2)}{w_2^2} < 0 \qquad (2.16a)$$

and when $s_1 = 0$,

$$\frac{\partial G^N}{\partial w_2} = -\frac{(1 - \alpha_2)h_2 y_2}{w_2^2} < 0 \qquad (2.16b)$$

Any effect of increases in the father's wage (w_1) on the provision of the child good is purely through an income effect; and there would indeed be no effect of w_1 (or y_1) if the father does not make transfers to his partner. Higher productivity in child rearing for the mother (i.e. higher h_2) clearly raises G^N in both cases.

2.3.2 Cooperative Equilibrium

As before, we assume that cooperation leads to a Pareto-efficient allocation of a couple's time. It must maximize the utility of one parent subject to the other achieving a given utility and to the resource and production constraints.[4] Solution to this problem implies

$$\frac{w_1}{h_1} \geq \frac{U_G^1(x_1^*, G^*)}{U_x^1(x_1^*, G^*)} + \frac{U_G^2(x_2^*, G^*)}{U_x^2(x_2^*, G^*)} \qquad (2.17a)$$

$$\frac{w_2}{h_2} \geq \frac{U_G^1(x_1^*, G^*)}{U_x^1(x_1^*, G^*)} + \frac{U_G^2(x_2^*, G^*)}{U_x^2(x_2^*, G^*)} \qquad (2.17b)$$

Again, if $w_2/h_2 \neq w_1/h_1$, only one of these can hold with equality. For example, if $w_2/h_2 < w_1/h_1$, then $t_1 = 0$ and (2.17b) holds with equality. This condition states that the marginal cost of providing the public child good equals the sum of the parents' marginal rates of substitution, which is the Samuelson condition for the efficient provision of public goods.

With $w_2/h_2 < w_1/h_1$, this is analogous to our formulation of the cooperative equilibrium in the basic model of Section 2.2.2 with $p = w_2/h_2$ and full family income Y_F replacing $y_1 + y_2$. Thus, all of the analysis there is directly applicable, but now we can also consider the impact of a higher wage for the parent producing the child good, which is the mother when $w_2/h_2 < w_1/h_1$.

With the particular utility functions assumed above, the efficient provision of the child good is

$$G^e = [(1 - \theta)(1 - \alpha_1) + \theta(1 - \alpha_2)](Y_F)\left(\frac{h_2}{w_2}\right)$$

$$\text{and } t_2^e = \frac{G^e}{h_2}, \ t_1^e = 0 \qquad (2.18)$$

where $\theta = \mu/(1 + \mu)$ is now the share of *full* family income allocated to the mother. In this cooperative model, increases in the mother's wage (w_2) give rise to a substitution effect, as well as to income and bargaining effects:

$$\frac{\partial G^e}{\partial w_2} =$$

$$\left\{[(1 - \theta)(1 - \alpha_1) + \theta(1 - \alpha_2)]T + (Y_F)(\alpha_1 - \alpha_2)\left(\frac{\partial \theta}{\partial w_2}\right)\right\}\left(\frac{h_2}{w_2}\right) - \frac{G^e}{w_2}$$

$$(2.19)$$

If, for example, $\alpha_1 > \alpha_2$ and the impact of the mother's wage on her bargaining power ($\partial\theta/\partial w_2$) is sufficiently large, a higher mother's wage could increase the provision of the child good, despite the fact that its cost of production increases with w_2.

How does the inefficient non-cooperative solution of Section 2.3.1 compare with the efficient cooperative one? Consider the case when $w_2/h_2 < w_1/h_1$ and $s_1 > 0$ in the Nash equilibrium and preferences are identical ($\alpha_1 = \alpha_2$). From (2.15) and (2.18), $G^N/G^e = 1 - \alpha_1 < 1$. Thus, the non-cooperative equilibrium produces too little of the public good when parents' preferences are represented by the particular utility function assumed above and they are identical. We would expect this to be the case when preferences differ as well, provided that the cooperative equilibrium provides each parent with a utility at least as high as the non-cooperative equilibrium (see next section).

Given that communication is possible within families, particularly when the parents live together with their children, and there is repeated interaction between parents, it is plausible that parents would exploit any opportunities to make one parent better off without making the other worse off. Thus, it is reasonable to assume that parents choose efficient allocations in this static model (Chiappori 1992; Bourguignon 1999).

Lundberg and Pollack (2001) show, however, that in a dynamic model in which current decisions affect future bargaining power, we cannot presume that outcomes are efficient. For example, the decision to have a child could reduce the woman's bargaining power relative to her husband in subsequent years, thereby discouraging her from having a(nother) child, even though both could be better off if she did. Efficient solutions can be guaranteed only if at least one partner is able to make a binding commitment concerning future allocations (i.e. to forgo the possibility of renegotiating). For example, there could be a commitment to compensate the mother for the loss in future bargaining power entailed by the decision to have a child. How such commitments can be made, through agreements, promises or threats, is a matter for further analysis. "Trust" between partners may, for example, be a way to enforce agreements and promises.[5] As noted by Schelling (1960, pp.134–135), "Trust is often achieved simply by the continuity of the relation between parties and the recognition by each that what he might gain by cheating in a given instance is outweighed by the value of the tradition of trust that makes possible a long sequence of future agreement." Trust between partners may be fostered by reaching mutually advantageous agreements on many "small issues" in advance of big decisions like childbearing.

This chapter only uses static models, and therefore, we assume that parents cooperate and choose efficient allocations. Bargaining determines which of them they choose.[6] Even in this situation, the non-cooperative equilibrium may have a role to play in determining the allocation of parents' time and money and the distribution of welfare between them.

2.4 Bargaining within Families

As noted earlier, by assuming different values of U^{2^*}, and substituting the solution into the father's utility function, we trace out the *utility possibility frontier* (UPF), illustrated in Figure 2.4, which corresponds to given values of w_1, w_2, h_1, h_2, y_1, y_2 and the parameters of the parents' utility functions. All of the points on the frontier represent efficient time allocations for the couple, with each implying a particular time allocation and distribution of welfare in the family. Which point will be chosen? The possibility of bargaining within the household was discussed above in relation to the income sharing rule θ, but a bargaining theory was not advanced. This section considers some of these theories.

Each partner has the alternative of not cooperating, providing an alternative level of utility, which we call their *threat points*. These could, for

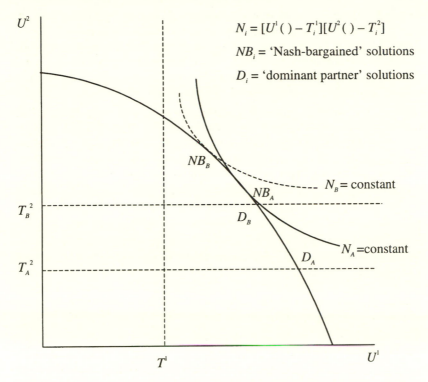

$$N_i = [U^1() - T_i^1][U^2() - T_i^2]$$

NB_i = 'Nash-bargained' solutions

D_i = 'dominant partner' solutions

Figure 2.4   Two bargaining rules: Nash bargaining and dominant partner.

example, be given by the non-cooperative equilibrium considered in Section 2.3.1. The possible cooperative solutions lie, therefore, between the two threat points, T^1 and T^2, indicated by the dashed lines in Figure 2.4. Corresponding to these threat points are minimum and maximum shares of full income allocated to the mother, θ. While this narrows the range of cooperative solutions, there are still an infinity of them.

In order to resolve the conflict between partners, and obtain a unique solution, some kind of bargaining rule is needed. We could assume that one parent is a "dominant partner", with the couple maximizing their utility. For example, if the father were dominant, he would offer his wife just enough to accept this arrangement, which would be her threat point.[7] In other words, he would choose the point on the UPF that would just induce her to cooperate, which would be point D_A in Figure 2.4.

Another assumption is that the preference orderings of the parents satisfy certain axioms proposed by Nash (1950a).[8] If those axioms are satisfied, then the equilibrium time allocation of the couple is that which maximizes the *product of the gains from cooperation*, where these gains are $U^1 - T^1$ and $U^2 - T^2$. Thus, with Nash bargaining the couple maximizes

$$N = [U^1(x_1, G) - T^1(w_1, w_2, y_1, y_2, h_1, h_2)]$$

$$\times [U^2(x_2, G) - T^2(w_1, w_2, y_1, y_2, h_1, h_2)]$$

subject to the resource and production constraints, where the threat points have been expressed as indirect utility functions. Indifference contours associated with the N function above are shown in Figure 2.4, and the Nash bargaining solution is illustrated as point NB_A. Changes in w_1, w_2, y_1, y_2, h_1 and h_2 alter the UPF, the threat points and the contours of the N function, producing a new equilibrium allocation and distribution of welfare between partners. An upward shift in one of the threat points, independent of w_1, w_2, y_1, y_2, h_1 and h_2, would increase that person's welfare relative to that of their partner. In Figure 2.4, NB_B and D_B are the Nash bargaining and dominant partner outcomes if the mother's threat point increased.

2.4.1 What Should Be the Threat Point in Bargaining Models?

Early formulations of household bargaining (e.g. Manser and Brown 1980; McElroy and Horney 1981) took the threat points to be the utility that each partner would achieve if the couple divorced. But Bergstrom (1996) called that into question, and we follow his argument here.

Consider a Rubinstein–Binmore multi-period bargaining game (Binmore 1985; Rubinstein 1982). Partners alternate in proposing how to "divide the cake", which in this context is utility from cooperation in the family which we normalize to be unity: $u_1 + u_2 = 1$, where u_j is the proposed utility of partner j in marriage. There is one time period between offers and each partner is impatient, discounting future utility by a factor of $\delta < 1$, yielding an inter-temporal utility function of $V_j = \sum \delta^t U_{jt}$, $j = 1, 2$, where U_{jt} is the utility of partner j in period t and the summation is from 0 to infinity. In any period in which they remain married but do not reach an agreement, partner j receives utility b_j. Because of the inefficiency of non-cooperative marriage shown above, $b_1 + b_2 < 1$. If either partner asks for a divorce, they will get m_1 and m_2, respectively, where $m_1 + m_2 < 1$.

Suppose again, for concreteness, that partner 2 is the wife and she makes the first offer $(u_1, u_2) > (m_1, m_2)$. The husband could (a) accept the offer, which implies that he will accept it in all future periods (there is a stationarity assumption); (b) refuse the offer and ask for divorce, which implies that $m_1 > u_1$ in all future periods; or (c) refuse and make a counteroffer in the next period. In *equilibrium*, it must be the case that the husband cannot do better by refusing and making a counteroffer; and his wife offers terms which leave her indifferent between accepting immediately and making a counteroffer, because she will want to make the smallest offer he will accept. It can be shown that the process has a unique equilibrium:

$$u_j^e = b_j + \frac{\delta(1 - b_1 - b_2)}{1 + \delta}, \qquad j = 1, 2 \tag{2.20}$$

If the time between offers is "small", $\delta \to 1$ and $u_j^e = b_j + (1 - b_1 - b_2)/2$, $j = 1, 2$; that is, the gains from cooperative relative to non-cooperative marriage are shared equally.

There are three cases to consider: (a) $b_j + (1 - b_1 - b_2)/2 > m_j$, $j = 1, 2$, in which case the divorce threat is not credible for either partner and the equilibrium is $u_j^e = b_j + (1 - b_1 - b_2)/2$, as illustrated in the top panel of Figure 2.5; (b) $b_1 + (1 - b_1 - b_2)/2 < m_1$, in which case the divorce threat is credible for the husband and $u_1^e = m_1$ and $u_2^e = 1 - m_1 > m_2$, as illustrated in the bottom panel of Figure 2.5; (c) $b_2 + (1 - b_1 - b_2)/2 < m_2$, in which case the divorce threat is credible for the wife and the equilibrium is $u_1^e = 1 - m_2 > m_1$ and $u_2^e = m_2$.

Case (a) corresponds to the cooperative Nash bargaining solution when the threat point is non-cooperative marriage (e.g. as in Lundberg and Pollack 1993). It maximizes $(u_1 - b_1)(u_2 - b_2)$ subject to $u_1 + u_2 = 1$, and so equilibrium is calculated as if (b_1, b_2) is the threat point. Thus, small changes in utility if divorced (m_j) have no impact on the outcome of bargaining, even if $m_1 > b_1$ and $m_2 > b_2$ (as illustrated in the top panel of Figure 2.5).

In the other two cases, the divorce threat is credible and relevant, but the outcome is *not* that produced by Nash bargaining with divorce utilities (m_1, m_2) as the threat point. The gains from marriage are not split equally, but one partner gets all of the surplus $(1 - m_j)$ and the other is indifferent between divorce and marriage.

The analysis suggests that the non-cooperative equilibrium examined in Section 2.3.1 can provide the threat point for the cooperative Nash bargaining model. As Chapter 8 explains, a non-cooperative model may also be a good representation of a divorced couple (s_1 would be interpreted as voluntary child support payments), but the budget constraints faced by each partner may differ from those of a married couple. For example, if welfare benefits are paid to divorced mothers (but not to married mothers), welfare benefits would be part of non-earned income (y_j) for a divorced mother, but not a married mother. As long as divorce is not a credible threat, changes in welfare benefits would not change the threat point in the Nash bargaining model, nor resource allocation and distribution within marriage.

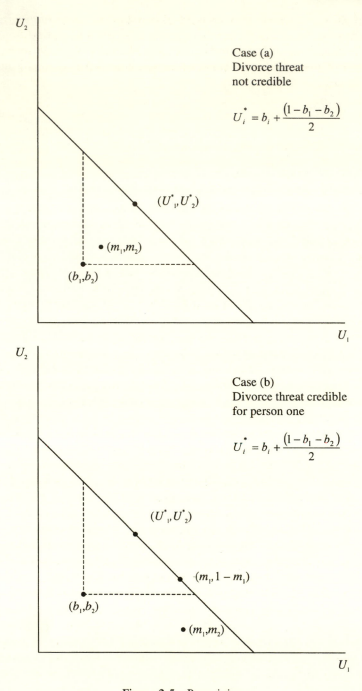

Figure 2.5 Bargaining.

If, however, divorce is a credible threat for the mother, the Nash bargaining solution would not be appropriate, and increases in welfare benefits for divorced mothers would directly improve her welfare in marriage. Thus, in this case the opportunities available to the mother if her relationship dissolved would affect allocation and distribution when the couple are together. Chiappori et al. (2002) provide evidence that divorce laws favourable to women increase married women's share of family income, which suggests that divorce is a credible threat for at least some portion of the population of married couples.

2.4.2 Threat Points and Income Shares: An Example

Suppose that the bargaining threat points come from the outcome of a non-cooperative equilibrium within a partnership, in which preferences and home production take the form assumed in Section 2.3. Assume further that $\alpha_1 = 0.7$, $\alpha_2 = 0.5$, $(w_1 T + y_1)/Y_F = 0.6$ (where $Y_F = (w_1 + w_2)T + y_1 + y_2$), $w_1/h_1 = 1.5$ and $w_2/h_2 = 1$; that is, the mother's preferences give more weight to the public good and she has the comparative advantage in producing it. In this case, the father would *not* make voluntary transfers, because his share of joint income is too low (the critical value is α_1). Then the level of the public good chosen in the non-cooperative equilibrium would be $G = (1 - \alpha_2)(w_2 T + y_2)/(w_2/h_2)$. As each partner must at least attain the utility available in the non-cooperative equilibrium, this implies minimum and maximum values for the share of full income allocated to the mother in the cooperative equilibrium, θ.[9] With the assumed parameter values, $0.24 < \theta < 0.34$. Note that this means that the mother's share of full income in the couple must be less than her relative contribution to joint full income; that is, $\theta < (w_2 T + y_2)/Y_F$. As the difference between the mother's private consumption (x_2) in the cooperative and non-cooperative equilibria is given by $\alpha_2[\theta Y_F - (w_2 T + y_2)]$, this means that her private consumption is lower in the cooperative equilibrium. Public good consumption is sufficiently higher in the cooperative equilibrium to compensate her for lower private consumption.[10] The minimum and maximum values are increasing in the woman's relative contribution to joint full income; for example, if this were 0.5, then $0.34 < \theta < 0.41$.

If the woman's share of joint full income is below $1 - \alpha_1$, then the man would make voluntary contributions to the child good, which is produced by the woman because of her comparative advantage. She is too poor to produce a high enough level of the public good without his transfers. In this case, the maximum and minimum values for θ in the cooperative equilibrium are independent of the distribution of full income between the partners; they only depend on the partners' preferences regarding the public good. With $\alpha_1 = 0.7$ and $\alpha_2 = 0.5$, $0.15 < \theta < 0.32$. For example, this equilibrium would emerge when $(w_1 T + y_1)/Y_F = 0.75$. If the man's and woman's preferences are reversed so that $\alpha_1 = 0.5$, $\alpha_2 = 0.7$, but her relative contribution to joint full income, $(w_2 T + y_2)/Y_F$, is again 0.4, the man would make transfers to her because of her comparative advantage and his relatively strong preference for the child good. In this case, $0.32 < \theta < 0.60$. In these two cases, it is possible that θ exceeds $(w_2 T + y_2)/Y_F$.

2.5 GAINS TO THE DIVISION OF LABOUR

Suppose now that a *private* good is produced with a person's time. Analogous to (2.9), let $G_1 + G_2 = h_1 t_1 + h_2 t_2$, where G_j is the amount of the home-produced private good consumed by person j, t_j is the amount of time that person j contributes to its production, and h_j is the productivity of person j's time. Assume that these two people have preferences represented by the utility functions $U^j = \alpha_j \ln(x_j) + \beta_j \ln(G_j) + \gamma_j \ln(z_j)$, $\alpha_j + \beta_j + \gamma_j = 1$, $j = 1, 2$ where z_j is person j's pure leisure. Also assume that person 2 has a comparative advantage in home production; that is, $w_1/h_1 > w_2/h_2$, where w_j is the wage rate of person j.

Suppose first that the two people do not cooperate. As person 2 has the comparative advantage in producing G, she will sell G_1 to person 1. Person 2 chooses x_2, z_2 and t_2 to maximize her utility subject to the demand for the home produced good by person 1 and her full income $w_2 T + y_2$, where T is total time available and y_2 is unearned income. She will charge (just under) w_1/h_1 for G_1, and person 1 will be willing to pay that price rather than produce G_1 himself. Person 1 chooses G_1, z_1 and x_1 to maximize his utility subject to this price and his full income, which is $w_1 T + y_1$. His choice of G_1 is $\beta_1(w_1 T + y_1)/(w_1/h_1)$. As a consequence, person 2 receives "profits on sales" of $s = (w_1/h_1 - w_2/h_2)\beta_1(w_1 T + y_1)/(w_1/h_1)$, implying utility from non-cooperation of U^{2nc}.[11] Thus, in the non-cooperative equilibrium, person 1 makes payments to person 2, because of her comparative advantage in home production.

Both people would be better off if they cooperate, provided person 2 receives an allocation in the cooperative equilibrium with $U^2 > U^{2nc}$. Letting θ again be person 2's share of joint full income when they cooperate, it must be the case that $\theta \geq (w_2 T + y_2 + s)/Y_F$, where $Y_F = (w_1 + w_2)T + y_1 + y_2$. That is, person 2 must receive a sufficiently large lump sum transfer in the cooperative equilibrium; otherwise she would not participate. For instance, if person 2 received a lump sum transfer of the same amount as her "profit on sales" in the non-cooperative equilibrium (s), person 1 would be better off in the cooperative equilibrium and person 2 would be just as well off.[12] The welfare gain arises because of the removal of the "distortionary tax" on the home-produced good entailed by moving from the non-cooperative to the cooperative equilibrium. There clearly is scope for bargaining over the amount of transfer in excess of s.

The cooperative equilibrium in this example also illustrates that observations on people's leisure are helpful for inferring the intra-household allocation. Compare two couples each of whom have the same set of preferences, identical wage rates and the same joint full income. Because $z_2 = \theta \gamma_2 Y_F / w_2$ and $z_1 = (1 - \theta)\gamma_1 Y_F / w_1$, the couple in which person 2 has more leisure must have allocated more of full income to person 2, and this may be related to differences in the composition of full income in the two families (e.g. $(w_2 T + y_2)/Y_F$ may be higher in the couple with higher z_2).[13] Leisure is particularly interesting because it can only be consumed by that particular person; it is an "exclusive good" in the terminology of Bourguignon (1999). But it is worth noting that it could well be the case that, within a couple, the marginal utility of one person's leisure depends on the amount of leisure consumed by the other, because they wish to undertake leisure activities together (to avoid "bowling alone"). This possibility has been ruled out by the particular preferences assumed in the example. If, instead, their preferences take the form $U^j = U^j(x_j, z_1, z_2, G_j)$, with $\partial U^j / \partial z_k \neq 0$, $j \neq k$, then it is not possible to make inferences about how they share full income from the observation of how much leisure each consumes. This is a case of inter-dependent preferences, discussed in Section 2.2, for which efficiency is not equivalent to the existence of a sharing rule.

2.6 SOME EMPIRICAL IMPLICATIONS

Traditional consumer theory has little to say about household behaviour if there is more than one adult in the household. It is usually assumed that the household behaves as if it is a single agent, allowing an application of the tools of consumer theory at the household level. This assumption, which is often called the "unitary model", or "consensus model", conflicts with the view that individualism is the foundation of microeconomic theory, because individualism clearly requires that we allow for different individuals to have different preferences (see Chiappori 1992). Thus, it is incorrect as a starting point for analysis. Rather we should investigate whether it is an acceptable simplification for empirical and policy purposes, and this requires that we start with an approach which allows for the preferences of all adults in the household to affect household choices. Such an approach has been adopted in this chapter, and we use it to examine how data may allow us to test the unitary model and to distinguish between alternative models of the household.

2.6.1 Income Pooling in Analyses of Household Consumption and Labour Supply

For simplicity, we continue to assume a two-adult household and to use the particular utility function introduced in Section 2.2 for illustration. From (2.7a*) and (2.7b*), the efficient levels of the public good and individual private consumption are given by

$$pG^e = [(1 - \alpha_1) + \theta(\alpha_1 - \alpha_2)](y_1 + y_2)$$

$$x_1^e = (1 - \theta)\alpha_1(y_1 + y_2) \qquad \text{and} \qquad x_2^e = \theta\alpha_2(y_1 + y_2) \qquad (2.21)$$

where $\theta = \mu/(1 + \mu)$ is again the income sharing rule.

The unitary model amounts to assuming that the sharing rule θ does not vary with individual incomes. Thus, one important implication of the unitary model is that consumption of the public good and each person's private consumption depend only on total family income. This is what is usually called the "income pooling" hypothesis: only joint household income should matter for allocation decisions and not who receives the income. In this example, it is as if there was a household utility function equal to $(1 - \theta)\alpha_1 \ln(x_1) + \theta\alpha_2 \ln(x_2) + [(1 - \alpha_1) + \theta(\alpha_1 - \alpha_2)] \ln(G)$.

In the general cooperative model individual incomes may matter. For example, from (2.21),

$$\frac{\partial G^e}{\partial y_j} = \frac{[(1 - \alpha_1) + \theta(\alpha_1 - \alpha_2)] + (y_1 + y_2)(\alpha_1 - \alpha_2)(\partial\theta/\partial y_j)}{p} \qquad (2.22)$$

$$\frac{\partial x_2^e}{\partial y_j} = \theta\alpha_2 + \alpha_2(y_1 + y_2)\frac{\partial\theta}{\partial y_j} \qquad (2.23)$$

The impact of individual incomes clearly comes through their effect on the income sharing rule. The way in which this operates is outside the scope of this general cooperative model. As indicated in Section 2.4, one way is through some bargaining process in which individual incomes determine the threat points, such as Nash bargaining. In contrast, the decision rule examined in the next chapter eliminates the impacts of individual incomes, making it equivalent to the unitary model.

While it is often difficult to identify consumption of particular individuals within a household, we can test the unitary model by studying the consumption of exclusive goods such as a person's pure leisure, provided that one person's utility does not depend on the leisure of the other. If the unitary model is correct, then only total full income of the household should matter for a person's consumption of leisure. Holding this constant, changes in a person's own unearned income should not affect that person's leisure. This is clear from the example of the previous section, in which person 2's leisure is given by $z_2 = \theta \gamma_2 Y_F / w_2$. If y_2 (unearned income) does not influence θ, then, holding Y_F constant, y_2 has no effect on z_2.

Household labour supply has been an important area in which the unitary model has been tested, and usually rejected (e.g. Fortin and Lacroix 1997; Lundberg 1988). A possible shortcoming of these studies is that it is impossible to distinguish leisure from other non-market time (e.g. home production) in the data available, making it necessary to assume that a person's utility is increasing in all non-market time.

Suppose we have data on expenditures on an exclusive good, like women's clothing, and that we can take individual incomes to be exogenous, an important assumption to which we return. If we find that individual incomes have no impact on expenditure on the good once we control for joint household income, then we cannot reject the unitary model, but it is not necessarily confirmed either. For example, if the true model is a non-cooperative one in which both parents contribute to the public good, then only their joint income matters: from (2.4b), the Nash equilibrium in this case is $x_1^N = [\alpha_1(1 - \alpha_2)(y_1 + y_2)]/(1 - \alpha_1 \alpha_2)$. Thus, finding no impact of individual incomes is also consistent with this non-cooperative model, which produces inefficient outcomes. It is also consistent with a Nash bargaining model in which the threat points come from a non-cooperative equilibrium in which both parents contribute to the public good, because in this case redistribution of incomes between parents would not affect the threat points.[14] If, however, we find that, in addition to joint income, individual incomes affect expenditure on the good, then we can reject the unitary model, but we also must reject these two alternative models.

In a recent empirical study, Browning and Lechene (2001) found that, in the range of individual shares of household income in which we would expect that both parents contribute to household public goods (i.e. when the shares are closer to equality), individual incomes matter for expenditure on exclusive goods like women's clothing and expenditure on household public goods like children's clothing. This is evidence against the unitary model and these two alternative models.

Implementing these tests is more difficult than it may first appear because most incomes are not exogenous. Earnings, which represent by far the largest component of family income, are clearly endogenous with respect to the household's time allocation decisions. It is clear from the household production model in Section 2.3 (and Section 2.5) that preferences (α_j) affect both earnings and the demand for the child good (and leisure).[15] Unearned incomes would appear to offer more promise, but they may not be exogenous with respect to past or present household behaviour. For instance, income from investments reflects to a considerable extent accumulated savings which is correlated with past labour supply, which reflects individual preferences, through which it would also be correlated with present labour supply and expenditure on the child good or leisure.

Suppose that we reject income pooling through the tests suggested in the previous section. We can test for efficiency, and therefore for the validity of the cooperative family model, by using the restrictions on the marginal propensities to consume derived in (2.8), which we now discuss in a more general framework.

2.6.2 Cooperation and the Costs of Children

The general cooperative model suggests a different approach to measuring the "costs of children". Following Bourguignon (1999), assume that the utility of the two parents, denoted as f and m for father and mother, takes the following form:

$$V^j = V^j[U^f(\mathbf{x}^f), U^m(\mathbf{x}^m), U^c(\mathbf{x}^c)], \qquad j = f, m \qquad (2.24)$$

where x^c represents the vector of goods consumed by children and $U^c(\ )$ the utility that their consumption gives to their parents; the $U^j(\ )$ are "private" utility indices for each parent and x^j is the vector of goods consumed by parent j; and $V^j[\ ]$ is "social utility" to parent j, which is a natural way to represent parents caring for their children and each other. The separability in each parent's preferences assumed in (2.24) means that each parent does not care how a given level of utility is obtained by the other parent, and that both parents have the same preferences among goods consumed by their children, but they may not value children's welfare equally. As children do not make decisions in this formulation, U^c is equivalent to a public good, like G earlier in the chapter.

A Pareto efficient allocation must maximize $V^f + \mu V^m$ subject to $y = y_f + y_m = p'(x^f + x^m + x^c)$, where y_j are individual incomes, p is a vector of prices and μ is a Lagrange multiplier. As in Section 2.2.3, the solution to this problem implies that the outcome for each parent's choice of x^j is equivalent to giving each a share of joint income and letting each choose x^j to maximize their private utility indices (U^j). The remainder of the budget is spent on x^c to maximize U^c. Thus, the sharing rule is now represented by two functions, $\theta^m[y, \mu(y_f, y_m, p, D)]$ and $\theta^f[y, \mu(y_f, y_m, p, D)]$, where D is a vector of K "distribution factors" (discussed in Section 2.2.2). The residual amount allocated to expenditure on children is

$y - \theta^m[y, \mu(y_f, y_m, p, D)] - \theta^f[y, \mu(y_f, y_m, p, D)]$.[16] Note again the common factor $\mu(y_f, y_m, p, D)$ in both components of the sharing rule.

For any good i consumed by the two parents and children, the household's demand function is

$$x_i(y_f, y_m, p, D) = F_i^f(\theta^f) + F_i^m(\theta^m) + F_i^c(y - \theta^m - \theta^f) \qquad (2.25)$$

where the arguments of θ^j have been omitted for simplicity. If we differentiate the demand function in (2.25) with respect to y_f and y_m and form the ratio of these derivatives, then we obtain, analogous to (2.8),

$$\frac{\partial x_i/\partial y_f}{\partial x_i/\partial y_m} = \frac{\partial \mu/\partial y_f}{\partial \mu/\partial y_m} = \frac{\partial x_j/\partial y_f}{\partial x_j/\partial y_m} \qquad \text{for all } i, j \qquad (2.26a)$$

$$\frac{\partial x_i/\partial D_k}{\partial x_i/\partial D_1} = \frac{\partial \mu/\partial D_k}{\partial \mu/\partial D_1} = \frac{\partial x_j/\partial D_k}{\partial x_j/\partial D_1} \qquad \text{for all } i, j, k = 2, \ldots, K \qquad (2.26b)$$

If these restrictions do not hold, then we must reject the cooperative model.

If the restrictions in (2.26) hold, then Bourguignon (1999) shows that in a number of plausible circumstances we can identify the sharing rule given by the functions θ^m and θ^f up to a constant. This means that we are able to say how changes in particular sources of income and distribution factors affect the consumption of each parent and expenditure on their children. For instance, it would tell us how much a child benefit paid to the mother would actually be spent on children, and how much it would change each parent's consumption and welfare.

2.6.3 Empirical Studies of Intra-Household Allocation

One of the first studies to estimate the "sharing rule" discussed in Section 2.2.3, by Browning et al. (1994), uses expenditure data from childless couples with both spouses in full-time employment from four Canadian family expenditure surveys. Their identification of the sharing rule (up to a constant) is based on the following assumptions: (a) that households achieve efficient allocations; (b) that preferences are "caring" in the sense of the separability in preferences assumed in (2.24); (c) that the private utility indices in (2.24) may include household public goods but they are separable in them (i.e. $U^j(x^j, G) = W^j(u^j(x^j), G)$, where G is a vector of household public goods); and (d) that men's and women's clothing are private goods.[17] The last assumption implies that wives (husbands) care about their husband's (wife's) clothing only to the extent that it contributes to the welfare of the husband (wife). Some may find this assumption objectionable, because they think people care how their spouses' dress. But the assumptions impose testable restrictions on the demand functions. A rejection of these restrictions can be taken narrowly as evidence that clothing is a public good, or more broadly that preferences take a less restrictive, "altruistic" form ($V^j = V^j(x^f, x^m, G)$), in contrast to the more restrictive assumption of "caring preferences".

The informal analysis by Browning et al. (1994) indicates that, after controlling for total expenditure in the demand function, among singles in full-time employment, a person's income does not affect his or her demand for clothing. But in couples with both spouses in full-time employment, the incomes of each person do affect the demands for men's and women's clothing. This difference in the effects of income variables between singles and couples is hard to explain if couples are also assumed to maximize a single utility function (i.e. the unitary model). The preliminary analysis also finds that, for a given level of total household income, less is spent on women's clothing in households in which the husband is better off relative to his wife.

They proceed to estimate a structural model of the demand for men's and women's clothing in households containing a childless married couple, which allows identification of the sharing rule. They cannot reject the restrictions implied by the identification assumptions; that is, it is acceptable to treat clothing as a private good in a model characterized by efficient households with caring preferences. Their estimates of the parameters of the sharing rule indicate that older and higher income partners receive more of total expenditure, and also that the wife receives proportionately more as total household expenditure increases (i.e. women receive more in wealthier households). While the share of the wife's expenditure increases with her share of household income, this "bargaining effect" is relatively modest: increasing her supply of household income from 25% of household income to 75%, her share in total expenditure increases by about 2%. The effect of total expenditure (wealth) on her share of expenditure is much more substantial: a 60% increase in total household expenditure increases the wife's share of it by 12%.

A less structural approach, but one that avoids making assumptions about the exogeneity of individual incomes, relies on a "natural experiment" arising from a policy change in the United Kingdom. Over the period 1977–1979, the Child Tax Allowance, which primarily went to the father through an increase in his take-home pay, was replaced by a single Child Benefit, which is paid directly to the mother. At the time, the change was perceived as a transfer of income "from the wallet to the purse". Under the unitary model, this would make no difference to expenditure patterns, but if individual income affects bargaining within the family, then the switch to paying child benefits to mothers should increase expenditure on women's clothing relative to expenditure on men's clothing. It may also increase the ratio of children's to men's clothing expenditure if mothers' preferences weight expenditure on children more than fathers' preferences. Lundberg et al. (1997) indeed find a substantial increase in spending on women's and children's clothing, relative to men's clothing, following the policy change. Not only is this strong evidence against the unitary model, but it suggests that children do better when mothers control more of family resources, that developments which improve women's earning opportunities affect the distribution of welfare within families and that it is possible to target policies on individuals within families.

Finally, in a very recent study, Chiappori et al. (2002) demonstrate the value of information on "distribution factors" affecting the sharing of income within the household. They use marriage market attributes and divorce laws as distribution factors in the context of a model of household labour supply. Their empirical application is not able to reject the efficiency hypothesis. Furthermore, the distribution factors generate new testable predictions concerning the relationship between the effect of any distribution factor and the impact of one spouse's wage on the labour supply of the other. These predictions are unlikely to be fulfilled unless the model is the correct one.

The analysis so far has taken the presence and number of children as given. Chapter 6 examines how such fertility decisions may be made. The next chapter investigates the implications of "caring" within families with very specific assumptions about family decision making.

NOTES

1. Strictly speaking, it may not always be the "best" that they can do in the absence of communication. As Schelling (1960, Chapter 3) shows, it may be possible to coordinate on a common choice without communication because the particulars of the case suggest one. The outcome of such tacit bargaining is determined by something that is fairly arbitrary. It arises because it is one of only a few outcomes that can serve as a coordinator.

2. Also, $[(\partial V^1/\partial U^1) + \mu(\partial V^2/\partial U^1)]U_x^1(x_1^e, G^e) = [(\partial V^1/\partial U^2) + \mu(\partial V^2/\partial U^2)]U_x^2(x_2^e, G^e)$.

3. Extension of the model to include leisure as another use of parents' time does not alter the main message of this section.

4. That is, an efficient allocation must maximize $U^1(x_1, G)$ subject to (a) $U^2(x_2, G) \geq U^{2*}$, (b) $(T - t_1)w_1 + (T - t_2)w_2 + y_1 + y_2 = x_1 + x_2$, (c) $G = h_1 t_1 + h_2 t_2$ and (d) $t_1 \geq 0, t_2 \geq 0$.

5. "Trust in another person" can be defined as having correct expectations about the actions of that person that affect one's own choice of action. A person is trusted to do something because you expect he(she) will *choose* to do it, not

merely because he(she) says he will. Various types of "commitment" (e.g. contracts and promises) alter your expectation of what he(she) will choose to do. See Dasgupta (1988).

6. Equivalently, we collapse the dynamic game to a one-stage cooperative game.

7. As Lundberg and Pollack (2001) point out, in a dynamic context the father's threat is not credible because he would not want to carry it out if called upon to do so. The father must commit to this allocation.

8. One of these is that the solution is invariant to positive linear transformations of the individual utility functions, which means that we are specifying *cardinal* utility functions, not just ordinal ones.

9. Denote utility in the non-cooperative equilibrium as U^{jnc} and that in the cooperative one as U^{jc}. For person 1, $U^{1c} \geq U^{1nc}$ requires that θ must satisfy $\alpha_1 \ln(1 - \theta) + (1 - \alpha_1)\ln[1 - \alpha_1 + (\alpha_1 - \alpha_2)\theta] \geq \alpha_1 \ln[(w_1 T + y_1)/Y_F] + (1-\alpha_1) \ln[(w_2 T + y_2)/Y_F] + (1-\alpha_1)\ln(1 - \alpha_2) - \alpha_1 \ln(\alpha_1)$, and for person 2, $U^{2c} \geq U^{2nc}$ requires that θ must satisfy $\alpha_2 \ln(\theta) + (1 - \alpha_2)\ln[1 - \alpha_1 + (\alpha_1 - \alpha_2)\theta] \geq (1 - \alpha_2)\ln(1 - \alpha_2) + \ln[(w_2 T + y_2)/Y_F]$.

10. If the model included leisure specifically, her leisure would also be smaller.

11. Her utility maximizing choices are $x_2 = \alpha_2(s + w_2 T + y_2)$, $z_2 = \gamma_2(s + w_2 T + y_2)/w_2$ and $G_2 = \beta_2(s + w_2 T + y_2)/(w_2/h_2)$, implying that $U^{2nc} =$ constant $+ \ln(s + w_2 T + y_2) + \beta_2 \ln(h_2) - (\beta_2 + \gamma_2)\ln(w_2)$.

12. The difference between person 1's utility in the cooperative equilibrium and that in the non-cooperative equilibrium is $\ln[\beta_1(w_1/h_1) + (1 - \beta_1)(w_2/h_2)] - \{\beta_1 \ln(w_1/h_1) + (1 - \beta_1)\ln(w_2/h_2)\} > 0$, because the logarithm function is concave.

13. These would also be the demands for leisure if G were a public good (i.e. $G_1 = G_2 = G$).

14. Similar remarks apply when we are studying expenditure on a public child good, like child's clothing, but in this case individual incomes may not affect expenditure in the general cooperative model because the parents' preferences are the same (see (2.22)).

15. The exogenous variables are not earnings, but individual "full incomes" ($w_j T + y_j$, where w_j is person j's wage rate, T is total time available and y_j is their non-earned income) and wage rates.

16. Note that here θ^j represents *amounts* of income rather than *share* of total income.

17. They are what they call *assignable* goods—private goods for which we can observe individual consumption.

CHAPTER THREE

Altruism in the Family

THE PURPOSE of this chapter is to examine the implications of a particular family decision-making rule. This rule is that the family maximizes the welfare of an "effective altruist". It has been an important part of the family economics literature (and indeed the economics literature more generally), and so despite the fact that it is a special case of the general cooperative (efficient outcomes) framework discussed in the preceding chapter, it is worthy of detailed investigation. In particular, the chapter considers the circumstances under which such a rule can produce efficient outcomes and reduce intra-family conflict.

In economic analysis, a person is said to be *altruistic* toward someone if his welfare depends on the welfare of that person. As the previous chapter indicated, in its most general form, we could define person 1 as altruistic toward person 2 if his(her) preferences are represented by the utility function $U^1 = U(x_1, x_2, G)$, where x_1 and x_2 are vectors of private goods consumed by persons 1 and 2, respectively, and G is a vector of public goods; that is, the preferences of the two people are interdependent.

But altruism is usually defined more narrowly; we have denoted this as "caring" preferences in the previous chapter. The altruist does not care how (in terms of x_2 and G) a given level of utility is obtained by his beneficiary. As in the Bergson–Samuelson social welfare function (Samuelson 1956), the altruist's "social" utility takes the form: $W^1 = W^1[U^1(x_1, G), U^2(x_2, G)]$, where $U^1(\ )$ and $U^2(\ )$ are "private" utility indices for each person, as in Section 2.2.3. Person 1 caring for (being altruistic towards) person 2 is represented by his utility being a positive function of her private utility (i.e. $\partial W^1 / \partial U^2 > 0$). Selfishness would be represented by $\partial W^1 / \partial U^2 = 0$. Clearly, the social utility function $W^1[\ ]$ could be defined over many beneficiaries. We shall identify "altruism" with such caring preferences in the remainder of the chapter.

Section 3.1 relates caring preferences and the operation of an effective altruist to the general cooperative (efficient outcomes) framework of the previous chapter, and Section 3.2 provides further discussion of the implications of effective altruism. Section 3.3 introduces the concept of "conditional transferable utility" with a view to deriving additional implications of effective altruism when preferences take that form in Section 3.4. Section 3.5 examines whether these implications carry over to preferences not characterized by transferable utility, while Section 3.6 considers the implications of a particular form of altruist's social preferences. In Sections 3.7 and 3.8, bequests and gifts from effective altruists are contrasted in terms of their efficiency implications, and Section 3.9 discusses a test of effective altruism in the context of the extended family. The chapter's analyses are summarized in a short concluding section.

3.1 Altruism and Bargaining

Altruistic (caring) preferences do not affect the conclusions derived from the general cooperative framework of the previous chapter. As Section 2.2.3 indicated, they only limit the relevant range of the utility possibility frontier expressed in terms of *private* preferences (Figure 2.3). In general, a bargaining rule is still needed to determine the point on the frontier that is chosen. Caring preferences do, however, have additional implications for how the impacts of individual incomes on efficient outcomes vary with respect to an individual's share of family income.

   To show this, we return to the basic model of Chapter 2, in which there is one private good, x_j, and one public good, G, which we can identify as expenditure on children. Suppose that a wife and her husband care for each other, and her share of joint income, $y_w/(y_w + y_h)$, is sufficiently large so that she is making transfers to her husband to ensure that his welfare is not too low. Using Becker's (1981) term, she is an *effective altruist*. Her social preferences are given by $W = W[U^w, U^h]$, and private preferences take the general form $U^j = U^j(x_j, G)$, $j = w, h$. Suppose the couple do not cooperate, but make voluntary contributions to the public good, as in Section 2.2.1. She chooses her contribution to the public good g_w and transfers to her husband s to maximize her utility subject to $y_w = s + pg_w + x_w$, his contribution to the public good g_h and $G = g_w + g_h$, where p is the price of the public good. He chooses g_h to maximize his utility $H = H[U^w, U^h]$ subject to $y_h + s = pg_h + x_h$. The first-order conditions in addition to the constraints are

$$W_w U_x^w = W_h U_x^h \tag{3.1a}$$

$$W_w U_G^w + W_h U_G^h = p W_w U_x^w \tag{3.1b}$$

$$H_w U_G^w + H_h U_G^h \leq p H_h U_x^h \tag{3.1c}$$

where $W_j = \partial W/\partial U^j$ and $H_j = \partial H/\partial U^j$.

   If he contributes to the public good, then (3.1c) holds with equality. Equations (3.1b) and (3.1c) then entail that $W_w U_x^w > W_h U_x^h$, because $W_w/W_h > H_w/H_h$ (see Section 3.4.1), in violation of (3.1a). Thus, if the wife makes transfers, she must be the only contributor to the public good (the strict inequality in (3.1c) holds). In effect, she chooses s and G to maximize her utility.

Combining (3.1a) and (3.1b), we obtain the Samuelson (1954) condition for the efficient level of the public good: $U_G^w/U_x^w + U_G^h/U_x^h = p$ (as in (2.6)). It is as if the spouses had cooperated because the husband is completely passive in these circumstances; he is too poor to affect the outcome.

As noted in the previous chapter, the definition of caring preferences imposes weak separability in the altruist's preferences. This separability implies that the choice (of x_h, x_w, G) that maximizes an *effective* altruist's utility can be broken down into two stages. First, find the allocations that maximize $U^w(x_w, G)$ for each $U^h(x_h, G)$. These satisfy the Samuelson condition and are efficient in terms of private preferences. The socially efficient allocation from the altruist's point of view will be found amongst these, and choosing it is the second stage of the problem. Thus, a necessary condition for efficiency in terms of the altruist's social preferences is efficiency in terms of private preferences. In other words, the altruist's socially efficient allocation is on the utility possibility frontier defined in terms of private preferences. Its position on the frontier corresponds to condition (3.1a), which can be written as $W_h/W_w = U_x^w/U_x^h = (-dU^h/dU^w)|_{\text{UPF}}$. This is the condition for tangency of the highest indifference curve $W[U^w, U^h] = \text{constant}$ and the utility possibility frontier in terms of private preferences.[1] In terms of Figure 2.3, this tangency point is A if person 2 is the wife.

Defining $\mu = W_h/W_w$, the first-order conditions (3.1a) and (3.1b) are the same as those for the general cooperative formulation of Section 2.2.2. However, in this range of the wife's share of family income (i.e. where she is an effective altruist), the sharing rule is independent of either spouse's individual income ($\partial\mu/\partial y_j = 0$, $j = w, h$). The conventional comparative static exercise applied to (3.1a) and (3.1b) then yields

$$\frac{\partial s}{\partial y_h} = \frac{-(\mu U_{xx}^h)d_{22} + d_{12}(\mu U_{xG}^h)}{D} \tag{3.2}$$

where $d_{22} = \mu U_{GG}^h + U_{GG}^w + p^2 U_{xx}^w - 2p U_{xG}^w < 0$, $d_{11} = \mu U_{xx}^h + U_{xx}^w < 0$ and $D = d_{11}d_{22} - d_{12}^2 > 0$ from the second-order conditions for a maximum, with $d_{12} = p U_{xx}^w + \mu U_{xG}^h - U_{xG}^w$ and $U_{xx}^j = \partial^2 U^j/\partial x_j^2$, $U_{xG}^j = \partial^2 U^j/\partial x_j \partial G$, etc. Also,

$$\frac{\partial s}{\partial y_w} = \frac{(U_{xx}^w)d_{22} - d_{12}(p U_{xx}^w - U_{xG}^w)}{D} \tag{3.3}$$

$$\frac{\partial G}{\partial y_h} = \frac{(\mu U_{xx}^h)d_{12} - d_{11}(\mu U_{xG}^h)}{D} \tag{3.4}$$

$$\frac{\partial G}{\partial y_{\mathrm{w}}} = \frac{-(U_{xx}^{\mathrm{w}})d_{12} + d_{11}(pU_{xx}^{\mathrm{w}} - U_{xG}^{\mathrm{w}})}{D} \tag{3.5}$$

The important predictions usually associated with effective altruism emerge from (3.2)–(3.5). First, from manipulation of (3.4) and (3.5), $\partial G/\partial y_{\mathrm{w}} = \partial G/\partial y_{\mathrm{h}}$; that is, expenditure on children only depends on joint family income $(y_{\mathrm{w}} + y_{\mathrm{h}})$, and so income redistribution between the parents has no effect on G. Individual consumption of the parents $(x_{\mathrm{w}}$ and $x_{\mathrm{h}})$ also depends on joint family income only. In other words, the position on the utility frontier in terms of private preferences (point A or B in Figure 2.3) is invariant to redistribution of income as long as the altruist remains effective. Second, from manipulation of (3.2) and (3.3), a redistribution of family income from the wife to the husband brings an equal reduction in transfers from her $(\partial s/\partial y_{\mathrm{h}} - \partial s/\partial y_{\mathrm{w}} = -1)$. Third, from (3.2), given additive separability between G and x_{h} (i.e. $U_{xG}^{\mathrm{h}} = 0$), an increase in the husband's income given the wife's income, must reduce transfers from her $(\partial s/\partial y_{\mathrm{h}} < 0)$, because both spouses' consumption must benefit from the increase in family income that arises from higher husband's income, and the only way that the wife can increase her consumption in this situation is to reduce transfers.

The first prediction means that individual income does not affect the efficient outcome when the wife's (or the husband's) share of joint family income is large enough. Because one of the spouses would be an *effective* altruist (i.e. making transfers to the other) when their incomes are sufficiently different, only joint income matters for consumption decisions in these circumstances.

If, however, their incomes are relatively similar, then neither spouse is "rich enough" relative to the other to make transfers to the other, in the sense that, $W_{\mathrm{w}} U_x^{\mathrm{w}} > W_{\mathrm{h}} U_x^{\mathrm{h}}$ in (3.1a), and similarly for the husband, $H_{\mathrm{h}} U_x^{\mathrm{h}} > H_{\mathrm{w}} U_x^{\mathrm{w}}$. That is, the marginal utility of the wife's private consumption exceeds her valuation of the marginal utility of her husband's private consumption, and similarly for her husband. As we know from Chapter 2, voluntary contributions to the public good alone will not produce an efficient outcome. They must cooperate to achieve efficient outcomes. If they do, then even after controlling for joint income, individual incomes may affect efficient consumption decisions, because of their impact on bargaining and the sharing rule, as discussed in Chapter 2.

This pattern of variation in the effects of individual incomes with the distribution of family income between spouses is indeed what Browning and Lechene (2001) find in their analysis of Canadian household expenditure data among married couples in which both spouses are in full-year, full-time employment. When the distribution of income within the family is skewed, they find that after controlling for total expenditure, the individual share of income does not affect expenditure on goods like children's and women's clothing; that is, the high income partner appears to behave as an effective altruist. This is the case for about half of the households in the sample. For the other half, the distribution of household income affects expenditure patterns. In particular, amongst this group, households in which the wife has a higher income share spend relatively more on women's clothing and children's clothing. The latter finding suggests that women's preferences favour children relative to men's. Thus, there is evidence of caring preferences for husbands and wives, but these only produce an effective altruist for about half of the sample. Caring preferences in conjunction with the assumption of efficient outcomes are equivalent to a bargaining rule that maximizes the utility of an effective altruist if there is one, and otherwise the couple bargain over the distribution of welfare in the family.

3.2 Implications of Effective Altruism

The analysis of the previous section indicated a number of interesting implications of a person being an *effective* altruist that are worth further discussion. These could apply to one spouse caring for the welfare of the other or parents caring for the welfare of their children, but to be concrete we shall continue to identify the wife as being an effective altruist toward her husband.

First, redistribution of income between her and her husband has no effect, provided that she remains an effective altruist. The previous section showed that such redistribution has no effect on the amount of the public good chosen or private consumption, because they only depend on joint income, not its distribution. The distribution of utilities is determined by (3.1a), and it is not altered by redistribution of income (provided that the wife remains an effective altruist). For example, shifting income from her to her husband would produce an offsetting reduction in transfers to him, leaving the distribution of utilities the same. In the context of the discussion of cooperative equilibria in the previous chapter, this means that the income sharing rule is independent of individual incomes; that is, the Lagrange multiplier μ is a constant in (2.7a) and (2.7b). If the redistribution from her to him were very large, she may cease being an effective altruist, in which case only part of the redistribution would be offset by a reduction in transfers to her husband.

Effective altruism also provides partial insurance. Suppose that the husband lost his job, causing a fall in his income. Because joint income falls, the utility possibility frontier would shift inwards. Both spouses' would suffer a fall in welfare. Part of his welfare decline would, however, be offset by higher transfers from his wife, and so she would absorb some of the decline in welfare. His reduction in utility would be smaller than if he was not the beneficiary of her altruism. If her income fell, she would reduce transfers to her husband, thereby partially offsetting the decline in her consumption and utility. Thus, effective altruism helps families insure their members. For the same reason, it also partially insulates them from targeted changes in taxes and benefits. For instance, shifting the payment of child benefits to mothers from fathers would have no effect.

In some circumstances, effective altruism can produce incentives for the beneficiary to act in the best interests of the family and reduce intra-family conflict. As a means to examining when maximizing an effective altruist's utility can produce these benefits, the next section introduces the concept of "transferable utility".

3.3 TRANSFERABLE UTILITY

There is *conditional transferable utility* if and only if preferences of every agent j can be represented by a utility function of the form $U^j = A(a)x_j + B_j(a)$, where x_j is person j's consumption of some private good x (e.g. "money" or a Hicksian composite commodity) and a is a vector of "actions" by all agents (Bergstrom and Cornes 1981; Bergstrom 1989). For example, for a married couple, a could be the choice of a public good or each spouse's consumption of some other private good, such as leisure. Note that the marginal utility of x_j is independent of the level of x_j, although it can depend on the actions a. For any two persons,

$$U^1 + U^2 = A(a)[x_1 + x_2] + B_1(a) + B_2(a) \qquad (3.6)$$

Equation (3.6) is the *conditional utility possibility frontier*, which is conditional on actions a, and the slope of the frontier is -1. It is clear from (3.6) that the sum of utilities is independent of the distribution of the private good (x), and independent of the distribution of utilities. Utility is transferable between individuals at a one-for-one rate through transfers of the private good.

In the context of the model of the previous section, conditional transferable utility requires that $U^j = U^j(x_j, G)$ can be written as $U^j = A(G)x_j + B_j(G)$, where private consumption by person j is denoted by x_j.[2] Thus, the "action" here is the choice of the public good. The marginal utility of x_j can depend on the level of G, but it is independent of the level of x_j. Individual variation in preferences for the public good are captured by the function $B_j(G)$.

An efficient allocation comes from maximizing U^1 subject to (i) $U^2 \geq U^{2^*}$ and (ii) $x_1 + x_2 + pG = y_1 + y_2$, where p is the price of the public good and y_j is person j's income. The first-order conditions for this problem entail that $A(G) = \mu A(G)$, where μ is the Lagrange multiplier on the efficiency constraint (i). As this equation implies $\mu = 1$, the efficient allocation arises from maximizing $U^1 + U^2 = A(G)[y_1 + y_2 - pG] + B_1(G) + B_2(G)$. Thus, an efficient allocation amounts to choosing the level of G so as to attain the highest possible conditional utility possibility frontier.

Of course, the first-order conditions for the efficient allocation problem also yield the Samuelson condition for the efficient level of the public good, which is now given by

$$p = \frac{A'(G)[y_1 + y_2 - pG] + B_1'(G) + B_2'(G)}{A(G)} \tag{3.7}$$

where $A'(G) = dA(G)/dG$, etc. Thus, the efficient level of G depends only on total income and relative prices and is independent of the distribution of income.

Substituting the optimal amounts of G and $x_1 + x_2$ into the conditional frontier yields the unconditional utility possibility frontier. Because these optimal amounts depend only on total income and p, this takes the form $U^1 + U^2 = g(y_1 + y_2, p)$, implying that the slope of the unconditional utility possibility frontier is also -1, and increases in joint income shift it outwards. As long as couples cooperate within marriage, total utility from the marriage is not affected by the distribution of utility between members of the couple when there is conditional transferable utility.

3.4 EFFECTIVE ALTRUISM WITH TRANSFERABLE UTILITY

Suppose, for example, that the wife in a couple is altruistic and the husband is selfish. With conditional transferable utility, her (caring) preferences are represented by $W = W[U^w, U^h]$, where $U^j = A(G)x_j + B_j(G)$, $j = h, w$, while his selfish preferences are simply represented by U^h. If she chooses the public good, her budget constraint is $y_w = s + x_w + pG$, and his is $x_h = s + y_h$, where s is transfers to her husband, with $s \geq 0$. She makes transfers to her husband and chooses the level of the public good to maximize W subject to these constraints.

The first-order conditions for the solution to this problem, which are equivalent to (3.1a) and (3.1b) with these particular preferences, are

$$W_w \geq W_h \tag{3.8a}$$

where $W_j = \partial W / \partial U^j$ and

$$pA(G)W_w = A'(G)\{W_w(y_w - s - pG) + W_h(y_h + s)\}$$

$$+ W_w B'_w(G) + W_h B'_h(G) \tag{3.8b}$$

Condition (3.8a) will hold with an equality when $s > 0$, and in this case (3.8b) becomes the Samuelson condition in (3.7). Thus, the wife's actions have achieved the utility possibility frontier in terms of the "private" utilities U^w and U^h, and the choice of the public good does not depend on the altruist's social preferences $W[U^w, U^h]$. The amount of the transfer to her husband is determined by her social preferences in conjunction with the linear utility possibility frontier with slope of -1, the position of which depends on $y_h + y_w$ and p.

The wife's social preferences are best achieved at the tangency of the highest indifference curve $W[U^w, U^h] =$ constant and the utility possibility frontier, as illustrated in Figure 3.1. At this tangency point, $W_w = W_h$. Having determined the optimum U^w and U^h, we work backwards and determine transfers to her husband as $s = [U^{h*} - A(G^*)y_h - B_h(G^*)]/A(G^*)$, where

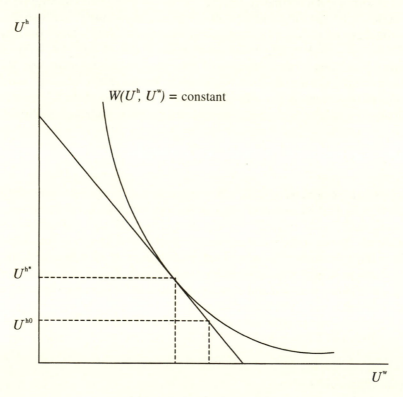

Figure 3.1 Altruistic wife.

U^{h*} is the optimum utility allocation from the tangency condition (3.8a) and G^* is the efficient amount of the public good from condition (3.8b). These transfers clearly decline with increases in her husband's income, holding joint income constant. Equivalently, $s = [A(G^*)(y_w - pG^*) + B_w(G^*) - U^{w*}]/A(G^*)$, and so transfers to her husband increase with increases in her income, given joint income.

These transfers are illustrated in Figure 3.1 in terms of utility by the movement from U^{h0} to U^{h*} along the utility possibility frontier, where U^{h0} is the utility the husband would achieve if the optimal amount of G were chosen, but his wife made no transfers. Both the husband and his wife are better off by moving from U^{h0} to U^{h*} through transfers from his altruistic wife, because she reaches a higher indifference curve in terms of her social preferences.

Like a benevolent dictator, the altruistic wife has achieved the efficient allocation by choosing the public good unilaterally and making transfers to her husband. The outcome would be the same if the wife let her husband choose the public good G. We have seen that the distribution of utilities is given by the tangency of her social indifference curve and the conditional utility possibility frontier. Let his share of the sum of utilities resulting from his wife's choice (i.e. the tangency point) be S^H, which is independent of the level of G. He would then wish to choose G to maximize $S^H(U^h + U^w) = S^H\{A(G)[y_h + y_w - pG] + B_h(G) + B_w(G)\}$. This results in the same choice of G that his wife would have made, which satisfies condition (3.8b) with $W_w = W_h$. Thus, he is content to let his altruistic wife choose G. There is no conflict concerning the choice of G, even though they may have different preferences (as reflected in $B_j(G)$).

She must, of course, have sufficient income to make transfers to her husband. If $W_w > W_h$ when $s = 0$, then she is "too poor to make transfers", in the sense that the marginal social utility of an increase in her own utility exceeds the marginal utility of any transfer of utility to him. In terms of Figure 3.1, this can occur if her private utility in the absence of transfers would be to the left of this tangency point, because of her low income. She has insufficient income to reach the tangency point. This is more likely to occur if her social indifference curves are steep (she is "not very altruistic"), in which case the tangency of the indifference curve and the conditional utility possibility frontier would be near the right end of the frontier.

In these circumstances, condition (3.8b) does not become the Samuelson condition. Letting $W_h/W_w|_{s=0} = \phi(y_h, y_w, p, G) < 1$, (3.8b) is

$$pA(G) = A'(G)[(y_w - pG) + \phi y_h] + B'_w(G) + \phi B'_h(G) \quad (3.9)$$

From (3.9) we see that now the distribution of income between the spouses matters for the choice of G, as does who chooses G. Also, social preferences matter for its determination, through ϕ. In these circumstances, the altruistic wife's actions will not be sufficient to achieve the efficient allocation. She must be an *effective altruist*, in the sense that $s > 0$, in order for her actions to be efficient.

For example, let $U^h = G(x_h - \beta)$ and $U^w = G(x_w - \alpha)$, which satisfy the conditions for conditional transferable utility. Also, let the wife's social preferences be given by $W[U^w, U^h] = (U^w)^\gamma (U^h)^{1-\gamma}$. When she is rich enough to make transfers, the couple achieve the efficient allocation $G = [y_h + y_w - (\alpha + \beta)]/2p$. If, however, she is "too poor" to make transfers, $\phi(y_h, y_w, p, G) = (1 - \gamma)(y_w - pG - \alpha)/\gamma(y_h - \beta) < 1$, and her choice of G is $(y_w - \alpha)/(1 + \gamma)p$. Thus, neither his preferences (β) nor his income are reflected in the choice of G. Also, in contrast to when she was an effective altruist, her social preferences (γ) matter for this choice. In this particular example, "too poor to make transfers" means that $(y_w - \alpha)/(y_h - \beta) < (1 + \gamma)/(1 - \gamma)$. This is more likely to be the case when y_w is lower relative to y_h, and when the wife is less altruistic (γ is larger).

3.4.1 The Rotten Kid Theorem

We have already seen that a selfish husband has the incentive to choose the efficient level of the public good, or alternatively is perfectly content to let his altruistic wife choose it, even though their preferences differ. More generally, both spouses would take actions that raise their *joint* income and avoid actions that lower it, because higher (lower) joint income shifts the utility possibility frontier outward (inward), thereby making both spouses better (worse) off. Even if an action increased the husband's income, he would avoid it if it lowered joint income, because transfers from his wife would decline sufficiently to reduce his utility. Indeed, he would take actions that lower his income if joint income increases. Again, the proviso is that his wife remains an effective altruist. If he had the opportunity for an income increase that exceeded his transfer from her, then he would take it, even if it lowered joint income.

This analysis also applies to parents' altruism toward their children. The impact of effective altruism on incentives is Becker's "Rotten Kid Theorem". Because a selfish beneficiary has an incentive to maximize joint family income, she is "led by the invisible hand of self interest to act as if she is altruistic toward her benefactor". (Becker 1981, p. 179). We could interpret the two private utilities in Figure 3.1 as belonging to two children toward whom their mother is altruistic. Her social preferences regarding the welfare of these two children are represented by the indifference curves. If she is making transfers to each child, then her transfers are used to distribute levels of welfare between her children.

These tend to have an equalizing influence on welfare levels: as one child's income increases relative to the other's she decreases her transfers to the child whose income increased and increases her transfers to the other child. Indeed, her actions would neutralize redistribution of income between the children. The Rotten Kid Theorem represents the incentive that each child has to maximize joint family income. Even if one child could take an action that would increase his own income, he would avoid doing so if it reduced joint family income.

The analysis has suggested that altruism tends to induce cooperative behaviour without retaliatory threats or negotiation. Extensive specialization and division of labour within families, particularly between men and women, encourages shirking of responsibilities and efforts to improve one's relative position. Because an effective altruist and her beneficiaries try to maximize joint family income, altruism encourages the division of labour and the efficient allocation of resources.

The utility of beneficiaries in effect "counts twice" (once for the altruist and once for her beneficiary). As a consequence, people are better off marrying people for whose welfare they care. That is, it is likely that a married couple will care for each other's welfare. In terms of our discussion so far, the husband's welfare is given by $H[U^w, U^h]$, where again $U^j = A(G)x_j + B_j(G)$, and the wife's is given by $W[U^w, U^h]$ above.

Such *reciprocal altruism* is illustrated in Figure 3.2. At e_1, the husband is an effective altruist, and he makes transfers to his wife to achieve the distribution of utilities at e_1. At e_2, she is an effective altruist, and she makes transfers to him. Note that e_2 is to the right of e_1 because both are likely to be more selfish than altruistic in the sense that when $U^h = U^w$, $\partial W/\partial U^w > \partial W/\partial U^h$ and $\partial H/\partial U^h > \partial H/\partial U^w$. For instance, when, as in the example above, $W[U^w, U^h] = (U^w)^\gamma(U^h)^{1-\gamma}$, this condition is that $\gamma > 0.5$. The condition for being an effective altruist ((3.8a) holding with equality) has $\partial W/\partial U^w = \partial W/\partial U^h$ at the optimum when the wife is an effective altruist, thereby implying $U^{h*} < U^{w*}$.

The equilibrium e_1 in Figure 3.2 occurs when the husband's income is high relative to that of his wife, and e_2 occurs when the wife is relatively rich. When one of the spouses is making transfers to the other, both would act to maximize their joint income. By providing two ranges of income over which an effective altruist is operating, joint income maximization is more likely when both spouses are altruistic.

If, however, the initial utilities in the absence of transfers are between these two points, neither spouse wishes to transfer to the other. Despite caring preferences, neither spouse would then be an effective altruist, because their incomes are too similar relative to the degree of their altruism. For example, if $W[U^w, U^h] = (U^w)^\gamma(U^h)^{1-\gamma}$ and $H[U^w, U^h] = (U^w)^{1-\gamma}(U^h)^\gamma$, and we assume the particular utility functions used earlier in this section ($U^h = G(x_h - \beta)$ and $U^w = G(x_w - \alpha)$), then she will make transfers (be an effective alturist) when $(y_w - \alpha)/(y_h - \beta) > (1 + \gamma)/(1 - \gamma)$, and he will be an effective altruist when $(y_w - \alpha)/(y_h - \beta) < (1 - \gamma)/(1 + \gamma)$. When $(y_w - \alpha)/(y_h - \beta)$ lies between $(1 - \gamma)/(1 + \gamma)$ and $(1 + \gamma)/(1 - \gamma)$, neither spouse is an effective altruist. When relative spouse's incomes are in this intermediate range, the benefits of effective altruism cannot be attained.

Efficient outcomes and the incentive of beneficiaries to maximize joint family income with an *effective* altruist making decisions are remarkable implications of altruistic behaviour. Reciprocal altruism will also tend to make welfare outcomes in the family more equal, as the richer spouse transfers income to the poorer one. But the existence of altruistic preferences per se does not eliminate conflict and generate efficient outcomes. We have seen that when initial welfare positions are more equal, an effective altruist may not emerge (Figure 3.2).

This may be of increasing importance because labour market developments have tended to produce more equal wage outcomes for men and women. When we incorporate household production and labour supply

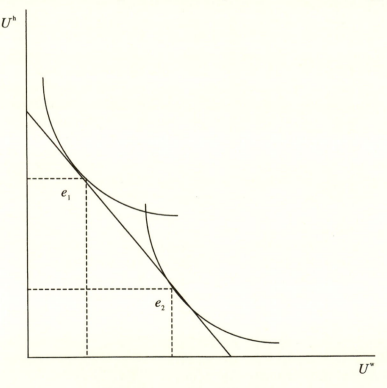

Figure 3.2 Reciprocal altruism.

decisions in the model, as, for example, in Section 2.3, then the relative income concept for each spouse is relative "full income" ($w_i T + v_i$, where w_i is the wage, T is total time available and v_i is non-labour income). More equal full incomes of spouses would operate against an effective altruist emerging. A middle-aged parent would, however, be more likely to be an effective altruist relative to his young adult child.

In any case, the implications of having an effective altruist for incentives are powerful. Do they carry over to preferences not characterized by conditional transferable utility?

3.5 Effective Altruism without Transferable Utility

Suppose we return to utility functions similar to those assumed in Chapter 2: $\ln(U^j) = \alpha_j \ln(x_j) + (1 - \alpha_j)\ln(G)$, $j = \text{h, w}$. Note that these do not satisfy the conditions for conditional transferable utility, because the marginal utility of x_i depends on the level of x_j. We shall assume the wife is an effective altruistic and her social preferences are again of the form $W = (U^w)^\gamma (U^h)^{1-\gamma}$. She chooses transfers to her husband and the public good to maximize W. The first-order conditions imply that $pG = (1 - \alpha)(y_h + y_w)$, where $\alpha = \gamma\alpha_w + (1 - \gamma)\alpha_h$, and $x_h = (1 - \gamma)\alpha_h(y_h + y_w)$. Thus, the logarithm of the husband's utility when his wife chooses G is $\ln(U_W^h) = \alpha_h \ln[(1 - \gamma)\alpha_h] + (1 - \alpha_h)\ln(1 - \alpha) + \ln(y_h + y_w)$.

Now suppose that, because of her altruism, the wife continues to make transfers to her husband, but he chooses the public good G. She chooses transfers to maximize her utility for a given level of G, and so her transfers are according to the following rule: $s = [(1 - \gamma)\alpha_h y_w - \gamma\alpha_w(y_h - pG)]/\alpha$. He chooses G to maximize his utility subject to this transfer rule. The first-order conditions entail that $pG = (1 - \alpha_h)(y_h + y_w)$ and $x_h = (1 - \gamma)\alpha_h^2(y_h + y_w)/\alpha$. Thus, the logarithm of his utility when he chooses G is $\ln(U_H^h) = \alpha_h \ln[(1 - \gamma)\alpha_h^2/\alpha] + (1 - \alpha_h)\ln(1 - \alpha_h) + \ln(y_h + y_w)$.

As long as the husband and wife's preferences differ ($\alpha_w \neq \alpha_h$), it matters who chooses the public good G, even though the wife is an effective altruist. To see this, note that

$$\ln(U_W^h) - \ln(U_H^h) = \alpha_h \ln\left(\frac{\alpha}{\alpha_h}\right) + (1 - \alpha_h)\ln\left(\frac{1 - \alpha}{1 - \alpha_h}\right) \qquad (3.10)$$

It is clear from (3.10) that the husband would prefer to choose G if and only if

$$\alpha_h \ln\left(\frac{\alpha_h}{\alpha}\right) > (1 - \alpha_h)\ln\left(\frac{1 - \alpha}{1 - \alpha_h}\right) \qquad (3.11)$$

This is always satisfied when $\alpha_w \neq \alpha_h$; that is, when his wife's preferences are different, he would prefer to choose the public good. Furthermore, the larger is γ (i.e. the less altruistic is his wife), the more he gains from choosing G himself.[3]

The example has shown that even when the wife is an effective altruist, there is a conflict about who chooses the public good when her preferences differ from her husband's. The selfish husband would be better off choosing the public good when their preferences are different, and the wife would be better off if she chose it. Furthermore, in contrast to the case of conditional transferable utility, because $pG = (1 - \alpha)(y_h + y_w)$ when she chooses it, the choice of the public good depends (through α) on the degree of altruism of the wife (γ), making resource allocation (public good) decisions interdependent with distribution decisions. Note that the difference in G between when he and she chooses it is $(\alpha - \alpha_h)(y_h + y_w)$. As we would expect, he would choose a larger (smaller) G than she would when $\alpha_w > \alpha_h$ ($\alpha_h > \alpha_w$).

The reason that this conflict occurs is that, in the absence of transferable utility, the slope of the conditional utility possibility frontier depends on G. In the particular example, along the frontier,

$$\left. \frac{dU^h}{dU^w} \right|_{UPF} = - \frac{\alpha_h}{\alpha_w} \frac{x_w^{1-\alpha_w}}{x_h^{1-\alpha_h}} G^{\alpha_w - \alpha_h} \qquad (3.12)$$

When $\alpha_w > \alpha_h$, the larger the choice of G, the steeper the conditional utility possibility frontier. A steeper frontier means that it is "cheaper" for the wife to supply U^h, in that a smaller reduction in her utility is required to increase his utility. Thus, the larger is G, the higher the U^h the wife will choose through her altruistic transfers, making a steeper frontier more favourable to the husband. We have seen that when $\alpha_w > \alpha_h$, he would choose a larger G than she would, and this provides an incentive for the husband to choose G. When $\alpha_h > \alpha_w$, the smaller the choice of G, the steeper the conditional utility possibility frontier. We have seen that when $\alpha_h > \alpha_w$, he would choose a smaller G than she would, which again provides an incentive for the husband to choose G. In either case, by choosing G he can twist the terms of redistribution along the frontier in his favour.

In general, the conflict on the choice of G (and in the more general case, actions a) occurs when the conditional utility possibility frontiers intersect; that is, different Gs (different actions) affect the slope of the frontier. As Figure 3.3 illustrates, the husband would prefer frontier UU to $U'U'$. When there is such an intersection, it is possible to construct benevolent preferences for the wife such that the husband's choice of G is against her interests.[4] Thus, effective altruism does not automatically align the

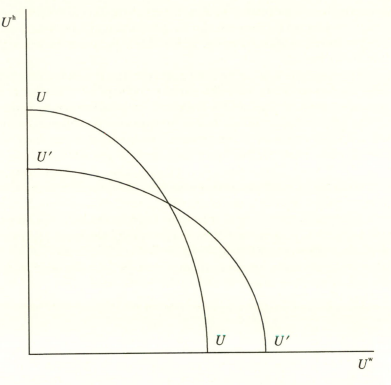

Figure 3.3 Conditional utility possibility frontiers intersecting.

interest of the beneficiary with those of the altruist, in contrast to what the Rotten Kid Theorem would suggest. Bergstrom (1989) shows that a *necessary* condition for such conflict to be avoided is that there is conditional transferable utility. Of course, in the general cooperative framework of the previous chapter, the question is not "who chooses" the public good, but "how it is chosen", particularly how does bargaining in a cooperative setting affect the choice.

3.6 RAWLSIAN ALTRUISTS

Bergstrom's analysis focussed on the type of "private" preferences required for the Rotten Kid Theorem to work. Jürges (2000) considers whether the form of "social preferences" matters. In particular, what if the altruist is "Rawlsian" in the sense that she wants the beneficiary to be at least as well off as herself? This has some intuitive appeal for a couple—one partner cannot be happy if the other is unhappy. It is also appealing when a parent is altruistic toward her children, because parents often state that they wish their children to be better off than themselves. Rawlsian preferences are also less demanding in the sense that the altruist only makes an *ordinal* judgement about her own utility compared to the beneficiary's, in contrast to the caring preferences assumed so far, which need to evaluate increments in own utility compared to the beneficiary's. That is, *cardinality* in utility was assumed in the foregoing analysis.

The Rawlsian altruist's social preferences are given by $W = \min\{U^w, U^h\}$, and private preferences take the general form $U^j = U^j(x_j, G)$. This social welfare function is not fully consistent with the definition of altruism given at the start of this chapter because $\partial W/\partial U^h > 0$ does not hold for every combination of U^w and U^h. It does, nevertheless, reflect altruistic behaviour in the everyday use of the term. The Rawlsian altruist delegates the choice of the public good (G) to her beneficiary and makes transfers to him to maximize her social welfare function. The welfare maximizing condition for the Rawlsian altruist is $U^w = U^h$, and this implies the following reaction function for the altruist's transfers as a function of the beneficiary's choice of the public good:

$$s'(G) = \frac{ds}{dG} = \frac{U^w_G + pU^h_x - U^h_G}{U^w_x + U^h_x} \tag{3.13}$$

where $U^w_G = \partial U^w/\partial G$, etc. The beneficiary maximizes his utility $U^h(y_h + s - pG, G)$ subject to (3.13). It is straightforward to show that the first-order condition for his problem is the Samuelson condition for the efficient level of the public good, namely $U^w_G/U^w_x + U^h_G/U^h_x = p$, as in (2.6).

Thus, we have shown that an altruist with Rawlsian social preferences can achieve, through her transfers, the efficient level of the public good irrespective of the form of the private preferences of the beneficiary and altruist. Rawlsian preferences are a limiting case of the wide class of CES-type welfare functions: $W(U_1, U_2) = [U_1^c + U_2^c]^{1/c}$, with $c \leq 1$. The parameter c indicates the degree of aversion to inequality between altruist and beneficiary's utility, with lower c indicating more inequality aversion. With $c = 1$, preferences are utilitarian, and as c approaches negative infinity preferences are Rawlsian. Analysis by Jürges (2000) indicates that the inefficiency of outcomes for general private preferences disappears as the altruist's aversion to inequality approaches infinity. This special class of social preferences is used in subsequent chapters.

3.7 Lazy Rotten Kids

The Rotten Kid Theorem of Section 3.4.1 suggests that parents should delay transfers to their children until late in their lifetime or indeed until after their death, because this provides children a long-run incentive to consider the interests of the entire family and maximize joint family income (e.g. Becker 1981, p. 188). Thus, it suggests that altruistic parents should use bequests rather than gifts.[5] Bergstrom (1989) showed that many of the implications of the Rotten Kid Theorem break down when beneficiaries suffer disutilities of effort; he called this the case of "lazy rotten kids". This section examines whether bequests are preferred to gifts in this situation.

Let the private utility index of the parents be given by $U^{\mathrm{p}}(x_{\mathrm{p}})$, where x_{p} is parents' consumption, and the private utility index of the child is given by $U^c(x_c, e)$, where x_c is the child's consumption and e is their work effort, with $U_e^c = \partial U^c/\partial e < 0$. We have seen at the outset of the chapter that efficiency in terms of these private preferences is a necessary condition for efficiency in terms of social preferences. Thus, the conditions for an efficient allocation come from maximizing $U^{\mathrm{p}}(x_{\mathrm{p}})$ for each $U^c(x_c, e)$ subject to $x_{\mathrm{p}} + x_c = y_{\mathrm{p}} + we$, where y_{p} is the parents' income, and w is the child's wage. It is straightforward to derive that the efficient allocation of child's effort must satisfy

$$U_x^c w = -U_e^c \tag{3.14}$$

where $U_x^c = \partial U^c/\partial x_c$. That is, the marginal gain from extra work must equal the marginal cost of work effort.

Now suppose that parents retain the last word by making bequests. Let their altruistic social preferences be given by the function $W[U^{\mathrm{p}}(x_{\mathrm{p}}), U^c(x_c, e)]$. They choose a bequest b to maximize W subject to $x_{\mathrm{p}} = y_{\mathrm{p}} - b$ and $x_c = we + b$, where b is the bequest transfer from parents to child, with $b \geq 0$. This implies that when $b > 0$,

$$W_{\mathrm{p}} U_x^{\mathrm{p}} = W_c U_x^c \tag{3.15}$$

where $W_{\mathrm{p}} = \partial W/\partial U^{\mathrm{p}}$, etc. Equation (3.15) in association with the budget constraints implies a bequest function $b(y_{\mathrm{p}}, ew)$, which is increasing in y_{p} and decreasing in ew. The child takes this transfer function as a constraint in maximizing his utility, so that he chooses e to maximize $U^c(ew + b(y_{\mathrm{p}}, ew), e)$. This implies

$$U_x^c \left[w + \frac{\partial b}{\partial e} \right] = -U_e^c \tag{3.16}$$

Because $\partial b/\partial e < 0$, the efficiency condition (3.14) is not fulfilled. The left-hand side of (3.16) is smaller than the left-hand side of (3.14), which implies lower child's effort when (3.16) is satisfied than when (3.14) is satisfied. As we might expect, bequests discourage effort by the child, because effort is costly and parents compensate through their bequests for exerting less effort. Because bequests are inefficient, altruistic parents clearly do not encourage their child to maximize family income, contrary to the Rotten Kid Theorem.

Suppose instead that parents pre-commit to a fixed transfer before the child chooses his(her) work effort, which we shall denote as a gift, g. So the child chooses his(her) effort to maximize $U^c(ew + g, e)$, which entails the first-order condition in (3.14). Because the gift only has an income effect, it elicits the efficient effort response. In choosing the amount of gift to make, parents take into account the child's effort response, $e = e(w, g)$, which is derived from the efficiency condition in (3.14). Thus, the parents choose g to maximize $W\{U^p(y_p - g), U^c[we(w, g) + g, e(w, g)]\}$, which implies the condition in (3.15).

This analysis indicates, therefore, that gifts (pre-committed fixed transfers) are preferable in the sense that they are efficient for the family. The child is clearly worse off than in the equilibrium with bequests, because he(she) could work less and obtain higher transfers with bequests, while the parents are better off. Thus, we cannot say that the gift equilibrium is a Pareto improvement on the bequest equilibrium, only that is efficient and the bequest equilibrium is not.

Jürges (2000) provides a fuller analysis of this situation, and he also shows that when the parents' social preferences are Rawlsian, the bequest and gift equilibra are the same, making both the parents and child indifferent between the timing of transfers. To see this, recall that $U^p = U^c$ is the welfare-maximizing condition for the Rawlsian altruist, and this implies the following reaction function for the bequest as a function of the child's choice of effort:

$$b'(e) = \frac{db}{de} = -\frac{U_e^c + wU_x^c}{U_x^p + U_x^c} \tag{3.17}$$

The child maximizes his utility $U^c(we + b(e), e)$ subject to (3.17), and this implies

$$\frac{[U_x^c w + U_e^c]U_x^p}{U_x^p + U_x^c} = 0 \tag{3.18}$$

In turn, (3.18) is only satisfied if (3.14) is satisfied, because $U_x^p/(U_x^p + U_x^c) > 0$. Thus, bequests from Rawlsian parents produce an efficient outcome, which is identical to that produced by giving gifts (i.e. fixed transfers).

3.8 THE SAMARITAN'S DILEMMA

The case of "lazy rotten kids" is an example of the general phenomenon of what Buchanan (1975) calls the "Samaritan's dilemma". It arises when a benefactor's generosity encourages beneficiaries to be less self-sufficient. Another example of this comes from an intertemporal allocation problem (e.g. see Bruce and Waldman 1990). Consider a model with only one consumption good, but it is consumed over two periods; that is, there are savings. Assume again that parents retain the last word by making bequests (in the second period of their life). Let their altruistic social preferences be given by the function $W[U^p(x_{p1}, x_{p2}), U^c(x_{c1}, x_{c2})]$, where $x_{pj}(x_{cj})$ is parents' (child's) consumption in period j. They choose a bequest b and their own savings s_p to maximize W subject to $x_{p1} = y_{p1} - s_p$, $x_{p2} = y_{p2} - b + (1 + r)s_p$, $x_{c1} = y_{c1} - s_c$ and $x_{c2} = y_{c2} + (1 + r)s_c + b$, where b is the bequest transfer from parents to child ($b \geq 0$), r is the interest rate, y_{ij} are incomes per period j ($i = p, c$) and s_c is the child's savings. This implies that when $b > 0$,

$$W_p U_2^p = W_c U_2^c \qquad (3.19)$$

where $W_p = \partial W / \partial U^p$, $U_2^c = \partial U^c / \partial x_{c2}$, etc.

$$U_2^p(1 + r) = U_1^p \qquad (3.20)$$

Equation (3.19) says that the parents equate their marginal utility of consumption in the second period to the second-period marginal utility of their child, adjusted by the degree of altruism implicit in their social preferences, W_c / W_p. Equation (3.20) is the usual condition for the optimal allocation of lifetime income to consumption in the two periods, which equates marginal utilities of consumption in the two periods adjusted by the interest rate. In association with the lifetime budget constraint, these two equations imply a bequest function $b(Y_p, y_{c2} + (1 + r)s_c)$, where $Y_p = y_{p1} + y_{p2}/(1 + r)$ is parents' lifetime income. Bequests are increasing in Y_p and decreasing in $y_{c2} + (1 + r)s_c$. The child takes this transfer function as a constraint in maximizing his utility, so that he chooses s_c to maximize $U^c[y_{c1} - s_c, y_{c2} + (1 + r)s_c + b(Y_p, y_{c2} + (1 + r)s_c)]$. This implies

$$(1 + r)U_2^c\left[1 + \frac{\partial b}{\partial(y_{c2} + (1 + r)s_c)}\right] = U_1^c \qquad (3.21)$$

The condition for an efficient level of the child's saving is analogous to (3.20). Because $\partial b / \partial(y_{c2} + (1 + r)s_c) < 0$, (3.21) implies that $(1 + r)U_2^c > U_1^c$, and so the parents' bequest behaviour produces too little saving by their child. The child over-consumes in the first period in order to be more impoverished and receive larger bequests in the second period.

The child does, however, have an incentive to maximize the joint income of the family with this bequest rule. To see this clearly, consider the following simple inter-temporal utility functions, $U^i = \ln(x_{i1}) + \ln(x_{i2})/(1 + \rho_i)$, where ρ_i is the discount rate, $i = p, c$. To further simplify, let $\rho_p = \rho_c = r$ and $\beta = W_c / W_p$, which indicates the relative weight of children in parents' social preferences. With these preferences, the first-order conditions above imply that the bequest function is

$$b = \frac{\beta(1 + r)Y_p - (2 + r)[y_{c2} + (1 + r)s_c]}{(\beta + 2 + r)} \tag{3.22}$$

and the child's consumption in the two periods is

$$x_{c1} = \frac{(1 + r)(Y_c + Y_p)}{(2 + r)} \quad \text{and} \quad x_{c2} = \frac{\beta(1 + r)(Y_c + Y_p)}{(2 + r)(\beta + 2 + r)} \tag{3.23}$$

where $Y_c = y_{c1} + y_{c2}/(1 + r)$.

The child has an incentive to take actions that increase joint income $Y_c + Y_p$ because such actions increase his consumption in both periods. Thus, the Rotten Kid Theorem operates to encourage the child to maximize joint family income, but the outcome is inefficient because the child's intertemporal consumption allocation is not efficient. Note that, with these preferences, the efficient allocation of the child's consumption across periods would have $x_{c1} = x_{c2}$, but with the parents' bequest behaviour, x_{c2} is a fraction of first-period consumption: $x_{c2} = \beta x_{c1}/(\beta + 2 + r)$.

Now consider what would happen if the parent pre-commits to gifts (g) in the first period. This is equivalent to giving the child an increase in his first-period income, and therefore his lifetime income. He allocates this efficiently between periods; thus, with first-period gifts from altruistic parents, there is no incentive to save too little. In choosing the amount of the first-period gift, parents' take into account the child's consumption response. With the special assumptions about preferences, the child's response function would be $x_{cj} = (1 + r)(Y_c + g)/(2 + r)$, $j = 1, 2$, and parents would make gifts according to the function $g = (\beta Y_p - Y_c)/(1 + \beta)$. Thus, the child's consumption in period j would be $x_{cj} = (1 + r)\beta(Y_c + Y_p)/[(2 + r)(1 + \beta)]$. This gives the child an incentive to choose actions in the first period that maximize joint family income. But once he has received the gift in the first period, he would wish to take actions that maximize his own income in the second period, even if it reduced joint family income, because such actions would raise his second-period consumption and lifetime utility. Thus, the Rotten Kid Theorem would break down because of the absence of second-period transfers.

This analysis indicates that second-period bequests would produce an inefficient outcome because of the Samaritan's dilemma, while first-period gifts would be inefficient because of the failure of the Rotten Kid Theorem. Even effective altruism fails to produce efficient outcomes in this situation, irrespective of whether transfers are given "early" or "late".

If per-period incomes were fixed, then inefficiencies associated with "rotten kid behaviour" can be ignored. As with "lazy rotten kids", the gift equilibrium is efficient for the family while the bequest equilibrium is not. But with gifts in the first period, the child's utility is lower than with bequests in the second period. The child would prefer bequests because he can manipulate them in his favour, while the parents prefer the pre-committed gift transfer in the first period. Furthermore, using the same methods as those leading to (3.17), it is easy to show that if parents have Rawlsian social preferences, second-period bequests produce an efficient outcome, which is the same as that produced by first-period gifts.

Finally, the inter-temporal consumption problem indicates another reason why gifts may be preferred to bequests. Suppose the child does not have access to capital markets in the first period while the parents do. Then altruistic parents making first-period gifts can produce an efficient outcome, while second-period bequests do not.

3.9 Testing for Effective Altruism between Generations

The empirical strategy for testing whether an extended family's decision rule is to maximize the utility of an effective altruist is clearest in a simple model of altruism of parents toward their children. In particular, each child's welfare depends on one private consumption good and the parents' welfare depends on their own private consumption and the welfare of each of their children. Altonji et al. (1992, p. 1180) show that "the basic test procedure carries over to more realistic dynamic models with multiple consumption goods, uncertainty, and endogenous labor supply."

Parents' welfare is, therefore, given by $W[U^p(x_p), U^1(x_1), ..., U^n(x_n)]$, where x_j is the consumption of the jth child, x_p is parents' consumption and U^j are their respective private utility indices. Parents choose transfers to each child, s_j, to maximize W subject to $x_p = y_p - \sum_j s_j$ and $x_j = y_j + s_j$, where $s_j \geq 0$, and y_j are the respective incomes $(j = 1, ..., n, p)$. This is equivalent to a combined budget constraint for the extended family of $\sum_j x_j = \sum_j y_j$. The solution to this problem implies that when, for all j, $s_j > 0$,

$$W_p U^{p'} = W_j U^{j'} = \lambda \qquad (3.24)$$

where $W_j = \partial W / \partial U^j$ and $U^{j'} = dU^j / dx_j, j = 1, ..., n, p$ and λ is the marginal utility of income associated with the combined income of the extended family. In other words, when the parents are effective altruists for every one of their children, they make transfers to equate the appropriately weighted marginal utility of consumption of themselves and every child in their family to the same marginal utility of income, which is unique to that (extended) family. In contrast, if the individual life-cycle model is correct, parents and children maximize their own utility subject to their own resources, and have different marginal utilities of income.

Thus, an altruistically linked extended family fully pools resources among its members in the sense that the division of the total income of the extended family among consumption of the family members is independent of the distribution of individual income among them. We can test that the extended family's decision rule is to maximize the utility of an effective altruist by testing whether parents resources, y_p, enter the parents' consumption equation and whether the child's resources, y_j, enter that child's consumption equation. If they do, then we must reject this decision rule (or any other one that would produce income pooling in the extended family). Rejection is consistent with the individual life-cycle model or a general cooperative model for the extended family.

In their study, Altonji et al. (1992) use data of parents matched together with at least a subset of their independent children drawn from the American Panel Study of Income Dynamics (PSID). The measure of consumption is food consumption. In their tests they use total income, non-labour income, home equity and wages rates as proxies for the resource position of particular extended family members. Each of these is a significant variable in explaining the consumption of extended family members even after controlling for the extended family's marginal utility of income. Thus, there is strong rejection of the altruism model when applied to the extended family. This is also the case for a sample consisting of "rich" parents and "poor" children, for whom parents would be expected to be an *effective* altruist (i.e. transfers are being made to every child).

The rejection of the decision rule of maximizing an effective altruist's utility in this study does not, however, mean that altruistically motivated transfers are not important. Even in the context of intergenerational transfers, condition (3.24) may not hold because of imperfect information about child's effort available to the parents, as studied in Section 9.4. Furthermore, transfers may be used to help adult children who face borrowing constraints to smooth their consumption early in their adult life, especially in the context of human capital investments, as explored more fully in Chapters 9 and 10. They may also be used to smooth consumption among households belonging to an extended family in response to the risks inherent in agricultural production. For instance, Rosenzweig (1988) finds that the response of household net transfers to deviations from longer-term income is larger when the household contains more daughters-in-law of the head.[6] While kinship links support such implicit insurance contracts because of the trust and information they engender, they also reflect altruism. Parents may also delay transfers until their death because they are concerned that their children will squander them and ask for more (Lindbeck and Weibull 1988). In this case, transfers would not equate the marginal utility of income across households of the extended family during the parents' life.

3.10 CONCLUSION

Maximizing the utility of an effective altruist is not sufficient to produce efficient allocations, or to eliminate conflicts about allocations and the distribution of welfare between partners. The association of efficiency and conflict resolution with altruistic behaviour is derived from simple models in which there is conditional transferable utility or a Rawlsian altruist. They do not arise automatically in more general settings.

Many of the powerful results stemming from the operation of an effective altruist do not extend beyond the transferable utility and Rawlsian altruist cases, and we have seen that a major empirical study rejects this family decision rule in the extended American family. Another study does find evidence of caring preferences for spouses within households, but among about half of the sample there was not an effective altruist. Nevertheless, altruism remains a valuable concept when discussing the interaction between individual preferences and family behaviour. Chapters 5 and 6 assume a paternalistic form of altruism in which parents are concerned with the adult incomes rather than the utility of their children. But we return to the altruism model in order to contrast it with non-altruistic motives for inter-generational transfers in Chapter 9, and also in the context of support for human capital investment and multi-generation households in Chapter 10.

NOTES

1. The altruist's choices in terms of the utility possibility frontier are discussed in more detail in Section 3.4, in which a particular type of private preferences is assumed.

2. Note that the particular specification of the utility function used often in Chapter 2 cannot be written in this form, and so it is not consistent with conditional transferable utility.

3. $\ln(U_W^h) - \ln(U_H^h)$ is decreasing in γ.

4. In the preceding example, the husband prefers to choose G for all values of her altruism parameter, γ.

5. Of course, this would not be the case if adult children face borrowing constraints at some points in their life.

6. In Chapter 7, we examine how this risk reduction motive may influence marriage decisions.

CHAPTER FOUR

Home Production and Investment

AS A FOUNDATION for analysis in subsequent chapters, this chapter analyses "home production", the division of parents' labour and their implications for the costs of home-produced goods, such as the child's human capital. In many respects this is a straightforward application of production and cost analysis from the theory of the firm. But the elaboration of certain aspects is helpful in the context of the economics of the family. These include the possibilities of "corner solutions" in the use of parents' time inputs and of investments that affect parents' productivity in the market or in home production. The first section develops the theory when parents' wages and home productivity are taken as given; the next section explores the implications of investments that change these; and the final section discusses some empirical applications of the concept of home production.

4.1 HOME PRODUCTION AND COSTS

Section 2.3 considered the allocation of time to the production of a "child good", G, which is a public good to the parents. It assumed a very special production function for G, which only used parents' time and led to one parent doing all of the home production and the other specializing in paid work. We now generalize this formulation, taking each parent's wage and home productivity as given in this section, and then allowing for investments in specialized human capital, which increase market or home productivity, in the next section.

The good G is assumed to be produced by combinations of purchased goods and services, x_c, mother's time, t_m, and father's time t_f: $G = g(x_c, t_m, t_f; S_m, S_f)$, where S_m and S_f are indicators of each parent's efficiency in home production, such as the mother's and father's education, respectively. The function $g(\cdot)$ exhibits constant returns to scale in x_c, t_m and t_f.

The parents cooperate to choose their own consumption, x_m and x_f, and inputs x_c, t_m and t_f in the production of G subject to their budget constraint, which is $x_m + x_f + p_c x_c = (T - t_m)w_m + (T - t_f)w_f + y$, to $0 \le t_j \le T$, $j = m, f$ and to $x_c \ge 0$, where w_j is parent j's wage rate, p_c is the price of goods used in the production of G, y is other family income, and each parent's total time is T. The parents' choices of their own consumption and G can be separated from their choices of inputs x_c, t_m and t_f in the production of G. The first stage of this two-stage problem is to minimize the total cost of producing G. That is, the parents choose x_c, t_m and t_f to minimize $p_c x_c + w_m t_m + w_f t_f$ subject to $G^* = g(x_c, t_m, t_f; S_m, S_f)$, $0 \leq t_j \leq T$, $j = $ m, f and $x_c \geq 0$, where G^* is a particular level of the child good. In the second stage, the parents cooperate to choose x_m, x_f and G subject to $y + (w_m + w_f)T = x_m + x_f + \pi G$, where π is the (marginal) shadow price of G implied by solution to the first stage problem.

The Kuhn–Tucker first-order conditions for the first stage problem are:

$$p_c + \mu_{0x} = \pi g_x \qquad (4.1a)$$

where $g_x = \partial g/\partial x_c$ and $\pi > 0$;

$$w_m + \mu_{0m} = \pi g_m + \mu_m \qquad (4.1b)$$

where $g_m = \partial g/\partial t_m$;

$$w_f + \mu_{0f} = \pi g_f + \mu_f \qquad (4.1c)$$

where $g_f = \partial g/\partial t_f$;

$$\mu_j(T - t_j) = 0, \qquad j = \text{m}, \text{f} \qquad (4.1d)$$

where $\mu_j < 0$ when $T = t_j$ and $\mu_j = 0$ when $T > t_j$;

$$\mu_{0x} x_c = 0, \qquad \mu_{0j} t_j = 0, \qquad j = \text{m}, \text{f} \qquad (4.1e)$$

where $\mu_{0j} = 0$ when the input is positive and $\mu_{0j} < 0$ when the input is zero.

Note that μ_j measures the impact on costs of relaxing the constraint $T = t_j$, and so $\mu_j < 0$, because relaxing the constraint reduces costs. Similarly, relaxing a binding non-negativity constraint would reduce costs, and so $\mu_{0j} < 0$.

When the constraint that $T = t_j$ is binding, $w_j/g_j < \pi$; that is, the marginal cost of G exceeds the ratio of parent j's wage relative to his(her) marginal product in the production of G. Given their low wage relative to their marginal productivity, it would be less costly to use more of their time in the production of G, but no more of their time is available. We can think of $w_j - \mu_j$ as the price of time of parent j, which is equated to the value of his(her) marginal product, πg_j. By performing the conventional comparative static exercise, it is easily shown that, when the constraint $T = t_j$ is binding, the production of more output (i.e. higher G) increases $w_j - \mu_j$ and the marginal cost of production, π, but a higher wage for parent j has no impact on the marginal cost.

In the first instance, we assume that neither parent specializes completely in home production (i.e. $t_j < T$). Then the first-order conditions can be written as $p_c \geq \pi g_x$, $w_m \geq \pi g_m$, and $w_f \geq \pi g_f$. If any of these expressions holds with a strict inequality, then that input is not used. For instance, if $w_f > \pi g_f$, then the father's price of time is too high relative to his home productivity and $t_f = 0$. Constant returns to scale in home production implies $G = x_c g_x + t_m g_m + t_f g_f$, and substituting from the first-order conditions, $\pi G = p_c x_c + w_m t_m + w_f t_f$. It follows that, in the neighbourhood of the cost minimizing choice of inputs,

$$d \ln(\pi) = \left(\frac{p_c x_c}{\pi G}\right) d \ln(p_c) + \left(\frac{w_m t_m}{\pi G}\right) d \ln(w_m) + \left(\frac{w_f t_f}{\pi G}\right) d \ln(w_f) \quad (4.2)$$

That is, proportionate differences in the marginal cost of G are a weighted average of the proportionate differences in input prices, with the weights being the share of that input's cost in the total cost of producing G. Differences in the price of inputs that contribute little to costs, perhaps because they are used very little due to their high price, have little influence on the cost of G.

For illustration, assume that the father's wage is too high relative to his home productivity, so that $t_f = 0$, and let $G = g(x_c, t_m, 0; S_m, S_f) = S_m{}^\phi [\alpha x_c{}^\rho + \beta t_m{}^\rho]^{1/\rho}$. That is, the production function takes the constant elasticity of substitution (CES) form with $\rho < 1$. With this specification, solution of the first stage problem above implies

$$\pi = S_m^{-\phi}[a^\sigma p_c^{1-\sigma} + \beta^\sigma w_m^{1-\sigma}]^{1/(1-\sigma)} \quad (4.3a)$$

$$\frac{w_m t_m}{\pi G} = \frac{\beta^\sigma w_m^{1-\sigma}}{\alpha^\sigma p_c^{1-\sigma} + \beta^\sigma w_m^{1-\sigma}} \quad (4.3b)$$

$$\frac{p_c x_c}{\pi G} = \frac{\alpha^\sigma p_c^{1-\sigma}}{\alpha^\sigma p_c^{1-\sigma} + \beta^\sigma w_m^{1-\sigma}} \quad (4.3c)$$

where $\sigma = 1/(1 - \rho)$ is the elasticity of substitution between mother's time and purchased goods and services in the production of G. Equations (4.3b) and (4.3c) indicate that the share of an input in the costs of producing G will rise with a higher price of that input if the elasticity of substitution is less than unity, and fall if it is larger than unity. When $\sigma = 1$, the share is constant (e.g. $w_m t_m / \pi G = \beta/(\alpha + \beta)$), and the production function takes the Cobb–Douglas form. Equation (4.3a) indicates that families with a more productive mother (say, because she is more educated) have a lower marginal cost of G when $\phi > 0$, and that the marginal cost of G is increasing in both p_c and the mother's wage.

4.2 Investments in Market and Home Productivity

Parents can make investments in their own human capital that improve their earning power or their productivity in producing their children's human capital. There is substantial evidence, for instance, that more experience in paid employment increases a person's wage. Suppose that this takes the form of simple learning-by-doing, so that $w_j = H(T - t_j)$, with $H'(T - t_j) = -dH/dt_j > 0$. Then the first-order conditions (4.1b) and (4.1c) become

$$H(T - t_m) - t_m H'(T - t_m) + \mu_{0m} = \pi g_m + \mu_m \qquad (4.1b^*)$$

$$H(T - t_f) - t_f H'(T - t_f) + \mu_{0f} = \pi g_f + \mu_f \qquad (4.1c^*)$$

The left-hand side of each of these expressions is the "full marginal cost" of the parent's time, which is decreasing in t_j. That is, the more time a parent spends in home production, the lower the marginal cost of doing so, because his or her wage will be lower. Or put differently, the more a parent works in paid employment, the higher his(her) wage and therefore the cost of his(her) time in home production. If learning-by-doing is sufficiently strong, so that $H'(T - t_j)$ is large enough, it leads to complete specialization in market production by one parent. If both members of the couple have exactly the same endowments and the same ability to invest (i.e. the learning-by-doing function $H(T - t_j)$ is the same for both parents) and each parent's time is equally productive in home production for given values of the other's time, then it does not matter which parent specializes in market production.

This can be shown graphically in the case where the only inputs are parents' time. The "isocost curve" gives the combinations of the mother's and father's time resulting in the same cost of production. Its slope is $dt_m/dt_f = -[H(T - t_f) - t_f H'(T - t_f)]/[H(T - t_m) - t_m H'(T - t_m)]$. With $H'(T - t_j) > 0$, the isocost curve is convex to the origin. The different combinations of parents' time that produce the same level of home production is given by the isoquant, the slope of which is $-g_f/g_m$, which is also convex to the origin. The cost minimizing combination of parents' time inputs is given by the tangency of the isocost curve and the isoquant. If $H'(T - t_j)$ is large enough, the isocost curve will be more convex to the origin than the isoquant and one parent will not contribute time to home production. This is illustrated in Figure 4.1, where t^* is the time input required for the optimal amount of G when only one parent contributes time to home production. If learning-by-doing is more moderate so that the opposite is true, then both parents contribute to home production when they have the same learning-by-doing function $H(T - t_j)$, as illustrated in Figure 4.2.

The linear production function of Chapter 2, $G = h_m t_m + h_f t_f$, assumes perfect substitutability between productivity-adjusted time inputs (i.e. $h_j t_j$). It has linear isoquants with slope $-h_f/h_m$, and so learning-by-doing in paid employment produces complete specialization by one parent in market work. We have seen in Chapter 2 that even with

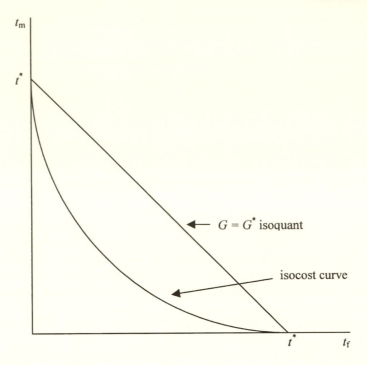

Figure 4.1 Learning-by-doing in paid employment and specialization in home production.

constant market wage rates (making the slope of the isocost curve $-w_f/w_m$), if one parent has a comparative advantage, then at least one parent completely specializes, and it is possible that both completely specialize. For instance, if $w_f/w_m > h_f/h_m$, then the isocost line has a steeper slope than the isoquant, and so there is a corner solution with $t_m = t^*$ and $t_f = 0$. This is also the case with a home production function that also contains goods inputs when there is perfect substitutability between parents' effective time inputs: $G = g(x_c, h_m t_m + h_f t_f)$, as, for instance, assumed by Becker (1981, Chapter 2). Given x_c, this production function also has linear isoquants.

When learning-by-doing is strong, small gender differences in wages could tip the balance in favour of complete specialization in paid work by one parent, even though they have exactly the same endowments and ability to invest and each parent's time is equally productive in home production. If, for example, sex discrimination in the labour market makes men's wages higher than women's for a given level of human capital, then specialized human capital investments could result in women doing all of the home production and men specializing in market

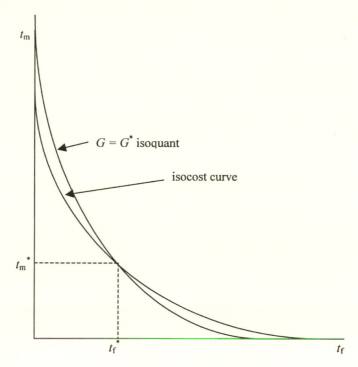

Figure 4.2 Learning-by-doing in paid employment without specialization.

production. Note that the isocost curves in Figure 4.1 would be steeper and non-symmetric. Conditions (4.1b*) and (4.1c*) would become, respectively, $H(T - t_m) - t_m H'(T - t_m) \le \pi g_m$ and $H(T) > \pi g_f$. If, indeed, it is optimal for the mother to specialize completely as well (i.e. $H(0) - TH'(0) < \pi g_m$), then the marginal cost of home production would be given by p_c/g_x, and changes in either parent's wage would have no effect on the cost of home production. For fathers, this would be because they contribute no time to home production, and for mothers, it is because they devote all of their time to home production.

Similar results emerge if home productivity increases with time spent in home production. For instance, the home production function could be $g(x_c, t_m^e, t_f^e)$, where t_m^e and t_f^e denote *effective* time in home production, and $t_j^e = \psi(t_j)$, $j = m, f$, with $d\psi(t_j)/dt_j > 0$. In this case, for given x_c, the isoquants are concave to the origin, while the isocost curve has a slope of -1 if both receive the same wage, as illustrated in Figure 4.3.

Thus, one or the other of the parents would do all of the home production and the other would specialize completely in market work. If the productivity-enhancing function $\psi(t_j)$ is the same for both parents and their effective time is equally productive (given the

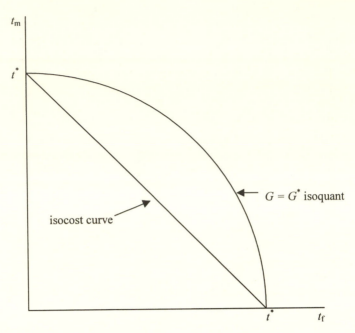

Figure 4.3 Learning-by-doing in home production and specialization in home production.

effective time of the other), then it does not matter who fully specializes. If, for example, the woman's role in childbearing gives her a comparative advantage in home production (implying a flatter, nonsymmetric isoquant in Figure 4.3), this could tip the balance toward her contributing all of the home production time when there is learning-by-doing in home production.

4.3 Empirical Examples of Household Production Functions

Household production theory is primarily used in the remainder of the book to represent family investments in human capital and "child quality" that require parents' time and goods. But it also aids in estimating and interpreting relationships that summarize more specific family activities, such as those that promote the health of family members and those that control fertility. The first of these that we consider is the production of "healthy infants", as indicated by birth weight. The second example is related to the health of family members through nutritional intake, and the third is the "reproduction function", which relates contraceptive use, natural fecundity and luck to the number of births.

4.3.1 Birth weight

The weight of a child at birth is related to a child's health. For example, low birth weight babies (less that 2.5 kg) have a much higher mortality rate at ages below one year (in excess of five times higher), and low birth weight children who survive have high rates of medical and developmental problems.

Rosenzweig and Wolpin (1995) estimate the production relationship between birth weight and eight "inputs" that the mother chooses. These are the age of the mother at birth, the mother's weight just preceding the pregnancy, her weight gain per week of gestation net of birth weight, whether the mother obtained prenatal care in the first trimester of pregnancy, the number of cigarettes she smoked during the pregnancy, whether she consumed alcoholic beverages during pregnancy, and for births after the first, the interval between the last birth and conception of the current birth. This is a fundamental biological relationship. Estimates of it address the important issue of whether postponing births can improve birth outcomes, such as birth weight. In particular, they provide an estimate of the biological effect of the age of mother on birth weight, holding constant other maternal behaviour. The estimates of the effects of the other behavioural inputs can provide a basis for prescriptive advice about behaviour such as gaining weight and smoking during pregnancy.

The difficulty in estimating this birth weight production function is that there are "endowments" of the mother and of her individual children that also affect birth weight, and these are likely to be correlated with the inputs that a mother chooses. Thus, ordinary least squares estimation of the production function is likely to produce biased estimates of it. To see this more clearly, consider the following simple specification of the production functions for a two-child family:

$$w_{ij} = \beta X_{ij} + \varepsilon_{ij}, \qquad i = 1, 2 \tag{4.4}$$

$$\varepsilon_{ij} = \rho \varepsilon_j + \nu_{ij} \tag{4.5}$$

where w_{ij} is the birth weight of the ith-order child to mother j; X_{ij} is a vector of inputs; ε_{ij} is the unobservable "endowment" of the ith child that affects his(her) birth weight, which is outside the control of the parents. Equation (4.5) is a type of Galton's law of heritability of endowments (see Becker and Tomes 1986), with regression to the mean across generations ($0 \leq \rho < 1$), where ε_j is the mother's endowment and ν_{ij} is an idiosyncratic endowment, which is not correlated with ε_j and with ν_{kj} (the analogous endowment for sibling k).

Resource allocation decisions during pregnancy, expressed solely in terms of endowments (ignoring, for example, prices), are given by

$$X_{1j} = \Pi\varepsilon_j \quad \text{and} \quad X_{2j} = \Pi\varepsilon_j + \gamma\nu_{1j} \qquad (4.6)$$

where Π and γ are conformable vectors of parameters.[1] The parameters in Π capture the mother's input response to her own endowment, while the γ measures the input response to child-specific idiosyncratic endowments. Equation (4.6) plausibly assumes that the child-specific endowment of a child not yet born cannot influence decisions, but parents may respond to information about the idiosyncratic endowments of children born previously in making input decisions concerning the curr ent child. Thus, allowance is made for sequential decision-making.

The covariance (vector) between X_{ij} and ε_{ij} is $\Pi\rho\,\mathrm{var}(\varepsilon_j)$. Given that there is heterogeneity in mother's endowments (i.e. $\mathrm{var}(\varepsilon_j) > 0$), this covariance disappears if and only if either $\Pi = 0$ or $\rho = 0$. It is, however, plausible that at least some of the inputs in X_{ij} depend on the mother's endowment ε_j, that is, $\Pi \neq 0$. For example, as we generally find that more educated women are less likely to smoke, mother's smoking is likely to depend on ε_j. If we believe that there exists a positive degree of "inheritability", through genetic and cultural transmission of endowments, then ρ is positive. The non-zero covariance between X_{ij} and ε_{ij} means that least squares estimates of (4.4) are not consistent. A least squares regression between differences in birth weight between siblings and differences in inputs between the siblings does not, in general, produce consistent estimates either, because the covariance between $X_{2j} - X_{1j}$ and $\varepsilon_{2j} - \varepsilon_{1j}$ is $-\gamma\,\mathrm{var}(\nu_{1j})$. This is non-zero if the first child's idiosyncratic endowment affects input choice for the second child (i.e. $\gamma \neq 0$) and there is heterogeneity in individual endowments.

Rosenzweig and Wolpin (1995) derive an estimator of the birth weight production function that allows for heterogeneity in mother's and child's endowments and for a response during the current pregnancy to the endowments of children born earlier.[2] Their data are from the National Longitudinal Surveys 1979 Youth Cohort. The raw data indicate that women giving birth at younger ages have lower birth weight babies. But the estimates of the production function indicate that mother's age has no significant impact on birth weight. They also find that cigarette smoking during pregnancy reduces birth weight and that women who weighed more just preceding pregnancy have heavier babies.

Their method also allows estimation of the response of behaviour to endowments (Π). For example, they find that women with propensities to have low birth weight children (lower ε_j) are significantly more likely to have their children when they are younger. Also, among mothers with the same endowment, those with a better-endowed first child (higher ν_{1j}) are more likely to have the second child earlier. Thus, all of the observed association between low birth weight and the child having a young mother can be explained by young mothers having relatively poor endowments that are transmitted to their children in terms of low birth weight; there is no biological effect on birth weight of young motherhood.

4.3.2 Nutrition

Information about the nutrition intake responses to prices and income is useful for the evaluation of the efforts to improve nutrition in developing countries through price subsidies and income-generation policies. In light of this policy focus, it is more helpful to use the household production framework to derive demand equations for nutritional intake of individuals in households, which are a function of prices, incomes and endowments, than to estimate the production functions themselves. We can think in terms of efficient household outcomes in the bargaining framework of Chapter 2, in which health affects individual welfare and the intra-household decision-making is constrained by a full income constraint and, inter alia, two types of production functions. The first is a biological *health production function* for each individual that relates his or her health to nutrition and other health-related inputs, conditional on health endowments of that individual, and the second is a *nutrient production function* for each individual that converts quantities of different foods into nutrients consumed.

The solution to the household's optimization and bargaining problem entails derived demand functions for different foods and other goods, and these can be substituted in the nutrition production functions to obtain nutrient consumption for each individual as a function of prices, wage rates, household full income, personal characteristics, health endowments of all household members and family- and location-specific variables. These latter variables can be considered to give rise to three types of "fixed effects" in the demand equations: individual, household and village, analogous to the mother-specific endowment ε_j of the previous section. The individual fixed effects include genetic endowments, such as inherited immunity to diseases, which may be correlated with household income. The household fixed effects include the quality of the household's water supply and housing and health and nutrition knowledge, and the village effects include soil and climatic characteristics that may be correlated with village-level prices and wage rates. Wage rates enter the demand function because of the role of time in household production, as in the production function $g(\ )$ earlier in the chapter.

Behrman and Deolalikar (1989) use data from rural south India to obtain estimates of these nutrient demand functions, and they allow responses to price and income to vary among four groups: men, women, boys and girls. There is strong evidence that unobserved household (and therefore village) and, to a smaller extent, individual, fixed effects are important in determining individual nutrient intakes. They find that when food prices rise, the nutrient intakes of women and girls fall by more than the household average, implying that the difficulties of poor agricultural seasons fall disproportionately on females. By the same token, women and girls enjoy a disproportionate share of the nutritional rewards from falling food prices. There is also evidence of strong substitution effects across foods, suggesting that subsidies on foods other than staples (e.g. sorghum or cassava) actually can reduce nutritional intake by encouraging consumption of "tastier" but less nutritious foods.

4.3.3 The Reproduction Function

As will become clearer in Chapter 6, it is useful to have estimates of the *exogenous* variation in fertility, which is not under parents' control. It can be used to infer how the costs of contraception influence fertility and human capital investment in the absence of direct measures of the prices of contraceptives, because couples with a higher propensity to conceive face higher costs of controlling fertility when control is costly. A "reproduction function" describes how the use of fertility control methods, age and other biological inputs affect conceptions or births; it describes the technology of birth production. Abstracting from other potential determinants of conception, such as frequency of sexual intercourse and breastfeeding, let the reproduction function take the following form for couple j in the ith period:

$$N_{ij} = \mu_j + \varepsilon_{ij} + \gamma(a + i) - \sum_{k=1}^{K} \beta_k Z_{ijk} \qquad (4.7)$$

where Z_{ijk} is the kth fertility control input (e.g. use of the contraceptive pill), with $\beta_k > 0$; $a + i$ is the age of the mother, and γ and the β_ks are biological–technical parameters to be estimated. Note that μ_j is a persistent fertility component specific to the jth couple (e.g. their fecundity), and ε_{ij} is an independently distributed, serially uncorrelated stochastic fertility component (e.g. luck). Together, $\mu_j + \varepsilon_{ij} + \gamma(a + i)$ is the exogenous component of fertility, unrelated to the couple's preferences and outside their control, while fertility control inputs (Z_{ijk}) are chosen by them and are thereby influenced by their preferences and the budget constraints that they face.

Ordinary least squares (OLS) estimates of the parameters in (4.7) are not consistent, because the choice of fertility control inputs depends on μ_j. Instrumental variable estimates of these parameters are consistent. They can use proxies for the prices of contraceptives, prices of other goods and incomes as instruments because, given the contraceptive methods chosen by the couple, these do not directly influence realized fertility, but do potentially affect the choice of methods. It is not, however, necessary to measure all of the relevant prices. This approach was pioneered by Rosenzweig and Schultz (1985, 1987). For example, in their study of Malaysian fertility (1987), they relate the conception rate (per month at risk to conceive) for a couple over the most recent five-year period as a function of the woman's age, the fractions of that period they used different types of contraceptives and the number of months the mother was continuously and exclusively breastfeeding any child from the time of the child's birth. They distinguish between three types of methods (Pill/IUD, Condom and "Ineffective methods"). Their instruments are the education levels of parents, husband's earnings and community-level information such as distances to a doctor, nurse, family planning clinic, private medical centre and a midwife.

The estimates of the β_ks represent the effectiveness of the various methods in reducing fertility. Their estimates are similar to those obtained when estimating the reproduction function for the United States (Rosenzweig and Schultz 1985), as we would expect if this is a biological–technical relationship rather than a behavioural one. For instance, it shows the Pill to be the most effective contraceptive method in Malaysia and that breast-feeding reduces the conception rate. OLS estimates would understate the effectiveness of the more effective methods such as the Pill because more fecund women (i.e. with higher μ_j) would employ this method.

It is possible to estimate the persistent component for couple j by taking the difference between average and predicted fertility over T periods; that is

$$\hat{\mu}_j = \frac{\sum_{i=1}^{T}\left\{N_{ij} - \hat{\gamma}(a + i) + \sum_{k=1}^{K}\hat{\beta}_k Z_{ijk}\right\}}{T} \tag{4.8}$$

where the symbol "$\hat{\,}$" indicates a parameter estimate. We shall return to the use of this estimate of μ_j in Chapter 6 to examine how variation in fertility outside a couple's control affects their fertility and other choices, such as human capital investment in their children and mother's labour supply. The next chapter examines investment in children's human capital when family size is taken as given.

NOTES

1. More generally, $X_{ij} = \Pi\varepsilon_j + \sum_{k=1}^{i-1} \gamma_k \nu_{kj}$.

2. In the two-child case, this estimator amounts to being an instrumental variable fixed effects estimator with inputs to the first child being instruments for the difference in inputs between siblings.

CHAPTER FIVE

Investments in and Financial Transfers to Children

THIS CHAPTER examines the links between generations, either through gifts and bequests to children or investment in their human capital, which affect their earnings and income when they become adults. It is particularly concerned with whether and how these two types of intergenerational transfer depend on parents' resources and other aspects of family background such as parents' education. Section 5.1 studies the intergenerational links when there is only one child. In Section 5.2, we analyze how intergenerational links may change when human capital investment is riskier than making financial transfers. Differences in parents' human capital investment between their children are considered in Sections 5.3 and 5.4 in the context of two models: the "wealth model" associated with Becker (1981) and the "separable-earnings transfer model" associated with Behrman et al. (1982). The empirical implications of these two models are discussed in Section 5.5, including ways in which the two models can be estimated and compared empirically.

5.1 FAMILY BACKGROUND AND CHILDREN'S ATTAINMENTS

Initially, assume that there is only one child. We now interpret the household public good of Chapter 2 as the income of the child as an adult, which is made up of his or her earnings, denoted as e, and income from gifts and bequests from parents, denoted as rb, where b is the amount of transfers (gifts or bequests) and r is the market interest rate. Earnings are determined by "educational attainments" resulting from parents' human capital investment in the child *over his entire childhood* and an "endowment" with which the child is born. We are not assuming that parents directly choose the child's educational level, but rather that human capital investments in their offspring during childhood strongly influence subsequent educational attainments. The model abstracts from the dynamics of these investments over childhood and treats educational attainments as the choice variable. For simplicity, we assume a particular earnings function $e = f(S, \varepsilon) = S^\gamma \varepsilon$, where S is the educational level achieved by the child, ε is the "earnings endowment" of the child and

$0 < \gamma < 1$. While, for concreteness, we shall continue to refer to S as educational level, all of what follows applies to other investments in the child's human capital, such as investments in health, which raise the child's earnings and welfare in adulthood. Thus, S can be interpreted as human capital in a wider sense than education.

The particular utility function assumed in Chapter 2, $U^j = \alpha_j \ln(x_j) + (1 - \alpha_j)\ln(e + rb)$ is also assumed here, where x_j is parent j's own consumption, $j = $ m for mother and $j = $ f for father. Strictly speaking, the parents' preferences are not *altruistic* in the sense of their use in Chapter 3, and might be called *paternalistic*. But to the extent that a child's income as an adult is an important component in his(her) standard of living, they do represent caring for the child's living standard as an adult.

5.1.1 Cooperative Equilibrium

We focus primarily on the cooperative model of the family, which produces efficient allocations. An efficient allocation in this context maximizes $U^f + \mu U^m$ subject to $y_f + y_m = x_f + x_m + b + p_s S$ and $b \geq 0$, where μ is a Lagrange multiplier, p_s is the unit cost of education and y_j is parent j's "full income"; that is, $y_j = w_j T + v_j$, where T is total time available, w_j is parent j's wage and v_j is j's non-labour income. S is assumed to be produced through home production combining parents' time and purchased good and services, where S now substitutes for G in the previous chapter. Thus, $p_s = \pi$ of the previous chapter. The level of education chosen by the parents must satisfy

$$p_s \leq \frac{\gamma S^{\gamma-1} \varepsilon}{r} \tag{5.1}$$

The right-hand side of (5.1) is the marginal return from educational investment and the left-hand side is the marginal cost.

PARENTS MAKING FINANCIAL TRANSFERS

If parents give transfers to their child, then (5.1) holds with equality and optimal investment in education is

$$S^* = \left(\frac{\gamma \varepsilon}{r p_s}\right)^{1/(1-\gamma)} \tag{5.2}$$

Note that in this case the child's educational level does not depend on parents' incomes. It only depends on the market interest rate, the cost of education and the child's earnings endowment.

The amount of transfers does, however, depend on parents' full incomes:

$$b^* = [(1 - \alpha_f) + \theta(\alpha_f - \alpha_m)]\left(y_f + y_m - p_s S^* - \frac{e^*}{r}\right) \qquad (5.3)$$

where the optimal level of human capital investment (S^*), given by (5.2), determines $e^* = S^* \gamma \varepsilon$; and $\theta = \mu/(1 + \mu)$ is the share of "net full income" allocated to the mother, where net full income is $y_f + y_m - p_s S^* - e^*/r$. If the mother's share is influenced by her own full income, y_m, then the distribution of joint full income between parents affects the amount of financial transfers to the child when parents' preferences differ ($\alpha_f \neq \alpha_m$). Thus, parents make an efficient investment in their child's education (through human capital investments during childhood) and then make financial transfers to their child according to their incomes and preferences.

There is substantial evidence that a child's education is correlated positively with that of his(her) parents. Equation (5.2) indicates that if parents give transfers, then mother's (father's) education S_m (S_f) only has a causal effect on her (his) child's education if it affects the cost of education p_s. There may nevertheless be a correlation between mother's (father's) and child's education because the child's endowment ε and S_m (S_f) are correlated. This correlation is likely to be positive because of genetics. In particular, the child's endowment is correlated with the endowments of his parents, and parents with larger endowments have higher educational attainments (as in (4.5) and (4.6)). The correlation between ε and S_m (S_f) may also arise because of "cultural transmission"; that is more highly educated parents provide a better environment (e.g. books around the house) for producing human capital in their children and this is part of the child's endowment ε. In these circumstances, the correlation between parents' and child's education would be a poor indication of the "effect" of raising parents' education on child's education, biasing it in favour of a positive "effect".

The analysis of the previous chapter indicates how parents' education may affect the cost of education p_s. Higher mother's education could raise both her wage w_m and her productivity in human capital investment. Let mother's wages be an iso-elastic function of her education: $w_m = a S_m^\delta$; and assume the CES production function of the previous chapter for the production of the child's human capital investment, S. It follows from (4.3a) and (4.3b) that the elasticity of the unit cost of the child's education with respect to mother's education is

$$\frac{d\ln(p_s)}{d\ln(S_m)} = -\phi + \delta\frac{w_m t_m}{p_s S} \qquad (5.4)$$

Whether the effect of higher mother's education on costs dominates the effect on productivity (ϕ) depends on the share of total costs represented by the mother's time ($w_m t_m / p_s S$) and the proportionate effect of education on her wage (δ).

Alternatively, consider the model of Chapter 2 in which S is produced by time inputs of the parents: $S = h_f t_f + h_m t_m$, where t_j is the time input of parent j. If, for example, the mother has a comparative advantage in human capital investment in her children (i.e. $w_m / h_m < w_f / h_f$), the unit cost of her child's human capital is w_m / h_m. If the mother's wage increases proportionately more than her home productivity with higher levels of her education, then the cost of human capital investment would increase, leading to a negative effect on child's education. If the opposite is the case, p_s declines and the effect is positive.

Similarly, the effect of the father's education on his child's education depends on its relationship to p_s. Analogously to the mother, it is clear that this relationship depends on the contribution of the cost of his time to the cost of human capital investment ($w_f t_f / p_s S$), the impact of his education on his wage and any effect of his education on his productivity in human capital investment. If his time contribution (t_f) is small, the correlation between a father's education and his child's would primarily represent a correlation between the child's endowment (ε) and the father's educational attainment (S_f), rather than any causal impact of father's education.

POOR PARENTS

If parents are too poor to make transfers, in the sense that the marginal utility of their private consumption exceeds the marginal utility of transfers, then the inequality in (5.1) holds. This means that parents do *not* invest in their child's human capital up to the point that the marginal return equals the marginal cost of education. They invest less than this amount, and the optimal investment depends on parents' full incomes:

$$S^* = \frac{\Phi(\gamma, \theta, \alpha_f, \alpha_m)(y_f + y_m)}{p_s} \tag{5.5}$$

where $\Phi(\gamma, \theta, \alpha_f, \alpha_m) = \gamma[(1-\alpha_f)+\theta(\alpha_f-\alpha_m)]/\{\gamma+(1-\gamma)[\alpha_f-\theta(\alpha_f-\alpha_m)]\}$ and θ is the share of family full income ($y_f + y_m$) allocated to the mother. Note that $\partial\Phi/\partial\theta > 0$ if $\alpha_f > \alpha_m$, and $\partial\Phi/\partial\theta < 0$ if $\alpha_f < \alpha_m$. That is, more of total full income will be allocated to human capital investment when the mother's share of income is larger if she puts a larger weight on the child's income in her utility function than the father does.

The impact of a mother's education (S_m) on human capital investment in her child for poor parents is

$$\frac{\partial S^*}{\partial S_m} = \frac{\partial y_m}{\partial S_m}\left[\Phi + \frac{\partial \Phi}{\partial \theta}\frac{\partial \theta}{\partial y_m}\right] - \frac{S^*}{p_s}\frac{\partial p_s}{\partial S_m} \tag{5.6}$$

From (5.6), we can see three separate effects of mother's education on the education of her child. First, there is *an income effect* (Φ), which is positive. Second, there is *a bargaining effect*, which is positive if mothers put more weight on the child's income than fathers ($\alpha_f > \alpha_m$) and higher education and income increases her bargaining power ($\partial \theta / \partial y_m > 0$). Thirdly, there is *a substitution effect*, which depends on any impact of mother's education on the cost of human capital investment in children, which was discussed above. The evidence that a child's education is correlated positively with that of his(her) mother among 'poorer parents' in Britain (Ermisch and Francesconi 2001a) suggests that any negative substitution effect is dominated by the two other effects in (5.6).

Behrman et al. (1999) use data from rural India before and during the "green revolution" to identify a productivity effect on the cost of human capital investment from the mother's education, such as suggested by ϕ in (5.4). They show that women's education contributed little to household income from either higher profitability in farming (while men's education did) or from wage employment in the non-agricultural sector. Thus, in this context, it is unlikely that higher mother's education increased either family income or her bargaining power in the household. This suggests that the income and bargaining effects are absent in (5.6). Furthermore, from (5.4), mother's education should reduce the cost of human capital investment through the productivity effect, thereby increasing investment in a child's education according to (5.6). It is not possible to do full justice to their study in the space available, but their within-household instrumental variable estimates, which take into account the influence of the father's preferences, indicate that having a mother who is literate but not a primary school graduate increases the study hours of children, and such mothers spend more time on home care, which includes child care.[1] Further, there is a higher demand for literate but not primary-schooled wives in areas with more rapid technical change (because of the green revolution) despite the absence of any financial return to female literacy in either the farm or non-farm sector.

It is, however, still possible that literate mothers have more bargaining power in the household because such mothers have better options outside marriage that are not adequately measured by labour market rewards. Behrman et al. (1999) show, however, that there is no impact of maternal literacy on expenditure on children's clothing, which we would expect if better educated mothers have more bargaining power. Also, in the absence of market returns to maternal literacy, if there were no productivity effect of literacy, but it increased women's bargaining power, it would impose a cost on men. We would, therefore, expect that dowries of literate, but not primary-schooled, women would be higher than those of other women, but the opposite is the case. That is, men are willing to pay for the higher productivity of literate women in human capital invest-ment in terms of requiring lower dowries in the marriage market. Thus, at least in rural India, there is evidence that there is a productivity effect from having a more educated mother, which tends to enhance the human capital of the next generation.

The impact of father's education (S_f) is analogous to that of mothers in (5.6). The bargaining effect of father's education would be negative if a father values his child's income less than the mother does $(\alpha_f > \alpha_m)$ and higher income increases his bargaining power $(\partial\theta/\partial y_f < 0)$. A substitution effect may be virtually absent $(\partial p_s/\partial S_f \cong 0)$ if father's time is used much less than mother's time in human capital investment in their children. Evidence of positive correlation between the education of father and child among "poorer parents" (e.g. Ermisch and Francesconi 2001a) suggests that the income effect dominates.

In general, when parents are too poor to make transfers, the effect of the child's endowment (ε) on education is made up of opposing influ-ences.[2] On the one hand, a higher endowment encourages human capital investment because it means a higher marginal return on investment. On the other hand, a higher endowment means that the child's income is higher, independent of investments. As this lowers the parents' marginal utility from human capital investment in their child, this encourages parents to substitute their own consumption for investment in their child. With the particular preferences and earnings function assumed above, these two effects exactly offset each other when parents have the same preferences $(\alpha_f = \alpha_m)$, or when the endowment does not affect the sharing rule (see (5.5)).[3] Thus, if parents do not make gifts or bequests, the correlation between parents' and child's education mainly represents a causal impact.

5.1.2 Non-Cooperative Equilibrium

The implications of the non-cooperative model are similar to those of the cooperative model. If at least one parent makes financial transfers, then the efficient level of education is attained, and it is given by (5.2). In this case, total financial transfers depend on total family income and not its distribution if both parents give transfers, but they will only depend on the income of the parent giving, if only one does so. The level of transfers will in either case be inefficient.

If neither parent makes transfers, then investment in their child's human capital depends on total family income if both parents make investments, but only on the income of the parent making human capital investments, if only one does. In either case, investment will not be effi-cient.

5.1.3 Further Analysis

In order to focus now on risk and differences in parents' investments between their children, the remainder of the chapter assumes that the share of family income allocated to the mother (θ) does not vary with the relative incomes of parents. With the particular utility function assumed above, this could be justified because both parents have the same preferences ($\alpha_f = \alpha_m$), or, more generally, it could be justified by the presence of an effective altruist who dictates the outcome (i.e. has all the bargaining power), as discussed in Chapter 3. Qualitatively, it is equivalent to assume that parents' preferences are represented by one utility function, describing their "consensus preferences", and that there is a joint family budget constraint. The next section examines the extent to which the conclusion that there is no impact of parents' resources on human capital investment if parents have sufficient resources to also make financial transfers (gifts and bequests) to their children is modified when human capital investment is risky.

5.2 RISKY HUMAN CAPITAL INVESTMENT AND PARENTS' RESOURCES

Investments in children may be riskier than many financial investments that the parents could make. The child's earning function $e = f(S, \varepsilon)$ is assumed to be characterised by $f_S = \partial f(S, \varepsilon)/\partial S > 0$, $f_\varepsilon = \partial f(S, \varepsilon)/\partial \varepsilon > 0$ and $f_{SS} = \partial^2 f(S, \varepsilon)/\partial S^2 < 0$. With probability π the human capital investment fails, and the child receives income of $e_0 + rb$, rather than $f(S, \varepsilon) + rb$, where r is a riskless interest rate and $e_0 = f(0, \varepsilon)$ is the unskilled wage.[4] Letting $z = e + rb$, the parents' "consensus preferences" are represented by the utility function $U(x, z)$, where x denotes their own consumption. Parents' expected utility is given by

$$E(U) = \pi U(x, e_0 + rb) + (1 - \pi)U(x, f(S, \varepsilon) + rb) \qquad (5.7)$$

The parents choose x, b and S to maximize their expected utility subject to $b \geq 0$ and $Y_F = x + b + p_s S$. Let $U_j = \partial U(x, z)/\partial j$, $j = x, z$, $U_j^S = U_j(x, f(S, \varepsilon) + rb)$ and $U_j^F = U_j(x, e_0 + rb)$. That is, U_j^S and U_j^F represent marginal utilities in the cases of success (S) and failure (F) of the human capital investment. Define $E(U_j) = \pi U_j^F + (1 - \pi)U_j^S$. Then the level of education chosen by the parents must satisfy

$$rp_s \leq \frac{(1 - \pi)U_z^S f_S}{E(U_z)} \qquad (5.8)$$

If the returns to human capital investment were certain ($\pi = 0$), then (5.8) becomes $rp_s \leq f_S$. In this case, the right-hand side of the inequality is simply the marginal return from educational investment and the left-hand side is the marginal cost, as in (5.1).

5.2.1 Parents Making Financial Transfers to Their Child

If parents give monetary transfers to their child (i.e. $b > 0$), then the first-order conditions imply that $E(U_x) = rE(U_z)$ and (5.8) holds with equality. If there is no risk of failure ($\pi = 0$), (5.8) implies that $rp_s = f_S$, which is familiar from the previous section. Thus, in the absence of risk, parents' income does not affect human capital investment, because human capital investment is carried to the point at which the marginal return from education equals its marginal cost. Furthermore, higher child endowments increase human capital investment if the marginal return increases with a higher endowment (i.e. $f_{S\varepsilon} = \partial^2 f(S, \varepsilon)/\partial\varepsilon\partial S > 0$), because $\partial S/\partial\varepsilon = -f_{S\varepsilon}/f_{SS}$. As in Becker and Tomes (1986) and Section 5.3, parents make efficient human capital investments in their child and then make transfers to their child according to their incomes and preferences.

Because $0 < [(1 - \pi)U_z^S]/E(U_z) < 1$ when $\pi > 0$, f_S is larger and human capital investment is smaller when there is uncertainty about its returns than when returns are certain. Parents' preferences now also matter for the human capital investment decision. The impact of parents' income on human capital investment is derived through the conventional comparative static analysis. Let $U_{jj} = \partial^2 U(x, z)/\partial j^2$, $j = x, z$, $U_{xz} = \partial^2 U(x, z)/\partial x\partial z$ and $E(U_{jj}) = \pi U_{jj}^F + (1 - \pi)U_{jj}^S$, where U_{jj}^k ($k = F, S$) is defined analogously to U_j^k above. For simplicity, assume additively separable preferences (i.e. $U_{xz} = 0$). Then

$$\frac{\partial S}{\partial Y_F} = r^2 p_s E(U_{xx})E(U_{zz})\frac{\left\{1 - \dfrac{U_{zz}^S/U_z^S}{E(U_{zz})/E(U_z)}\right\}}{D} \tag{5.9}$$

$$\frac{\partial b}{\partial Y_F} = \frac{E(U_{xx})(1 - \pi)[(1 - r)f_S U_{zz}^S + U_z^S f_{SS}]}{D} \tag{5.10}$$

where $D > 0$ by the second-order conditions for a maximum, which also require $U_{jj} < 0$, $j = x, z$. Equation (5.10) indicates that financial transfers increase with parents' income. A necessary and sufficient condition for $\partial S/\partial Y_F > 0$ is that $U_{zz}^S/U_z^S > U_{zz}^F/U_z^F$. Under this condition $(U_{zz}^S/U_z^S) < [E(U_{zz})/E(U_z)]$ in (5.9), and the quantity in curly brackets is positive.

The Arrow–Pratt measure of *absolute* risk aversion defined relative to child's income is $A^{zk}(x, z) = -U_{zz}^k/U_z^k$, $k = F, S$. Thus, the condition for $\partial S/\partial Y_F > 0$ translates into $A^{zF}(x, z) > A^{zS}(x, z)$, which will be true if absolute risk aversion is declining in the child's income outcome ($\partial A^{zk}(x, z)/\partial z < 0$). That is, parents will increase the level of (risky) human capital investment when their own income is larger if they are less averse to risk when the child's income is larger. While the latter may appear to be a reasonable assumption, it is not difficult to find plausible utility functions for which it is not true (e.g. a quadratic specification for $U(x, z)$).

The impact of child endowments is less clear in the presence of risk.

$$\frac{\partial S}{\partial e} = (1 - \pi)$$

$$\times f_{\varepsilon} f_S U_{zz}^S \frac{E(U_{xx})[(1 - \pi)U_z^S/E(U_z) - 1] + r^2[(1 - \pi)(U_{zz}^S) - E(U_{zz})]}{D}$$

$$-f_{S\varepsilon} U_z^S \frac{E(U_{xx}) + r^2 E(U_{zz})}{D} \tag{5.11}$$

The first term on the right-hand side of (5.11) is negative, and the second is positive (for $f_{S\varepsilon} > 0$). The first term reflects the parents' risk aversion. A higher child endowment increases the child's income in the "success" state, which lowers the marginal utility of child's income (U_z^S) and discourages human capital investment. Stronger risk aversion by parents (larger $|U_{zz}|$), lowers $(1 - \pi)U_z^S/E(U_z)$ and makes the size of $E(U_{zz})$ exceed that of $(1 - \pi)U_{zz}^S$ by more, thereby increasing the size of the negative first term. Thus, with risky human capital investments, it is possible that higher child endowments reduce investment.[5]

5.2.2 Parents Too Poor to Make Monetary Transfers

If parents are too poor to make transfers, in the sense that the expected marginal utility of their private consumption exceeds the expected marginal utility of transfers (i.e. $E(U_x) > rE(U_z)$), then the inequality in (5.8) holds. Their human capital investment satisfies the following condition:

$$f_S = \frac{p_S E(U_x)}{(1 - \pi)U_z^S} \tag{5.12}$$

If there is no risk of failure ($\pi = 0$), (5.12) becomes $f_S = p_S U_x/U_z$.

Compared to the case of certain returns, f_S is higher and human capital investment is lower when there is a risk of failure. For these relatively poor parents,

$$\frac{\partial S}{\partial Y_F} = \frac{p_s E(U_{xx})}{B} \tag{5.13}$$

where $B < 0$ by the second-order conditions. Thus, poor parents always increase their human capital investment as their income rises. Comparison of (5.9) and (5.13) indicates that the impact of parents' income on investment in the child's human capital is likely to differ substantially between "wealthy" parents making transfers and "poor" parents not making transfers. For instance, if absolute risk aversion does not decline with parents' income, $\partial S/\partial Y_F \leq 0$ for wealthy parents, while $\partial S/\partial Y_F > 0$ for poor parents.

As originally shown by Becker and Tomes (1986), a higher child endowment could either increase or decrease human capital investment when parents are too poor to make transfers:

$$\frac{\partial S}{\partial \varepsilon} = (1 - \pi)\frac{\{- f_\varepsilon f_S U_{zz}^S - f_{S\varepsilon} U_z^S\}}{B} \tag{5.14}$$

On the one hand, a higher endowment means that the child will be richer, which lowers the parents' marginal utility of additional investment in their child (the first term in the curly brackets). On the other hand, a higher child endowment increases the marginal return to human capital investment (the second term in the curly brackets). If the former effect dominates, a higher endowment would reduce investment. When $U(x, z)$ takes a log-linear form and $e = f(S, \varepsilon) = S^\gamma \varepsilon$ (as in the previous section), these two effects exactly offset each other, and so $\partial S/\partial \varepsilon = 0$.

Comparison of (5.11) and (5.14) indicates that the impact of the child's earnings endowment on human capital investment can differ substantially between "wealthy" and "poor" parents. It is not clear whether the endowment has a bigger impact for poor or for wealthy parents. Even the direction of the impact is ambiguous for both groups.

In summary, when returns are uncertain, parents' resources can also have a causal impact on human capital investment among wealthier parents, because of variation in parents' absolute risk aversion with child's income, and this impact could be in either direction. The next section considers the allocation of human capital investment and financial transfers among children in the context of the "wealth model" of investment in children proposed by Becker (1981), which is very similar to the cooperative model with financial transfers being made.

5.3 WEALTH MODEL

Let parents' preferences be represented by $U(x_P, e_1 + rb_1, e_2 + rb_2)$, where x_P is total parental consumption, e_i is the earnings of the ith child when an adult, b_i are transfers to that child, r is the market interest rate, and we assume a two-child family for simplicity. Parents maximize their utility subject to earnings functions $e_i = f(S_i, \varepsilon_i)$, where ε_i is the "earnings endowment" of the ith child and S_i is the educational level achieved by that child (or human capital investment in that child), and to a parental resource constraint: $Y_F = x_P + p_s(S_1 + S_2) + b_1 + b_2$, where Y_F is total family full income and p_s is the cost per unit of education. The solution to this problem implies

$$U_x \geq rU_1 \quad \text{and} \quad U_x \geq rU_2 \tag{5.15}$$

where $U_x = \partial U/\partial x_P$ and $U_i = \partial U/\partial(e_i + rb_i)$, $i = 1, 2$.

$$U_1 f_{S1}(S_1, \varepsilon_1) = U_x p_s = U_2 f_{S2}(S_2, \varepsilon_2) \qquad (5.16)$$

where $f_{Si}(S_i, \varepsilon_i) = \partial f/\partial S_i$, $\partial^2 f/\partial S_i^2 < 0$ and $\partial^2 f/\partial S_i \partial \varepsilon_i > 0$.

We say that parents' preferences exhibit *equal concern* if the parents are indifferent to the labels on earnings–transfer assignments between their children, and we assume that this is the case. When parents make monetary transfers to each child (i.e. $b_i > 0$, $i = 1, 2$), then both equalities in (5.15) hold and $e_1 + rb_1 = e_2 + rb_2$, because $U_1 = U_2 = U_x/r$. Equation (5.16) then implies that $f_{S1}(S_1, \varepsilon_1) = rp_s = f_{S2}(S_2, \varepsilon_2)$; that is, parents invest in the human capital of each child up to the point that the marginal return equals the product of the market interest rate and the cost of education. It also implies that $S_2 > S_1$ and $e_2 > e_1$ if $\varepsilon_2 > \varepsilon_1$, and this is shown graphically in Figure 5.1. That is, parents invest more in the human capital of the more able child, who then ends up with higher earnings. From the fact that $e_1 + rb_1 = e_2 + rb_2$ when both expressions in (5.15) hold with equality, it follows that the less able child will be *fully* compensated by higher monetary transfers in the form of gifts and bequests.

For ease of comparison with the next section, we again assume the particular earnings function of the first section: $f(S_i, \varepsilon_i) = S_i^\gamma \varepsilon_i$, with

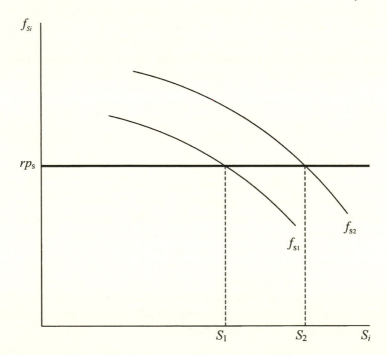

Figure 5.1 Optimal education, parents making monetary transfers.

$0 < \gamma < 1$. With this specification, the solution to the parents' optimization problem implies

$$\ln \frac{S_1}{S_2} = \frac{1}{1 - \gamma} \ln \frac{\varepsilon_1}{\varepsilon_2} \tag{5.17}$$

Thus, in the wealth model, parents always *reinforce endowment differences* between their children in the sense that the proportionate difference in educational attainments is larger than the proportionate difference in endowments, because $1/(1 - \gamma) > 1$. But parents fully compensate the poorer-endowed child with financial transfers. While the "wealth model" is a static model, in the perfect capital market version of the standard human capital investment model, marginal returns to education would be the same for *all children in all families*, which is also the case here when each child receives transfers and the unit cost of education (p_s) does not vary among families.

Parents may not, however, be sufficiently wealthy to satisfy both expressions in (5.15) with equality. Suppose, for example, that $\varepsilon_1 < \varepsilon_2$ and $f_{S1}(S_1, \varepsilon_1) < f_{S2}(S_2, \varepsilon_2)$ throughout the range of S_i, as in Figure 5.2, and that parents' income only is sufficient to make transfers to one child.

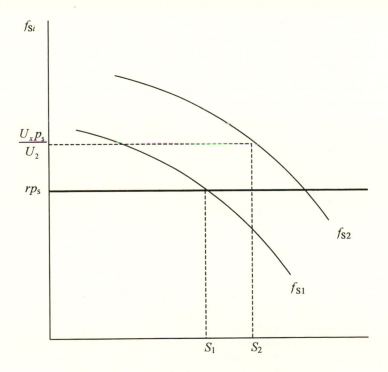

Figure 5.2 Optimal education, "poorer" parents.

Then $U_x > rU_2$ while $U_x = rU_1$. It then follows that $f_{S1}(S_1, \varepsilon_1) = rp_s$ while $f_{S2}(S_2, \varepsilon_2) > rp_s$. In words, parents invest in the poorer-endowed child to equate the marginal cost and return and also make a gift or bequest to him or her. The better-endowed child receives no gift or bequest, and educational attainment is less than the efficient level, which equates the marginal cost and return, but larger than investment in the poorer-endowed child. If parents are even poorer, then we may have both $U_x > rU_2$ and $U_x > rU_1$, implying that no gifts or bequests are made. In this case, investment in neither child is efficient ($f_{Si}(S_i, \varepsilon_i) > rp_s$, $i = 1, 2$). In both these cases of limited parental resources, it is clear from the appearance of U_i and U_x in (5.16) that parental preferences play an important role in investment in children's human capital. The next section considers a model that particularly focuses on the role of preferences. It provides an extension of the wealth model with "poor parents".

5.4 Separable Earnings–Transfers (SET) Model

This model, first presented by Behrman et al. (1982), assumes that parents' preferences have earnings of children separable from parents' consumption and from transfers; that is, parental utility is given by $U = U(x_P, W(e_1, e_2), V(b_1, b_2))$, where $W(\ )$ is the sub-utility function representing parental welfare from children's earnings and $V(\ )$ is the sub-utility function for parental welfare from gifts and bequests to children. Maximization of parental utility subject to the resource and earnings function constraints is equivalent to a three-stage problem in which parents first allocate Y_F between x_P and total expenditures on children. They then allocate the latter between transfers ($R_b = b_1 + b_2$) and total expenditures which affect earnings ($R_S = p_s(S_1 + S_2)$). Finally they allocate transfers between children to maximize $V(b_1, b_2)$ subject to $R_b = b_1 + b_2$, and they choose children's educational levels to maximize $W(e_1, e_2)$ subject to the earnings functions and $R_S = p_s(S_1 + S_2)$. In light of the symmetric nature of the gift/bequest budget constraint ($R_b = b_1 + b_2$), equal concern implies that transfers are divided equally between children.

For tractability and ease of comparison with the existing literature, we assume the particular specifications of the earnings and welfare functions used by Behrman et al. (1982). Let $W(e_1, e_2) = [\delta_1 e_1^c + \delta_2 e_2^c]^{1/c}$, with $c \le 1$ (i.e. a CES form). The parameter c indicates the degree of aversion to inequality between children's earnings, with a lower c indicating more inequality aversion. Note that this is the utility function introduced in the discussion of Rawlsian preferences at the end of the Chapter 3. The parameters δ_j ($j = 1, 2$) are utility weights for individual children. Equal concern means that $\delta_1 = \delta_2$. The earnings function is again $e_i = S_i^\gamma \varepsilon_i$.

With these specifications, the solution to the parents' optimization problem implies

$$\ln \frac{S_1}{S_2} = \frac{1}{1 - \gamma c} \ln \frac{\delta_1}{\delta_2} + \frac{c}{1 - \gamma c} \ln \frac{\varepsilon_1}{\varepsilon_2} \qquad (5.18)$$

With equal concern for the two children, the first term on the right-hand side disappears. Unequal concern shifts resources in favour of the child with the larger preference weight.

The inequality aversion parameter, c, determines whether parents' human capital investments *reinforce*($c > 0$) or *compensate* ($c < 0$) for differences in children's endowments. With reinforcement, the ratio of education levels is larger than the ratio of earnings endowments, and with compensation the opposite is the case. In the case of "Cobb–Douglas" preferences, $c \to 0$, and educational levels do not depend on child endowments and are the same for each child if there is equal concern When there is unequal concern, the shift in resources to the favoured child is larger the less is the concern about equity (i.e. the larger is c) and the greater is the elasticity of earnings with respect to education (γ).

Substituting the optimal education level in the earnings functions, we obtain

$$\ln \frac{e_1}{e_2} = \frac{\gamma}{1 - \gamma c} \ln \frac{\delta_1}{\delta_2} + \frac{1}{1 - \gamma c} \ln \frac{\varepsilon_1}{\varepsilon_2} \qquad (5.19)$$

When $c \to -\infty$, $\ln(e_1/e_2) = 0$, implying $e_1 = e_2$. In words, if parents are extremely averse to inequality between children, they will invest in the human capital of the poorer-endowed child so as to eliminate differences in earnings between children.

When $c = 1$, there is no inequality aversion, and proportionate earnings differences are the same as proportionate education differences when there is equal concern (cf. (5.18) and (5.19)). If, however, parents' preferences favour one of the children, earnings differences are proportionately less than education differences because of diminishing returns to human capital investment ($\gamma < 1$).

At the latter extreme, when, $c = 1$, parents maximize the sum of the earnings of their children; that is, they are utilitarian. Then educational choices only depend on efficiency considerations: equal marginal returns to education for *all children in a family*. The results are the same as in the wealth model (cf. (5.17) and (5.18)). While the "separable earnings–transfers model" is a one-period model, the imperfect capital market version of the standard human capital investment model is similar to it when parents have no aversion to earnings inequality among children.

At the opposite extreme, as $c \to -\infty$, only equity considerations matter. These Rawlsian parents fully compensate their lesser-endowed child with education so as to achieve the same earnings as the better-endowed child. In between these extremes, educational choices reflect both equity and efficiency considerations (i.e. both the c parameter and earnings function parameter, γ).

When combined with the resource constraint, and assuming "equal concern", the first-order condition in (5.18) implies, for the ith child with sibling k:[6]

$$\ln(S_i) = \frac{c}{1 - \gamma c}\left\{\frac{(\varepsilon_i/\varepsilon_k)^{c/1-\gamma c}}{1 + (\varepsilon_i/\varepsilon_k)^{c/(1-\gamma c)}}\right\}\ln\frac{\varepsilon_i}{\varepsilon_k} + \ln\frac{R_S}{p_s} \qquad (5.20)$$

Define the coefficient of $\ln(\varepsilon_i/\varepsilon_k)$ in (5.20) as the function $\phi(\varepsilon_i/\varepsilon_k)$, and note that $\phi(\varepsilon_i/\varepsilon_k)$ has the same sign as $c/(1 - \gamma c)$, but is smaller in size. Note that this outcome is similar to that which would be obtained in the cooperative model of the first section when parents make no gifts or bequests and $\alpha_f = \alpha_m = \alpha$; that is, from (5.5),

$$\ln(S^*) = \ln\frac{\gamma(1 - \alpha)}{\gamma(1 - \alpha) + \alpha} + \ln\frac{y_f + y_m}{p_s} \qquad (5.21)$$

The amount of resources devoted to human capital investment, R_S, is equal to $\{[\gamma(1 - \alpha)]/[\gamma(1 - \alpha) + \alpha]\}(y_f + y_m)$. As there is only one child, there is no scope for compensation or reinforcement and so the first term of (5.20) is absent. Furthermore, the individual earnings endowment does not influence the child's education, because educational investment is not carried to the point at which the marginal return from education equals its marginal cost. In both models, resources and preferences determine the level of education chosen.

5.5 ESTIMATING THE RETURN TO EDUCATION IN THE LABOUR MARKET

The impact of education on earnings, or the return to education, is of particular interest in economics because education is one of the major ways in which one generation affects the standard of living of its successor. It is important to consider how parents' decisions that influence the amount of education may affect the empirical analysis that attempts to estimate this impact.

5.5.1 Separable Earnings–Transfer (SET) Model

Equation (5.20) for optimal educational investment for the ith child with sibling k is augmented by allowing for error in the measurement of educational attainments; this has received considerable attention in the literature. Let S_{if} denote measured education, where a subscript for the family (f) has been added for clarity. Then let $\ln(S_{if}) = \ln(S_{if}^*) + \mu_{if}$, where S_{if}^* is the true level of education and μ_{if} is measurement error, with $E[\mu_{if}] = E[\ln(\varepsilon_{if})\mu_{if}] = E[\ln(\varepsilon_{kf})\mu_{if}] = 0$, where $E[.]$ is the "expectations operator". As the earnings function is expressed in terms of the true level of education, we have the following model of children's educational choice and earnings:

$$\ln(S_{if}) = \phi\left(\frac{\varepsilon_{if}}{\varepsilon_{kf}}\right)[\ln(\varepsilon_{if}) - \ln(\varepsilon_{kf})] + \ln\frac{R_{Sf}}{p_{sf}} + \mu_{if} \qquad (5.22)$$

$$\ln(e_{if}) = \gamma\ln(S_{if}) + \ln(\varepsilon_{if}) - \gamma\mu_{if} + \nu_{if} \qquad (5.23)$$

where, as above,

$$\phi\left(\frac{\varepsilon_{if}}{\varepsilon_{kf}}\right) = \frac{c}{(1 - \gamma c)} \frac{(\varepsilon_{if}/\varepsilon_{kf})^{c/(1-\gamma c)}}{1 + (\varepsilon_{if}/\varepsilon_{kf})^{c/(1-\gamma c)}}$$

and ν_{if} reflects "luck" in the labour market, with $E[\ln(\varepsilon_{if})\nu_{if}] = E[\nu_{if}] = E[\nu_{if}\mu_{if}] = 0 = E[\ln(\varepsilon_{if})]$.

Treating $\phi(\varepsilon_{if}/\varepsilon_{kf})$ as a constant and taking expectations in (5.23) *conditional* on education,

$$E[\ln(e_{if})|S_{if}] = \gamma\ln(S_{if}) +$$

$$E\left\{\ln(\varepsilon_{if}) - \gamma\mu_{if} + \nu_{if}\middle|\ln(S_{if}) = \phi[\ln(\varepsilon_{if}) - \ln(\varepsilon_{kf})] + \ln\frac{R_{Sf}}{p_{sf}} + \mu_{if}\right\}$$

$$= \gamma\ln(S_{if}) + \left[\phi\{\mathrm{var}[\ln(\varepsilon_{if})] - \mathrm{cov}[\ln(\varepsilon_{kf}), \ln(\varepsilon_{if})]\}\right.$$

$$\left.+\mathrm{cov}\left[\ln(\varepsilon_{if}), \ln\frac{R_{Sf}}{p_{sf}}\right] - \gamma\mathrm{var}(\mu_{if})\right]\frac{\ln(S_{if})}{\mathrm{var}[\ln(S_{if})]} \qquad (5.24)$$

where var[ ] and cov[ ] represent "variance" and "covariance" respectively.

The second term on the right-hand side of (5.24) is a "sample selection term" (see Heckman 1979; Garen 1984), reflecting the endogeneity of educational choice, and the "probability limit" of the ordinary least square (OLS) estimator of γ is[7]

$$\mathrm{plim}\,\gamma_{\mathrm{ols}} =$$

$$\gamma + \frac{\phi\{\mathrm{var}[\ln(\varepsilon_{if})] - \mathrm{cov}[\ln(\varepsilon_{kf}), \ln(\varepsilon_{if})]\} + \mathrm{cov}[\ln(\varepsilon_{if}), \ln(R_{Sf}/p_{sf})] - \gamma\mathrm{var}(\mu_{if})}{\mathrm{var}[\ln(S_{if})]}$$

$$(5.25)$$

Even in the absence of measurement error, OLS estimates of γ will be biased because of correlation between parental resources and children's earnings endowments and because parents respond to variation in children's earnings endowments in making educational choices for their children (namely, ϕ is different from zero).

In the case of identical twins, $\varepsilon_{if} = \varepsilon_{kf}$ and $\text{var}[\ln(\varepsilon_{if})] = \text{cov}[\ln(\varepsilon_{kf}), \ln(\varepsilon_{if})]$, making the OLS bias equal to $\text{cov}[\ln(\varepsilon_{if}), \ln(R_{Sf}/p_{sf})]$ in the absence of measurement error. This would also be the OLS bias in a one-child family. Thus, with samples of identical twins (or one-child families), we would expect that, after adjusting for measurement error, any bias from using OLS would be upward, because of positive correlation between parents' and children's endowments and positive correlation between parents' endowments and real resources devoted to human capital investment in their children, R_{Sf}/p_{sf}.

In the case of other siblings (including non-identical twins), the direction and magnitude of OLS bias also depends on $\phi\{\text{var}[\ln(\varepsilon_{if})] - \text{cov}[\ln(\varepsilon_{kf}), \ln(\varepsilon_{if})]\}$. If parents' educational choices *reinforce* earnings endowments, then $\phi > 0$, while if parents' choices *compensate* for differences in children's endowments, then $\phi < 0$. It follows that, because $\text{cov}[\ln(\varepsilon_{kf}), \ln(\varepsilon_{if})] < \text{var}[\ln(\varepsilon_{ij})]$, in the absence of measurement error, when parents reinforce endowments, the OLS estimator of γ is biased upward by more than among identical twins (or one-child families). But when parents compensate for differences in their children's earnings endowments, any upward bias in the OLS estimator is smaller than that for identical twins (or one-child families), and the bias could be downward.

Thus, provided that measurement errors are drawn from the same distribution for both samples (so that $\text{var}(\mu_{if})$ is the same), if parents compensate for (reinforce) endowment differences between children, the OLS estimator from a sample of identical twins is larger (smaller) than that from a sample from the general population (or a sample of non-identical twins or siblings). This comes about because reinforcement or compensation is impossible with identical twins (or one-child families), but it would appear among the general population.

Taking differences between siblings removes the influence of family resources relative to the cost of education R_{Sf}/p_{sf} on educational attainments (see (5.22)). The probability limit of the ordinary least-squares estimate of γ based on sibling differences in earnings and education, γ_{dif},

$$\text{plim}\,\gamma_{\text{dif}} = \gamma + \frac{4\phi\{\text{var}[\ln(\varepsilon_{if})] - \text{cov}[\ln(\varepsilon_{kf}), \ln(\varepsilon_{if})]\} - 2\gamma\,\text{var}(\mu_{if})}{\text{var}[\ln(\Delta u_{f1})]}$$

$$(5.26)$$

where $\Delta u_{f1} = 2\phi[\ln(\varepsilon_{if}) - \ln(\varepsilon_{kf})] + \Delta\mu_f$ and $\Delta\mu_f = \mu_{if} - \mu_{kf}$.

Note that, even in the absence of measurement error, γ_{dif} does not converge to the true value of γ. The direction of the bias will reflect the operation of compensation ($\phi < 0$) or reinforcement by parents ($\phi > 0$).

5.5.2 Wealth Model

Section 5.3 showed that when parents make gifts or bequests to each child, the optimal level of education does not depend on family resources, but only on that child's earnings endowment and on the marginal cost of education to the family. From (5.2),

$$\ln(S_{if}) = \frac{1}{1-\gamma}[\ln(\gamma\varepsilon_{if}) - \ln(rp_{sf})] \tag{5.27}$$

Taking conditional expectations of the earnings function in this model, we obtain

$$E[\ln(e_{if}) \mid S_{if}] = \gamma\ln(S_{if})$$

$$+E\left\{\ln(\varepsilon_{if}) - \gamma\mu_{if} + \nu_{if} \mid \ln(S_{if}) = \frac{1}{1-\gamma}[\ln(\gamma\varepsilon_{if}) - \ln(rp_{sf})] + \mu_{if}\right\}$$

$$= \gamma\ln(S_{if}) + \{\mathrm{var}[\ln(\varepsilon_{if})] - \mathrm{cov}[\ln(\varepsilon_{if}), \ln(p_{sf})]$$

$$- \gamma\mathrm{var}(\mu_{if})\}\frac{\ln(S_{if})}{(1-\gamma)\,\mathrm{var}[\ln(S_{if})]} \tag{5.28}$$

Thus, similar issues arise in this model. Namely, we again find a "selection term" in the conditional earnings equation, (5.28), and, even in the absence of measurement error, OLS estimates of γ are usually biased:

$$\mathrm{plim}\,\gamma_{\mathrm{ols}} = \gamma + \frac{\mathrm{var}[\ln(\varepsilon_{if})] - \mathrm{cov}[\ln(\varepsilon_{if}), \ln(p_{sf})] - \gamma\mathrm{var}(\mu_{if})}{(1-\gamma)\,\mathrm{var}[\ln(S_{if})]}$$

In this model, the bias arises because of any correlation between the cost of education in the family and children's earnings endowments and because of variation in children's earnings endowments. Families whose parents have higher endowments are likely to both have better-endowed children and lower costs of making investment, thereby by suggesting that $\mathrm{cov}[\ln(\varepsilon_{if}), \ln(p_{sf})] \le 0$. In this case, the bias is positive in the absence of measurement error.

A sibling–difference estimator would eliminate the impact of the marginal cost of education in the family (rp_{sf}), but the probability limit of this estimator also does not converge to the true value of γ, as the following shows:

$$\mathrm{plim}\,\gamma_{\mathrm{dif}} = \gamma + \frac{2\dfrac{\mathrm{var}[\ln(\varepsilon_{if})] - \mathrm{cov}[\ln(\varepsilon_{kf}), \ln(\varepsilon_{if})]}{1-\gamma} - 2\gamma\mathrm{var}(\mu_{if})}{\mathrm{var}(\Delta u_{f2})} \tag{5.29}$$

where $\Delta u_{f2} = [\ln(\varepsilon_{if}) - \ln(\varepsilon_{kf})]/(1-\gamma) + \Delta\mu_f$.

5.5.3 Comparing the Two Models Empirically

It may be possible to distinguish between the two models with siblings samples. If measurement error is not too large, then the coefficient of the selection term in (5.29) is positive. Thus, if we find a negative value for the selection coefficient, we can reject the wealth model. Ermisch and Francesconi (2000a) indeed find a negative coefficient in their sibling difference estimates, thereby favouring the separable earnings–transfer (SET) model and suggesting that parents act to compensate for differences in the children's endowments. If $cov[\ln(\varepsilon_{if}), \ln(p_{sf})] \leq 0$, estimation of a negative selection coefficient in a conventional sample would also favour rejection of the wealth model.

It may still be possible to draw some conclusions about the relative merits of the two models when we do not have data on siblings or do not find a negative selection coefficient. This can be done by comparing the coefficient of the selection term estimated from a sample of one-child families with that estimated from a sample of people with siblings. In the wealth model, these two coefficients should be the same. In the SET model, the selection coefficient from a sample of people with siblings must be smaller (larger) than the coefficient in the only-child sample when there is compensation (reinforcement). Such a difference would suggest that the SET model is more likely to be valid than the wealth model. Ermisch and Francesconi (2000a) indeed find that the selection coefficient estimated from a sample of people with siblings is negative and statistically significant, while the estimate of this coefficient from an only-child sample is virtually zero.

5.5.4 The Value of Samples of Twins

Whether you have samples of siblings or conventional population samples, consistent estimates of the impact of education on earnings rely on having some variables that affect the level of education achieved and are not correlated with individual endowments (or differences in them between siblings), but do not affect earnings directly. That is, some "instrumental variables" for education are needed. These allow identification of the "selection coefficient" in the models outlined above, and so they also provide an estimate of whether there is compensation or reinforcement of endowments in the SET model. For instance, in the estimates using differences between siblings by Ermisch and Francesconi (2000a), their instrument for identifying the selection coefficient is whether or not a sibling had experienced a one-parent family. Some may argue that this could have direct effects on earnings as well as affecting education, or that it is correlated with differences in endowments, and so it is not a valid instrument.

Behrman et al. (1994) rely on weaker assumptions to identify the impact of education on earnings and whether there is compensation or reinforcement by using two samples of twins, one containing "identical" (monozygotic) twins and the other "fraternal" (dizygotic) twins. They estimate the parameters of a relatively general intra-family allocation model, which takes the following linear form:

$$S_{if} = \psi_1 a_{if} + \psi_2 a_{kf} + \eta h_f + s_f + u_{if} \qquad (5.30)$$

$$e_{if} = \beta S_{if} + h_f + a_{if} + v_{if} \qquad (5.31)$$

where h_f represents genetic and other endowments that are common among all children in a family; a_{if} represents an idiosyncratic endowment specific to the ith child; s_f represents the joint influence of exogenous features of the family environment, including prices, family income, parents' human capital, etc.; η is the effect of the family-specific earnings endowment on education decisions; u_{if} is a random factor that affects education but not earnings directly; and v_{if} again reflects labour market luck. We ignore measurement errors for simplicity, but Behrman et al. (1994) incorporate them in their analysis.

Compared to this model, a linear version of the SET model represented by (5.22) and (5.23) is more restrictive. It assumes that $\psi_1 = \phi$, $\psi_2 = -\phi$, and $\eta = 0$, where the endowment ε_{if} in (5.22) and (5.23) is $h_f + a_{if}$. This is because, in the SET model, resources and not the *level* of endowment, determine the level of education chosen by parents.

Denote differences between a pair of identical twins by the superscript M and differences between fraternal twins by the superscript D. Then, obtaining an expression for $\Delta e_{if} = e_{if} - e_{kf}$ after substituting (5.30) into (5.31), and calculating variances and the covariance for ΔS_{if} and Δe_{if}, we obtain

$$\text{var}(\Delta e_{if}^M) = 2\beta^2 \text{var}(u_{if}) + 2\text{var}(v_{if}) \qquad (5.32a)$$

$$\text{var}(\Delta S_{if}^M) = 2\text{var}(u_{if}) \qquad (5.32b)$$

$$\text{cov}(\Delta e_{if}^M, \Delta S_{if}^M) = 2\beta\text{var}(u_{if}) \qquad (5.32c)$$

Dividing (5.32c) by (5.32b), we obtain a consistent estimate for β based on differences between identical siblings, $b^M = \text{cov}(\Delta e_{if}^M, \Delta S_{if}^M)/\text{var}(\Delta S_{if}^M)$. This is the estimate of the impact of education on earnings obtained by applying OLS to the difference in earnings between the twins, which from (5.31) is given by $\Delta e_{if} = \beta \Delta S_{if} + \Delta v_{if}$, owing to their identical endowments.

Of course, data on identical twins would not allow us to estimate how families respond to differences between children in endowments. Here is where the sample of fraternal twins comes into the analysis. Two plausible assumptions are required to identify the compensation or reinforcement response of parents: (1) that the impact of education (β) is the same for all individuals, as is commonly assumed; and (2) that the *individual-specific* elements of (5.30) and (5.31), namely u_{if} and v_{if}, are drawn from the same distribution for identical twins as for other siblings, including fraternal twins.

Calculating variances and the covariance for the fraternal twin pairs,

$$\text{var}(\Delta \varepsilon_{if}^{D}) = 2\beta^2 \, \text{var}(u_{if}) + 2 \, \text{var}(v_{if}) + 2(1 + \beta\psi_1 - \beta\psi_2)^2 \, \text{var}(a_{if})$$
(5.33a)

$$\text{var}(\Delta S_{if}^{D}) = 2 \, \text{var}(u_{if}) + 2(\psi_1 - \psi_2)^2 \, \text{var}(a_{if}) \qquad (5.33b)$$

$$\text{cov}(\Delta e_{if}^{D}, \Delta S_{if}^{D}) = 2\beta \, \text{var}(u_{if}) + 2(\psi_1 - \psi_2)(1 + \beta\psi_1 - \beta\psi_2)^2 \, \text{var}(a_{if})$$
(5.33c)

Taking the difference between the respective variances and covariance for the two types of twins, we obtain, in particular,

$$\text{var}(\Delta e_{if}^{D}) - \text{var}(\Delta e_{if}^{M}) = 2(1 + \beta\psi_1 - \beta\psi_2)^2 \text{var}(a_{if}) \qquad (5.34a)$$

$$\text{cov}(\Delta e_{if}^{D}, \Delta S_{if}^{D}) - \text{cov}(\Delta e_{if}^{M}, \Delta S_{if}^{M}) = 2(\psi_1 - \psi_2)(1 + \beta\psi_1 - \beta\psi_2)^2 \text{var}(a_{if})$$
(5.34b)

Dividing (5.34b) by (5.34a), we obtain a consistent estimate of $\psi_1 - \psi_2$; that is, we can identify whether or not parents compensate for or reinforce differences in endowments between children of the same family, because $\psi_1 - \psi_2 > 0$ indicates reinforcement and $\psi_1 - \psi_2 < 0$ indicates compensation. If this were strictly an individual model, so that $\psi_2 = 0$, then we could identify the own-endowment effect, ψ_1, directly. A negative estimate of $\psi_1 - \psi_2$ would clearly favour a family model over an individual one. Note that we did not have to make any assumption about the covariance of h_f and s_f in order to identify $\psi_1 - \psi_2$ and β. In other words, we did not have to find any variables that affect education and are not correlated with the family-specific endowment, but do not affect earnings directly (i.e. elements feeding into s_f).

It is useful to formulate the estimate of $\psi_1 - \psi_2$ differently. Letting b^{D} be the OLS estimate of β from the differences between fraternal twins (i.e. $b^{D} = \text{cov}(\Delta e_{if}^{D}, \Delta S_{if}^{D})/\text{var}(\Delta S_{if}^{D}))$, we obtain

$$\psi_1 - \psi_2 = \frac{1 - R}{b^{D} - b^{M}} \qquad (5.35)$$

where $R = \text{var}(\Delta S_{if}^{M})/\text{var}(\Delta S_{if}^{D})$. Given that $R < 1$, because identical twins are more alike than fraternal ones, whether or not there is reinforcement or compensation depends on whether or not b^D exceeds b^M. As noted earlier in the discussion following (5.25), this is because reinforcement or compensation is impossible with identical twins, but it could appear among the fraternal twins and siblings more generally. Recalling that b^M is a consistent estimate of β, if there is reinforcement, b^D would be an upwardly biased estimate of β (i.e. $b^D - b^M > 0$). This is because a more favourable endowment for one of the pair would be reinforced by more educational investment in that person, thereby conflating the influence of endowment differences on earnings with the influence of differences in education. With compensation for endowment differences, b^D would underestimate β ($b^D - b^M < 0$) for analogous reasons.

The expression for b^D in terms of the underlying parameters of the model in (5.30) and (5.31) reiterates why sibling differences are usually not sufficient to identify the impact of education on earnings. From (5.33b) and (5.33c),

$$b^D = \frac{\beta \operatorname{var}(u_{if}) + (\psi_1 - \psi_2)[1 + \beta(\psi_1 - \psi_2)]^2 \operatorname{var}(a_{if})}{\operatorname{var}(u_{if}) + (\psi_1 - \psi_2)^2 \operatorname{var}(a_{if})} \tag{5.36}$$

Unless parents do not respond to endowment differences ($\psi_1 = \psi_2$), or there is no variation in idiosyncratic endowments ($\operatorname{var}(a_{if}) = 0$), which is the case for identical twins, b^D does not provide a consistent estimate of β.

The estimates of $\psi_1 - \psi_2$ in the analyses using two sources of twin samples by Behrman et al. (1994) are positive, thereby indicating reinforcement. This result is consistent with both an individual model and a family model. This contrasts with the results indicating compensation within families obtained by Ermisch and Francesconi (2000a), but their estimates depend on stronger identification assumptions.

Notes

1. They bring to bear a range of data and analyses to address the issue of the productivity effect of home teaching by more educated women, taking into account preferences for a child's education in the home and in the marriage market. Note that these impacts of having a literate mother who is not a primary school graduate are relative to both illiterate *and* primary school graduates, suggesting that primary-schooled women devote more time to activities in which schooling has a financial return.

2. See the discussion around (5.14) when it is assumed that parents have the same preferences.

3. A higher child endowment reduces the amount of child education required to achieve a given level of the mother's utility if mothers put a larger utility weight on child's income than fathers do.

4. The possibility that e_0 increases with the endowment ε is considered below.

5. If the endowment ε also increases earnings in the "failure" state, then there is another negative term in (5.11), thereby reducing $\partial S/\partial \varepsilon$ further.

6. This comes from a first-order expansion around a given $(\varepsilon_{if}/\varepsilon_{kf})$ of the solution $\ln(S_{if}) = -\ln[1 + (\varepsilon_{kf}/\varepsilon_{if})^{\alpha c/(1-\beta c)}] + \ln(R_f{}^c/p_s)$.

7. Loosely speaking, the probability limit, or *plim*, is the value to which the estimator converges *with probability one*, or *almost surely*, as the sample size approaches infinity.

CHAPTER SIX

Economic Theories of Fertility

ECONOMIC theories of fertility have been around for over two hundred years. The ideas advanced by Thomas Malthus are the best known. In a few words, Malthus' view was that fertility was determined by the age at marriage and frequency of coition during marriage, because methods for controlling fertility other than abstinence were not well known at the time. He argued that an increase in people's income would encourage them to marry earlier and have sexual intercourse more often. In addition, an increase in income would cause a decline in child mortality, enabling more children to survive childhood. Modern economic theories of fertility date from a paper by Gary Becker (1960), which generalized and developed the Malthusian theory.

6.1 CHILD QUALITY AND FERTILITY

Becker's seminal contribution pointed out that the psychic satisfaction parents receive from their children is likely to depend on the amount that parents spend on children as well as the number of children that they have. This has been a foundation of the analysis in the previous chapters, in which we have taken the number of children as given. For short, Becker calls children who have more spent on them "higher quality" children, hastening to add "that 'higher quality' does not mean morally better." (Becker, 1960, p. 211) The basic idea is that if parents voluntarily spend more on a child, it is because they obtain additional satisfaction from the additional expenditure. It is this additional satisfaction that is called "higher quality".

The concept of "child quality" continues to be an important element in the economic analysis of fertility. The characterization of "child quality" has moved in the direction of identifying child quality with the lifetime well-being of the child, which, as the previous chapter has shown, can be increased by investing more in the child's human capital or by the direct transfer of wealth to the child. That is, the parents receive more satisfaction from having children who are better off throughout their life, and they make monetary transfers and human capital investments to influence their child's lifetime standard of living. Thus, we could think of child quality as the child's "quality of life", as an adult as well as during his or her childhood.

Having incorporated the quality dimension of reproduction decisions, the well-developed model of consumer choice can be applied to them. Parents are assumed to choose the best combination of the number of children, their quality and the parents' own standard of living subject to the lifetime income that the parents have and the prices that they face in markets. An increase in parents' income is expected to increase both the quantity and quality of children. In light of the tendency for people to increase the quality of most consumer durable goods proportionately much more than the quantity of such goods when their income increases, Becker argued that this is also likely to be the case for children. Thus, Becker's contention is that the income elasticity of the number of children ("quantity") is small compared to the income elasticity of child quality. Put somewhat differently, an increase in parents' income may increase the amount spent on children substantially, but this would mainly take the form of higher quality rather than more children. The introduction of the child quality concept generalizes the Malthusian theory, which only allows responses to income along the quantity dimension.

6.1.1 Quantity–Quality Interaction

A new twist to the quantity–quality model was added in the influential papers by Willis (1973) and Becker and Lewis (1973). They assumed that parents view child quantity and quality as substitutes and that parents treat all their children equally, in the sense that child quality is the same for each child.

In terms of the analysis in the previous chapter, child quality could be equated to income as an adult, earnings plus gifts and bequests ($e + rb$ in Chapter 5). We have seen that the "production" of income as an adult requires parental time and purchases of good and services, including in the latter direct financial transfers to children. Here we will abstract from the difference between direct transfers and investments in a child's human capital, which was the focus of the previous chapter, and define directly a production function for child quality (Q), or income as an adult, in terms of parents' time and purchases of good and services.

It is assumed that parents choose the same level of child quality for each child, and that production can be described by the constant returns to scale production function

$$Q = f\left(\frac{x_c}{N}, \frac{t_{mc}}{N}, \frac{t_{fc}}{N}\right) \tag{6.1}$$

where x_c is the total amount of goods and services and t_{mc} and t_{fc} are the total amounts of mother's and father's time, respectively devoted to the production of child quality, and N is the number of children. Total expenditure on children is, therefore, $\pi_C NQ = \pi_C f(x_c, t_{mc}, t_{fc})$, where π_C is the marginal cost of children.

Application of the analysis leading to (4.2) implies that the marginal cost of children depends on the prices of inputs into its production, namely

$$d \ln(\pi_C) = \frac{p_c x_c}{\pi_C NQ} d \ln(p_c) + \frac{w_m t_{mc}}{\pi_C NQ} d \ln(w_m) + \frac{w_f t_{fc}}{\pi_C NQ} d \ln(w_f) \quad (6.2)$$

where w_i is the wage rate of parent i and p_c is the price of purchased goods and services. This assumes that both parents work in the market sometime during the childrearing part of their marriage.

The parents' standard of living Z, or "parental consumption" for short, is also produced by combining parents' time and purchased goods and services. Let $Z = g(x_z, t_{mz}, t_{fz})$, where $g(\ )$ exhibits constant returns to scale. As the impact of differences in preferences between parents for decisions has already been explored in Chapters 2 and 5, we assume consensus preferences represented by the utility function $U(Z, N, Q)$. We also assume for the moment that fertility can be controlled without cost. Then a newly married couple is assumed to choose N, Q and Z to maximize their utility subject to the lifetime budget constraint

$$Y = \pi_Z Z + \pi_C NQ \quad (6.3)$$

where π_Z is the marginal cost of parental consumption, which depends on input prices analogously to (6.2). The solution to this problem implies that

$$U_N = \lambda \pi_C Q = \lambda p_N \quad (6.4a)$$

$$U_Q = \lambda \pi_C N = \lambda p_Q \quad (6.4b)$$

$$U_Z = \lambda \pi_Z \quad (6.4c)$$

where $U_k = \partial U / \partial k$, $k = N, Q, Z$, are marginal utilities, and p_N and p_Q are the marginal costs of the number and quality of children, respectively. The marginal utility of income is λ.

Equations (6.4a) and (6.4b) show that the product NQ in the budget constraint implies that the cost (or "shadow price") of an additional child is proportional to the level of child quality, and the cost ("shadow price") of raising child quality is proportional to the number of children the parents have. As a consequence, there is an important interaction between family size and child quality. Suppose, for example, that there is an exogenous increase in the parents' desired level of child quality, say as a consequence of technological changes which raise the rate of return on human capital investment. This raises the shadow price of children,

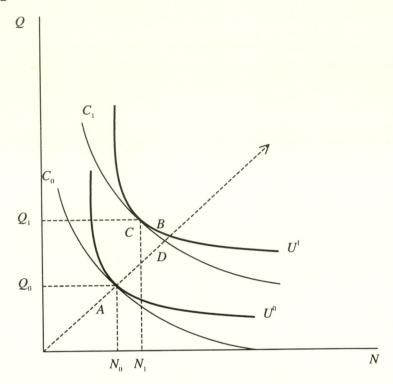

Figure 6.1 Quantity–quality interaction.

which lowers family size, which in turn lowers the shadow price of child quality, which in turn raises child quality, which raises the shadow price of children further, and so on. Thus, a cumulative process favouring child quality and reducing fertility ensues.

Figure 6.1 illustrates the impact of the non-linear budget constraint. The optimal choice of N and Q is given at point A, at which the indifference curve U_0 is tangent to the budget constraint $C_0 = NQ = [Y - \pi_Z Z(Y, \pi_Z, \pi_C)]/\pi_C$, where C_0 is the parents' real expenditure on children and $Z(Y, \pi_Z, \pi_C)$ is the demand function for parents' consumption. Maximization of utility implies that the indifference curve must be more convex than the budget constraint, which means that child quality and quantity cannot be *close* substitutes for one another. As is clear from (6.4a) and (6.4b), at the tangency point, $U_N/U_Q = p_N/p_Q = Q/N$.

Now suppose that there is an increase in income Y, so that the new budget constraint is $C_1 = NQ$. If the income elasticities of child quality and quantity were equal, then the new optimum would be at point D, where the ratio N/Q is the same as at A. If, as argued above, the quality income elasticity exceeds the one for quantity, then Q/N rises, thereby increasing p_N/p_Q, and the new optimum is at point C. There has been a small increase in N and a large increase in Q. This total effect can be decomposed into a *pure income effect*, holding p_N/p_Q constant, from point A to B, and an *induced substitution effect*, from point B to C, arising from the induced increase in p_N/p_Q. Thus, higher income produces only a small increase in the number of children because the pure income effect on fertility is partially offset by the substitution effect against fertility induced by the higher cost of an additional child associated with higher quality.

The induced substitution effect may be sufficiently large to produce a decline in fertility when income increases. It may, therefore, appear that the income elasticity of fertility is negative, even though children are "normal goods", in the sense that parents want more of them when parental income increases. The reason is that the true income elasticity is defined with relative prices constant, but, because of the interaction, we cannot hold the ratio of the shadow price of an additional child to that of child quality constant when we measure the elasticity. The measured income elasticity of family size is more likely to be negative (even though the true elasticity is positive), the more responsive is child quality to changes in income relative to the responsiveness of fertility (i.e. the higher is the quality elasticity relative to the quantity elasticity), and the better substitutes are child quality and parental consumption for family size (see the Appendix for details).

The interaction between child quality and fertility does not derive from assuming that child quality and quantity are *close* substitutes for one another. Indeed, we have seen that just the opposite must be the case, because if both fertility and child quality are to be non-zero, as they must, then they cannot be close substitutes. Nevertheless, the interaction is stronger when they are better substitutes.

The budget constraint in (6.3) can be generalized to incorporate costs of the number of children that do not depend on child quality and costs of quality that do not depend on the number of children: $Y = \pi_Z Z + \pi_C NQ + \pi_N N + \pi_Q Q$. As an example of the former, a decline in the cost of averting births, say because of the introduction of the oral contraceptive pill, would increase the marginal cost of a birth (π_N) without affecting the marginal cost of child quality. This would raise Q/N and p_N/p_Q, which produces an induced substitution effect favouring child quality and lowering fertility further. Lower contraception costs and other increases in π_N can, therefore, produce *large* increases in child quality and further large declines in fertility. Thus, family size can be highly responsive to changes in prices and incomes, even though children have no close substitutes.

6.1.2 Testing the Quantity–Quality Interaction Model

The interaction model is more restrictive than the assumption that parents obtain satisfaction from the quality of children as well as their number. It requires that the product of quantity and quality appears in the budget constraint of parents, which means that they are substitutes and that parents want the same quality for each child. In general, it is difficult to test the interaction model, but Rosenzweig and Wolpin (1980) derive a test based on the occurrence of twins, which provides random exogenous variation in the number of children. Their measure of child quality is the average educational attainments of children in the family, and they find that twins are associated with lower schooling levels for the other children. This finding supports the hypothesis that quantity and quality are substitutes, but it is not sufficient to test the interaction model. They show, however, that under plausible restrictions on parents' preferences, the negative impact of twins on the other children's educational attainments is sufficiently large to reject the interaction model with their household data from India. While supporting quality–quantity substitution, these results cast doubt on the simplifying assumption of uniform quality across children in a family. Differences in educational investment between sons and daughters in some countries also point to the need for a more general formulation of the quantity–quality model. The previous chapter has shown that "poorer parents" (i.e. those not making financial transfers) do not equalize the adult incomes of their children, which could be taken as a measure of child quality.

6.2 The Cost of Children

Consumer theory tells us that, like any other price, a higher marginal cost of children π_C ought to reduce both fertility and child quality. The factors affecting this cost are closely associated with the key role of parental time, especially the mother's, in the rearing of and investment in children. The foundations for this analysis were laid in a paper by Mincer (1963) and in Becker's (1965) theory of time allocation, and Willis (1973) built on them in his analysis.

The concept of "household production", discussed in Chapter 4, is important in understanding what influences the cost of children. Following Becker (1965), we have assumed that Q and Z cannot be purchased directly in the market. Rather, the parents' standard of living and child quality are both produced within the household by combining parents' own time and purchased goods and services, as in (6.1). It is the cost of these inputs that determines the cost of child quality relative to the cost of the parents' living standard. From (6.2),

$$d\ln\left(\frac{\pi_C}{\pi_Z}\right) = (q_{mC} - q_{mZ})d\ln(w_m) + (q_{fC} - q_{fZ})d\ln(w_f) \quad (6.5)$$

where $q_{mC} = (w_m t_{mc}/\pi_C NQ)$ and $q_{fC} = (w_f t_{fc}/\pi_C NQ)$ are the parents' respective shares in the costs of producing Q, $q_{mZ} = (w_m t_{mz}/\pi_Z Z)$ and $q_{fZ} = (w_f t_{fz}/\pi_Z Z)$ are their shares in the cost of producing Z, and purchased goods and services are taken as the numeriare (i.e. $p_c = p_z = 1$).

Parental time in the production of child quality is primarily the mother's time, and the rearing of children is assumed to be *time-intensive* relative to other home production activities in the sense that $q_{mC} > q_{mZ}$. That is, the proportion of the total cost of producing children represented by the value of the mother's time input to children is larger than the proportion of the total cost of producing the parents' standard of living represented by the value of her time input to that production. Thus, the unit cost of children relative to the cost of the parents' living standard is directly related to the mother's cost of time. If she has ever been in paid employment, her cost of time is the wage she could earn in employment (i.e. her foregone earnings). From (6.5), we see that the higher her wage, the higher the cost of an additional child and of additional quality per child relative to the cost of improving the parents' living standard (Z). The relative cost of children clearly also depends on the father's wage as long as $q_{fC} \neq q_{fZ}$.

The parents' lifetime budget constraint is $x_c + x_z = (T - t_{mc} - t_{mz})w_m + (T - t_{fc} - t_{fz})w_f + y$ and $0 < t_{ij} \leq T$, where y is other family income, and each parent's total time is T. This can be written in terms of "full income"

$$Y = (w_m + w_f)T + y = (t_{mc} + t_{mz})w_m + (t_{fc} + t_{fz})w_f + x_c + x_z$$

$$= \pi_z Z + \pi_C NQ$$

Equations (6.4a)–(6.4c), along with the budget constraint, continue to be necessary conditions for the parents to maximize $U(Z, N, Q)$ with respect to their budget and the production relations for Z and Q. These give rise to a demand function for children. As we have already analyzed the quantity–quality interaction, let us simplify by letting $U(Z, N, Q) = U(Z, NQ)$.[1] Then

$$d\ln(NQ) = \psi_C S_{YY} d\ln(y) + [\psi_C S_{mY} - \sigma S_Z(q_{mC} - q_{mZ})]d\ln(w_m)$$

$$+ [\psi_C S_{fY} - \sigma S_Z(q_{fC} - q_{fZ})]d\ln(w_f) \quad (6.6)$$

where σ is the elasticity of substitution in consumption between Z and NQ ($\sigma > 0$); ψ_C is the elasticity of NQ with respect to full income; $S_Z = \pi_Z Z/Y$; and $S_{yY} = y/Y$ and $S_{iY} = w_i(T - t_{ic} - t_{iz})/Y$, $i = \text{m, f}$, are shares of full income.

Equation (6.6) suggests that men's and women's wages should have important effects on fertility and child quality. Higher wages mean higher income for the parents, encouraging them to have more children and to invest more in the human capital of each child or to make larger monetary transfers to them (i.e. higher quality). These effects are represented by the terms $\psi_C S_{mY}$ and $\psi_C S_{fY}$. Clearly the income effects are proportional to that parent's share of full income.

Higher wages also mean more income lost by those caring for children and investing in their human capital. Because it is plausible that children are relatively more time intensive than other home production, we expect $q_{mC} > q_{mZ}$. Higher mother's wages give rise to a substitution effect of $-\sigma S_Z(q_{mC} - q_{mZ})$, which is negative. Thus, higher women's wages raise the opportunity cost of a child as well as increasing family income. If the opportunity cost effect of women's wages dominates their effect on family income, higher women's wages reduce family size and child quality.

Higher men's wages mainly affect childbearing through their effect on the couple's income. Although there is also a substitution effect from higher men's wages, it is likely to be small or positive. For instance, if the man has a comparative advantage in market work and wages increase with work experience, then the discussion in Chapter 4 suggests that $q_{fC} = q_{fZ} = 0$, so that there would be no substitution effect. In a less extreme case, it may still be likely that his time in both types of home production is small, so that $q_{fC} - q_{fZ}$ is also small. It could also be the case that, because of his wife's comparative advantage in child-rearing, his home time is mainly allocated to the production of the parent's standard of living (Z), so that $q_{fC} < q_{fZ}$, implying a positive substitution effect. It is this line of reasoning that produces an expectation that an increase in the ratio of women's to men's wages would reduce fertility.

The fraction of the mother's time supplied to the labour market, ($T - t_{mc} - t_{mz})/T$ is also a choice variable, which depends on the wage that she can earn and her partner's wage and non-earned income. Women who can earn high wages, or whose partners do not earn very much, tend to devote a high proportion of their time to the labour market and remain childless.

At the other extreme, women who could only earn low wages, or who have partners whose earnings are high, do not work in the labour market at all (i.e. the constraint that $T \geq t_{mc} + t_{mz}$ is binding) and have large families. For this group, their opportunity cost of time is above their wage rate, as we saw in Chapter 4. Higher husband's wages or non-earned income increase the couple's demand for children, which increases the wife's opportunity cost of time and π_C.[2] For these women, women's wages have no impact on the cost of children or their fertility, and higher men's wages increase the cost of children relative to that of Z, because home production time is scarce for these women (they cannot increase it by reducing time in paid employment) and the production of child quality is assumed to be time-intensive relative to other household production activities. Thus, because of this substitution effect encouraging lower fertility, higher husband's wages would have a smaller effect on fertility among this group of couples than among couples in which the woman spends some time in paid employment.

In between these two extremes are women who combine childbearing with paid employment. Increasingly, this is the bulk of the female population in industrialized countries. Within this group, there would tend to be a negative correlation between family size and the fraction of their life they spend in paid employment. This is a correlation between two choice variables. Variation in wages and preferences drive both variables.

6.3 Purchased Child Care and Fertility

So far we have included purchased child care (e.g. childminders, nannies and creches) in the composite input of 'purchased goods and services', thereby concealing some of the implications of the choice of a combination of parents' time and purchased child care. In order to focus on this issue, assume that fathers are not involved in home production $(t_{fc} = t_{fz} = 0)$. We now use t_{mc} in the child quality production function (6.1) to denote *total time* for child care (rather than just mother's time), some of which can be purchased outside the household at price p per unit, but it is not a perfect substitute for the mother's time. In particular,

$$t_{mc} = H + h(M),$$

$$0 < h'(M) < 1, \ h''(M) < 0, \ h(0) = 0 \ (h'(M) = dh/dM, \text{ etc.})$$

(6.7)

where H is the amount of the mother's time devoted to children, M is the amount of time purchased in the market, and $h(M)$ is a function converting purchased time inputs into units equivalent to mother's time. It is plausible that as more child-care time is purchased, additional purchased time becomes a poorer substitute for mother's time; thus the assumption that $h''(M) < 0$. Because each child may require a minimum amount of mother's time, k, it is also the case that $H \geq kN$ as well as $M \geq 0$.

We focus on the case in which mothers work in the market sometime. Then the fundamental equation for the division of child-care time between the mother and outside care is

$$h'(M) = \frac{p - \mu_M/\lambda}{w_m - \mu_H/\lambda N} \tag{6.8}$$

where μ_H and μ_M are the Lagrange multipliers (shadow prices) associated with the inequality constraints $H \geq kN$ and $M \geq 0$, respectively. These are zero when the constraint is satisfied with an inequality and positive if satisfied with an equality.

Because mother's time and purchased care are not perfect substitutes, it is likely that the parents use both sources of care. That is, $H > kN$ and $M > 0$; then (6.8) becomes $h'(M) = p/w_m$. This is illustrated as tangency point A in Figure 6.2. The parents adjust their purchases of child care so that the marginal contribution of an extra hour of M equals the ratio of the price of child care to the mother's wage.

If the price of market child care is sufficiently low, say because of subsidies, then w_m may exceed $p/h'(M)$ for all values of M. Then child care above the minimum contribution of the mother is entirely provided from purchased time ($M = t_{mc} - kN$). This situation could also arise

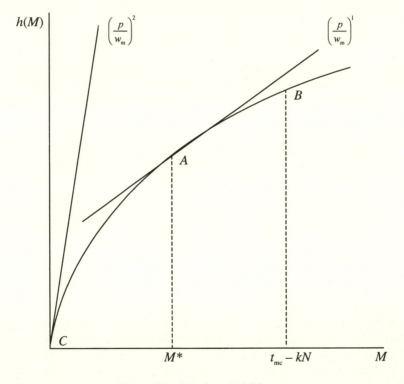

Figure 6.2 Purchased child care.

from a high value of the mother's time. It is illustrated as point B in Figure 6.2. Conversely, if the mother's wage is low or the market price of child care is high, the mother's value of time would be less than $p/h'(0)$, and no child care would be purchased, as at point C in Figure 6.2.

With the incorporation of purchased child care, and assuming an interior solution ($M > 0$ and $H > kN$), (6.6) becomes

$$d \ln(NQ) = \psi_C S_{yY} d \ln(y) + [\psi_C S_{mY} - \sigma S_Z(q_{HC} - q_{mZ})] d \ln(w_m)$$

$$-q_{MC}[\psi_C S_C + \sigma S_Z] d \ln(p) \qquad (6.9)$$

where $q_{HC} = w_m H/\pi_C NQ$, $q_{MC} = w_m h(M)/\pi_C NQ$, $S_C = \pi_C NQ/Y$ and now $S_{mY} = w_m(T - H - t_{mz})/Y$. From (6.9), the effect of a higher price of child care is to reduce fertility and child quality. The larger is the share of children's costs contributed by purchased child care (q_{MC}), the stronger is this effect. If the mother does not use outside care ($M = 0$), then its price clearly has no effect. It is noteworthy that even though children may be more time intensive than the production of Z in the sense that $w_m t_{mc}/\pi_C NQ > q_{mZ}$, the substitution effect of a higher mother's wage could still be positive if purchased child care time is a large enough proportion of child care time so as to make $q_{HC} < q_{mZ}$.

Equation (6.9) indicates a tendency for the impact of the mother's wage on fertility to vary with the level of wages and the price of market child care. At low wages, and high prices of child care, it is more likely that $w_m < p/h'(0)$, and so no child care is purchased. In these circumstances, q_{HC} is relatively high, because all child-care time is provided by the mother, making the substitution effect of the mother's wage in (6.9) negative and larger in size. It is then more likely that a higher mother's wage reduces family size and child quality.

At a somewhat higher wage, child care is also purchased. While by no means certain (Ermisch 1989), this creates a tendency for $q_{HC} - q_{mZ}$ to fall as the mother's wage increases, thereby reducing the size of the (negative) substitution effect. Thus, the impact of the mother's wage on fertility and child quality becomes less negative (or it may turn positive) at higher levels of the wage. A lower price of child care also reduces the size of the substitution effect of the mother's wage and makes it more likely that her wage has a positive effect on fertility, because lower p tends to lower q_{HC}. When child care is heavily subsidized, such as in countries like Sweden, a higher mother's wage may encourage larger families.

Women with very high wage levels find that $w_m > p/h'(M)$ for all values of $H > kN$, so that $H = kN$. In this situation, the marginal cost of children, π_C, is not affected by changes in the wage, only the price of child care.[3] Thus, a higher mother's wage only has an income effect, leading to larger family size and child quality.

In sum, the possibility of purchasing child care, an imperfect substitute for the mother's time in child-rearing, weakens the link between a woman's wage and the cost of an additional child. Mothers with high wages tend to purchase a much larger proportion of child-care time. For them, higher wages have little effect on the cost of children, making it more likely that they increase fertility by raising family income. Similarly, in countries with heavily subsidized child care, mothers contribute much less of child care themselves, making it more likely that women earning higher pay have larger families. At low to moderate levels of wages, a higher mother's wage tends to reduce fertility, but its negative impact attenuates as her wage rises, or the price of child care falls, because mothers purchase a larger proportion of child-care time. The impact of the price of child care on fertility displays a similar interaction, becoming more negative as the mother's wage rises.

Nevertheless, when examining changes over time, the cost of purchased child care and women's wages tend to move together, because women's labour is such an important input to the provision of child-care services. Thus, over time we may still expect women's pay relative to men's and fertility to be negatively related, because higher women's pay raises the cost of children.

There have been many empirical studies that use the theoretical framework of Section 6.2 to structure their statistical analysis. These are surveyed in Hotz et al. (1997) and Schultz (1997). In order to illustrate the difficulties in testing some of the predictions of the models of Sections 6.2 and 6.3, two of my own studies are used as examples. One uses British cross-section data containing retrospective marriage, fertility and work histories to estimate the impacts of mother's wage and father's earnings on family size at the 15th anniversary of the marriage and on the number of months the mother was in paid employment over these 15 years (Ermisch 1989). The other exploits time series variation in British wages and fertility during 1950–1983 (Ermisch 1988).

The hourly wage that a woman can earn is important in the theories discussed above. Often a mother's educational attainment is used as a measure of this wage because of the association between hourly earnings and education. In Ermisch (1989), a small extension of this idea is used. The measure of the mother's wage is taken to be the hourly wage that a woman with particular human capital characteristics could earn in full-time employment *at the time of marriage*. It is calculated by first estimating an earnings function from cross-section earnings data, relating hourly earnings in full-time employment to a woman's educational qualifications, part-time employment experience, full-time employment experience and years out of employment, controlling for non-random selection into full-time employment at a point in time. This earnings function is evaluated at the time of marriage for each woman, using educational attainments and work experience accumulated to that time. An important shortcoming of this measure is that any unmeasured attributes that affect a woman's educational attainments and work experience at marriage (e.g. ability, motivation) may be correlated with her preferences. As a consequence, the estimated impact of the mother's wage on family size may not measure the impact of *exogenous* variation in mother's wages. For instance, it is likely that women who prefer smaller families also obtain higher qualifications and work more in full-time employment before marriage, thereby biasing the size of the estimated impact of her wage on family size upward. This problem is likely to afflict other measures of her wage that rely on her personal characteristics, such as education and work experience.

Keeping this strong possibility of bias in mind, the estimated impact of a woman's estimated full-time wage at marriage on family size 15 years later is strongly negative for most women, but it becomes smaller (less negative) at higher levels of the wage, as the model of this section suggests. A higher woman's wage also increases a woman's employment after marriage, with the positive impact diminishing at higher levels of the wage. Higher husband's earnings increase family size and reduce the amount of time after marriage that his wife is in paid employment.[4] While these results are in line with the predictions of the theoretical models of this section and the preceding one, the source of variation in measured parents' wages makes the results suspect, because it is difficult to make a credible defence that this variation is exogenous. A similar criticism can be directed at many empirical studies of fertility and mother's employment.

Time series variation in average wages may be a more creditable source of exogenous variation in parents' wages that can be used to estimate their effects on fertility. Ermisch (1988) relates annual conditional birth rates by birth order (i.e. births of a given order relative to the population at risk to have a birth of that order) for each age group to the following variables: net (after tax) women's real hourly earnings in manual occupations, net men's real weekly earnings in manual occupations, the unemployment rate, real house prices, child allowances received for an additional birth and the proportion of the cohort at risk for a given order birth in that age group. The estimation uses econometric techniques developed from the theory of co-integrated time series to deal with the non-stationarity of most of the data series. These techniques yield information about equilibrium relationships while retaining flexibility in estimating the dynamics of fertility.

This analysis finds that one of the strongest influences on birth rates is women's net real hourly earnings relative to men's net real weekly earnings. At almost every age and birth order, higher net women's wages reduce the likelihood of a birth while higher men's net earnings increase it. Thus, there is strong evidence that, by raising the cost of an additional child, higher women's wages reduce the likelihood of another birth, but couples respond to higher men's earnings by having more children and having them sooner. Use of the parameter estimates to simulate steady-state equilibria indicates that a higher women's relative wage would reduce average family size, with a particularly large fall in the proportion of women with three children and a large rise in childlessness. *Holding the relative wage constant*, higher men's real net earnings also reduce family size slightly because women's hourly earnings are also higher, thereby raising the cost of children sufficiently to offset the effect of higher income. The analysis also indicates that more generous child allowances increase the chances of third and fourth births and also encourage earlier motherhood. Nevertheless, a costly doubling of child allowances would only moderately increase family size.

Thus, this analysis of changes in British fertility over time provides strong support for an important influence of the cost of children and income on fertility decisions. The next section takes another approach to testing the economic model of fertility. It uses household-level data, but does not rely on indicators of parents' wages, the exogeneity of which is often questionable. Even if community-level wages are used instead of estimates of individual's wages, migration between communities in response to wage differentials can make adult wages endogenous in fertility decisions. For example, women whose preferences favour smaller families may move to areas with higher wages because they expect to work in paid employment more, thereby producing a negative correlation between community-level wages and fertility that does not reflect a negative impact of wages on fertility.

6.4 CHILD LABOUR, CONTRACEPTION AND FERTILITY

In addition to being of interest in its own right, this section argues that the impacts of child wages on fertility and child quality in an environment in which children often work, provide further tests of the economic model of fertility. In order to focus on this aspect of fertility decisions, we abstract from the use of parents' time in producing child quality and their own living standard and assume that child's human capital is produced by expenditures by parents and a child's own time in human capital investment activities, like school. More formally, $h = h(x, t)$, where x is the amount of goods and services allocated to each child, t is the amount of the child's own time and the production function $h(\ )$ exhibits constant returns to scale. Child quality is taken to be income as an adult, which is assumed to be proportional to a child's human capital: $Q = \alpha h$, where α is the rate of return on human capital. Also, the parents' standard of living is directly purchased in the market, and there is a direct cost of a child, p_N. In addition, there are costs associated with averting births, p_c, with the total expenditure associated with averting births being $p_c[N^{max} - N]$, where N^{max} is the number of births that would occur if no contraception was practiced.

As in Chapter 4, parents choose x and t to minimize the cost of producing a given amount of human capital per child, and as earlier, this gives rise to a marginal cost of each child's human capital equal to π, with $d\ln(\pi) = (px/\pi h)d\ln(p) + (wt/\pi h)d\ln(w)$, where w is the child's wage and p is the price of goods and services used in the production of a child's human capital. Then parents maximize $U(N, Q, Z)$ subject to the budget constraint, $Y + wNT = N(p_N + \pi h) + Z + p_c[N^{max} - N]$ and $0 \le t \le T$, where Y is the parents' income and T is the maximum time available from each child. Assuming each child works sometime as a child, the solution to this problem implies

$$\frac{\alpha U_Q}{U_N} = \frac{\pi N}{p_N + \pi h - p_c - wT} \tag{6.10}$$

That is, the marginal rate of substitution between each child's income as an adult and family size must equal the marginal cost of human capital, πN, relative to the cost of an additional child, $p_N + \pi h - p_c - wT$. Note that a higher child wage and a higher cost of contraception encourage larger families by reducing the net cost of an additional child. A higher marginal cost of human capital investment increases both the price of human capital and the cost of an additional child, while the cost of human capital is larger in a larger family and the cost of an additional child is larger when human capital investment per child is larger.

Performing the conventional comparative static exercise, we find that

$$\frac{\partial N}{\partial w} = S_{NN}(t - T) + S_{QN}\frac{Nt}{h} + \frac{\partial N}{\partial Y}N(T - t) \tag{6.11a}$$

$$\frac{\partial N}{\partial p_c} = -S_{NN} - \frac{\partial N}{\partial Y}[N^{max} - N] \tag{6.11b}$$

$$\frac{\partial N}{\partial \alpha} = -\frac{S_{NQ}(N\pi)}{\alpha} \tag{6.11c}$$

$$\frac{\partial N}{\partial p_N} = S_{NN} - \frac{\partial N}{\partial Y}N < 0 \tag{6.11d}$$

where the S_{ij} are the Hicksian compensated substitution effects.[5] Maximization implies that $S_{jj} < 0$, and we shall assume that children are normal goods ($\partial N/\partial Y > 0$). The only clear prediction is that a higher direct cost of a child reduces family size (6.11d). If, however, we also assume, as the evidence in Rosenzweig and Wolpin (1980) indicates, that children and child quality are net substitutes (i.e. $S_{QN} > 0$), then higher child wages increase family size (6.11a), and a higher return to human capital reduces it (6.11c). Lower contraception costs tend to reduce family size if the income effect of lower contraceptive costs is not too strong, which is more likely in environments in which family size is high.

The impacts of these same parameters on human capital investment per child are given by

$$\frac{\partial h}{\partial w} = S_{QN}(t - T) + S_{QQ}\frac{Nt}{h} + \frac{\partial h}{\partial Y}N(T - t) \qquad (6.12a)$$

$$\frac{\partial h}{\partial p_c} = -S_{QN} - \frac{\partial h}{\partial Y}[N^{\max} - N] \qquad (6.12b)$$

$$\frac{\partial h}{\partial \alpha} = -\frac{S_{QQ}(N\pi)}{\alpha} > 0 \qquad (6.12c)$$

$$\frac{\partial h}{\partial p_N} = S_{QN} - \frac{\partial h}{\partial Y}N \qquad (6.12d)$$

The only clear prediction here is that a higher return to human capital investment increases human capital per child (6.12c). When child quality and quantity are net substitutes, lower contraception costs raise human capital investment in children (6.12b). Also, under this condition, the substitution effect of a higher child wage tends to reduce human capital investment, but the income effect of a higher wages tends to increase it (6.12a). The size of this income effect clearly depends on the amount that a child works ($T - t$).

The theory predicts, therefore, that a change in child wages tends to affect fertility and human capital investment in opposite directions, because of the symmetry of substitution effects. Indeed, the Hicksian substitution effects of child wages must be in opposite directions. It is a stronger test of the theory to examine the impacts of child wages on these two outcomes rather than just one of them. We would certainly reject the theory if child wages had a negative effect on fertility, and there would be doubts about it if child wages increased both fertility and human capital investment, because this would only be consistent with the theory if there were a strong income effect of child wages on human capital investment.

Rosenzweig (1990) produces evidence from three countries, India, Indonesia and the Philippines, that indicate that the mean child wage rate in the community in which the household lived is positively related to the number of children ever born, while it is negatively related to the school enrolment rate (India and Indonesia) or schooling attainment (Philippines). In contrast to adult wages, the wage rates of young children are unlikely to be influenced by human capital investments, and families are unlikely to move between communities in response to differences in child wage rates. That is, community-level child wage rates can more credibly be treated as exogenous than adult wages. There may still be concern that in communities in which preferences favour longer schooling or smaller families, child labour supply is smaller and consequently the child wage is higher. This would tend to understate estimated child wage effects on both fertility and human capital investment. But Rosenzweig (1990) shows that instrumental variable estimates using community-level instruments produce similar estimated effects and a statistical test accepts exogeneity of child wages.

These estimates support the economic theory of fertility and human capital investments, which has further implications for policy and for the impacts of technological developments like the "green revolution". For instance, a family planning programme that reduces the cost of using contraception tends to raise human capital investment as well as to reduce fertility. Also, we see from (6.11c) and (6.12c) that technological change that raises the return from human capital investment also reduces fertility and raises human capital investment. Rosenzweig (1990) exploits the exogenous variation in the degree of introduction of the higher-yielding grain varieties in the early 1960s in India to provide support for these predictions. He finds that the returns to education were higher in areas that used this green revolution technology, and that these areas experienced a significantly larger fall in fertility during 1961–1971 than areas not affected by the new technology. The former areas also experienced a moderately larger decline in the proportion of men with no schooling in farm households. Taken together, the theory and the supporting empirical evidence indicate that increases in the returns to human capital investment associated with technical change lead to simultaneous reductions in fertility and increases in human capital investment in children, thereby accounting for important stylized facts of economic development.

6.5 CHILD MORTALITY RISK AND FERTILITY

The ultimate manifestation of low child quality is a child not surviving to adulthood. In light of the *demographic transition* (i.e. the change from a high fertility–high child mortality environment to a low fertility–low mortality one), an interesting question is how fertility responds to changes in the "risk" of child mortality. Because parents may know the risk, but not exactly how many of their children will die for any given number of births, this is a problem of choice under uncertainty.

Following Cigno's (1998) formulation, let parents have the following separable utility function, $U = u(z) + v(n)$, where z denotes parental consumption, n is the number of children who survive to become adults, and $u(z)$ and $v(n)$ are strictly concave sub-utility functions. These preferences mean that children who die in childhood are not a source of utility to their parents. Each birth has survival chances, which can be represented by a probability distribution with mean equal to the survival probability s. The number of *surviving* children, n, is the outcome from subjecting the number of births, b, to this random survival process. Denote the probability density function of n, conditional on b and s, as $f(n, b, s)$. Then the expected utility of parents is given by

$$E(U) = u(z) + \int_0^b v(n)f(n, b, s)dn \equiv u(z) + g(b, s) \qquad (6.13)$$

Thus, $g(b, s)$ is the expected utility from having b births when, on average, sb, survive.

We assume that each birth has a fixed cost c. Then the parental budget constraint is $y = z + cb$, where y is parental income. Parents choose b to maximize $E(U) = u(y - cb) + g(b, s)$. This implies that

$$c = \frac{g_b}{u'} \qquad (6.14)$$

where $g_b = \partial g/\partial b$ is the marginal expected utility from an additional birth and u' is the marginal utility of parents' consumption. That is, parents have children up to the point where the cost of a birth equals the marginal rate of substitution between births and parents' own consumption. From (6.14) we obtain

$$\frac{db}{ds} = -\frac{g_{bs}}{D} \qquad (6.15)$$

where $D = c^2 u'' + g_{bb} < 0$ is the second-order condition for a maximum. Because g_{bs} is the effect of the survival rate on the marginal expected utility of a birth, it must be non-negative. It then follows from (6.15) that $db/ds \geq 0$. A higher probability of child survival reduces the price of a surviving birth, thereby encouraging higher fertility.

Suppose now that parents can influence the chances that their own children survive to become adults (an element of child quality) by spending more on each child. Thus, the cost of a birth, c, is now chosen by the parents, and the probability density function of n is now conditional on b, s and c, and is denoted as $f(n, b, s, c)$. Parents now choose b and c $(z = y - bc)$ to maximize their expected utility, which is given by

$$E(U) = u(z) + \int_0^b v(n)f(n, b, s, c)dn \equiv u(z) + g(b, s, c) \qquad (6.16)$$

Their optimal choice must satisfy

$$c = \frac{g_b}{u'} \qquad \text{and} \qquad b = \frac{g_c}{u'} \qquad (6.17)$$

Thus, in addition to procreating up to the point where the cost of a birth equals the marginal rate of substitution between births and parents' own consumption, parents raise c to the point that the marginal rate of substitution between expenditures on each child born and parents' own consumption equals the marginal cost of such expenditure, which is equal to the number of births. From the conditions in (6.17), we obtain

$$\frac{db}{ds} = \frac{-(g_{cc} + b^2 u'')g_{bs} + g_{cs}(g_{bc} + cbu'' - u')}{A} \qquad (6.18)$$

$$\frac{dc}{ds} = \frac{-(g_{bb} + c^2 u'')g_{cs} + g_{bs}(g_{bc} + cbu'' - u')}{A} \qquad (6.19)$$

The second-order conditions for a maximum entail that the determinant A is positive and that $g_{cc} + b^2 u''$ and $g_{bb} + c^2 u''$ are negative. Note that the effect of c on the marginal utility of an additional birth, U_b, is $dU_b/dc = g_{bc} + cbu'' - u'$, and because c is a cost, we expect $g_{bc} + cbu'' - u'$ to be positive.

If exogenous factors affecting child survival substitute for parents' expenditure to improve their children's chances of survival, then we expect $g_{cs} < 0$. It is clear from (6.18) that, under these conditions, it is *possible* that a higher survival rate *reduces* the number of births $(db/ds < 0)$; the negative second term in (6.18) could outweigh the positive first term. In addition, for g_{bs} small enough, (6.19) indicates that parents would reduce their own expenditure when the survival rate increases.

If, however, these exogenous survival-enhancing factors are complementary with parents' own expenditure to reduce mortality risk (i.e. $g_{cs} > 0$), then $db/ds \geq 0$ and $dc/ds \geq 0$. That is, parents would both increase their fertility and their expenditure on each child when the chances of survival are better.

Cigno (1998) shows, for a particular utility function and probability distribution, that g_{bs} decreases as s increases, becoming zero at a survival probability of about 90%. In other words, the larger the survival probability, the smaller is the effect of an increase in that probability on the marginal expected utility from an additional birth. This pattern is likely to be true more generally. When g_{bs} is smaller and $g_{cs} < 0$, it is more likely that $db/ds < 0$ and $dc/ds < 0$ (see (6.18) and (6.19)).

Thus, in this model in which parents can influence their own children's survival chances, an exogenous reduction in child mortality may either raise or lower fertility. When the level of child mortality is high (i.e. a low survival rate), reductions in it are likely to raise both fertility and expenditures on children to enhance their chances of survival. When, however, the level of child mortality is already low, further reductions in it are likely to reduce both fertility and expenditures on children that reduce their risk of mortality. It is only in this latter case that reductions in child mortality lead to reductions in fertility, in line with the correlation we observe in the demographic transition.

Sah (1991) takes a different approach from the analysis above, treating the number of children as a discrete variable in the context of a general function relating utility to the number of surviving children, inclusive of all benefits and costs. He assumes that parents choose the number of births to maximize their expected utility, which is the weighted sum of the utilities of having particular numbers of surviving children, with the weights being the probabilities of obtaining that number of surviving children from a given number of births (analogous to the $f(n, b, s)$ probability density function when n is treated as a continuous variable).

Suppose first that only surviving children bring costs and benefits. Sah shows that the number of births the parents have cannot increase with an increase in the probability that the child survives to adulthood. Parents may wish to have more births when survival chances are low, because some may die before adulthood and they will not have enough time to replace them in their fecund period, but their incentive to practice such *hoarding* is less when survival chances are better. Thus, their fertility will not be higher when child survival is more likely.

As in Cigno's model, a cost may, however, be incurred by a birth regardless of whether or not the child survives. In this case, a higher probability of child survival also has the effect of reducing the price of a surviving birth, thereby encouraging higher fertility. Sah finds that this effect will be dominated by the hoarding effect above if parents are sufficiently risk averse, or there is a "target fertility level", in the sense that the marginal utility of the last child is non-positive if all the children from an optimally chosen number of births were to survive. If either of these conditions hold, better survival chances for children tend to reduce fertility.

Unless child mortality is expected when the mother is older, replacement is a better response to child mortality risk than hoarding, because the latter involves a larger deviation from what the parents would have done in the absence of child mortality. Thus, it is likely that the effect of the survival probability on fertility is mainly through its impact on the effective price of surviving children. Wolpin (1984) was the first to incorporate uncertainty about child survival into a sequential, dynamic fertility model, which permits analysis of the replacement in response to child deaths and the effect of infant mortality risk on fertility. In Wolpin's (1984) empirical analysis of mortality in the first 18 months of life in Malaysia, he indeed finds that a higher survival probability *increases* the number of children ever born. This is in line with the predictions of Cigno's model with exogenous survival chances, or his model with endogenous survival and relatively high infant mortality.

6.6 DYNAMIC FERTILITY MODELS

The theories discussed so far are "static" in nature, the relevant time unit being the parents' lifetime. If we wish to consider decisions about the timing of births, imperfect fertility control, or the consequences of unexpected outcomes like birth control failure or child mortality, a dynamic model is needed.

In principle, dynamic models incorporating a sequence of decisions and imperfect, costly fertility control are more realistic than the static theories discussed above. In practice, they usually have to make special assumptions to obtain predictions of behaviour. Their predictions often depend on what is assumed about parents' ability to borrow and save. One of two polar assumptions has been made in the literature: either parents can borrow and save as they choose ("perfect capital markets") or they cannot do so at all (i.e. they must consume all of their current income).

In one of the earliest dynamic fertility models, by Heckman and Willis (1976), a couple's fertility is controllable by the contraceptive strategies they adopt, but control is not perfect. Because it is assumed that couples start obtaining satisfaction from children as soon as they are born, they wish to have their children early. Couples may, however, find it best to adopt a 'precautionary' contraceptive strategy early in their partnership in order to reduce the risk of having more children than they would have chosen to have if fertility control were perfect and free. Such a strategy would result in postponing the age at first birth. If people cannot borrow or save and their incomes rise with age, they would also wish to practice contraception in order to postpone childbearing to a time when the marginal benefit of income for parental consumption is lower (when they can "better afford" children). Subsequent spacing of births (rather than having children as quickly as possible) would also be a response to this tension between their desire to have children early and the economic incentive to have them later, when parents' income is higher. The more rapid the increase in income with age, the greater the incentive to postpone the start of childbearing and to space births. In other words, births are timed in order to 'smooth' parental consumption over time.

Another common (but not universal) feature of dynamic models is allowance for the possibility that a woman's current participation in paid employment improves her future earning capacity (as in Chapter 4), and that absence from employment may reduce her pay when she returns to employment. Thus, a mother's absence from paid employment because of a birth has two costs: a loss of current earnings and a loss of future earning potential. An early example of such a model is that of Moffitt (1984).

Even when there are perfect capital markets, couples may choose to postpone childbearing because these opportunity costs of childbearing are higher when the woman is younger and on the steep part of her career earnings profile. Women in jobs in which previous work experience has little effect on earnings have less incentive to postpone. In addition, if the care of young children is particularly intensive in the mother's time, then a birth produces a temporary increase in the value of her time in the home to a level above the value of her time in the labour market, causing her to leave paid employment. It also increases the cost of an additional child, encouraging her to postpone the next birth until the value of her time declines sufficiently through the ageing of the child. Thus, even with perfect capital markets, there is an economic incentive to space births. An unexpected birth, because of contraceptive failure, would generate similar incentives for the mother to leave paid employment temporarily and postpone having another child.

The death of a child encourages its replacement, because the marginal benefit of an additional child is likely to increase when a child dies. Replacement makes fertility increase with the experience of child mortality.

In order to explore more formally the consequences of imperfect fertility control and child mortality in a dynamic model and provide some empirical estimates of them, consider the following simple two-period model of Rosenzweig and Schultz (1987). Following the discussion in Chapter 4, there is a "reproduction function" that relates the number of births to the resources devoted to fertility control and factors affecting conception that are outside the couple's control. Let the number of births in the ith period be given by $N_i = N(Z_i) + \mu + \varepsilon_i$, $i = 1, 2$, where Z_i is the amount of resources devoted to fertility control (e.g. use of the contraceptive pill) in the ith period, μ is a persistent fertility component specific to the couple (e.g. their fecundity), and ε_i is a serially uncorrelated stochastic fertility component (e.g. luck). We expect, of course, that more fertility control resources reduce births ($\partial N/\partial Z = N_Z < 0$) and that resources may have a declining marginal effect ($\partial^2 N/\partial Z^2 = N_{ZZ} < 0$). Contraceptive resources can be purchased at price P_Z per unit.

Parents' preferences are represented by the inter-temporal utility function $U(N_1, X_1) + V(N_1 + N_2, Q, X_2)$, where X_i is parents' consumption in the ith period, and Q is child quality per child, investments in which are made in the second period, and for simplicity we assume Q is purchased at price P_Q per unit and does not require parents' time. The parents maximize their expected utility over these two periods subject to the reproduction function above and the budget constraints in each period, $Y_1 = X_1 + P_Z Z_1$ and $Y_2 = (N_1 + N_2)QP_Q + X_2 + P_Z Z_2$; that is, it is assumed that parents cannot borrow or save, one of the polar assumptions discussed above. This problem can be solved backwards; that is, starting in the second period. Suppose by this time that the parents know their fecundity parameter μ (and that ε_2 is not stochastic for simplicity). Their problem in the second period, when the fertility outcome in the first period is known, is just to maximize $V(N_1 + N_2, Q, X_2)$ subject to the reproduction function and their second period budget constraint.

The first-order conditions for the second period maximization problem include the following:

$$\frac{V_Q}{V_X} = (N_1 + N_2)P_Q \qquad (6.20a)$$

where $V_Q = \partial V/\partial Q$, etc.

$$\left[\frac{V_N}{V_X} - P_Q Q\right] N_Z = P_Z \qquad (6.20b)$$

Equation (6.20a) is the now familiar condition that the marginal rate of substitution between child quality and parental consumption equals the shadow price of child quality, which is proportional to the number of children. Equation (6.20b) implies that at the optimum choice of second period fertility control, the marginal rate of substitution between children and parental consumption (V_N/V_X) is less than the shadow price of an additional child ($P_Q Q$), because $N_Z < 0$ and fertility control is costly. That is, a couple would have more children than they would if fertility control were free; if it were free they would equate the marginal rate of substitution with the shadow price of children. Using the first-order conditions, we can derive the effects of the cost of fertility control on the use of control in the second period and child quality:

$$\frac{\partial Z_2}{\partial P_Z} = S_{ZZ} - Z_2 \frac{\partial Z_2}{\partial Y_2} \qquad (6.21a)$$

$$\frac{\partial Q}{\partial P_Z} = S_{ZQ} - Z_2 \frac{\partial Q}{\partial Y_2} \tag{6.21b}$$

where S_{ZZ} is the Hicksian compensated substitution effect of the price of fertility control on its use (i.e. $\partial Z_2/\partial P_Z|_{dV=0}$), and S_{ZQ} is the Hicksian compensated cross-substitution effect of the price of fertility control on child quality (i.e. $\partial Q/\partial P_Z|_{dV=0}$).

Maximization implies that S_{ZZ} is negative, and we expect that more fertility control will be purchased when second-period income is higher. Thus, (6.21a) indicates that $\partial Z_2/\partial P_Z < 0$. The sign of the cross-substitution effect is not predicted by optimizing behaviour, but as a higher price of fertility control is a subsidy to childbearing, it tends to increase family size and thereby the price of child quality. This suggests that S_{ZQ} is negative because child quality and the number of children are likely to be substitutes.[6] As child quality is a normal good, we therefore expect from (6.21b) that a higher cost of fertility control reduces child quality. A practical problem with testing these predictions of the model is that it is difficult to measure the price of fertility control and it is not likely to vary in cross-section data. We can, however, assess the effects of imperfect fertility control by studying the effects of the couple's persistent fertility component (μ), fecundity for short, on the level of second-period fertility control and child quality (human capital investment in children).

In order to make the expressions for these effects simpler, assume that preferences are separable in parents' consumption, in the sense that $V_{XN} = 0 = V_{XQ}$, where $V_{XN} = \partial^2 V/\partial X \partial N$, etc. Then

$$\frac{\partial Z_2}{\partial \mu} = 2\left(\frac{S_{ZQ}(\lambda P_Q - V_{QN}) - N_Z S_{ZZ} V_{NN}}{\lambda} \right) - 2P_Q Q\left(\frac{\partial Z_2}{\partial Y_2} \right) \tag{6.22a}$$

$$\frac{\partial Q}{\partial \mu} = 2\left(\frac{S_{QQ}(\lambda P_Q - V_{QN})/\lambda - N_Z S_{ZQ} V_{NN}}{\lambda} \right) - 2P_Q Q\left(\frac{\partial Q}{\partial Y_2} \right) \tag{6.22b}$$

where λ is the marginal utility of income ($=V_X$), and S_{QQ} is the compensated own-substitution effect of child quality, which must be negative.

From (6.22a), the own-substitution effect (the second term in brackets) tends to increase resources devoted to fertility control, because N_Z is negative and the marginal utility of children is declining at the optimum. But if $\lambda P_Q > V_{QN}$, which would, for example, be the case with separability in preferences such that $V_{QN} = 0$, the cross-substitution effect (the first term in brackets) tends to reduce fertility control, because higher fecundity raises the marginal cost of child quality, which encourages higher fertility, thereby discouraging fertility control. The income effect of higher fecundity (the last term in (6.22a)) also reduces fertility control because higher fecundity necessitates more expenditure on child quality

$(P_Q Q(N_1 + N_2))$, which reduces the couple's ability to afford spending on fertility control.

Provided that $\lambda P_Q > V_{QN}$, (6.22b) indicates that the own-substitution effect (the first term in brackets) tends to reduce child quality because higher fecundity raises the marginal cost of child quality, and this effect is reinforced by the income effect. But the cross-substitution effect (the second term in brackets) tends to increase child quality because the marginal utility of an additional child declines.

While the effects of fecundity on contraceptive use and child quality are both ambiguous, depending on the particular preference structure, they do indicate responses of both variables to variation in fecundity.[7] If the cross-substitution effect and the income effect on contraceptive use are not too large, higher fecundity increases contraceptive use and reduces child quality. We now consider some empirical estimates of these effects.

In Chapter 4, we discussed estimation of the reproduction function by Rosenzweig and Schultz (1987), based on Malaysian data, including estimation of the persistent couple-specific fertility (fecundity) component, μ. Their analysis also relates the estimate of μ to the number of children ever born and the efficiency of contraception. They find that more fecund couples adopt more efficient contraceptive methods, as suggested by (6.22a), but they also have more children; that is, they cannot fully offset the impact of fecundity on their fertility through their own actions, but they reduce it. In line with what (6.22b) suggests, they also find that the average child's completed schooling and birth weight (a proxy for health human capital) are lower for more fecund couples (computed across all of the couple's children).

In this framework, a birth control failure is represented by a higher value of the transitory fertility component, ε_1. The impacts of such a failure on fertility control in the second period and child quality are made up of the same components as those of the impacts of the persistent fertility component, given in (6.22a) and (6.22b), but are one-half the size. Similarly, the death of a child is represented by a lower value of ε_1. Thus, from (6.22a) and (6.22b), a child's death tends to reduce fertility control in the second period and to increase child quality if the cross-substitution effect (S_{ZQ}) and the income effect on contraceptive use are not too large.

6.7 Non-Marital Fertility

In the last decade, economic analysis of fertility shifted away from the paradigm of the stable married couple making fertility decisions as a single entity. This probably reflects the fact that, in many countries, a substantial proportion of children are born outside marriage. The latter development suggests that men and women should be treated as individual agents in fertility decisions and that fertility and marriage decisions need to be considered together. Chapter 7 analyses non-marital childbearing in the context of a marriage market matching model.

A relatively unexplored area is childbearing within cohabiting unions, which has grown in importance in many countries. It undoubtedly shares some of the features of the analysis of non-marital fertility, as explained in Chapter 7, but it also may share aspects of the analysis of marital fertility. However, there are probably also unique features of cohabiting unions that are important for fertility decisions. One is their high risk of dissolution, which is also relevant to marital fertility in high-divorce countries. In light of it, we need to treat the fertility decision as a problem of choice under uncertainty in which each partner is an individual agent whose preferences, expectations and resources influence the decision. This aspect is considered in Chapter 8.

APPENDIX: CHILD QUANTITY–QUALITY INTERACTION

With general (consensus) preferences represented by $U(Z, N, Q)$,

$$d \ln(N) = \psi_{NY} d \ln(Y^R) + \varepsilon_{NN} d \ln(p_N) + \varepsilon_{NQ} d \ln(p_Q) + \varepsilon_{NZ} d \ln(\pi_Z)$$

$$(6A.1)$$

where ψ_{NY} is the income elasticity of N with respect to *real* full income, which is defined as $Y^R = Y/(S_Z \pi_Z + S_C \pi_C)$, and so $d \ln(Y^R) = S_{yY} d \ln(y) + S_{mY} d \ln(w_m) + S_{fY} d \ln(w_f)$, where $S_{yY} = y/Y$, $S_{iY} = w_i(T - t_{ic} - t_{iz})/Y$, $i = $ m, f, are shares of full income. Each ε_{Nj} is a compensated price elasticity for N. Using the fact that $\varepsilon_{NZ} = -(\varepsilon_{NQ} + \varepsilon_{NN})$, and the definitions of p_N and p_Q in (6.4),

$$(1 - \varepsilon_{NQ}) d \ln(N) = \psi_{NY} d \ln(Y^R) + (\varepsilon_{NN} + \varepsilon_{NQ}) d \ln\left(\frac{\pi_C}{\pi_Z}\right) + \varepsilon_{NN} d \ln(Q)$$

$$(6A.2)$$

Similarly, $\varepsilon_{QZ} = -(\varepsilon_{QQ} + \varepsilon_{QN})$ and

$$(1 - \varepsilon_{QN}) d \ln(Q) = \psi_{QY} d \ln(Y^R) + (\varepsilon_{QQ} + \varepsilon_{QN}) d \ln\left(\frac{\pi_C}{\pi_Z}\right) + \varepsilon_{QQ} d \ln(N)$$

$$(6A.3)$$

Equations (6A.2) and (6A.3) can be used to solve for $d \ln(N)$. By the definition of the partial elasticity of substitution in consumption,[8] $\sigma_{NQ} = \varepsilon_{NQ}/S$ and $\sigma_{QN} = \varepsilon_{QN}/S$, where $S = \pi_c NQ/(Y + \pi_C NQ)$, and $\sigma_{NQ} = \sigma_{QN}$. By the assumption of substitution between quantity and quality, $\sigma_{NQ} > 0$. Of course, both σ_{NN} and σ_{QQ} are negative.

After some manipulation, it follows that

$$d\ln(N) = \{(1 - S\sigma_{NQ})\psi_{NY} - (S\sigma_{NQ} + (1 - S)\sigma_{NZ})\psi_{QY}\}\frac{d\ln(Y^R)}{D}$$

$$+\{S\sigma_{NQ}(1 - S) + S\sigma_{NN}(1 + S\sigma_{QQ})\}\frac{d\ln(\pi_C/\pi_Z)}{D} \qquad (6A.4)$$

where $D = (1 - S\sigma_{NQ})^2 + S^2\sigma_{QQ}\sigma_{NN} > 0$ by the second-order conditions for a maximum; $d\ln(Y^R)$ was given above, and, as before,

$$d\ln\left(\frac{\pi_C}{\pi_N}\right) = (q_{mC} - q_{mZ})d\ln(w_m) + (q_{fC} - q_{fZ})d\ln(w_f) \qquad (6A.5)$$

where $q_{xC} = (p_c x_c/\pi_C NQ)$, $q_{mC} = (w_m t_{mc}/\pi_C NQ)$ and $q_{fC} = (w_f t_{fc}/\pi_C NQ)$ are shares in the costs of producing Q, and $q_{xZ} = (x_Z/\pi_Z Z)$, $q_{mZ} = (w_m t_{mz}/\pi_z Z)$ and $q_{fZ} = (w_f t_{fz}/\pi_z Z)$ are shares in the cost of producing Z, with adult purchased goods and services taken as the numeriare (i.e. $p_z = 1 = p_c$).

It follows from (6A.4) that $\partial\ln(N)/\partial\ln(Y^R) < 0$ if

$$\frac{\psi_{NY}}{\psi_{QY}} < \frac{S\sigma_{NQ} + (1 - S)\sigma_{NZ}}{1 - S\sigma_{NQ}} \qquad (6A.6)$$

This inequality is more likely to be satisfied if the income elasticity of quantity is much smaller than the income elasticity of child quality; and/or if N and Q, or N and Z, are strong substitutes (i.e. σ_{NQ} and/or σ_{NZ} are "large").

Using (6A.4), (6A.5) and the expression for $d\ln(Y^R)$ above,

$$d\ln(N) = \frac{\psi S_{yY} d\ln(y)}{D} + [\psi S_{mY} + \beta(q_{mC} - q_{mZ})]d\ln(w_m)$$

$$+[\psi S_{fY} + \beta(q_{fC} - q_{fZ})]d\ln(w_f) \qquad (6A.7)$$

where $\psi = \{(1 - S\sigma_{NQ})\psi_{NY} - (S\sigma_{NQ} + (1 - S)\sigma_{NZ})\psi_{QY}\}/D$, which is a combination of the income elasticities of fertility and child quality, and $\beta = \{S\sigma_{NQ}(1 - S) + S\sigma_{NN}(1 + S\sigma_{QQ})\}/D$, which depends on three elasticities of substitution: the "own elasticities" of fertility and child quality and the cross elasticity between the two.

Note that, from (6A.7), the sign of the substitution effect of the mother's wage, given by $\beta(q_{mC} - q_{mZ})$, is now ambiguous, even if $q_{mC} > q_{mZ}$. The reason is that a higher wage increases the prices of both child quality and quantity. Because the positive elements of β, $S\sigma_{NQ}(1 - S)$ and $S^2\sigma_{NN}\sigma_{QQ}$, are both multiplied by the product of fractions, $S(1 - S)$ and S^2, respectively, these terms are likely to be smaller in size than $S\sigma_{NN}$, thereby making the substitution effect negative. In any case, the substitution effect is dampened, making it more likely that a higher mother's wage increases fertility.

NOTES

1. With these very specialized preferences, the division of NQ between N and Q is indeterminate. A derivation of the comparative static results for general preferences over N, Q and Z, analogous to (6.6), is given in the Appendix. The derivation of the special case leading to (6.6) should be clear from that derivation.

2. Recall from Chapter 4 that $w_m - \mu_m$ is the price of time of the mother when the time constraint is binding at T, where $\mu_m < 0$ is the impact on the costs of children (NQ) from relaxing the time constraint. The production of more NQ increases $w_m - \mu_m$ and the marginal cost of NQ, π_C, when the time constraint is binding, but a higher wage for the mother has no impact on the marginal cost.

3. In this case, $\pi_C = p/f_t h'(M) < w_m/f_t$, where $f_t = \partial f/\partial t_{mc}$.

4. A measure of the father's annual earnings 25 years after leaving full-time education is constructed from a function relating earnings to educational qualifications, occupation and age. This measure has two important shortcomings: it cannot separate the effect of being from a particular birth cohort from the effect of age, and unmeasured traits of a man that affect his lifetime earnings cannot be identified. These important sources of variation in lifetime earnings are, therefore, ignored.

5. Note that $\partial\pi/\partial w = t/h$.

6. The model implies that $S_{ZQ} = \{(V_{QN} - \lambda P_Q)N_Z + (N_1 + N_2)P_Q(P_Z + P_Q Q N_Z)V_{XX}\}/D$, where λ is the marginal utility of income, $V_{QN} = \partial^2 V/\partial Q \partial N$, $D < 0$ from the second-order condition for a maximum, $V_{XX} = \partial^2 V/\partial X^2 < 0$ because of diminishing marginal utility, and $P_Z + P_Q Q N_Z < 0$ from the first-order condition (6.20b). If $\lambda P_Q > V_{QN}$, the cross-substitution effect S_{ZQ} is negative.

7. The ambiguity concerning the direction of the effects of fecundity is enhanced relative to (6.22a) and (6.22b) when $V_{XN} \neq 0$ and $V_{XQ} \neq 0$.

8. For example, $\sigma_{NQ} = -[\partial\ln(N)/\partial\ln(Q)]/[(\partial\ln(p_N)/\partial\ln(p_Q)]$.

CHAPTER SEVEN

Matching in the Marriage Market

THIS CHAPTER examines how marriages are formed and who marries whom. Section 7.1 considers the process of search for a partner when there are search frictions, and Section 7.2 studies equilibrium in a marriage market with these frictions. Section 7.3 studies who marries whom when there are no frictions, corresponding to Becker's original theory, and compares the predictions of this model with models containing frictions or non-transferable utility. As noted in the previous chapter, childbearing outside marriage has become very important in many countries in recent years. The link between marriage market frictions and pre-marital childbearing is examined in Section 7.4.

7.1 SEARCHING FOR A PARTNER

The process of finding a spouse is one on which information is scarce, and it takes time to gather it and choose the best option. These market frictions affect who marries whom, the gains from each marriage and the distribution of gains between spouses. In order to analyse the impacts of these frictions, we consider a stylized world in which contacts with people of the opposite sex in the "marriage market" are assumed to occur according to a "Poisson process" with parameter α. This means that the expected number of contacts over a time period Δ is $\alpha\Delta$, and the probability that a person contacts n people in the period is $A(n, \Delta) = (\alpha\Delta)^n \exp(-\alpha\Delta)/n!$, which is the Poisson density function. Denoting $o(\Delta)$ as the probability that more than one person of the opposite sex is contacted in the interval Δ, this formulation has the important property that $o(\Delta)/\Delta \to 0$ as $\Delta \to 0$.

We interpret contacts as marriage proposals or offers, letting α_j be the rate at which woman j receives offers of marriage from men. Suppose that she can tell instantly what her utility would be if she married this particular man, and denote it as x per unit of time. The likelihood of receiving such an offer can be described by the probability that she receives an offer less than x (i.e. the distribution function for offers to woman j), which we denote by $F_j(x)$. For instance, suppose that the maximum marriage offer she can receive is x_j^* and the minimum one is $\underline{x}_j$. Also assume that offers between these limits are equally likely. Then $F_j(x) = (x - \underline{x}_j)/(x_j{}^* - \underline{x}_j)$; that is, x has a uniform distribution.

We first derive the expected discounted lifetime utility if woman j marries a man who offers x (the "value of being married" for short), which is denoted as $V_{jM}(x)$. It is assumed that she obtains b_j utility per unit of time while single, and that the probability that the marriage subsequently dissolves in a period of time Δ is $\delta\Delta$.

Denoting V_j as her expected discounted lifetime utility when single (the "value of being single") and r as her discount rate,

$$V_{jM}(x) = \frac{[x\Delta + \delta\Delta V_j + (1 - \delta\Delta)V_{jM}(x)]}{(1 + r\Delta)} + o(\Delta) \qquad (7.1)$$

The first term in the brackets is the utility obtained from being married to this man during the interval Δ. The second is the product of the probability of divorcing (re-entering the single state) during Δ and the value of being single, and the final term in the brackets is the product of the probability of remaining married during Δ and the value of being married. Manipulating (7.1), dividing by Δ and letting Δ become very small ($\Delta \rightarrow 0$), we obtain

$$V_{jM}(x) = \frac{[x + \delta V_j]}{(r + \delta)} \qquad (7.2)$$

Note that when the risk of divorce is very small ($\delta \rightarrow 0$), $V_{jM}(x) = x/r$.

The value of marriage (to a man offering x) declines as the risk of divorce increases, because $\partial V_{jM}(x)/\partial\delta = r(V_j - x/r)/(r + \delta)^2$ and $V_j < x/r$ if the woman would marry a man offering x. If we rewrite (7.2) as $V_{jM}(x) = [x - \delta(V_{jM}(x) - V_j)]/r$ it is clear that divorce generates a utility loss $V_{jM}(x) - V_j$ that must be taken into account in calculating the value of marriage.

We can now derive the value of being single, V_j. Over the next short interval of time, a single woman j obtains utility of $b_j\Delta$, and the probability that she gets a marriage offer from a man is $\alpha_j\Delta$. She will clearly only marry a man who offers x if the value of being married to him ($V_{jM}(x)$) is at least as great as V_j. Thus,

$$V_j = \frac{[b_j\Delta + (1 - \alpha_j\Delta)V_j + \alpha_j\Delta E_j\max\{V_j, V_{jM}(x)\}]}{(1 + r\Delta)} + o(\Delta) \qquad (7.3)$$

where E_j is the "expectations operator" for woman j, which calculates the mean over the distribution $F_j(x)$. The $o(\Delta)$ term captures what happens if more than one marriage offer is obtained. Rearranging, dividing by Δ and letting Δ become very small ($\Delta \rightarrow 0$), we obtain

$$rV_j = b_j + \alpha_j[E_j\max\{V_j, V_{jM}(x)\} - V_j] \qquad (7.4)$$

The flow value of search, $R_j = rV_j$, equals the utility flow while single plus the expected payoff generated by using the optimal search strategy. The latter is the "option value" of remaining single.

Substituting for $V_{jM}(x)$ from (7.2) and using $R_j = rV_j$, (7.4) becomes

$$R_j = b_j + \alpha_j \frac{[E_j \max\{R_j, x\} - R_j]}{(r + \delta)} \tag{7.5}$$

From (7.5) it is clear that the optimal search strategy has the "reservation payoff" property—accept offers when $x \geq R_j$ and reject them otherwise. The standard reservation offer equation (7.5) can be rewritten as

$$R_j = b_j + \frac{\alpha_j}{r + \delta} \int_{R_j}^{\infty} (x - R_j) dF_j(x) \tag{7.6}$$

The integral represents the expected gain from a marriage offer under the optimal search strategy. As it falls as R_j increases, (7.6) provides a unique solution for R_j given b_j, α_j, r, δ and $F_j(x)$.

For example, if $F_j(x)$ is the uniform distribution described above, then (7.6) becomes

$$R_j = b_j + \frac{\alpha_j(x_j^* - R_j)^2}{2(r + \delta)(x_j^* - \underline{x}_j)} \tag{7.7}$$

In this case, the parameters of $F_j(x)$ are just x_j^* and $\underline{x}_j$, and it is clear that R_j is a function of b_j, α_j, r, δ and these two parameters. Differentiation of (7.7) indicates that higher values of b_j, α_j, x_j^* and $\underline{x}_j$ increase the reservation payoff R_j. That is, higher utility when single, faster arrival of marriage offers and a higher maximum or minimum offer all increase the advantages of setting a higher standard of marriage offer, above which the woman accepts. They allow her to be choosier when selecting a husband. A higher discount rate lowers the reservation payoff, as women are more impatient to receive the benefits from marriage, and so less choosy about whom they marry. A higher divorce rate has the same effect as a higher discount rate, reducing the perceived benefits from waiting for a better match. Because a higher divorce risk makes it more likely that a woman will return to the single state, she is less choosy about whom she marries.

The probability that a single woman marries in a small interval, or the "hazard rate" of marriage, is

$$\theta_j = \alpha_j[1 - F_j(R_j)] \tag{7.8}$$

For short, call this the marriage rate. The mean waiting time to marriage is $1/\theta_j$. Higher utility when single, a higher minimum or maximum offer, a lower discount rate and a smaller divorce risk lower the marriage rate and increase the time spent single, because they raise the reservation offer, R_j. Faster arrival of marriage offers (higher α_j) has two opposing effects on the marriage rate. Its direct effect is partially offset by its positive effect on R_j. The net effect of receiving offers faster is to increase the marriage rate and reduce the waiting time to marriage.

The direction of most of these effects is the same for distribution functions other than the uniform distribution, with the special case considered above providing a flavour of the results. But looking at marital search from only the woman's (or man's) point of view begs the question of the source of individual differences in arrival rates α_j and the distribution of marriage offers $F_j(x)$. These depend on the behaviour of the opposite sex. The next section draws on the analysis of Burdett and Coles (1997, 1999) and addresses this in a simple framework that illustrates the main issues. It derives a steady-state equilibrium in the marriage market when there are two types of people of each sex.

7.2 Matching in the Marriage Market

Assume that there are equal numbers of single men and single women, N, in the marriage market. Let single people contact singles of the opposite sex according to a Poisson process with parameter α. There are two types of people, "goods" (G) and "bads" (B), and when people meet they observe the other's type. In order to keep computation of the steady state simple, we assume that if they marry, they stay married for life (i.e. $\delta = 0$). The payoff to marrying a G is x_G/r, while the payoff to marrying a B is x_B/r, where $x_G > x_B > 0$ and r is the discount rate. Women's and men's utility flow while single is normalized to zero, and the proportion of both men and women in the market who are good is λ. No bargaining over the surplus from marriage is allowed.

7.2.1 Nash Equilibria

A Nash equilibrium in this model requires that all are using optimal search strategies, which have been described in the preceding section. Given a steady-state number and distribution of types in the marriage market, it will describe who is willing to match with whom. A central issue is whether a G-woman (G-man) is willing to marry a B-man (B-woman).

Using the methods of the previous section and noting that everyone wants to marry a G-person, the flow value of being a single G-person of either sex is

$$rV_G = \alpha\lambda\left(\frac{x_G}{r} - V_G\right) + \alpha(1 - \lambda)\left[\max\left(\frac{x_B}{r}, V_G\right) - V_G\right] \qquad (7.9)$$

The first term on the right-hand side is the product of the probability of meeting a G-person and the gain from marrying that person. The second term is the product of meeting a B-person and any gain from marrying them. If $x_B/r \geq V_G$, a G-person will marry a B-person. Everyone will marry the first person that they meet, and their value of being single is

$$V_G^m = \alpha\frac{[\lambda(x_G/r) + (1 - \lambda)(x_B/r)]}{\alpha + r} \qquad (7.10)$$

If, however, $x_B/r < V_G$, then a G-person will only marry another G-person. In this case, the value of being single is

$$V_G^a = \frac{\alpha\lambda(x_G/r)}{\lambda\alpha + r} \qquad (7.11)$$

Thus, the best strategy of a G-person will be to reject a B-person if and only if $V_G^a > V_G^m$, which implies that

$$x_B < \frac{x_G\alpha\lambda}{r + \lambda\alpha} \qquad (7.12)$$

This is illustrated in Figure 7.1, in which equality of x_B with the right-hand side of (7.12) is graphed in $x_B - x_G$ space for given values of α, λ and r. In area **B**, G-men only marry G-women, while in area **A** people marry the first person that they meet.

Equation (7.12) can be rewritten as $\alpha\lambda > rx_B/(x_G - x_B)$, and so such "perfect assortative mating" requires that there be a "sufficiently high" proportion of G-people in the market (λ) and a sufficiently high encounter rate (α) to make it worthwhile to continue to search for a G-person. How "high" depends on the flow value of being married to a B-person (x_B) relative to the lifetime gain in marrying a G-person rather than a B-person $(x_G - x_B)/r$. For instance, note that at a high discount rate, this lifetime gain will be relatively small, and so it is not worth waiting for a G-person to come along. In general, when the inequality in (7.12) is not satisfied, there is a "mixing equilibrium", with everyone marrying the first person that they meet.

Now consider the value functions for B-people. If G-people will marry B-people (the inequality in (7.12) is not satisfied), all people have the same value of being single, $V_B = V_G^m \leq x_B/r$. If however G-people will not marry B-people (i.e. (7.12) holds), B-people have no choice; they can only marry a B-person, and $V_B = \alpha[(1 - \lambda)(x_B/r)]/(\alpha(1 - \lambda) + r)$.

Of course, the value of λ is determined in equilibrium as a consequence of the behaviour in the marriage market. The following analysis considers a steady-state equilibrium in which exogenous inflows of singles must equal outflows to marriage.

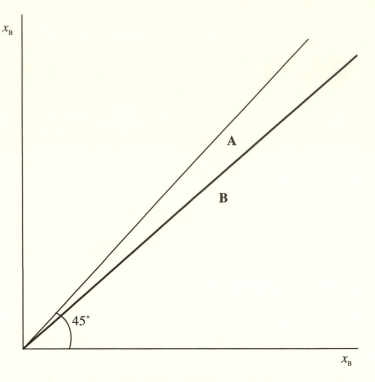

Figure 7.1   Matching strategies of G-people.

7.2.2 Steady-State Equilibrium

First consider an equilibrium in which people of the same type only marry each other (*perfect assortative mating*), and so condition (7.12) must be satisfied. Assume that the exogenous inflow of single men and women into the marriage market is at the instantaneous rate g, and proportion π of these are G-type. Equating exits (into marriage) with inflows of each type, yields

$$\alpha \lambda \lambda N = \pi g \quad \text{and} \quad \alpha (1 - \lambda)(1 - \lambda)N = (1 - \pi)g \qquad (7.13)$$

for G-people and B-people, respectively.

These equalities yield the steady-state equilibrium condition that implicitly defines the equilibrium value of λ as a function of π:

$$\pi = \frac{\lambda^2}{[\lambda^2 + (1 - \lambda)^2]} \qquad (7.14)$$

This equilibrium λ in the perfect assortative mating equilibrium is denoted as λ^*. It is a strictly increasing function of π, with a critical

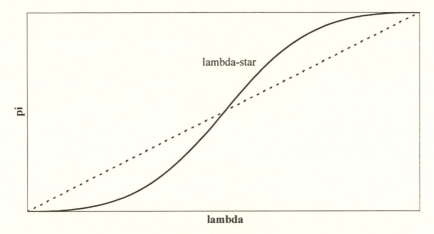

Figure 7.2   Equilibrium proportion of G-people in the marriage market (λ) with perfect assortative mating.

value of 0.5 for π that has $\pi < \lambda^*$ for values of π less than 0.5 and $\pi > \lambda^*$ for values of π above 0.5. This function is shown as the curved line in Figure 7.2.

If π is small *and there is perfect assortative mating*, then the exit rate to marriage of G-people is lower than the exit rate of B-people. Thus, single G-people accumulate relative to the number of single B-people, and in a steady state $\lambda^* > \pi$. Of course, λ^* must satisfy the inequality in (7.12). If π is relatively large, single B-people accumulate in the marriage market, causing $\lambda^* < \pi$ in equilibrium.

In a *mixing equilibrium*, $\alpha\lambda N = \pi g$ and $\alpha(1 - \lambda)N = (1 - \pi)g$. This implies that $\lambda = \pi$ and $N = g/\alpha$, but of course the condition for a mixing equilibrium requires that $\pi \le r x_B/\alpha(x_G - x_B)$.

When π is less than 0.5 and $\pi \le r x_B/\alpha(x_G - x_B) < \lambda^*$, both a mixing equilibrium and a perfect assortative mating equilibrium exist for the same set of parameters (π, g, α, r, x_G, x_B). As explained by Burdett and Coles (1999), these multiple equilibria arise from a "sorting externality". People do not take into account that when they marry they change the composition of singles in the market, which changes the expected returns to search for the remaining singles. In the present model, if G-people are willing to marry B-people, they match relatively quickly, implying that there are relatively few single G-people in the steady-state equilibrium. Because of the scarcity of single G-people, G-people prefer to marry B-people rather than to continue to search for one of their own. Thus, there is a mixing equilibrium in which the equilibrium proportion of single G-people is $\pi \le r x_B/\alpha(x_G - x_B)$. The sorting externality is that when marrying a B-person, G-people do not take into account that this reduces the probability of meeting a G-person for the remaining G-singles.

If, however, G-people will only marry their own kind, then they match relatively slowly, implying that their equilibrium proportion is higher. As a consequence, it pays to continue to search for a G-person rather than marry a B-person. There is a perfect assortative mating equilibrium with the equilibrium proportion of single G-people being $\lambda^* > rx_B/\alpha(x_G - x_B) \geq \pi$.

The search and matching framework explicitly takes into account frictions in the marriage market. Elimination of these frictions corresponds to a situation in which α/r becomes large, either because contacts are made very quickly or because people are very patient (their discount rate is very low). It is clear that when this happens, the inequality in (7.12) will always be satisfied, no matter how small the additional utility there is from marrying a G-person. Given π, the equilibrium proportion of single G-people in the marriage market will be λ^*, given by (7.14).

Burdett and Coles (1997, 1999) show that these results generalize when there are many types of people. Suppose there is a generally agreed ranking of men and women by "quality" and that a person's utility from the marriage is equal to her(his) partner's "quality". They show that people of higher quality tend to marry each other. Indeed, marriages take place within quality "classes", with the number of classes being larger when the rate of encounters between single men and women is larger.[1] As the contact rate becomes very large, there is again perfect assortative mating.

This framework has been extended by Sahib and Gu (2002) to incorporate cohabiting unions, which are used to learn the true value of the partner's quality. Cohabiting unions also occur between members of the same "class", and there is overlap between the classes formed by marital unions and those formed by cohabiting unions. The reservation quality of a man for a marriage exceeds the reservation *expected* quality of a man for forming a cohabiting union. In that sense, people are more choosy when forming marriages than cohabiting unions. After a period of cohabitation, during which she learns about the man's quality (and vice versa), a woman may reject the man as a husband. Men who turn out to be of a lower quality class than the woman will be rejected, and men will reject women who turn out to be of a lower quality class than themselves.

7.3 BECKER'S THEORY OF MARRIAGE

The discussion in this chapter has not introduced any notion of what couples do within marriage, which was the focus of earlier chapters. So far in this chapter, people's utility from marriage depends on their "type" of partner, which would be characterized by various attributes associated with their "attractiveness" as a husband or wife. It has been assumed that utility is *not transferable* between spouses. We have seen that if frictions are not too large, positive assortative mating by attractive attributes emerges. In Becker's (1981) theory of marriage, there are no frictions, but assortative mating arises because people's attributes, such as education, are either complements or substitutes in the production of utility within marriage.

7.3.1 Marriage Market Equilibrium

Becker's theory is an application of the solution to the "assignment problem" (Koopmans and Beckman 1957). A marriage market equilibrium (a 'stable assignment') is one in which (i) there is no married person who would rather be single, and (ii) there are no two persons who prefer to form a new union. These two criteria can be easily applied when there is *transferable utility*, because then we can assign a unique "output" measure to each marriage. With non-transferable utility, which was assumed in the previous section, an individual who would obtain large gains from a match with a given partner cannot compensate that potential partner to ensure the match is made. Allowing transferable utility implies a price mechanism that ensures that jointly efficient matches are made.

Chapter 3 discussed the concept of transferable utility in some detail. As noted there, one source of the gains from marriage is the existence of a public household good, G. In this context, *conditional transferable utility* requires that $U^j = U^j(x_j, G)$ can be written as $U^j = A(G)x_j + B_j(G)$, where private consumption by person j is denoted by x_j, and so

$$U^i + U^j = A(G)[x_i + x_j] + B_i(G) + B_j(G) \qquad (7.15)$$

Thus, the sum of utilities is independent of the distribution of the private good, and independent of the distribution of utilities. Utility is transferable between individuals at a one-for-one rate through transfers of the private good. It follows that as long as couples cooperate within marriage, total utility from the marriage is not affected by the distribution of utility between members of the couple.

The "output" measure associated with each potential marriage is, therefore, the total utility produced by the marriage of man i to woman j, denoted as $Z_{ij} = U^i + U^j$. The condition for optimal assignments is that the set of marriages formed maximizes aggregate output, which in this case is total utility from all marriages. This is illustrated with a population of two people of each sex, all of whom prefer marriage to the single state. Let v_{ij} be the utility that male i receives if he marries woman j. Her utility from this marriage is $u_{ij} = Z_{ij} - v_{ij}$. In order for the assignment that has man 1 married to woman 2 and man 2 married to woman 1 to be optimal it must be the case that condition (ii) above holds; that is,

$$v_{21} + u_{12} \geq Z_{22} \tag{7.16}$$

$$v_{12} + u_{21} = Z_{12} - u_{12} + Z_{21} - v_{21} \geq Z_{11} \tag{7.17}$$

If (7.16) does not hold, then man 2 and woman 2 can form a union and redistribute utilities so as to improve over any possible values of v_{21} and u_{12}. If (7.17) fails to hold, then man 1 and woman 1 can form a union with a distribution of utilities that improves on v_{12} and u_{21}. Adding conditions (7.16) and (7.17),

$$Z_{12} + Z_{21} \geq Z_{11} + Z_{22} \tag{7.18}$$

Thus, from (7.18), the optimal assignment maximizes total utility. This condition is also sufficient for people marrying their opposite number to be an optimal assignment. If it is satisfied, then we can find values of v_{21} and u_{12} that ensure that (7.16) and (7.17) hold. By a similar argument, people marrying their same number would be optimal if and only if the weak inequality in (7.18) is reversed.

Suppose that each person is endowed with a single attribute, m_i for men and f_i for women, which has a positive effect on total utility from the marriage. This may arise because of home production or household public goods. Let $Z_{ij} = Z(m_i, f_j)$, and rank people by their endowment, with $m_2 > m_1$ and $f_2 > f_1$. From (7.18), people marrying their opposite number is an optimal assignment if and only if

$$Z(m_1, f_2) - Z(m_1, f_1) \geq Z(m_2, f_2) - Z(m_2, f_1) \tag{7.19}$$

or equivalently

$$Z(m_2, f_1) - Z(m_1, f_1) \geq Z(m_2, f_2) - Z(m_1, f_2) \tag{7.20}$$

That is, the incremental contribution to utility of a higher value of the female (male) attribute is larger for a smaller value of the male (female) attribute. In other words, there is a negative interaction between the two sex-specific traits. People marrying their same number (like marrying like) requires a positive interaction in the production of total utility from the marriage.

Positive assortative mating is, therefore, associated with a positive interaction in the production of total utility from the marriage, and negative assortative mating with a negative interaction. A positive (negative) interaction means that the attributes are complements (substitutes) in the production of total utility in the marriage, in the sense that the marginal product of one person's attribute is increasing (decreasing) in the attribute of the spouse: $\partial Z_{ij}^2 / \partial m_i \partial f_j > 0 \ (<0)$.

Suppose, for example, that m_i and f_j are the man's and woman's income, respectively (y_i and y_j) and the simple household model considered above applies, with $U^k = A(G)x_k + B_k(G)$. It can be shown that $\partial Z^2_{ij}/\partial y_i \partial y_j = \partial Z_{ij}{}^2/\partial y_i^2 > 0$, provided that the income elasticity of demand for the public good is not zero (Lam 1988). Thus, positive assortative mating on income would be optimal when the gains from marriage arise from the joint consumption of public goods. Spouses' incomes are complementary in the production of total utility because it is optimal to match spouses who have similar incomes and therefore similar demands for the public good.

Equations (7.16) and (7.17) restrict the division of the gains from marriage, but, in general, they do not determine them uniquely. Bargaining within marriage determines their exact division, and as discussed in Chapter 2, the outcome will depend on the bargaining rule adopted. There are, however, some circumstances in which the marriage market dictates the distribution of the surplus from marriage. For example, if all women have the same endowment of the attribute f, and if the number of women exceeds the number of men, then the only marriage market equilibrium will be one in which all women get the common value of being single. That is, men reap all the gains from marriage.

More generally, this reasoning suggests that the division of the marriage surplus should be responsive to differences in the relative number of men and women in the market. It is, of course, difficult to observe this division. But in societies in which there are "bride prices" (capital or lump sum transfers to brides or their families from grooms or their families) or "dowries" (transfers from women or their families to grooms), it is easier to observe differences or changes in the surplus division. As first noted by Becker (1981, p. 86), there may be rigidities in the surplus division during marriage because of household public goods. Bride prices and dowries allow the flexibility to adjust the surplus division to marriage market conditions.[2]

In a population with declining mortality, younger cohorts will be larger than older ones. If, as is the case, women tend to marry older men, there will be a surplus of women in the marriage market, because the women belong to a younger and larger cohort than men. The size of this surplus will depend on the rate of population growth and the average age difference between spouses. We would expect dowries to increase when population growth is faster because of competition for scarce grooms. Households with older potential brides would be willing to outbid the families of younger brides, because the younger ones have a longer time available to marry, and so the surplus of women is also relaxed by a smaller age difference between spouses when population growth is faster. Expressing the dowry as a function of the differences between the traits of brides and grooms and the sex ratio (women aged 10–19 to men aged 20–29) in the district in which the marriage took place, Rao (1993) finds that a larger surplus of women significantly increases the dowry paid to the groom.[3]

7.3.2 Transferable Utility with Frictions

With frictions in searching for a partner, it is no longer the case that complementary inputs necessarily generate positive assortative mating. Burdett and Coles (1999) examine a model in which there is transferable utility, Nash bargaining over the surplus generated by a marriage and the two types of person are complementary in production, in the sense that total output is maximized if G-people only marry G-people of the opposite sex. Without matching frictions (i.e. α/r is very large), the only equilibrium is perfect assortative mating and it is efficient. When there are matching frictions, there can be a mixing equilibrium, but more importantly there can also be "negative assortative mating" in the sense that there is a type that rejects those of the opposite sex of the same type. For instance, if B-people are very unproductive, the proportion of G-people in the market (λ) is less than one-half and there are search frictions, there is an equilibrium in which B-people will not marry B-people of the opposite sex and G-people marry B-people. This comes about because B-people can extract sufficient surplus from marriages to G-people that they prefer not to marry their own kind because their joint production would be so small, and G-people can bargain for a large enough share of the surplus to be willing to marry B-people.

In this model, the division of the gains from marriage is jointly determined with the type of equilibrium that emerges (who marries whom). Furthermore, the surplus division depends on the parameters that give rise to matching frictions (α and r) and the equilibrium proportion of G-people in the marriage market (λ), because these parameters influence the value of further search. In the absence of search frictions, the equilibrium outcome is socially efficient. But, as is the case in the model of Section 7.2 with non-transferable utility, search frictions produce sorting externalities, which lead to an inefficient matching equilibrium. When a man and woman meet, they only match if it is jointly efficient to do so, but by leaving the marriage market they change the composition of types in the market, which affects the expected returns to search for single persons in the market. Their failure to take into account the impact of their match on the welfare of singles in the market produces the inefficiency.

Reality is clearly in between the extreme assumptions of non-transferable and transferable utility. The latter assumption allows us to capture in a simple way the idea that each partner can compensate the other for their actions or attributes. The simplification is that such compensation can be made without affecting the total utility coming from the marriage. When there are no matching frictions, the decision about whom to marry can be separated from bargaining about the distribution of welfare within marriage. It is effectively a separable two-step process: first choose a spouse so as to obtain the highest utility frontier, and then bargain within marriage to choose a point on the frontier to regulate the division of the gains from marriage. This separability breaks down when there are market frictions (i.e. whom to marry depends on what the bargaining outcome within marriage would be), and some of the predictions about the conditions for positive or negative assortative mating on attributes which affect total utility also break down under these conditions.

The assumption of non-transferable utility recognizes that it is often impossible to effect compensation by simple monetary transfers. Also, it is easier to analyse matching frictions in a model with non-transferable utility, and such frictions are more realistic. We have seen that it is possible to generate positive assortative mating, sorting externalities and multiple marriage market equilibria in such a model. Section 7.4 considers an equilibrium with childbearing outside marriage, which is generated by frictions in the marriage market.

7.3.3 Risk and Marital Sorting

In the agricultural sector, income risk has a strong spatial component. Risk pooling would need to take the form of transfers of resources across geographic areas characterized by a low covariance of income. But distance raises problems of monitoring performance, which is required because people's income outcomes are partly a consequence of their own actions (i.e. there is a problem of "moral hazard"). One way in which a family can diversify its sources of income while using kinship bonds to monitor performance is to locate its members in areas with a low covariance in income. Marriage across villages in which one of the marital partners migrates to the household of the other partner provides such insurance.

This hypothesis, put forward by Rosenzweig and Stark (1989), implies a particular assortative mating pattern. The "permanent" attributes or endowments influencing the level and variability of incomes of the families of the bride and groom will be similar, but the correlation between income outcomes will be as low as possible. Close matching by permanent endowments of parents' households is desirable because a difference in endowments that affects susceptibility to risk (such as the size of landholdings) leaves the better-endowed family poorly insured. Families facing greater income risk (given their wealth) will be more willing to send their offspring away to marry. It is also expected that wealthier families, who are better able to insure themselves, will be less likely to marry their sons and daughters in this way, and so marriage involving families living far apart should be less common among wealthier families. This contrasts with a prediction of the search-theoretic marriage model when there is positive assortative mating on wealth, as we would expect, for example, because of household public goods (see Section 7.3.1). As wealthy families are rare in a given area, this model would predict that children of wealthier parents would search for a spouse over a larger geographic area. Thus, the wealth–distance relationship provides a strong test of the risk model against the traditional search model of marriage.

Rosenzweig and Stark (1989) test their hypothesis with unique longitudinal data (over a 10-year period) from southern India, where it is common for women to move between villages at the time of their marriage. They find that the correlation between villages in daily rainfall, mean farm profits and agricultural wages declines with distance between villages, thereby indicating scope for risk pooling by marriages between families in different villages. There are significant positive correlations between permanent characteristics of the origin households of the bride and groom, such as father's schooling and land holdings, as predicted by both the risk model and conventional marriage models. Their analysis of household food consumption indicates that, for given variability in farm profits, the variability of household food consumption declines significantly with the number of married women resident in the household and the distance between the origin households of the marital partners; that is, marital ties across villages help smooth consumption. Using direct evidence on inter-household transfers, Rosenzweig (1993) shows that net transfers to the household are more likely the smaller is current household income, and the impact of income on transfers is larger in size for households with more married women resident in the household and more absent daughters.

They also find that farm households with more variable profits have a larger mean distance between the origin village of resident daughters-in-law and that of the sample household.[4] Furthermore, this mean marriage distance is smaller for wealthier households, as measured by their inherited land holdings. This latter finding is inconsistent with the conventional marital-search model, but conforms to the prediction of the risk-insurance model of marriage.

7.4 Childbearing outside Marriage

At first thought it may appear odd to discuss non-marital fertility in the context of forming marital unions. But, in Britain at least, it has historically been associated with courtship. The fact that premarital childbearing tended to be higher when marriage ages were lower, and that the age at first "illegitimate" birth was approximately equal to the age at first marriage (Laslet 1980; Oosterveen et al. 1980), suggest that it was part of the courtship process. In times when general marriage opportunities were good, there would be more courtship, hence more sexual activity, and more risk of non-marital births when, for a number of reasons, a particular marriage failed to take place. Wrightson (1980, p. 190) interprets the illegitimacy ratio in 17th century England as "an index of the degree of disjunction between socially acceptable premarital sexual activity and particular marital opportunities."

Although there were fluctuations in the percentage of births outside marriage in Britain during the 400 years preceding 1975, it was only slightly larger in 1975 (9%) than in the mid-19th century (7%). This contrasts with 40% of births in 2000. The United States and at least five other European countries had a percentage of births outside marriage of at least 30% in 1997 (Kiernan 1999)[5], with the US percentage tripling since 1970. In both the United States and Britain, this increase is associated with the rise in cohabiting unions (Ermisch 2001). As these unions are short-lived before either dissolving or being converted into marriage, non-marital childbearing also appears to be associated with modern courtship. So why do women choose to have a child outside marriage? While the absence of reliable contraception may have produced many unplanned pregnancies, and the risks of and taboos against abortion may have made the outcome of premarital pregnancies clear in past times, it is less clear why a large percentage of contemporary women have a birth outside marriage. We first consider a static theory put forward by Willis (1999) and then discuss a dynamic model of search for a marital partner with frictions that is in the spirit of a model of courtship.

7.4.1 A Static Theory of Out-of-Wedlock Childbearing

We again take expenditures on children ("child quality") to be a public good to the parents. As a consequence, men fathering children may choose to make transfers to the mother, even if they do not live together. Assume, as argued in the next chapter, that the amount of transfer is determined in a non-cooperative way: the mother has custody and chooses child expenditures and her own consumption taking transfer payments from the father as given. Fathers choose transfers and their own consumption, taking into account how the mother reacts to such a transfer. Then a father would voluntarily make a transfer if his income is large relative to the mother's income and he cares sufficiently for the well-being of his child. But the mother, father and child could be even better off if the couple cooperated in their decisions (see Chapter 2). Because of difficulties in monitoring expenditures, cooperation would be facilitated by the parents marrying. Thus, these relatively affluent fathers would usually not want to father children outside marriage.

Earlier in the chapter it was shown that, in a frictionless marriage market, the collective good nature of child expenditures would encourage the highest income man to marry and have a child with the highest income woman, the next highest income couple would marry and have a child, and so on. That is, there would be positive assortative mating on income. If there were more men than women, then all women would marry and the men with the lowest incomes would remain single. If the number of women exceeded the number of men, and if women at the lower end of the income distribution had incomes which were sufficiently high that they would want to raise children with their own resources, then fatherhood outside marriage would be free. If low-income men can father children by more than one woman, out-of-marriage fatherhood may be more advantageous for them than marrying a low-income woman. The single low-income mothers gain by becoming mothers rather than remaining childless.

Thus, there may be what Willis (1999) calls an "out-of-wedlock equilibrium" in which men with low incomes seek to father children outside marriage and women oblige them in preference to remaining childless. This outcome requires there to be an excess of unmarried women relative to unmarried men, and is more likely if men's wages are not much higher than women's and low-income men believe that the combination of women's earnings and government transfer programs are adequate to raise children without their help. Thus, this theory explains fertility outside marriage as a rational choice by low-income men and women, while at the same time higher income couples choose to have children within marriage. This is clearly consistent with the long-established tendency for non-marital childbearing to be disproportionately among poorer members of society, which goes back to at least the 16th century in Britain (e.g. Oosterveen et al. 1980; Smout 1980).

In the world described by this model, people either marry or remain single forever. But a large proportion of women who have a child outside marriage eventually marry, although it may take them longer. For instance, analysis by Lichter and Graefe (2001) and Upchurch et al. (2001) indicates that, at each age, never-married women who are mothers are much less likely to marry than childless never-married women, and that this is a causal effect. Furthermore, a model with search frictions is a more natural approach for examining the matching and courtship process, which the evidence above suggests is intimately related to non-marital childbearing decisions.

7.4.2 Frictions and Childbearing outside Marriage

The model of this subsection allows for women to marry after spending some time as a single mother, for frictions in marital sorting and for an out-of-wedlock childbearing equilibrium with the same number of men and women in the market. Indeed, an equilibrium with non-marital child-bearing depends upon such frictions in the marriage market. The model follows the search and matching framework introduced earlier in the chapter.

Assume that single, childless women encounter men according to a Poisson process with parameter α_w, but the encounter process for single women who have a child is characterized by parameter $\beta \alpha_w$ $(0 < \beta \le 1)$. This assumption is consistent with the fact that single mothers take longer to marry than childless women. Single men encounter single women at a rate α_m.

Again, there are two types of people, "goods" (G) and "bads" (B), and the payoff to marrying a G is x_G/r, while the payoff to marrying a B is x_B/r, where $x_G > x_B > 0$ and r is the discount rate. These payoffs include the utility from having children within marriage. Women's and men's utility flow while single and childless is normalized to zero. If, however, a single woman has a child, she is assumed to receive a utility flow of b_c, where $0 < b_c < x_B$. The assumption that $b_c < x_B$ is consistent with all parties, man, woman and child, being better off if childbearing takes place within marriage, because of cooperation and coordination of resources in marriage. It is assumed that men are always willing to become fathers and that there is at most one child born outside marriage to a woman. Finally, denote the probability that, given a contact is made, a single woman meets a G-man as λ_m, and the probability that a single man meets a G-woman conditional on a contact being made is λ_w.

This model is similar to that analysed in Section 7.2, with the addition of the possibility of having a child outside marriage. The trade-off involved in becoming a single mother is that a woman's utility while single is increased, but her rate of encountering potential husbands is lower (i.e. her marital search is slowed down). Again, a central issue is whether a G-woman (G-man) is willing to marry a B-man (B-woman). Another key issue is whether each type of woman will have a child with a man whom she does not wish to marry, or who does not wish to marry her.

MARRIAGE AND CHILDBEARING DECISIONS OF G-PEOPLE

Standard models of marital search, like those examined in Sections 7.1 and 7.2, produce the "value functions" that give the flow values per period of being single childless (rV_{is}) or a single mother (rV_{ic}) for each type of woman ($i = G, B$) and of being single and childless (rU_{is}) for each type of man ($i = G, B$).[6]

The marriage choices of G-women and G-men are not constrained by others. If a G-woman meets a G-man, they will marry. The flow value of being a single mother for a G-woman is, therefore,

$$rV_{Gc} = b_c + \beta\alpha_w\lambda_m\left(\frac{x_G}{r} - V_{Gc}\right) + \beta\alpha_w(1 - \lambda_m)\left[\max\left(\frac{x_B}{r}, V_{Gc}\right) - V_{Gc}\right]$$

(7.21)

The first term on the right-hand side is per period utility of being a single mother; the second is product of the probability of meeting a G-man and the gain from marrying him; and the final term is the product of the probability of meeting a B-man and the gain from taking the best option—either marrying him or continuing to search. The flow value of being single and childless for a G-woman can be decomposed in a similar manner:

$$rV_{Gs} = \alpha_w\lambda_m\left(\frac{x_G}{r} - V_{Gs}\right) + \alpha_w(1 - \lambda_m)\left[\max\left(\frac{x_B}{r}, V_{Gc}, V_{Gs}\right) - V_{Gs}\right]$$

(7.22)

The main difference is that she obtains lower utility per period, but meets men at a faster rate than single mothers because $\beta < 1$.

If a G-woman rejects a B-man as a husband, but has a child with him, it must be the case that $x_B/r < V_{Gc}$. Defining $B(b_c, x_G) = (\beta\alpha_w\lambda_m x_G + b_c)/(\beta\alpha_w\lambda_m + r)$, (7.21) indicates that $B(b_c, x_G)$ is the flow value of being a single mother in this case.[7] If a G-woman rejects a B-man as a husband when she meets one, but does not have a child with him, $x_B/r < V_{Gs}$, and her flow value of being single and childless would be, from (7.22), $A_w(x_G) = \alpha_w\lambda_m x_G/(\lambda_m\alpha_w + r)$. Thus, for her best option to be having a child it must be the case that $B(b_c, x_G) > A_w(x_G)$. It follows that a G-woman rejects a B-man as a husband but has a child with him, if and only if

$$x_B < B(b_c, x_G) = \frac{b_c + \beta\alpha_w\lambda_m x_G}{r + \beta\alpha_w\lambda_m}$$

(7.23)

and

$$x_G < C(b_c) = \frac{b_c(r + \lambda_m\alpha_w)}{\lambda_m(1 - \beta)\alpha_w}$$

(7.24)

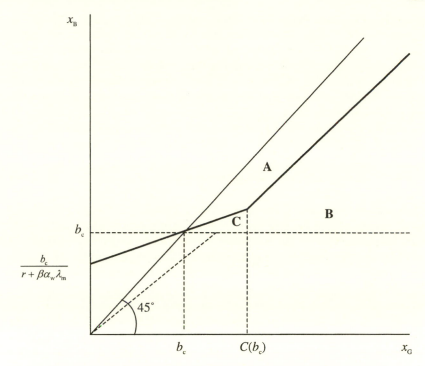

Figure 7.3   Marriage and childbearing decisions of G-women.

In order for her best option to be to reject a B-man as both a husband and a father, it must be the case that $A_w(x_G) \geq B(b_c, x_G)$ and also that $x_B < A_w(x_G)$. This implies that

$$x_B < A_w(x_G) \quad \text{and} \quad x_G \geq C(b_c) \tag{7.25}$$

If, in contrast, $x_B \geq \max\{B(b_c, x_G), A_w(x_G)\}$ a G-woman would marry a B-man, and there would be no childbearing outside marriage.

The relationship equating x_B with $\max\{B(b_c, x_G), A_w(x_G)\}$ is graphed as the kinked curve in x_G–x_B space in Figure 7.3. The kink occurs at $x_G = C(b_c)$, at which $B(b_c, x_G) = A_w(x_G)$. Given that the other parameters are held constant, Figure 7.3 shows what a G-woman would choose for possible combinations of x_G and x_B. As $x_G > x_B$ by assumption, the only possible combinations are below the 45-degree line. Childbearing outside marriage by G-women takes place if and only if the values of x_G and x_B lie in the area denoted by C. In this area, the inequalities (7.23) and (7.24) are satisfied and also $x_B > b_c$. Thus, a G-woman will choose to have a child outside marriage with a B-man if x_G is not much larger than x_B, and x_B is not much larger than b_c. In area **B**, where x_G

exceeds $C(b_c)$, the return when a G-man is found is large enough to discourage her from slowing down her search for him by having a child. In area **A**, where x_B is close to x_G, a G-woman is better off marrying a B-man than waiting for a G-man to come along.

The discussion so far has indicated that a necessary condition for child-bearing outside marriage in this model is that G-men and G-women only want to marry each other. Analysis along similar lines for men, who only have a choice of whether to marry or not, indicates that this will be the case if and only if[8]

$$x_B < A_m(x_G) = \frac{x_G \alpha_m \lambda_w}{r + \lambda_w \alpha_m} \qquad (7.26)$$

This was illustrated in Figure 7.1. Comparison of Figures 7.1 and 7.3 indicates the role of the additional option for women, which produces the kink in the curve.

How high the lifetime gain in marrying a G-woman rather than a B-woman $((x_G - x_B)/r)$ must be to make it worthwhile to continue to search for a G-woman depends on the probability of meeting a G-woman in the market (λ_w) and the encounter rate for men (α_m), higher values of these making it more likely that G-men only marry G-women. It is shown below, that in the steady state, these two variables depend upon whether or not each type of woman has a child outside marriage when she meets a man of the opposite type. A high discount rate leads to a violation of inequalities (7.23), (7.25) and (7.26), and so a high discount rate precludes childbearing outside marriage.

MARRIAGE AND CHILDBEARING DECISIONS OF B-PEOPLE

If G-women are willing to marry B-men, then B-men act exactly like G-men.[9] Suppose, however, that G-women are not willing to marry B-men. Then a B-man will always marry a B-woman because it is better than remaining single forever.

If G-men will marry B-women $(x_B/r \geq U_{Gs})$, then B-women act exactly the same as G-women because they face the same constraints. In this case, it is possible that neither G-women nor B-women want to marry B-men, and that B-women have a child by a B-man when they meet, provided inequalities (7.23) and (7.24) are satisfied. We do not consider this possibility because there would not be a steady-state equilibrium—B-men would never marry (see Burdett and Ermisch 2002). Thus, if G-men will marry B-women, we assume that all women will marry B-men, and there is no childbearing outside marriage.

If, however, G-men will not marry B-women $(x_B/r < U_{Gs})$, B-women can only marry a B-man. In this case, when a B-woman meets a G-man, she has the option to have a child with him. The value of search if she has a child is $V_{Bc}^0 = [\beta\alpha_w(1 - \lambda_m)(x_B/r) + b_c]/[\beta\alpha_w(1 - \lambda_m) + r]$.[10] If her best option is not to have a child, her value of search would be $V_{Bs}^0 = [\alpha_w(1 - \lambda_m)(x_B/r)]/[\alpha_w(1 - \lambda_m) + r]$. Thus, she has a child when she meets a G-man if and only if $V_{Bc}^0 > V_{Bs}^0$, in which case the parameters must satisfy

$$x_B < D(b_c) = \frac{[r + (1 - \lambda_m)\alpha_w]b_c}{(1 - \lambda_m)(1 - \beta)\alpha_w} \qquad (7.27)$$

This inequality provides, therefore, the condition under which B-women have children outside marriage. Given the other parameters, for x_B above $D(b_c)$, the return from marrying a B-man is large enough for it to be worthwhile for a B-woman to wait until a B-man is found rather than slowing down her search by having a child with a G-man. For $x_B < D(b_c)$, having a child with a G-man while she searches is the better option, because the return when she finds a B-man to marry is not that much greater than being a single mother.

If the speed of the marital search process (α_w) were increased sufficiently, the probability of observing a single mother at a point in time would be zero; thus, effectively, childbearing outside marriage disappears. That is, it is only worthwhile to have a child while searching if there are sufficient frictions in marital search and matching. The equilibrium values of λ_m, λ_w, α_w and α_m are derived in the following analysis, which considers steady-state equilibria in which exogenous inflows of singles must equal outflows to marriage.

STEADY-STATE EQUILIBRIUM

The aim of this subsection is to illustrate the determination of a steady-state equilibrium. The discussion focuses on an equilibrium in which G-women do not have children outside marriage but B-women do.[11] We have seen that this will only take place if people of the same type marry each other ("perfect assortative mating"), and so condition (7.26) must be satisfied. In this type of equilibrium, the fathers of children born outside marriage are, of course, G-men, who reject B-women as marriage partners. This equilibrium is consistent with the empirical evidence noted earlier that shows that women who bear children outside marriage have poorer attributes, such as lower educational attainments and poor job prospects, if being a B-woman is associated with these poor attributes.

The basic arithmetic of the determination of the steady-state values of λ_m, λ_w, α_w and α_m is similar to that in Section 7.2. As discussed there, the exogenous inflow of single men and single and childless women into the marriage market is $g\Delta$ per interval Δ, and a proportion π of these are

G-type. Let N be the number of single men and single women in the marriage market; U^B is the number of single childless B-women ("unattached"), and S^B is the number of B-women who are single mothers. Then $U^B + S^B = (1 - \lambda)N$, where λ is the steady-state proportion of G-men and G-women in the market (note that the flows into marriage for each type must be the same for men and women). Compared to earlier, there are two new aspects to the determination of the steady state.

First, there are two types of flow out of the single childless state for B-women: (i) into marriage with a B-man, $\alpha_w(1 - \lambda)U^B$ (i.e. the product of the probability of meeting a B-man and U^B), and (ii) into single motherhood, $\alpha_w \lambda U^B$ (i.e. the product of the probability of meeting a G-man and U^B). Equating flows into and out of the single and childless state, $(1 - \pi)g = \alpha_w U^B$. Also, flows into single motherhood must also equal flows out of single motherhood into marriage: $\alpha_w \lambda U^B = \beta \alpha_w (1 - \lambda)S^B$, where the right-hand side is the product of the probability that a single mother meets a B-man and the number of single mothers.

Second, we introduce the concept of a "matching function", which gives the number of encounters between men and women as a function of what we shall term the *effective* numbers of men and women. For men, the actual number and effective number are the same, as all single men face the same encounter rate. But single women with children face a lower encounter rate than childless single women, making the effective number less than the actual number.

The details are somewhat tedious, and are worked out in the Appendix. The probability that, given a contact is made, a man encounters a G-woman (λ_w) is now larger than λ, because the B-women who are single mothers contact men at a slower rate. Correspondingly, the encounter rate for men in the steady state must be smaller than that for childless single women ($\alpha_m < \alpha_w$), because the single mothers among the single female population encounter men at a slower rate ($\beta < 1$). The steady-state equilibrium condition that implicitly defines the equilibrium value of λ as a function of π and β can be rewritten as

$$\pi = \frac{\lambda^2}{\lambda^2 + k_B(1 - \lambda)^2} \tag{7.28}$$

where k_B is the average ratio of a B-woman's encounter rate to α_w, with $k_B = \beta/[\beta(1 - \lambda) + \lambda]$.

As illustrated by the curved line in Figure 7.4, the equilibrium λ, denoted $\lambda(\pi,\beta)$, is a strictly increasing function of π. There is a critical value for π that depends on β, $\pi_c(\beta)$, that has $\pi < \lambda(\pi, \beta)$ for values of π less than $\pi_c(\beta)$, and $\pi > \lambda(\pi, \beta)$ for values of π above it. In Figure 7.4, it is assumed that $\beta = 0.5$, which implies that $\pi_c(\beta)$ is about 0.4. If π is small, then the exit rate to marriage of G-people is lower than the exit rate

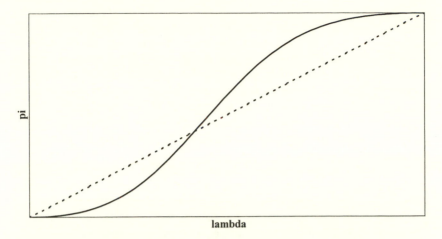

Figure 7.4 Equilibrium proportion of G-people in the marriage market (λ), when only B-women have non-marital births.

of B-people. Thus, single G-people accumulate relative to the number of single B-people, and in a steady state $\lambda(\pi, \beta) > \pi$. If π is relatively large, single B-people accumulate in the marriage market, causing $\lambda(\pi, \beta) < \pi$ in equilibrium. The equilibrium $\lambda(\pi, \beta)$ is also increasing in β, because single motherhood lasts for a shorter time when β increases, implying fewer single B-women in the marriage market relative to G-women.

In order for this steady state to be sustained by the search strategies described above, the variables, $\lambda(\pi, \beta)$, λ_w, α_w and α_m, must satisfy condition (7.26) for perfect assortative mating and conditions (7.27) and (7.25) for non-marital childbearing by B-women but not by G-women. The shaded area in Figure 7.5 shows the combinations of x_G and x_B that satisfy these conditions for a given values of b_c, π and β, and therefore support an equilibrium in which B-women have non-marital births but G-women do not (note $A_w(x_c) = A_m(x_G)$).

The proportion of B-women who become single mothers in this model is λ; thus, $(1 - \lambda)\lambda$ of all women become single mothers. The average duration of single motherhood is $1/[\beta\alpha_w(1 - \lambda)]$, and the median duration is $\ln(0.5)/\ln[1 - \beta\alpha_w(1 - \lambda)]$. Thus, in this model, there is not a dichotomy between women who marry and single mothers; the latter may also eventually marry but in a steady state there is a proportion (S^B/N) who are single mothers as a consequence of their pre-marital childbearing.

Is it possible to have an equilibrium in which G-women have births outside marriage, but B-women do not? Conditions (7.24) and (7.27) indicate that this would require that both $x_G/b_c < (r + \lambda\alpha_w)/[\lambda(1 - \beta)\alpha_w]$ *and* $x_B/b_c \geq [r + (1 - \lambda)\alpha_w]/[(1 - \lambda)(1 - \beta)\alpha_w]$. This is only

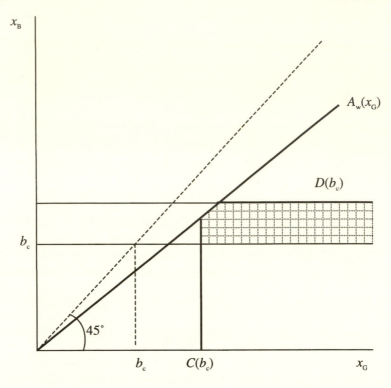

Figure 7.5 Parameters (x_G, x_B) that sustain equilibrium with only B-women having non-marital births.

possible if $\lambda < 0.5$. Thus, a steady-state value of λ in excess of 0.5 would be sufficient to rule out an equilibrium of this type. We now show that even if $\lambda < 0.5$, the ratio x_B/x_G that satisfied both of these conditions would be too large to satisfy condition (7.26) for perfect assortative mating, which is required to produce childbearing outside marriage.

From conditions (7.24) and (7.27), in order for only G-women to have non-marital births, it must be the case that $x_G/b_c < (r + \lambda\alpha_w)/[\lambda(1 - \beta)\alpha_w]$ and $x_B/b_c \geq [r + (1 - \lambda)\alpha_w]/[(1 - \lambda)(1 - \beta)\alpha_w]$. This implies that $x_B/x_G > \lambda[r + (1 - \lambda)\alpha_w]/[(r + \lambda\alpha_w)(1 - \lambda)]$. In order for there to be any non-marital births, there must be perfect assortative mating, which means, from condition (7.26), that $x_B/x_G < \alpha_m\lambda/(r + \lambda\alpha_m)$. Thus, because $\alpha_m < \alpha_w$, if we can show that

$$\frac{\alpha_w\lambda}{r + \lambda\alpha_w} < \lambda\frac{r + (1 - \lambda)\alpha_w}{(r + \lambda\alpha_w)(1 - \lambda)} \tag{7.29}$$

then $\alpha_m\lambda/(r + \lambda\alpha_m) < \lambda[r + (1 - \lambda)\alpha_w]/[(r + \lambda\alpha_w)(1 - \lambda)]$, in which case it is not possible for only G-women to have non-marital births.

Suppose that (7.29) is not true. Then $\alpha_w \lambda/(r + \lambda\alpha_w) \geq \lambda[r + (1-\lambda)\alpha_w]/[(r + \lambda\alpha_w)(1 - \lambda)]$, which implies that $(1 - \lambda)\alpha_w\lambda \geq \lambda[r + (1-\lambda)\alpha_w]$, which implies that $0 \geq \lambda r$, but this is not possible. Thus, (7.29) is true.

Thus, we conclude that if G-women have children outside marriage, so do B-women. In other words, if the return for G-women from waiting childless to marry a G-man is insufficient (relative to the utility of being a single mother) to discourage them from having a pre-marital birth, then this must also be the case for B-women, because of the lower returns to finding a man to marry among B-women.

The steady-state equilibrium conditions when both G-women and B-women have children outside marriage (fathered by B-men and G-men, respectively) are given in Burdett and Ermisch (2002) along with the characterization of the other possible steady states. This equilibrium has a higher steady-state proportion of G-people in the marriage market (λ) than in the one in which only B-women have non-marital births (for any given values of π and β). This is because the single population now contains G-women who become single mothers and therefore remain single longer. Burdett and Ermisch (2002) show that this equilibrium only exists if the discount rate is small enough, and even in this case, there is only a small set of combinations of x_G and x_B that satisfy the conditions that must hold for this equilibrium.

EMPIRICAL SUPPORT

An important implication of the model when there is an equilibrium with non-marital childbearing is that couples who find each other to be mutually acceptable marriage partners (two people of the same type) wait to have children within marriage, while women who are rejected by the man as a wife (or reject the man as a husband in an equilibrium in which G-women have non-marital births) have a child outside marriage. This suggests that sexual relationships that produce a child outside marriage should be much less likely to lead to marriage than those that do not. In general, it is difficult to observe the outcomes of relationships, but we can observe the outcome of cohabiting unions.

In Britain, about three-fourths of people cohabit in their first live-in partnership (rather than marry directly), and births in cohabiting unions make up 60% of the non-marital births. Following Sahib and Gu (2002), we can incorporate cohabiting unions in the framework of the model by considering them as a way to learn the true value of the partner's 'quality' (type G or B in the model). As predicted by the non-marital childbearing equilibria of the model, the cohabiting unions that produce children in Britain are much less likely to be converted into marriage and more likely to break up than childless ones (Ermisch and Francesconi 2000b). About 65% of these fertile unions dissolve, compared with 40% of childless unions. Brien et al. (1999) also find that American cohabiting white women who fail to marry by the time a child is born have marriage rates below those among cohabiting women who did not have a birth.

The conditions for B-women to have children outside marriage (inequalities in (7.26) and 7.27)) are more likely to be satisfied if x_B is lower. It is, for instance, plausible that the value of x_B is lower in labour markets in which the unemployment rate is higher, because higher unemployment particularly affects the incomes of people with poorer attributes. If that is the case, an equilibrium with non-marital childbearing among B-women is more likely to emerge in such labour markets. For instance, it will emerge for lower values of b_c. This suggests that non-marital birth rates will be higher in labour markets with higher unemployment rates. Empirical analysis using experimental data by Olsen and Farkas (1990) indicates that poorer local employment opportunities indeed encourage pre-marital childbearing and discourage the formation of unions, which delays marriage. Such a link between women's non-marital childbearing decisions and labour market conditions was also suggested by Wilson (1987).

7.5 Intergenerational Links through Marriage Markets

Chapter 5 analysed the links between generations, either through gifts and bequests to children or investment in their human capital, which affect their earnings and income when they become adults. Human capital investment can also affect a child's attractiveness in the marriage market as an adult. This affects their income through the matching process, including the probability of remaining single. Aiyagari et al. (2000) address this issue with a model that combines a number of ingredients from the models of matching in the marriage market discussed above in conjunction with explicit consideration of investment in children. This section outlines their approach and its implications for how the marriage market forges links between generations. It also provides a link to the next chapter, which focuses on divorce.

They assume that people live for two periods. Each woman has two children (one of each sex) attached to her throughout the two periods of the model, and children become adults afterwards. People differ in their "productivity type", which affects how much they can earn in the labour market, and, importantly, their type can change over time. At the beginning of each period, there is a marriage market for single people. In the first period, a person can marry if they find an acceptable spouse who also finds them acceptable. In the second period, single people can marry and married couples can divorce, but there is no chance of remarrying. Given the assumption about women's childbearing, never-married single mothers may be created in the first period as a by-product of marriage decisions. That is, if a woman does not receive an acceptable marriage offer, then she will become a single mother. Similar to the model of the previous section, search friction causes single motherhood, but in contrast to it, there is no separate decision about childbearing outside marriage.

When a couple is married, preferences are such that both spouses value a public consumption good for the family (produced through their market earnings and a value to the particular match), their own leisure (the only private good) and human capital investment in their children (similar to Chapter 5). But it is assumed that only the mother values the investment if they separate. Investment in children is produced with combinations of the public consumption good and the mother's time. The gains from marriage come from the joint consumption economies associated with the public good, from the "match value", which is only known after they marry, and from the father's positive valuation of human capital investment in children when he is married. Search for a partner to obtain these gains is subject to friction because there is a random draw with the probabilities of meeting different types being related to the available singles of each type in each period. Furthermore, marriage decisions must be made in the absence of knowledge of the "match value" and people's productivity in the next period, although they know the probability distributions associated with these.

For reasons of tractability, the time allocations for a married couple are assumed to be determined non-cooperatively according to a (static) Nash equilibrium (as, for example, in Section 2.3), thereby producing an inefficient allocation within marriage. This assumption sits uncomfortably with the arguments of Chapter 2 concerning efficiency within marriage. It also means that, in effect, there is non-transferable utility, because the Nash equilibrium entails that each spouse's utility in a marriage is a function of the productivity types of the man and woman and the match value. Because the latter is only known after marriage, there are unique values of man's and woman's expected utility of a match for each particular combination of man's and woman's current productivity type.

Divorce occurs when there is a "poor match value" (as in the models of the next chapter), or a person's productivity type changes sufficiently. Behaviour within marriage cannot respond to the divorce risk (in contrast to the analysis in Section 8.4), because in the model there is no way to transfer resources through time, either through saving or borrowing, or through investment in a person's own human capital. Divorced fathers are forced to pay some proportion of their income to their ex-wife, and single and divorced mothers who do not work receive welfare benefits from the state.

In the absence of search frictions, and change in a person's productivity type over time and variation in match value, there would be perfect assortative mating according to productivity type, as we would expect from Becker's theory (Section 7.3.1), because of the joint consumption economies available within marriage.[12] In the model, it is optimal to match spouses who have similar productivity and therefore similar demands for the public goods.[13] Without search frictions and welfare benefits, there would be no never-married mothers unless there were more women than men, as in Willis' model in Section 7.4.1, although one-parent families would still be created through divorce.

The special assumptions of the model allow the determination of a stationary equilibrium in a marriage market incorporating search frictions, uncertainty about match values and future productivity and household investment in children, in the context of which it is possible to study intergenerational income mobility. It is not possible to solve the model analytically, but the results of its simulation (under some special assumptions) are suggestive. First, the search frictions entail that low productivity types do not marry.[14] This means that low productivity women become single mothers, as is the case in the models of the previous section. Thus, single mothers have low income for two reasons: because they have only one income and because they are drawn from the low end of the productivity type distribution.

The model helps explain income persistence across generations. Children from low-income families receive lower human capital investment, tending to make them poor when they grow up. This occurs because they earn less themselves, but they also are relatively unattractive in the marriage market, thereby attracting low productivity mates or none at all. We have seen that women in this situation are more likely to become single mothers, producing low investment in their children's human capital, thereby continuing the "cycle of disadvantage". Thus, single motherhood and divorce make an important contribution to the process of intergenerational income mobility.

Aiyagari et al. (2000) also use their model to study the impact of varying child support from divorced fathers on marriage market and income outcomes. In contrast to the next chapter, child support is entirely involuntary in their model, because divorced fathers are assumed to no longer care about investment in their children (perhaps because they no longer live with them). It is a tax imposed by a child support agency. More child support directly increases the living standards of children in divorced one-parent families, and it also makes divorce less attractive to men. In addition, the larger investment in children from divorced families makes them more attractive mates when they become adults, thereby reducing the incidence of single motherhood and divorce among them. The simulation of setting a higher proportion of father's income for child support indicates that, because of these long-run effects, both men and women are better off in an equilibrium with larger child support payments. This arises because parents, particularly fathers, are poor agents for their children, and the higher child support "tax" alleviates this problem. Clearly, the conclusions depend on what has been assumed about how parents "care" for their children's welfare and other aspects of the model (e.g. inefficient marriage).

The next chapter considers divorce, child support and their impact on children in much more detail, but from an individual decision-making point of view rather than market equilibrium. It is able to allow for richer modelling of individual decision-making in terms of investments in children, divorce and child support, including forward-looking behaviour in the presence of divorce risk.

Appendix: Steady State Equilibrium

Let N be the actual number of single men and single women in the marriage market. Keeping things simple, we use a constant returns to scale Cobb–Douglas *matching function* with equal exponents, which relates the number of encounters (e) between men and women to what we shall term the *effective* numbers of men (N_m) and women (N_w): $e = \Omega N_m^{0.5} N_w^{0.5}$. Thus, because $\alpha_m N_m$ men contact single women per unit of time and $N_m = N$, $\alpha_m = e/N = \Omega(N_w/N)^{0.5}$ and $\alpha_w = \Omega(N_w/N)^{-0.5}$. Assume that the exogenous inflow of single men and single and childless women into the marriage market is $g\Delta$ per interval Δ, and a proportion π of these are G-type.

The discussion focuses on an equilibrium in which people only marry people of the opposite sex of the same type, and G-women do not have children outside marriage but B-women do. Because the flows into marriage for each type must be the same for men and women, the steady-state proportion of G-men and G-women among the actual number of single men and women is the same and is denoted by λ.

Let U^B be the number of single childless B-women ("unattached"), and let S^B be the number of B-women who are single mothers. Then $U^B + S^B = (1 - \lambda)N$. There are two types of flow out of the single childless state for B-women: (i) into marriage with a B-man, $\alpha_w(1 - \lambda)U^B$ (i.e. the product of the probability of meeting a B-man and U^B), and (ii) into single motherhood, $\alpha_w \lambda U^B$ (i.e. the product of the probability of meeting a G-man and U^B). Equating flows into and out of the single and childless state,

$$(1 - \pi)g = [\alpha_w(1 - \lambda) + \alpha_w\lambda]U^B = \alpha_w U^B \qquad (7A.1)$$

In the steady state, flows into single motherhood must also equal flows out of single motherhood into marriage:

$$\alpha_w\lambda U^B = \beta\alpha_w(1 - \lambda)S^B \qquad (7A.2)$$

where the right-hand side is the product of the probability that a single mother meets a B-man and the number of single mothers. Substituting for U^B in (7A.2), we obtain $\alpha_w\lambda[(1 - \lambda)N - S^B] = \beta\alpha_w(1 - \lambda)S^B$, and so

$$S^B = \frac{\lambda(1 - \lambda)N}{\beta(1 - \lambda) + \lambda} \qquad \text{and} \qquad U^B = (1 - \lambda)\frac{\beta(1 - \lambda)N}{\beta(1 - \lambda) + \lambda} \qquad (7A.3)$$

Because single mothers make contacts at a slower rate than childless single women, their presence in the market is scaled by β. Thus, the *effective* number of women searching in the marriage market is

$$N_w = \beta S^B + U^B + \lambda N = \{(1 - \lambda)\beta + \lambda[(1 - \lambda)\beta + \lambda]\}\frac{N}{\beta(1 - \lambda) + \lambda} \qquad (7A.4)$$

Thus, the probability that a man contacts a G-woman, conditional on a contact being made, is $\lambda_w = \lambda N/N_w$. Note that λ_w exceeds λ because $\beta < 1$. That is, a man is more likely to contact a G-woman when some B-women have children outside marriage than when they do not. Let k_{Bs} be the steady-state proportion of single B-women who are childless; thus, $k_{Bs} = U^B/(1 - \lambda)N$ and $1 - k_{Bs} = S^B/(1 - \lambda)N$. Define $k_B = k_{Bs} + \beta(1 - k_{Bs})$, which is the average ratio of a B-woman's encounter rate to α_w. From (7A.3), $k_B = \beta/[\beta(1 - \lambda) + \lambda]$, and so, from (7A.4),

$$N_w = [(1 - \lambda)k_B + \lambda]N \qquad \text{and} \qquad \lambda_w = \frac{\lambda}{(1 - \lambda)k_B + \lambda} \qquad (7A.5)$$

The total number of contacts must be the same for men and women, which means that $\alpha_m N = \alpha_w N_w$. Thus,

$$\alpha_m = \alpha_w[(1 - \lambda)k_B + \lambda] \qquad (7A.6)$$

This means that, in the steady state, the encounter rate for men must be smaller than that for childless single women, because $\beta < 1$.

For men, equating exits (into marriage) with inflows of each type, yields $\alpha_m\lambda_w\lambda N = \pi g$ and $\alpha_m(1 - \lambda_w)(1 - \lambda)N = (1 - \pi)g$ for G-men and B-men, respectively. That is, the product of the probability that a G-man (B-man) meets a G-woman (B-woman) and the number of G-men in the steady state equals the number of G-men (B-men) entering the marriage market. Equations (7A.5) and (7A.6) imply that $\alpha_m \lambda_w = \alpha_w \lambda$ and $\alpha_m(1 - \lambda_w) = \alpha_w(1 - \lambda)k_B$. Thus, substituting for $\alpha_m \lambda_w$ and $\alpha_m(1 - \lambda_w)$, the steady-state flow conditions for G-men and B-men, respectively, are

$$\alpha_w \lambda^2 N = \pi g \quad \text{and} \quad \alpha_w(1 - \lambda)^2 k_B N = (1 - \pi)g \qquad (7A.7)$$

There is an analogous condition for G-women when they do not have children outside marriage: $\alpha_w \lambda^2 N = \pi g$.

Using the two steady-state flow conditions to eliminate N, the following steady-state condition is obtained:

$$\pi = \frac{\lambda^2}{\lambda^2 + k_B(1 - \lambda)^2} \qquad (7A.8)$$

Because $k_B = \beta/[\beta(1 - \lambda) + \lambda]$, this condition implicitly defines the equilibrium value of λ as a function of π and β. Note that if the parameters are such that B-women do not have children outside marriage, the average ratio of a B-woman's encounter rate to α_w is unity (i.e. $k_B = 1$) and the steady-state condition is the same as (7.12).

NOTES

1. Burdett and Coles (1999, p. F320) note that this "class result" holds for some more general utility functions than the one assumed here.

2. Zhang and Chan (1999) argue that dowries and bride price are fundamentally different because dowries go to the new couple, while bride price goes to the bride's parents.

3. The average groom's age at marriage was 21.1 while the average age of the bride was 14.4, and on average women aged 10–19 in the district exceeded the number of men aged 20–29 by 22%.

4. A household's mean and variance of profits is instrumented by the interactions of the village monthly rainfall variances for the key agricultural months (July–October) and *inherited* land holdings.

5. The European countries in excess of 30% were Austria, France, Finland, Denmark, Sweden and Iceland, and Ireland had 27% of births outside marriage.

6. This section draws substantially on Burdett and Ermisch (2002), in which there is a fuller analysis.

7. In this case, her value of being single and childless is $\alpha_w[\lambda_m(x_G/r) + (1 - \lambda_m)V_{Gc}]/(\alpha_w + r)$.

8. Note that this is the same condition as the inequality in (7.12) from the model without non-marital childbearing. A G-man's value of being single is given by $rU_{Gs} = \alpha_m \lambda_w(x_G/r - U_{Gs}) + \alpha_m(1 - \lambda_w)[\max(x_G/r, U_{Gs}) - U_{Gs}]$.

9. The value function for single B-men is $rU_{Bs} = \alpha_m \lambda_w \theta^{GBm}(x_G/r - U_{Bs}) + \alpha_m(1 - \lambda_w)\theta^{BBm}[\max(x_B/r, U_{Bs}) - U_{Bs}]$, where θ^{ijm} is the probability that a j-type man gets a marriage offer from an i-type woman.

10. The value functions for single B-women with and without children, respectively, are

$$rV_{Bc} = b_c + \beta\alpha_w\lambda_m\theta^{GB}\left(\frac{x_G}{r} - V_{Bc}\right) + \beta\alpha_w(1 - \lambda_m)\theta^{BB}\left[\max\left(\frac{x_B}{r}, V_{Bc}\right) - V_{Bc}\right]$$

$$rV_{Bs} = \alpha_w\lambda_m\left\{\theta^{GB}\left(\frac{x_G}{r} - V_{Bs}\right) + (1 - \theta^{GB})[\max(V_{Bc}, V_{Bs}) - V_{Bs}]\right\} + \alpha_w(1 - \lambda_m)$$

$$\times\left\{\theta^{BB}\left[\max\left(\frac{x_B}{r}, V_{Bc}, V_{Bs}\right) - V_{Bs}\right] + (1 - \theta^{BB})[\max(V_{Bc}, V_{Bs}) - V_{Bs}]\right\}$$

where θ^{ij} is the probability that a j-type woman gets a marriage offer from an i-type man. Note that $x_B > b_c$ implies $x_B/r > V_{Bc}$. In the case considered, $\theta^{GB} = 0$ and $\theta^{BB} = 1$.

11. Similar to the multiple equilibria discussed in Section 7.2, there are parameter values for which you could have either an equilibrium in which each person marries the first person they meet, or an equilibrium in which some B-women have a child outside marriage.

12. In contrast to Becker's theory, the individual utility functions that are assumed in the analysis do not satisfy the conditions for transferable utility, and so there is not a unique "output" or "total utility" from each marriage.

13. While the cost of the mother's time in human capital investment in her children is higher for higher productivity women, this is outweighed by the higher level of public consumption in families with higher productivity mothers, which also enters the production function for human capital investment.

14. Thus, the common empirical finding that married men earn more than single men is likely to at least partly reflect this selection into marriage.

CHAPTER EIGHT

When Forever Is No More: Divorce and Child Support

WHEN ANALYSING matching in the marriage market in the previous chapter, we assumed, for simplicity, that there was no divorce. But, of course, divorce rates are high in many Northern European countries and in the United States. For instance, in Great Britain four out of every ten marriages are expected to end in divorce. There is particular interest in divorces involving children, including payment of child support to mothers, children's welfare and investment in their human capital. The analysis is clearly also relevant to the implications of the dissolution of cohabiting unions, within which childbearing has become more common.

8.1 CHILD SUPPORT FOLLOWING DIVORCE IN THE ABSENCE OF EX ANTE CONTRACTS

The revelation of new information about either spouse or the match is a potential catalyst for divorce. We can build this into our analysis by assuming that there is a random variable θ that affects utility when married, and we normalize so that $\theta = 0$ when divorced.

As in Chapter 6, we identify expenditures on children and investments in their human capital as child quality, denoted as Q. This is a public good to the parents. We abstract from the fertility decision here, but return to it later in the chapter. In order to focus on the main issues, it is assumed initially that Q can be purchased at a unitary price, that the husband's utility is given by $U_h = U_h(Q, x_h) + \theta$, and his wife's utility is given by $U_w = U_w(Q, x_w) + \theta$, where x_h and x_w are private consumption of the husband and wife, respectively.

Assume that the parents cooperate when married. Then the Pareto-efficient allocation is achieved by maximizing the husband's utility subject to his wife's utility being at least some level U_w^m, (i.e. $U_w(Q, x_w) + \theta \geq U_w^m$) and the resource constraint, $x_h + x_w + Q = y_w + y_h$, where y_h and y_w are husband's and wife's income, respectively. The first-order conditions are

$$U_{hx} = \mu U_{wx} = \lambda \tag{8.1a}$$

$$U_{hQ} + \mu U_{wQ} = \lambda \tag{8.1b}$$

where $U_{hx} = \partial U_h / \partial x_h$ etc., $\mu > 0$ is the gain to the husband's utility from lowering U_w^m, and λ is the marginal utility of income. Combining (8.1a) and (8.1b), we obtain the now familiar Samuelson condition for the efficient choice of public goods,

$$\frac{U_{hQ}}{U_{hx}} + \frac{U_{wQ}}{U_{wx}} = 1 \tag{8.2}$$

Ninety percent of children of divorced parents live with their mother. We could, following Weiss and Willis (1985), incorporate the determination of custody into the analysis, but we shall simply assume that after divorce the mother obtains custody of the children. In addition, we assume that she decides the level of child quality, Q. Her former husband, the children's father, can only influence Q by making transfers to his former wife. This is often called the "Stackelberg model", with the ex-wife being the leader and her former husband following by adjusting his transfer in the knowledge of how much of such transfers she spends on Q. This approach is plausible because the father cannot usually monitor the division of his transfer between expenditure on child quality and own consumption of his former wife, particularly expenditures on young children.[1] Thus, transfers are determined at the time of divorce by what is sometimes called "bargaining in the shadow of the law" (Mnookin and Kornhauser 1979). This ex post contract is self-enforcing.

Thus, the mother chooses child quality and her own consumption to maximize U_w subject to $y_w + s^d = x_w + Q$, where s^d is a transfer from her former husband. The first-order condition for her problem is that her marginal utility from expenditure on child quality equals her marginal utility from her private consumption, or

$$\frac{U_{wQ}}{U_{wx}} = 1 \tag{8.3}$$

Comparison of (8.2) and (8.3) indicates that the allocation of resources to child quality is not efficient. This is because the mother does not internalize the effect of her choices on the utility of the father. The inefficiency can be interpreted as an *agency* problem—the father can only indirectly affect child quality through his ex-wife's choices.

In order to illustrate how the allocation decisions in the married and divorced states affect divorce, consider a particular example. Let $U_h = Q(x_h - \beta) + \theta$ and $U_w = Q(x_w - \alpha) + \theta$. These utility functions satisfy the condition for utility to be transferable (see Chapter 3), which is helpful for presenting the main ideas. With these utility functions, (8.2) implies that child quality when married, Q^m, is

$$Q^m = \frac{y_h + y_w - (\alpha + \beta)}{2} \tag{8.4}$$

Using (8.4) and the budget constraint, total utility is $U_h + U_w = 2\theta + [y_h + y_w - (\alpha + \beta)]^2/4$.

In the divorced state, with the particular utility function assumed, condition (8.3) is that $x_w - \alpha = Q$. Substituting from her budget constraint,

$$Q^d = \frac{y_w + s^d - \alpha}{2} \tag{8.5}$$

Her former husband takes (8.5), which shows how she will react to transfers from him, as a constraint on his decision. He chooses s^d to maximize U_h subject to (8.5), $y_h = s^d + x_h$ and $s^d \geq 0$. If his income is below $y_w + \beta - \alpha$, he will make no transfers. Given that his income is large enough that $s^d > 0$, the first-order condition implies

$$s^d = \frac{y_h - y_w + \alpha - \beta}{2} \tag{8.6}$$

Clearly, he will transfer more the higher his income and the lower is hers. He will also transfer more if his preferences favour child quality more than hers (i.e. $\alpha - \beta$ is higher). A key feature of the mother's child quality choice, (8.5), is that he must transfer \$2 to obtain \$1 more expenditure on child quality. In other words, he faces a higher effective price for child quality when divorced than when he was married (at which time \$1 of expenditure bought \$1 of child quality). We should, therefore, expect him to spend less on child quality, resulting in a lower provision of Q.

Substituting from (8.6) into (8.5), we indeed find that, even when $s^d > 0$,

$$Q^d = \frac{y_h + y_w - (\alpha + \beta)}{4} \tag{8.7}$$

Comparison of (8.4) and (8.7) indicates that child quality has been halved relative to when the couple were married. Using (8.7) and their respective budget constraints, the former husband's utility is easily derived to be $U_h = [y_h + y_w - (\alpha + \beta)]^2/8$, while his former wife's utility is $U_w = [y_h + y_w - (\alpha + \beta)]^2/16$. Her utility is, therefore, lower than his if they divorce. This is consistent with the finding that mothers fare less well after divorce than fathers (e.g. see Duncan and Hoffman 1985, 1988; Jarvis and Jenkins 1999).

Given our assumption of transferable utility, the parents will divorce when $U_h + U_w$ in the divorced state exceeds $U_h + U_w$ when married, or, with our particular utility functions, they will divorce when

$$\theta < -\frac{[y_h + y_w - (\alpha + \beta)]^2}{32} \tag{8.8}$$

Note that the couple remains married for some negative values of θ. This is because it is worthwhile to stay married in order to avoid the loss of efficiency associated with divorce if the negative "shock" to the marriage is moderate. The efficiency loss from divorce, arising from the father's lack of control over child quality, is the decline in total utility, $U_h + U_w$, which is $EL = [y_h + y_w - (\alpha + \beta)]^2/16$. If θ has distribution function $G(\theta)$, then the probability of divorce is $G(-EL/2)$. It is clearly smaller the higher is either spouse's income, because the efficiency loss from lack of cooperation in deciding on the public good is larger for a larger demand for the public good, and the demand increases with the income of either spouse. For the same reason, the probability of divorce is smaller if the parents' preferences are more favourable toward child quality (i.e. $\alpha + \beta$ is lower).

The father's effective price for child expenditure is also affected by the government income support system when the mother's income is low enough for her to receive state support. Her income y_w is likely to be primarily made up of benefit payments, and benefits are withdrawn at the rate t. Equation (8.5) then becomes

$$Q^d = \frac{y_w + (1 - t)s^d - \alpha}{2} \tag{8.5b}$$

The father has less incentive to make payments than before, because he now must spend $\$2/(1 - t)$ to increase expenditure on his children by $\$1$. Clearly, if the benefit withdrawal rate were $\%100$ (i.e. $t = 1$), child support payments do not affect expenditure on children and he would have no incentive to transfer money to the mother. A "disregard" of a certain amount of child support for the purposes of state benefit, would, however, give the father an incentive to make payments up to the "disregarded" amount.

Equations (8.6) and (8.7) now become

$$s^d = \begin{cases} \frac{1}{2}\left[y_h - \beta - \frac{(y_w - \alpha)}{1 - t}\right], & \text{for } y_h > \beta + \frac{y_w - \alpha}{1 - t} \\ \text{otherwise,} & 0 \end{cases} \tag{8.6b}$$

$$Q^d = \frac{(1 - t)y_h + y_w - (\alpha + (1 - t)\beta)}{4} \qquad \text{for } y_h > \beta + \frac{y_w - \alpha}{1 - t} \tag{8.7b}$$

A higher benefit withdrawal rate clearly reduces transfers to the mother and also expenditure on children. Higher benefit payments, which raise y_w, "crowd out" child support from the father in the sense that higher benefits paid to the mother reduce child support from the father, even if

$t = 0$; in our example, $\partial s^{d}/\partial y_{w} = -1/2(1 - t)$, for $t < 1$. Note that for a high enough benefit withdrawal rate ($t > 0.5$ in this example), the crowding out is more than dollar for dollar. Nevertheless, Q^{d} always increases with higher benefits to the mother (see (8.7b)).

The disincentive to child support transfers implied by the agency problem is consistent with the relatively low levels of child support observed in Britain. For instance, during the 1990s only 25% of fathers made child support payments directly to the custodial mother, although another 20% made payments to his parents-in-law or directly to his children (Smith 2002). Given that he made child support payments, they represented about 17 percent of a father's earnings on average.

The lower expenditure on children in families in which the parents have split is likely to also mean lower investment in the children's human capital when they are young, which may affect children's development and achievements. This suggests that children who have experienced a family break-up may have lower achievements than children brought up in an intact family. A concern when investigating this empirically is that the estimated association between childhood family structure and children's achievements might be spurious because of the mutual association that family structure and children's outcomes share with some unmeasured true causal factor. For example, the association between having experienced life in a single-parent family and, say, experiencing difficulties in the labour market may not be necessarily the result of family structure during childhood. Rather, differences in labour market success may simply reflect the characteristics of families in which the children of single mothers are brought up, some of which we cannot measure.

Ermisch and Francesconi (2001b) show that the effect of family structure on outcomes can be identified by comparing siblings in the same family if family structure does not respond to differences between siblings in "endowments" (e.g. intelligence). On this assumption, estimates that relate differences in achievements between siblings to differences in their family structure experience would measure the causal impact of childhood family structure on young adults' achievements. But note that, in addition to inherent differences between siblings (e.g., one born with a disability), differences between siblings in their "endowments" include differences over time in parental attitudes and behaviour which may affect both family structure and children's outcomes.[2] In any case, the "sibling-difference" estimates control for more aspects of family background than the traditional estimates that rely on comparisons between families, making them less contaminated by unmeasured factors associated with both family structure and children's outcomes.

Ermisch and Francesconi (2001b) find that young adults who experience lone parenthood as children have significantly lower educational attainments. It is also associated with a number of other disadvantageous outcomes for young adults, including a higher risk of unemployment, a higher risk of having a child before a woman's 21st birthday, a higher chance of being a heavy smoker and higher likelihood of experiencing psychological distress in early adulthood. Most of these unfavourable outcomes are more strongly associated with an early family disruption (in pre-school ages), which is more likely for those born in cohabiting unions.

8.2 CHILD SUPPORT FOLLOWING DIVORCE WITH EX ANTE CONTRACTS

Is it possible to obtain a better outcome if the couple makes a contract specifying transfers between spouses in the married and divorced states (s^m and s^d) and to children (Q^m and Q^d) at the beginning of the marriage? Following Weiss and Willis (1993), we derive what they call a "quasi-efficient contract" that takes the form of a set of contingent transfers. It recognizes that even if a divorce court can enforce a transfer specified ex ante, it cannot enforce an allocation between child quality and the custodial parent's consumption following divorce. It is, therefore, assumed that cooperation ceases and the mother has custody of the children in the event of divorce. The couple anticipates at the time of marriage that this "agency problem" will arise if they divorce and devises a set of transfers to insure each partner against this contingency. This quasi-efficient contract is ex post inefficient, but it is efficient ex ante. We simplify by assuming that θ takes on only two values: $\theta = \theta^m > 0$, which is high enough to ensure the marriage continues, and $\theta = \theta^d < 0$, which is low enough to produce a divorce. The probability that $\theta = \theta^m$ is denoted as p, and $E(\ )$ below is the expectations operator. Because we are dealing with risky choices, we assume that the utility functions are concave, implying that each spouse is risk averse.

The optimal set of contingent transfers, s^m, s^d, Q^m, Q^d, which constitute the quasi-efficient contract, are those which maximize

$$E(U_h) = (1 - p)U_h(Q^d, y_h - s^d) + p[U_h(Q^m, y_h - s^m) + \theta^m]$$

subject to

(a) $E(U_w) = (1 - p)U_w(Q^d, y_w + s^d - Q^d) + p[U_w(Q^m, y_w + s^m - Q^m) + \theta^m] \geq U_w^*$

(b) $U_w(Q^m, y_w + s^m - Q^m) + \theta^m \geq U_w(Q^d, y_w + s^d - Q^d)$

(c) $U_h(Q^m, y_h - s^m) + \theta^m \geq U_h(Q^d, y_h - s^d)$

(d) Q^d is the solution to the mother maximizing $U_w(Q^d, y_w + s^d - Q^d)$, implying $Q^d = f(y_w + s^d)$.

The first constraint is that the mother's expected utility must at least equal a level $U_w{}^*$, which may arise because of negotiations within the marriage or reflect marriage market options available to the wife. Constraints (b) and (c) are participation constraints, and we will assume that θ^m is large enough for these to hold with an inequality; that is, each spouse would be better off in the marriage if θ^m were realized. Finally, constraint (d) says that the mother has custody if the couple divorces, and she determines child quality in this situation.

The first-order conditions for these contingent transfers are:

    (i) $\mu U_{wx}^m = U_{hx}^m$ $[s^m]$

    (ii) $\mu[U_{wQ}^d f' + U_{wx}^d(1 - f')] + U_{hQ}^d f' = U_{hx}^d$ $[s^d]$

    (iii) $U_{hQ}^m + \mu U_{wQ}^m = \mu U_{wx}^m$ $[Q^m]$

    (iv) $U_{wx}^d = U_{wQ}^d$ $[Q^d]$

    (v) $E(U_w) = U_w^*$ $[\mu]$

where $U_{hx} = \partial U_h/\partial x_h$ etc., $f' = df/ds^d$, $\mu > 0$ is the gain to the husband's utility from lowering $U_w{}^*$, and the superscript indicates the state at which these derivatives are evaluated (marriage or divorce).

Combining (i) and (iii), we obtain the Samuelson condition for efficient provision of the public good, child quality, in the married state: $U_{hQ}{}^m/U_{hx}{}^m + U_{wQ}{}^m/U_{wx}{}^m = 1$, which is condition (8.2). Combining (ii) and (iv), we obtain the condition for transfers to the mother if the couple divorces (s^d): $(U_{hx}^d - \mu U_{wx}^d)/U_{hQ}^d = f'$. In order to obtain further insights into the nature of these transfers, it is helpful to reformulate the problem in terms of the utility levels assigned to the woman in the married and divorced states, U_w^m and U_w^d.

In the married state, the first-order conditions (8.1a) and (8.1b), along with the constraints $U_w(Q, x_w) + \theta \geq U_w^m$ and $x_h + x_w + Q = y_w + y_h$, provide solutions for x_h, x_w and Q as a function of U_w^m. From these, we obtain the husband's utility as a function of his wife's; that is, we obtain the utility possibility frontier in the married state: $U_h = V(U_w^m, \theta^m, y_w + y_h)$. The frontier is clearly further out for higher values of θ^m.

In the divorced state, we can derive a second best utility frontier by minimizing the cost, $x_h + x_w + Q$, of achieving a given level of the wife's utility, U_w^d. This gives rise to the first-order condition in (8.3), from which we derive x_w and x_h, and therefore U_h as a function of U_w^d. Thus, we have the utility frontier in the divorced state: $U_h = \psi(U_w^d, y_w + y_h)$.

We can now restate the problem at the outset of this section in the following terms: maximize $(1 - p)\psi(U_w^d, y_w + y_h) + pV(U_w^m, \theta^m, y_w + y_h)$ subject to (a) $(1-p)U_w^d + pU_w^m \geq U_w{}^*$, (b) $V(U_w^m, \theta^m, y_w + y_h) \geq \psi(U_w^d, y_w + y_h)$ and (c) $U_w^m \geq U_w^d$. Again assuming that θ^m is large enough to make constraints (b) and (c) ineffective, the solution to this problem implies

$$\frac{\partial \psi(U_w^d, y_w + y_h)}{\partial U_w^d} = \mu = \frac{\partial V(U_w^m, \theta^m, y_w + y_h)}{\partial U_w^m} \qquad (8.9)$$

Equation (8.9) says that the optimal contract assigns the wife utilities in the married and divorced states so that the slope of the utility possibility frontier within marriage is the same as the slope of the utility frontier if divorced. These slopes are equalized by transferring resources between the married and divorced states through the adjustment of s^m and s^d. Having determined the optimal utility assignments, we can obtain the optimal values of x_h, x_w and Q in the married and divorced states through their dependence on U_w^m and U_w^d derived above, and these yield the values of s^m and s^d.

In order to illustrate, assume that the utility functions take the following form for each spouse, $U_i = Q^\phi x_i^\gamma + \theta^m$, $i = h, w$ and $\phi + \gamma < 1$ (for concavity). In this case, the first-order conditions imply that $Q^m = \phi[y_h + y_w]/(\phi + \gamma)$, $x_w^m = [(U_w^m - \theta^m)/(Q^m)^\phi]^{1/\gamma}$, $x_h^m = y_h + y_w - Q^m - x_w^m$, and $s^m = y_h - x_h^m$. By substituting these in the utility functions, we obtain the utility possibility frontier $V(U_w^m, \theta^m, y_w + y_h)$. Once we have determined U_w^m, we can solve for the full allocation of resources in the married state and s^m. Note that higher θ^m will reduce s^m and raise the husband's utility for any given value of U_w^m.

In the divorced state, the first-order conditions imply $Q^d = \phi x_w^d/\gamma$. Substituting in the woman's utility function, $x_w^d = [(\phi/\gamma)^{-\phi} U_w^d]^{1/(\phi+\gamma)}$, $x_h^d = y_h + y_w - (\phi + \gamma)x_w^d/\gamma$, and $s_d = y_h - x_h^d$. By substituting these in the utility functions, we obtain the utility possibility frontier $\psi(U_w^d, y_w + y_h)$. We have, therefore, the full allocation of resources in the divorced state as a function of U_w^d.

The choice of U_w^m and U_w^d, given by the "equal slope condition" in (8.9), is illustrated in Figure 8.1, where the slopes of the two frontiers are equal at e and e', respectively. Note that the divorce frontier has a maximum at U_w^B, but it would never be efficient for the divorce settlement to be at levels of her utility in the divorced state lower than U_w^B, because both parties can gain by a feasible change. Also, if the choice of custody would also be at issue, if would not be efficient for the wife to take custody at levels of U_w^d below U_w^B (see Weiss and Willis 1985).

The utility allocation corresponding to the maximum at U_w^B is indeed the one that would emerge from the ex post contract discussed in the preceding section (the Stackelberg model). Given the wife's income and the utility function parameters, there is a one-to-one mapping of the wife's utility level in the divorced state to the transfer from her ex-husband. Thus, the divorce frontier corresponds to different values of the divorce transfer from the husband. He chooses the transfer to maximize his utility, and that occurs at U_w^B. This is the minimum transfer that induces her to take custody. Clearly, the quasi-efficient contingent transfers' contract provides a larger transfer and higher utility for the wife (but lower for the husband) than the ex post contract.

The contingent transfers' contract provides optimal risk sharing, given the agency problem that occurs in the event of divorce, encapsulated in constraint (d). The divorce settlement s_d tends to prevent a large discrepancy between the wife's utility in the two states, but it only provides partial insurance. In other words, the divorce transfer to the mother is tied "to the standard of living to which the she and the child were accustomed within marriage." (Weiss 1997, p. 116). This is the insurance motive for divorce settlements.

A fully efficient contract would require that all agreements on transfers made at the time of marriage, including transfers to children, are binding and that cooperation can be maintained after a divorce, so that resource allocation is efficient in both the marriage and divorce states. Such a contract would provide the husband and wife with the same consumption and the same child quality in both states, thereby

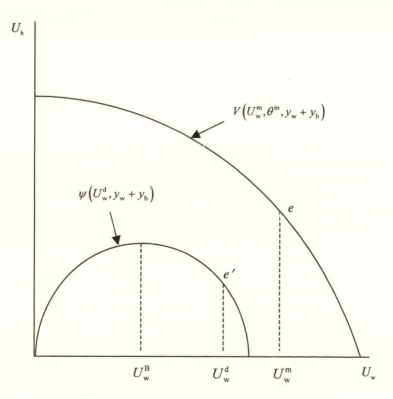

Figure 8.1 Optimal risk sharing contract.

providing full insurance. With the fully efficient contract, the utility frontier in the divorce state lies above the divorce frontier implied by the quasi-efficient contract (beyond the intersection with the U_w axis). The efficient contract is characterized by a utility allocation in the divorce and marriage states that satisfies an equal slope condition analogous to (8.9). In terms of Figure 8.1, the divorce-utility allocation in the efficient contract is to the left of that in the quasi-efficient contract. Both the husband and the wife obtain higher utility from the fully efficient contract than they would from the ex post contract, and the husband attains higher utility than he would under the quasi-efficient contract. The wife obtains a higher utility level under a quasi-efficient contract than she would under an efficient contract because, in order to overcome the agency problem, the husband must give his wife more resources to obtain the desired level of child quality.

In contrast to the quasi-efficient contract, the ex post transfers pay no attention to the options within marriage and fail to share risks optimally.[3] The mother and children bear more of the risk of divorce than the father. Divorce will be less likely when there is not a contingent transfer contract, because the efficiency losses from divorce are larger. For instance, we have seen from the inequality in (8.8) that some marriages in which $\theta < 0$ survive because divorce is discouraged by efficiency losses. With the contingent transfer contract, resources are allocated more efficiently in the divorced state, thereby reducing the efficiency-loss incentive to remain married and raising the probability of divorce. In this sense, there are too few divorces with the ex post transfers relative to the quasi-efficient contract.

The problem with such a marriage contract is that it is not likely to be enforceable. For instance, suppose the couple turns out to be well matched in the sense that $\theta = \theta^m$. Nothing prevents either spouse from trying to renegotiate the marriage contract. Courts are not likely to intervene in disputes within marriage. Now suppose that $\theta = \theta^d$, so that the couple divorce. The husband may have an incentive to renege on the contract because his utility is higher if he makes transfers according to the ex post rule. While the courts are interested in transfers after divorce, they usually confine their intervention to general guidelines or formulae concerning child support, alimony and property division. Thus, the transfers that the courts mandate are likely to be less than that specified in a contingent transfer contract. Such a contract is not, therefore, likely to be feasible, but it may influence voluntary agreements at divorce.

In their empirical analysis of divorce settlements, Weiss and Willis (1993) allow for spouses' resources at both the time of marriage and the time of divorce to influence the total divorce transfer from the husband to the wife.[4] The presence of implicit ex ante contracts is revealed by an independent influence of the initial conditions, holding conditions at the time of divorce constant. They use data from a cohort of American whites who graduated high school in 1972 and who were observed up to 1986 (the National Longitudinal Study of the High School Class of 1972). Their analysis controls for non-random selection into the sample of divorces. The total divorce transfer is made up of the present value of child support payments (alternatively child support obligation), the total net value of property received by the wife and the present value of expected alimony payments, less the wife's expenditure on lawyers. The largest component is child support, and alimony is by far the smallest. On average, the total divorce transfers are small, making up only 13% of the total resources of families with children who divorce. They are not sufficient to equalize resources between the two divorced spouses. The relatively low child support payment is in part due to imperfect enforcement, an issue to which we return below.

Their analysis finds that incomes of the husband and wife at the time of marriage affect divorce settlements, holding their incomes at divorce constant. This suggests that divorce settlements are influenced by ex ante considerations. Among couples with children, upon whom we focus, this result is driven by a positive impact of the wife's current income at the time of marriage on the divorce settlement; husband's income at marriage does not have a significant effect (see their Table 3A). In contrast, higher income of the husband and lower income of the wife at divorce increase the divorce settlement, as we would expect if the settlement were determined by ex post bargaining at the time of divorce. Thus, there seem to be aspects of both ex ante and ex post contracting in divorce transfers.

Weiss and Willis (1993) rearrange these estimated income effects to help interpret them (see their Table 3B). They distinguish between initial incomes and *changes* in them between the dates of marriage and divorce, interpreting the effects of *changes* as the impact on contingent transfers in response to new information acquired during marriage. They focus on the sum of husband's and wife's income ("total resources") and the difference between their incomes, computing the impacts of initial values of these and changes in them during marriage. Higher levels of initial total resources and higher growth in them during marriage both raise divorce settlements. Holding initial total resources and changes during marriage fixed, a wife who had a lower current income at the time of marriage relative to her husband obtains a higher divorce settlement. This suggests that a husband does not use a larger ex ante bargaining power to reduce his transfers to his wife in the event of divorce. It may be interpreted as a compensation for the wife's investment in marriage. Holding initial conditions constant, a husband who experiences higher growth in income relative to his wife during marriage makes a larger transfer to his wife at divorce. This may reflect insurance for unanticipated changes in income, compensation to his wife for her loss of earning capacity during marriage and also his demand for child quality, which requires a larger transfer the greater the discrepancy in the couple's incomes. Weiss and Willis (1993, p. 655) conclude as follows: "It seems that courts in the United States internalize ex ante considerations that are related to the wife's accustomed standard of living and her investments during marriage but do not internalize the influence of her opportunities outside marriage, as reflected by her earning capacity at the time of marriage."

This empirical analysis treats changes in the wife's income as exogenous. But her labour force participation and earning power may react to the anticipation of a small divorce transfer. If this is the case, the estimates of the impact of her income at divorce (or changes in it during marriage) would overstate the true effect because she acts to increase her income in response to the low expected divorce settlement. That is, her income is higher at divorce because the divorce settlement is lower, not just the other way around. The next section explores the implications of this possibility.

8.3 INVESTMENTS AND DIVORCE

We proceed under the assumption that only ex post transfers are feasible or operative, and again the mother has custody if a divorce occurs. The main issue to be investigated is whether the possibility of divorce in the future affects current employment and fertility behaviour. Consider a two-period model (used by Weiss 1997) in which child quality is produced by a combination of parents' time and expenditures on goods and services: $Q_j = (\delta t_{wj} + \phi t_{hj})^\gamma e_j^{1-\gamma}$, $j = 1, 2$, where t_{ij} is parent i's time input into the production of child quality in period j and e_j are goods inputs. The utility functions in each period are those assumed in Section 8.1: $U_{wj} = Q_j(x_{wj} - \alpha) + \theta_j$ and $U_{hj} = Q_j(x_{hj} - \beta) + \theta_j$. In the first period, the couple are married, each parent's wage, W_{i1} ($i = h, w$), is given, and θ_1 is normalized to zero. In the second period, new information produces a new value of θ, and the second period wage benefits from learning by doing in the first period: $W_{i2} = W_{i2}(h_{i1})$, where $h_{i1} = T - t_{i1}$ and $W'_{i2} = dW_{i2}/dh_{i1} > 0$. Also, $\theta_2 = 0$ if the parents divorce. For simplicity, there is no saving or borrowing, and so this learning-by-doing investment is the only way to move income between periods.

The problem is solved backwards from the second period. θ_2 is observed and W_{i2} is given. There are two possible states, remain married or divorce. In the married state, the efficient allocation is the solution to the following problem: maximize U_{h2} subject to the child quality production function, to $U_{w2} \geq U_w^*$ and to $(W_{h2} + W_{w2})T =$

$W_{h2}t_{h2} + W_{w2}t_{w2} + x_{h2} + x_{w2} + e_2$, where T is the total time available. The first-order conditions for this problem imply that the marginal utility of income is Q_2 and

$$\frac{(x_{h2} + x_{w2} - \alpha - \beta)\gamma}{\delta t_{w2} + \phi t_{h2}} \leq \frac{W_{h2}}{\phi} \tag{8.10a}$$

$$\frac{(x_{h2} + x_{w2} - \alpha - \beta)\gamma}{\delta t_{w2} + \phi t_{h2}} \leq \frac{W_{w2}}{\delta} \tag{8.10b}$$

$$e_2 = (x_{h2} + x_{w2} - \alpha - \beta)(1 - \gamma) \tag{8.10c}$$

Only one of (8.10a) and (8.10b) can hold with equality. If we assume that the mother has the comparative advantage in child quality production, then $W_{h2}/\phi > W_{w2}/\delta$, and only (8.10b) holds with equality. Thus, $t_{h2} = 0$, $Q_2 = (\delta t_{w2})^\gamma e_2^{1-\gamma}$ and $t_{w2} = (x_{h2} + x_{w2} - \alpha - \beta)\gamma/W_{w2}$. Using the second period budget constraint, $x_{h2} + x_{w2} = [(W_{h2} + W_{w2})T + \alpha + \beta]/2$. Substituting for Q_2 and $x_{h2} + x_{w2}$ in the sum of husband's and wife's utilities, the sum of utilities in the marriage state is

$$(U_{h2} + U_{w2})^m = K[(W_{h2} + W_{w2})T - (\alpha + \beta)]^2 \ W_{w2}^{-\gamma} + 2\theta_2 \tag{8.11}$$

where $K = [(\delta\gamma)^\gamma(1 - \gamma)^{1-\gamma}]/4$.

If the couple divorces, then the mother chooses Q_2, e_2 and t_{w2} to maximize her utility subject to $s^d + W_{w2}T = W_{w2}t_{w2} + e_2 + x_{w2}$ and $Q_2 = (\delta t_{w2})^\gamma e_2^{1-\gamma}$. This implies that $t_{w2} = \gamma(s^d + W_{w2}T - \alpha)/2W_{w2}$, $e_2 = (1 - \gamma)(s^d + W_{w2}T - \alpha)/2$ and $x_{w2} = (s^d + W_{w2}T + \alpha)/2$.

The former husband chooses s^d to maximize his utility subject to these functions determining e_2 and t_{w2}, and therefore Q_2, to his budget, $s^d + x_{h2} = W_{h2}T$ and to $s^d \geq 0$. Assuming that his full income is large enough relative to hers so that this last constraint is not binding, solution to his problem implies $s^d = [(W_{h2} - W_{w2})T + \alpha - \beta)]/2$. Substituting in the mother's reaction functions, $t_{w2} = \gamma[(W_{h2} + W_{w2})T - (\alpha + \beta)]/4W_{w2}$, $e_2 = (1 - \gamma)[(W_{h2} + W_{w2})T - (\alpha + \beta)]/4$ and $x_{w2} = [(W_{h2} + W_{w2})T + 3\alpha - \beta]/4$. His own private consumption is $x_{h2} = [(W_{h2} + W_{w2})T - \alpha + \beta]/2$.

With this information we can calculate the utilities of the former husband and wife by substituting in their utility functions:

$$U_{h2}^d = \frac{K}{2}[(W_{h2} + W_{w2})T - (\alpha + \beta)]^2 \ W_{w2}^{-\gamma} \tag{8.12a}$$

$$U_{w2}^d = \frac{K}{4}[(W_{h2} + W_{w2})T - (\alpha + \beta)]^2 \ W_{w2}^{-\gamma} \tag{8.12b}$$

The couple will divorce in period 2 if $(U_{h2}^d + U_{w2}^d) - (U_{h2} + U_{w2})^m > 0$, or

$$\theta_2 < \left(\frac{3K}{4} - K\right)[(W_{h2} + W_{w2})T - (\alpha + \beta)]^2 \frac{W_{w2}^{-\gamma}}{2} = \theta^* \qquad (8.13)$$

The threshold value θ^*, given by the right-hand side of (8.13), is negative because of the loss of efficiency arising from the lack of cooperation between parents after divorce, and again we see from (8.12a) and (8.12b) that the man's utility after divorce is higher than the woman's.

It is now possible to frame the couple's problem in their first period of marriage. For simplicity, we assume that there is no discounting. They choose t_{w1} and e_1 to maximize the sum of the spouses' expected utilities over the two periods; that is they maximize

$$U^* = (\delta t_{w1})^\gamma e_1^{1-\gamma}[W_{h1}T + W_{w1}(T - t_{w1}) - e_1 - \alpha - \beta]$$

$$+\left\{[1 - G(\theta^*)]K + \frac{3K}{4}G(\theta^*)\right\}$$

$$\times [(W_{h2} + W_{w2})T - (\alpha + \beta)]^2 W_{w2}^{-\gamma} + 2\int_{\theta^*}^{\infty} \theta dG(\theta) \qquad (8.14)$$

For ease of exposition, define $X_1 = W_{h1}T + W_{w1}(T - t_{w1}) - e_1 - \alpha - \beta$, $G(\theta)$ is a distribution function and $G(\theta^*)$ is the probability of divorce. Then the first-order conditions are

$$\frac{\gamma X_1 Q_1}{t_{w1}} + B[(2 - \gamma)W_{w2}T - \gamma W_{h2}T + \gamma(\alpha + \beta)]\left(\frac{\partial W_{w2}}{\partial t_{w1}}\right) = Q_1 W_{w1}$$
$$(8.15a)$$

$$(1 - \gamma)X_1 = e_1 \qquad (8.15b)$$

where B depends on the second period wages, the parameters of the model and the distribution $G(\theta)$. After some manipulation using (8.15a) and (8.15b),

$$t_{w1} = \gamma\frac{(W_{h1} + W_{w1})T - (\alpha + \beta)}{2(W_{w1} - Z^*)} \qquad (8.16)$$

where $Z^* = B[(2 - \gamma)W_{w2}T - \gamma W_{h2}T + \gamma(\alpha + \beta)](\partial W_{w2}/\partial t_{w1})/Q_1$. Note that Z^* is akin to an adjustment to the first period wage reflecting the impact of learning by doing on second period wages. If, for example, Z^* were negative, it would be like facing a higher wage in the first period, thereby encouraging the mother's paid employment.

If couples were myopic, maximizing the sum of first period utilities without taking into account that time allocations in the first period affect second period wages, then Z^* would be absent from (8.16). The effect of taking into account the uncertain marriage outcome in the second period depends on the sign of Z^*. Learning by doing means that $\partial W_{w2}/\partial t_{w1} < 0$, and if the woman works in paid employment at all in the second period (i.e. $t_{w2} < T$), then $(2 - \gamma)W_{w2}T - \gamma W_{h2}T + \gamma(\alpha + \beta) > 0$. Thus, the sign of B is crucial for the effect of the risk of divorce on the first period time allocation of the woman. Two terms in the expression for B are positive, and the third term is negative.

The last term captures the effect of the first period time allocation on the efficiency loss from divorce. More paid employment by the mother in the first period (i.e. lower t_{w1}) raises the second period wage, which increases the efficiency loss associated with divorce and decreases the threshold value θ^*. Thus, it also lowers the probability of divorce. The larger efficiency loss from a divorce in the second period discourages paid employment by the mother during marriage in the first period (i.e. higher t_{w1}). But a higher second period wage increases utility in the second period in both the divorced and married states, thereby encouraging more paid employment by the mother in the first period. The net effect is ambiguous.

If, as is likely, the effect operating through the larger efficiency loss from divorce is of second-order importance, then learning-by-doing in the labour market encourages more paid employment during the first period by the mother, and, by raising the effective cost of child quality, a lower production of child quality in the first period. If, as in Chapter 6, fertility is chosen in the first period, we could interpret Q_1 here as NQ in Chapter 6. Then learning-by-doing would also tend to decrease fertility. Weiss (1997) has called these "defensive investments". More paid employment (lower fertility and child quality in the first period) is undertaken to increase utility in the second period, when utility outcomes are uncertain.

If divorce did not cause an efficiency loss, then $\theta^* = 0$, implying a higher probability of divorce than above. In this case, $B > 0$ and $Z^* < 0$, and Z^* is smaller than before. From (8.16), this means that $W_{w1} - Z^*$ is larger and t_{w1} is smaller. In this sense, a higher probability of divorce encourages more paid employment by the mother during marriage, and lower fertility and child quality in the first period. But there is no structural equation in which divorce risk affects fertility. In their empirical analysis, Lillard and Waite (1993) assume that the fertility rate within marriage is a function of the "hazard rate" of divorce (roughly speaking the probability of divorce at a given time conditional on the marriage surviving up to that time). Such a specification could not be rationalized in terms of the dynamic model above.

There have been a number of studies examining the impact of children on divorce (e.g. Lillard and Waite 1993). In the context of this model, (8.13) indicates that the second period divorce probability is a function of (endogenous) second period parents' wages and the parameters of the spouses' utility functions and of the household production function for children and child quality. There is not a structural equation in which first period fertility affects the second period divorce probability. We could, however, think in terms of a *conditional* divorce probability equation, conditional on (pre-determined) first period fertility. *Exogenous variation* in fertility would affect the probability of divorce through its effect on parents' second period wages. If the mother has the comparative advantage in home production, higher fertility (less paid employment by the mother) in the first period lowers her second period wage, which reduces the efficiency loss associated with divorce and *raises* the probability of divorce. Estimates by Lillard and Waite (1993) and Böheim and Ermisch (2001) indeed find that additional children beyond the first increase the risk of divorce, but there are other studies that suggest the opposite relationship.

A large number of empirical studies have examined the impact of divorce, or experience of living in a single parent family, on investment in children, as for example indicated by their educational attainments. How can we interpret such an impact? In the model above, parents whose preferences favour more investment in children also have a different probability of divorce, because the efficiency loss caused by divorce is altered, partly because the mother's second period wage is lower. Thus, the probability of divorce is endogenous. But the impact of an actual divorce can still be given a meaningful causal interpretation. Take two sets of parents that are identical in every respect. Their preferences, wages, etc., generate the same endogenous child expenditure in the first period and probability of divorce in the second. But one couple divorces because of a "bad draw" on the stochastic component of marital utility (i.e. a low θ_2). That couple will have lower child expenditure in the second period than the couple that stays together. It will be $[(W_{h2} + W_{w2})T - (\alpha + \beta)][(\delta\gamma)^{\gamma}(1 - \gamma)^{1-\gamma}]W_{w2}^{-\gamma}/2$ if they stay married and one-half of that if they divorce. This is a legitimate causal effect of divorce. Estimating this effect may, however, be difficult, because different couples have different threshold values (θ^*) for the stochastic element that triggers divorce. Even a sibling-differences' approach, such as used by Ermisch and Francesconi (2001b) and discussed earlier in the chapter, may fail to identify the causal impact of divorce because the siblings have different fathers.

8.4 CHILD SUPPORT ORDERS AND THEIR ENFORCEMENT

Courts or government agencies often stipulate a minimum level of child support payments. Enforcement is not, however, likely to be perfectly effective. In the high quality administrative data used by Del Boca and Flinn (1995) and Flinn (2000), 38% of absent fathers pay exactly the child support order and 11% pay more than this amount. That leaves one-half who do not comply with the order; indeed, 37% of the fathers pay no child support.[5] In the model of Del Boca and Flinn (1995), fathers are assumed to have varying costs of non-compliance with the order. These can be thought of as a future penalty on the father if he does not comply with the child support order, such as a fine or a reduction in visiting time with the child. In other respects their model is similar to the non-cooperative one in the first section of the chapter. For fathers who would voluntarily pay more than the order, the order has no impact. But among fathers who would voluntarily pay less than the order, those whose costs of non-compliance are high relative to the difference between the amount of the order and what they would have paid anyway pay the ordered amount. Others for whom the ordered amount is very different from what they would have paid, or who have low costs of non-compliance, do not comply with the order and pay what they would have in the absence of a court order. Actual payments depend on parents' preference parameters, which contribute to the determination of what fathers voluntarily wish to pay, the relation between this and the child support order and the father's cost of non-compliance.

As demonstrated in the first section, divorced parents and their children could be better off if they could come to a cooperative agreement on resource allocation. There are, of course, a continuum of such efficient allocations, each involving different amounts of transfers from the father to the mother and entailing different levels of expenditure on children. In Flinn's (2000) analysis, the court can resolve this issue by, in effect, "suggesting" a given cooperative allocation indirectly through the child support order. It works as follows. The court announces the child support order, and if the cooperative allocation implied by that order gives each of the parents higher utility than they would obtain in a non-cooperative equilibrium (i.e. the one assumed in the first section), then they implement this cooperative equilibrium; if not, the non-cooperative equilibrium is observed. In either case, the outcome is unique and we know the cooperative equilibrium was chosen if the child support transfer is exactly equal to the court support order. While the order is exogenous, the child support payment is endogenous as long as some parents opt for the non-cooperative equilibrium.

This can be illustrated with the simple model of the first section, in which parents' incomes are exogenous and the utility functions when divorced are $U_h = Q(x_h - \beta)$ and $U_w = Q(x_w - \alpha)$ for the former husband and wife, respectively. It was shown there that the husband's and wife's utility in the non-cooperative equilibrium are $U_h^n = [y_h + y_w - (\alpha + \beta)]^2/8$ and

$U_w^n = [y_h + y_w - (\alpha + \beta)]^2/16$, respectively. Thus, the cooperative equilibrium would be chosen if and only if it provides utility for the respective parent that at least reaches these levels. If they are induced to cooperate by the child support order, then, as shown in (8.4), child expenditures would increase to $Q^c = [y_h + y_w - (\alpha + \beta)]/2$. Given these utility functions, the maximum child support transfer that he would pay in the cooperative equilibrium would be $s_{max} = y_h - \beta - U_h^n/Q^c$, and the minimum transfer that the wife would accept would be $s_{min} = U_w^n/Q^c - (y_w - \alpha - Q^c)$. Substituting for Q^c, U_h^n and U_w^n, these are

$$s_{max} = \frac{3(y_h - \beta) - (y_w - \alpha)}{4} \qquad (8.17a)$$

$$s_{min} = \frac{5(y_h - \beta) - 3(y_w - \alpha)}{8} \qquad (8.17b)$$

Let $y_h = 12$, $y_w = 6$, $\alpha = 4$ and $\beta = 6$. From the derivations in the first section, it is easy to calculate that transfers in the non-cooperative equilibrium are $s^d = 2$ and expenditures on children are $Q^d = 2$. This implies that father's and mother's utility in the non-cooperative equilibrium are 8 and 4, respectively. With cooperation, child expenditures would increase to $Q^c = 4$. It is readily computed that the maximum child support transfer that he would pay in the cooperative equilibrium would be 4. Similarly, the minimum child support transfer the mother would accept in the cooperative equilibrium is 3. Thus, if the court sets the father's transfer at $s^d = 3.5$, both parents would agree to cooperate, even though this is above the transfer he pays in the non-cooperative equilibrium. The efficiency gains from cooperation are sufficient for the father to agree to cooperate (his utility increases from 8 to 10). Suppose, however, that court orders set child support at 20% of the father's income, so that $s^d = 2.4$ is the court-ordered transfer. The mother would not agree to cooperate, despite the fact that the order exceeds what she receives in the non-cooperative equilibrium (because her utility would fall from 4 to 1.6), and the non-cooperative equilibrium would prevail, with the child support payment being 2. The efficiency gain from cooperation is not sufficient to compensate her for the reduction in control over resource allocation relative to the non-cooperative equilibrium. Similarly, if the court set the child support payment at 5, the father would not comply, and the non-cooperative equilibrium would be implemented.

It is clear from (8.17) that whether the child support award induces cooperative behaviour between divorced parents depends on their preferences (the parameters α and β in the particular utility functions assumed here) and the parents' respective income levels, because these determine the minimum and maximum of the range of orders that induce cooperation.

With the particular preferences assumed in this example, the width of the range of court orders in which cooperation is chosen is $[(y_h - \beta) + (y_w - \alpha)]/8$. This is clearly increasing in the parent's income levels and decreasing in the selfishness of their preferences (i.e. decreasing in β and α), because the efficiency gain from cooperation is larger when the demand for child quality is higher.

This model has implications for the impact of perfect enforcement of child support orders. If all of the divorced parents were in the non-cooperative equilibrium, perfect enforcement would either increase child support transfers and expenditure on children or have no effect on them (because the father already paid more than the ordered amount). If, however, some of them were induced by the child support order to implement the cooperative equilibrium when there was no enforcement, perfect enforcement would reduce expenditure on children among this group of parents. The reason is that perfect enforcement changes the order of s from being a suggested efficient outcome to the starting point of a non-cooperative game between the parents in which their income distribution shifts to $y_h - s$ for the father and $y_w + s$ for the mother. The result is a non-cooperative equilibrium, which produces lower expenditures on children than in a cooperative one. For instance, with the preferences assumed above, expenditures on children are given by (8.7) if the father pays more than the ordered amount and by (8.5) if he pays exactly the ordered amount. In either case, the amount of child expenditure is lower.[6] The reason for this is that with perfect enforcement the court becomes an agent for income redistribution rather than an arbitrator who leads some couples to an efficient allocation. By guaranteeing the mother's child support, she loses an incentive to spend at the cooperative level. Thus, in this model, perfect enforcement increases expenditures on children for some families and reduces them for others, with the net impact unclear.

Empirical analyses of divorced mother's labour supply have often expressed it as a function of child support transfers (e.g. Ermisch and Wright 1991). In terms of the model of Section 8.3, this is the conditional labour supply function

$$h_{w2} = T - \frac{\gamma(s^d + W_{w2}T - \alpha)}{2W_{w2}}$$

or

$$h_{w2} = T\frac{(2 - \gamma)}{2} - \gamma\frac{s^d}{2W_{w2}} + \frac{\alpha\gamma}{2W_{w2}} \tag{8.18}$$

Thus, such a specification has a clear theoretical interpretation. But the treatment of s^d as exogenous in such analyses would be questionable. For instance, suppose that the preference parameter α varies (randomly) among mothers. Then, because $s^d = [(W_{h2} - W_{w2})T + \alpha - \beta)]/2$, s^d is correlated with the random component of the labour supply equation, (8.18), which is $\alpha\gamma/2W_{w2}$. In particular, an estimator that treats s^d as not correlated with α would understate the size of the true impact of child support transfers from the former husband on the former wife's labour supply, $-\gamma/2W_{w2}$. This is because women with higher α both receive higher transfers from their former husband and have higher labour supply. They also have higher second period wages (which operate to reduce s^d) but this is a second-order effect.

As discussed above, court orders might mandate a certain minimum level of child support payments s_m^d. Provided that these are enforced, divorced fathers then face an additional constraint in their utility maximization problem, which is $s^d \geq s_m^d$. If the s^d chosen by a father exceeds s_m^d, then nothing in the analysis above changes; the court ordered constraint is not binding on such fathers. If, however, a father would have paid less than s_m^d, then $s^d = s_m^d$, and s^d is no longer correlated with the preference parameter α. In this case, treating s^d as exogenous would provide consistent estimates of γ. In practice, any sample of divorced fathers would be likely to contain a mix of these two types of fathers. Furthermore, the discussion above has shown that when there is not perfect enforcement and the court orders only "suggest" a cooperative equilibrium, the amount of child support actually paid is endogenous, as it depends on the preferences of fathers and mothers.

The existence of child support orders could not only affect the labour supply of divorced mothers and expenditure on their children, but also the probability of divorce. The next section considers when and how the law concerning divorce and property settlements affects the probability of divorce.

8.5 Divorce and the Law

In a pioneering paper, Peters (1986) contrasted the impact of divorce law in two models of marital contracting. The analysis (implicitly) assumes conditional transferable utility, so that there is a unique "value" (or "output") associated with each marriage (see Chapter 7). In the first model, each spouse has information about the other's opportunities outside marriage, and they are free to bargain. In this case, the law has no effect on the divorce rate, because bargaining can redistribute the gains to marriage in a way that insures that divorce only occurs when the value of the marriage is less than the sum of the values of the spouses' outside opportunities (an efficient outcome). Divorce settlements would, however, vary with the law to achieve efficiency. In the second model, neither partner knows the other's outside opportunities. Each has an incentive to misrepresent them, and one possible response to this is to contract for a fixed division of the value of the marriage. This can produce inefficient divorces, and the probability of divorce is higher when the law allows unilateral divorce rather than requiring mutual consent. If we do not restrict ourselves to preferences satisfying conditional transferable utility, then even when all outcomes are efficient, the divorce law and the law concerning property division inside and outside marriage can have impacts on the probability of divorce. We now consider the conditions under which this happens.

For a given couple, there are *utility possibility sets* associated with marriage and divorce. Denote these as M and D, respectively. These are defined by the combined resources of the couple, and they give the feasible levels of utility that can be achieved in each state. Their boundaries are the respective utility possibility frontiers in each state, which we denote as B^M and B^D, respectively. An example of these was given in Figure 8.1 for a particular realization of the match variable $\theta = \theta^m$, and the utility possibility frontier for marriage in the model of the first section above (B^M) satisfies $U_h + U_w = 2\theta + [y_h + y_w - (\alpha + \beta)]^2/4$, while B^D satisfies $U_h + U_w = 3[y_h + y_w - (\alpha + \beta)]^2/16$.

Divorce law confers certain rights concerning marital dissolution. These dissolution rights define, for each spouse, an outside option. For a law that allows unilateral divorce, the outside option is divorce. Either spouse can, without consent of the other, force a dissolution of the marriage. With a law requiring mutual consent for divorce, the outside option is marriage. Either party can refuse to divorce, and without consent of the other, force the marriage to continue. Following Clark (1999), we assume that exercising the option is irrevocable and that the outcome is efficient in the sense that neither party can be made better off without making the other worse off (i.e. no Pareto improvement is left unexploited).

If the outside option is exercised, then the couple will reach an efficient agreement on the allocation of resources, giving a utility pair (U_h, U_w) denoted by m^* if marriage is the outside option and d^* if it is divorce. Marital property law affects where m^* lies on the utility possibility frontier, and divorce settlement (alimony) law affects where d^* lies on its utility possibility frontier. If the divorce law requires mutual consent, there is no reason for the wife (husband) to agree to divorce unless she (he) gets at least $U_w^{m^*}$ ($U_h^{m^*}$). Thus, divorce will not occur if $m^* \notin D$ ($\in$ means "an element of" and $\notin$ means "not an element of"). If, however, $m^* \in D$, then divorce offers the opportunity for at least one party to be better off if divorced. Transfers between spouses can be used to induce both spouses to consent to a divorce. Under a law requiring *mutual consent*, divorce occurs if and only if $m^* \in D$.

Under a divorce law allowing unilateral divorce, the utility pair associated with d^* provides the minima that the wife and husband would accept. If, therefore, $d^* \notin M$, then the marriage cannot be saved. If $d^* \in M$, then there will exist a range of marital allocations that make both spouses better off in marriage compared to d^*. Under a *unilateral* law, divorce occurs if and only if $d^* \notin M$.

In general, $m^* \in D$ and $d^* \notin M$ are not equivalent, and neither necessarily implies the other. It is only in the case in which set M is entirely contained within set D, or D is entirely contained within M that the law does not matter. For instance, the utility possibility frontiers in Figure 8.2 imply that the marriage continues whatever the divorce law, because $m^* \notin D$ and $d^* \in M$, and Figure 8.3 implies that divorce occurs whatever the divorce law, because $m^* \in D$ and $d^* \notin M$. With the utility possibility frontiers in Figure 8.4, $m^* \notin D$ and $d^* \notin M$. Thus, divorce would occur under a unilateral divorce law, but not with a divorce law requiring mutual consent. In contrast, in Figure 8.5, $m^* \in D$ and $d^* \in M$. In this case, divorce would occur if the law required mutual consent, but not if there was a unilateral divorce law. In these latter two cases, a change in the law would affect whether a couple divorces or not.

This analysis indicates that divorce law matters for the outcome of the marriage when the utility possibility frontiers intersect. In Figures 8.2 and 8.3, the divorce law does not matter. Only the relative magnitudes of the

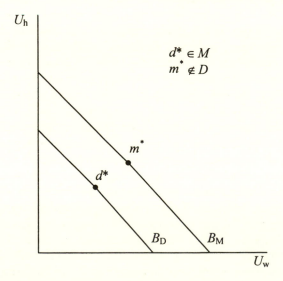

Figure 8.2 Marriage continues irrespective of the divorce law.

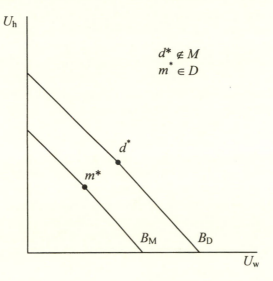

Figure 8.3 Divorce occurs irrespective of the divorce law.

spouses' gains and losses from divorce matter for the outcome. In Figure 8.2, the marriage frontier lies outside the divorce frontier. Even if, for example, the husband would gain from divorce, his wife would be able to compensate him for staying in the marriage by some change in the way the marriage is conducted. Thus, even if there were unilateral divorce, he

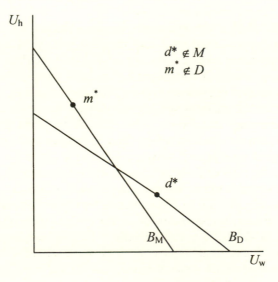

Figure 8.4 Divorce occurs under unilateral divorce law only.

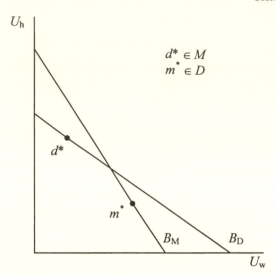

Figure 8.5 Divorce occurs under mutual consent divorce law only.

would not seek a divorce. In effect, he sells his right to divorce under a unilateral divorce law. In Figure 8.3, in which the marriage frontier lies within the divorce frontier, a husband who gains from divorce is able to compensate a wife who loses from divorce by a suitable divorce settlement so that she would also be better off from divorce. Thus, even under a mutual consent law, they would divorce. In effect, she sells her right to the marriage under a mutual consent law.

This result, when utility possibility frontiers do not intersect, can be viewed as an application of the Coase theorem, which asserts that, in the absence of significant transaction costs or asymmetry in information, the allocation of resources is unaffected by property rights. The analysis in Section 8.1 assumed transferable utility. We have seen in Chapter 3 that this implies that the utility possibility frontier is linear with a slope of -1 in both the marriage and divorce states. Clearly then, the utility possibility frontiers cannot intersect when there is transferable utility, and so divorce law does not matter in this case. It is in the interest of both parties to maximize the sum of their utilities, and the divorce rule is simply to divorce if this sum is higher after divorce than in marriage.

More generally, divorce law does matter for divorce decisions, and the outcome is efficient. In the discussion of the optimal marriage contract in Section 8.2, we defined a match variable θ that shifted the utility possibility frontier in marriage. In our analysis, we assumed it took on only two values, one of which was sufficiently low for the marriage frontier to be contained within the divorce frontier for relevant values of U_w, and the other put it beyond the divorce frontier (as in Figure 8.1). More generally, the marriage frontier could have intersected the divorce frontier for other values of θ.

Furthermore, because laws on marital property and divorce settlements affect m^* and d^*, such laws also affect divorce decisions. For example, with a unilateral divorce law, divorce does not occur in Figure 8.5, but if the law governing divorce settlements changed so that d^* moved to the right of the intersection point (so that $d^* \notin M$), then the couple would divorce under either type of divorce law.

In their analysis of the probability of divorce and divorce settlements, Weiss and Willis (1993, 1997) group states into four legal regimes. These rank states according to the degree of emphasis given to fault as a ground for divorce and as a determinant of property division.[7] They find that among couples with children, the legal regime has no effect on the probability of divorce, but divorce settlements are much larger in a state in which it is possible to choose fault or no fault grounds for divorce. This could reflect an attempt by fathers to buy their way out of marriage more quickly by admitting fault. Among childless couples, the less attention is given to fault consideration the higher the probability of divorce, and the husbands pay higher settlements to their ex-wives. Weiss and Willis (1993, p. 656) suggest that the latter relationship may be because some of the no-fault laws broaden the scope of marital property. This is consistent with the importance of the laws governing property division for divorce decisions, mentioned in the previous paragraph.

Friedberg (1998) uses longitudinal data on divorce rates for each state of the United States over the period 1968–1988 to study the impact of divorce laws. She finds that the US divorce rate would have been 6% lower in 1988 if no type of unilateral divorce had been adopted in the states that switched. The type of unilateral divorce rate adopted by the state also mattered. The unilateral law with least strings—without separation requirements or fault considerations in property division— raised the divorce rate the most. But other unilateral laws also tended to increase divorce, the next largest impact being the one without separation requirements but with fault property division. This is strong evidence supporting the importance of the law in affecting the probability of divorce, which is consistent with the marriage and divorce utility possibility frontiers intersecting.

NOTES

1. An alternative way to model the non-cooperative behaviour of the former spouses is to assume that it is the outcome of a "Cournot game", such as in the

voluntary contributions equilibrium in Chapter 2. This would be more appropriate if the parents can transfer directly to their children, such as education expenses and various child-specific expenses. In fact Del Boca and Flinn (1994) use this model to frame their empirical analysis of divorced mothers' expenditure.

2. For example, the father may develop an alcohol addiction, giving rise to a situation in which an elder sibling spends only a small part of his childhood with an alcoholic father while the youngest has one for most of his(her) childhood. The father's alcohol problem may directly affect investment in the youngest child, and his(her) parents may also divorce because of it, thereby causing correlation between individual 'endowments' and family structure.

3. With the particular utility functions assumed here, the ex post transfer is $s^d = (\phi y_h - \gamma y_w)/(\phi + \gamma)$ and $Q^d = \phi^2(y_h + y_w)/(\phi + \gamma)^2$.

4. In the theoretical model above, spouses' incomes were assumed to be constant during marriage, and the only change was in the stochastic component of utility, θ.

5. The data are a sample of divorce cases in Wisconsin over the period 1980–1982.

6. In the latter case, the difference between child expenditure in the cooperative equilibrium and that in the perfect enforcement non-cooperative one is $(y_h - \beta - s)/2$, where s is the ordered amount. Note that $y_h - \beta - s > 0$, because according to (8.17a) the cooperative equilibrium would not have been implemented if this were not true.

7. State laws specify three types of grounds for divorce: (1) fault; (2) no fault; and (3) choice of fault or no fault, where no fault applies after a specified period of separation ranging from 6 months to 3 years. The property division rules are classified into four categories: (1) equal division (2) equitable division with fault considerations ruled out; (3) equitable division with fault one of the considerations; and (4) division based on which spouse holds title to the property.

Non-Altruistic Family Transfers

IN CHAPTER 3, it was shown that transfers motivated by altruism between living persons, or "gifts" for short, can be more efficient than bequests in a number of situations. Furthermore, more than half of the value of private transfers in the United States are such inter vivos transfers (Kotlikoff and Summers 1981; Cox and Raines 1985). This chapter focuses on inter vivos transfers that are not motivated by altruism, even though the donor may have altruistic preferences. Section 9.1 considers self-interested transfers in an extended family transfer system in which fertility and transfers are determined in the context of a set of family rules of conduct. Section 9.2 explores transfers from parents in exchange for "services" from children that cannot be purchased in a market, and Section 9.3 examines family loans from parents, who have access to a capital market, to children who cannot borrow on the market. Section 9.4 considers the interaction between transfers from parents to their children and the unobservable labour market effort of children.

9.1 THE FAMILY AS A SUBSTITUTE FOR THE CAPITAL MARKET

How much of family transfer behaviour can we explain by pure self-interest? To address this question, we consider a model in which people only have children because they are needed to transfer resources through time. Assume that each person lives for three periods of equal duration—youth, middle-age and old-age—and that their welfare depends on their own consumption only. Denote c_i^t as consumption in the ith period of a person born at date t, and the utility of that person is given by $U^t = U(c_1^t, c_2^t, c_3^t)$. Suppose that the person only earns income y^t in the second period. Because of diminishing marginal utility of consumption in any given period, the person's utility would be higher if he(she) can transfer resources from the second to the first and third periods. In the usual model of consumer theory, this is accomplished by borrowing and lending in the capital market. But suppose there is no such market, or that the person does not have access to it, say because of difficulties in monitoring loans or very large transaction costs. An extended family network including three generations at different stages of life could substitute for a capital market by arranging loans to its young members from its middle-aged ones and enforcing repayment one period later when the young borrowers in the previous period have become middle-aged and the middle-aged lenders in the previous period have become old. How might such an intra-family transfer system work?

As Cigno (1991) argues, the family may set rules of conduct such that no member would be better off outside the family transfer system than within it. Childbearing is assumed to occur in the "middle-age" period of our model. Denote by n^t the ratio of the number of family members born at $t + 1$ to the number born at t; that is, n^t is the family size per head of generation t. Letting d^t be the amount transferred to the older generation during the middle-age of generation t, the budget constraints for generation t in their middle-age and old-age are

$$c_2^t + d^t + c_1^{t+1}n^t = y^t \tag{9.1}$$

$$c_3^t = d^{t+1}n^t \tag{9.2}$$

The first constraint indicates that the middle-aged spend their income on their own consumption, transfers to their parents and transfers to their children. Thus, consumption in one's first period of life, for a person born in generation t, must come out of the income of someone from generation $t - 1$, while the second constraint indicates that consumption in old-age must come from the income of someone from generation $t + 1$. Having a larger family would tend to increase the transfers that must be made to children when the person is middle-aged, but it also tends to increase the transfers received in old-age. There will also be a physiological constraint on fertility; that is

$$0 \le n^t \le m \tag{9.3}$$

The family rules would prescribe d^t and c_1^t for each generation. It is useful to define

$$\rho^t = \frac{d^t}{c_1^t} \tag{9.4}$$

The value of ρ^t is the ratio of transfers received in old age to expenditures on children for generation $t - 1$; thus, the rate of return to having a child for a member of generation $t - 1$ is $\rho^t - 1$, which can also be viewed as the implicit rate of interest on intra-family loans. Using (9.2) and (9.4), we can rewrite (9.1) as

$$c_1^t + \frac{c_2^t}{\rho^t} + \frac{c_3^t}{\rho^t \rho^{t+1}} = \frac{y^t}{\rho^t} \tag{9.5}$$

This is equivalent to a lifetime budget constraint of a consumer who has access to a capital market in which the interest rate is $\rho^t - 1$ in the first period of life and $\rho^{t+1} - 1$ in the second period. If this were the case, utility maximization would imply that he(she) would borrow to finance consumption in the first period to the point at which

$$\frac{U_1^t}{U_2^t} = \rho^t \tag{9.6}$$

where $U_1^t = \partial U/\partial c_1^t$, etc. and he(she) would lend in the second period so that

$$\frac{U_2^t}{U_3^t} = \rho^{t+1} \tag{9.7}$$

Equations (9.4), (9.6) and (9.7) imply

$$\frac{U_1^t}{U_2^t} = \frac{U_2^{t-1}}{U_3^{t-1}} = \frac{d^t}{c_1^t} \tag{9.8}$$

We can now describe how the "family rules" must be set. For ease of exposition, consider a set of rules for a steady state in which $y^t = y$ for all t. If the family rules prescribe to generation t, the transfer levels to children and parents of $\underline{c_1}$ and $\underline{d}$, respectively, each member of that generation would then maximize utility by choosing $c_2^t = \underline{c_2}$ and $c_3^t = \underline{c_3}$ to satisfy (9.8) and the constraints (9.1)–(9.3), and therefore, $n^t = \underline{c_3}/\underline{d} = \underline{n}$. Furthermore, if a member of generation t had been able to decide how much to borrow as a child at the implied rate of interest $\underline{d}/\underline{c_1} - 1$, he(she) would have chosen $c_1^t = \underline{c_1}$. Members of generation t would rather not pay $\underline{d}$ to their parents (generation $t - 1$), but since everyone needs the family transfer rules to survive in old-age, the prospect of receiving no support from the family in old-age deters any member from disobeying the rules.

In order to illustrate the family rules and the constraints on them, assume that the inter-temporal utility function takes the Cobb–Douglas form; that is, $U(c_1^t, c_2^t, c_3^t) = \alpha_1 \ln(c_1) + \alpha_2 \ln(c_2) + \alpha_3 \ln(c_3)$, with $\sum \alpha_j = 1$. If the physiological constraint (9.3) is not binding, then the steady-state solution is

$$\underline{c_1} = \frac{\alpha_1 y}{\rho} \tag{9.9a}$$

where $\rho = \underline{d}/\underline{c_1}$,

$$\underline{c_2} = \alpha_2 y \tag{9.9b}$$

$$\underline{c_3} = \rho \alpha_3 y \tag{9.9c}$$

$$\underline{d} = \alpha_1 y \qquad\qquad (9.9\text{d})$$

$$\underline{n} = \frac{\alpha_3 \rho}{\alpha_1} \qquad\qquad (9.9\text{e})$$

In this example, the family rules take a simple form: transfer a fixed proportion (α_1) of income when middle-aged to one's elderly parents, and transfers to children are the present value of transfers to the old using the intra-family interest rate to calculate present value (i.e. $\underline{c_1} = \underline{d}/\rho$). Note that the fertility rate $\underline{n}$ increases with the intra-family interest rate implied by the family rules. Larger transfers to the elderly relative to transfers to children increase the fertility required to sustain the family system.

Once established, these rules would persist over generations until there is a change of circumstances outside the family. Each generation would, of course, prefer that transfers to it when a child ($\underline{c_1}$) be as large as possible and that its transfers to aged parents when middle-aged ($\underline{d}$) be as small as possible. But as everyone passes from youth to old-age, no generation would agree to a change in the rules that would reduce its own consumption in old-age. The implicit intra-family interest rate at which a generation "lends" in middle-age to finance its own consumption in old-age is the same at which the next generation "borrows" from the middle-aged. The conditions in (9.8) are indeed the first-order conditions for a Pareto-optimum constrained by (9.1)–(9.3). It is not possible to devise a different set of family rules that makes any generation better off without making another generation worse off.

Now suppose that the family has access to a capital market, but that nobody outside the family would lend to a child. The middle-aged now have a choice between providing for their old-age by lending in the capital market or by staying within the family system and "lending" to their children, awaiting transfers from them in old-age. The intra-family rate of interest must, therefore, be at least as large as the market interest rate, but we now show that it must indeed be larger.

By the time that they reach middle-age, any generation t has already consumed $\underline{c_1}$. If they made the transfer $\underline{d}$ to their parents dictated by the family rules, their budget constraint would be

$$c_2^t + \frac{c_3^t}{\rho} = y - \underline{d} \qquad\qquad (9.10)$$

where $\rho = \underline{d}/\underline{c_1}$. If, however, they did not pay anything to their parents and lent to the market at the interest rate $r - 1$, their budget constraint would be

$$c_2^t + \frac{c_3^t}{r} = y \qquad\qquad (9.11)$$

If $\rho = r$, then generation t would clearly be better off by lending to the market than remaining in the family system. A threat of no support from the family in old-age is no longer a deterrent, because they can make their own provision for old-age through the market. The middle-aged people of generation t would default on their obligation to their parents under the family rules. To avoid this, the implicit rate of interest in the family system $(\rho - 1)$ must be set high enough to make a middle-aged member at least as well off as they would be from lending on the market.

The determination of this minimum ρ is illustrated in Figure 9.1. It is the value of ρ that places the middle-aged person on the same indifference curve that would be achieved by lending on the market at interest rate $r - 1$. In particular, it is the absolute value of the slope of the line with intercept on the c_2 axis of $y - \underline{d}$ that is tangent to the same indifference curve as the line with absolute slope r and intercept y. The family interest rate is, therefore, always higher than the market one.

Put differently, ρ must satisfy

$$V(\underline{c}_1, y, r) \leq V(\underline{c}_1, y - \underline{d}, \rho) \tag{9.12}$$

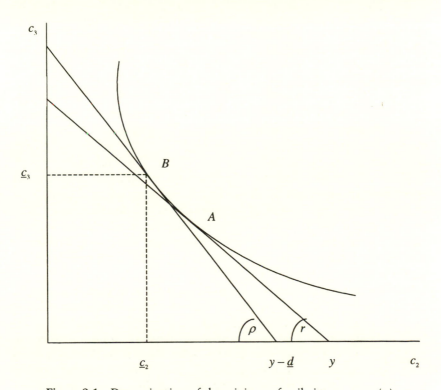

Figure 9.1 Determination of the minimum family interest rate (ρ).

where $V(\ )$ is the indirect utility function resulting from maximizing utility with respect to either (9.11) or (9.10), respectively. If the family rules set ρ large enough, constraint (9.12) may not be binding (with equality). But it is also possible that constraint (9.12) is not consistent with the biological constraint (9.3). It was noted earlier in the context of our example, (9.9e), that the equilibrium fertility rate increases with ρ. Thus, it may not be possible to find an intra-family interest rate $\rho - 1$ high enough to satisfy (9.12) because the fertility rate (n^t) required to do so would be too high to satisfy (9.3).

Returning to our example, if the physiological constraint (9.3) is not binding and the family rules stipulate that the intra-family interest rate should be as low as possible (i.e. (9.12) holds with equality), then the steady-state solution is

$$\rho = \frac{r}{\beta} \tag{9.13}$$

where $\ln(\beta) = (\alpha_2 + \alpha_3)\ln(\alpha_2 + \alpha_3)/\alpha_3$, implying $0 < \beta < 1$.

As we would expect from the earlier discussion, the intra-family interest rate increases with the market rate. Also, as the market, and therefore, family interest rate, increases, transfers to children for their consumption fall ((9.9a)) while consumption in old-age rises ((9.9c)). These results are independent of the particular utility function assumed, and reflect an inter-temporal substitution effect as interest rates rise, favouring consumption later in life.

In the particular example, fertility increases with the interest rate according to (9.9e). While this need not be the case for all preferences, it does illustrate the constraints on the family system of transfers. For a market interest rate large enough, $r\alpha_3/\alpha_1\beta$ would exceed the maximum family size m, and the family system would break down because the intra-family interest rate could not compete with market rate. That is, the current middle-aged could achieve higher consumption in their old-age by lending at the market rate of interest than having m children per head and adhering to the family transfer rules. Whether this indeed can happen clearly depends on preferences, with it being more likely when consumption during childhood receives less weight in people's preferences (i.e. $\alpha_3/\alpha_1\beta$ is larger).

The opening of a capital market offering a sufficiently high interest rate, or an unexpected rise in the interest rate to such a level in an existing market, toll the death knell for the family system of transfers. Childbearing would also cease in this model of selfish persons. In broad terms, the prediction of this model is consistent with the observation that the growth of the financial sector (or introduction of a state pension system) tends to coincide with a sharp fall in fertility and a decline in private transfers from the middle-aged to their elderly parents. As Cigno (1991) notes, the fact that fertility does not fall to zero, even for couples who make no contribution to the consumption of their own parents (and expect their children to do the same), suggests that the demand for children is not entirely derived from the need for transfers from them to finance consumption in old-age. At least for some couples, children enter the utility function of their parents in some form, as assumed in Chapter 6.

Cigno and Rosati (1992) provide evidence for Italy (1931–1987) that higher market interest rates and better access to capital markets reduce fertility, which is consistent with this non-altruistic model, but not with altruistic behaviour. They conclude that the availability and attractiveness of market or state-provided alternatives to the family as a provider of old-age support significantly affect saving and reproductive decisions in a manner consistent with the model outlined above.

9.2 TRANSFERS IN EXCHANGE FOR SERVICES

Adult children can provide "services" to their parents that do not have clear market substitutes, such as companionship, attention and conforming their behaviour to their parents' wishes. An increase in such services tends to reduce a selfish child's well-being because it undermines his or her independence and may use scarce non-working time. Here we follow Cox (1987) and develop a model in which inter vivos transfers may have an exchange motive—financial transfers from parents in exchange for services from children. A static framework suffices for studying when such transfers arise and the observable implications of transfers motivated by exchange.

The parents are assumed to have consensus preferences. Let x_p be the parents' consumption, x_c be the child's consumption, and S is "services" provided by the child to the parents ($S \geq 0$). The parents' "private" utility index is given by $U^p(x_p, S)$, where $\partial U^p/\partial S = U_S^p > 0$, and the child's welfare is represented by the utility function $U^c(x_c, S)$, where $\partial U^c/\partial S = U_S^c < 0$. The parents may have altruistic (caring) "social" preferences, which are represented by $W = W[U^p, U^c]$. Of course, the child and parent must both be willing to participate in this transfer-service arrangement, and this gives rise to another two constraints: $U^c(x_c, S) \geq U^c(y_c, 0)$ and $W[U^p(x_p, S), U^c(x_c, S)] \geq W[U^p(y_p, 0), U^c(y_c, 0)]$, where y_p and y_c are parents' and child's income, respectively. These "participation constraints" say that the parents' and child's utility in the transfer-service arrangement must be at least as high as that outside it.

As explained in Chapter 3, the weak separability in the parents social preferences $W[U^p, U^c]$ implies that the socially efficient allocation will be found amongst those that are efficient in terms of private preferences; that is, amongst the allocations that maximize $U^p(x_p, S)$ for each $U^c(x_c, S)$ subject to $y_p + y_c = x_p + x_c$ and the participation constraints. Following the approach used in Chapter 2, we can characterize the efficient outcome in general terms by maximizing $U^p(x_p, S) + \mu U^c(x_c, S)$ subject to $y_p + y_c = x_p + x_c$, where μ is a Lagrange multiplier that reflects a weighting of child's utility relative to parents, which may be an outcome of bargaining and/or altruism of parents. In general, μ is a function of individual incomes and the utility function parameters; it determines where on the utility possibility frontier the efficient allocation is located. The solution to this problem gives rise to the conditions for the efficient choices for consumption (x_p and x_c) and of child services (S):

$$U_x^p = \mu U_x^c \tag{9.14a}$$

$$U_S^p = -\mu U_S^c \tag{9.14b}$$

Cooperation between the parents and the child involves transfers to satisfy the first of these conditions, which equates the marginal utility of the parents' consumption with the product of the marginal utility of their child's consumption and the weight given to child's utility. Presuming that the parents are sufficiently richer than their child, parents make financial transfers T to satisfy (9.14a). The second condition indicates that the parents' marginal utility of services is equated to the weighted marginal disutility of services to the child. Combining these two equations,

$$\frac{U_S^p}{U_x^p} = -\frac{U_S^c}{U_x^c} \tag{9.15}$$

That is, at the efficient choice of S, the parents' marginal rate of substitution between child services and consumption equals their child's.

Assuming, for simplicity, additive separability of the parents' private utility index (i.e. $U_{Sx}^p = 0$), the conventional comparative static exercise applied to (9.14a) and (9.14b) yields

$$\frac{\partial T}{\partial y_c} =$$

$$\frac{-(\mu U_{xx}^c)(\mu U_{SS}^c + U_{SS}^p) + (\mu U_{xS}^c)^2 + [\mu U_{xS}^c U_S^c - (\mu U_{SS}^c + U_{SS}^p)U_x^c](\partial \mu / \partial y_c)}{D} \tag{9.16}$$

where $U_{SS}^j = \partial^2 U^j / \partial S^2$, $U_{xS}^j = \partial^2 U^j / \partial x_j \partial S$, etc., $D = (\mu U_{SS}^c + U_{SS}^p)$ $(\mu U_{xx}^c + U_{xx}^p) - (\mu U_{xS}^c)^2 > 0$, $(\mu U_{SS}^c + U_{SS}^p) < 0$ and $(\mu U_{xx}^c + U_{xx}^p) < 0$ from the second-order conditions for a maximum. Also,

$$\frac{\partial T}{\partial y_p} = \frac{(U_{xx}^p)(\mu U_{SS}^c + U_{SS}^p) + [\mu U_{xS}^c U_S^c - (\mu U_{SS}^c + U_{SS}^p)U_x^c](\partial \mu / \partial y_p)}{D}$$

$$(9.17)$$

$$\frac{\partial S}{\partial y_c} = \frac{-(\mu U_{xS}^c)(U_{xx}^p) + [\mu U_{xS}^c U_x^c - (\mu U_{xx}^c + U_{xx}^p)U_S^c](\partial \mu / \partial y_c)}{D} \quad (9.18)$$

$$\frac{\partial S}{\partial y_p} = \frac{-(\mu U_{xS}^c)(U_{xx}^p) + [\mu U_{xS}^c U_x^c - (\mu U_{xx}^c + U_{xx}^p)U_S^c](\partial \mu / \partial y_p)}{D} \quad (9.19)$$

The terms in (9.16)–(9.19) involving $(\partial \mu / \partial y_p)$ and $(\partial \mu / \partial y_c)$ can be interpreted as reflecting bargaining behaviour in the family, and so we expect that $(\partial \mu / \partial y_p) \leq 0$ and $(\partial \mu / \partial y_c) \geq 0$, because a person's bargaining power is likely to increase with their share of income. For instance, if Nash bargaining (see Chapter 2) were the relevant bargaining solution, then the threat points in the Nash bargain would be the values of parents' and child's utilities if the participation constraints were binding (with equality), and these increase with the individual incomes of parents' and child, respectively.

If, for example, the child's preferences are also additively separable ($U_{xS}^c = 0$), then, according to (9.16), an increase in the child's income has two clear, but opposing, effects on transfers from parents. It tends to reduce them because, when the child's income increases, the consumption of the parents must increase to equate the marginal utilities of consumption of parents' and children (condition (9.14a)). But a higher child's income tends to increase his(her) bargaining power, which shifts the distribution of utilities and income in his(her) favour, thereby tending to increase transfers from parents. Similarly, according to (9.17), an increase in the parents' income tends to increase transfers because of the equal weighted marginal utility condition (9.14a), but more bargaining power for the parents works in the opposite direction. With $U_{xS}^c = 0$, (9.18) and (9.19) indicate that there are only bargaining effects of individual income changes on child services: a higher child's (parents') income reduces (increases) child services.

Thus, in the general cooperative framework, a higher child's income could either reduce or increase transfers from parents depending on the size of the bargaining effect relative to the first effect mentioned above. There is not in fact a sharp distinction between altruism and exchange motives for transfers in this general cooperative framework. The child's utility if he(she) does not participate in the arrangement is always influencing outcomes. It should, therefore, not be surprising that the parents' altruistic preferences are not sufficient to produce the clear predictions of the effects of parents' and the child's individual incomes on transfers that are associated with Becker's (1981) analysis of altruism (discussed in

Chapter 3). To obtain them for general preferences, we need to assume that the parents' dominate the bargaining arrangement; that is, they choose transfers and child services to maximize *their* utility. This is also what was assumed by Becker (1981).

As shown in Section 3.1, this specialization of the problem is equivalent to treating μ above as independent of either the parents' or the child's individual income $(\partial\mu/\partial y_j = 0,\ j = \mathrm{p,c})$. Indeed $\mu = W_c/W_p$, where $W_j = \partial W/\partial U^j$. From (9.16)–(9.19), it is clear that the important predictions usually associated with altruism emerge. First, $\partial S/\partial y_c - \partial S/\partial y_p = 0$; that is, child services only depend on joint family income $(y_c + y_p)$, and so income redistribution between parents and child has no effect on S. The individual consumption of parents and child $(x_p$ and $x_c)$ also depend on joint family income only. Second, a redistribution of family income from the parents to the child brings an equal reduction in transfers from parents $(\partial T/\partial y_c - \partial T/\partial y_p = -1)$. Third, given additive separability, an increase in the child's income given parents' income, must reduce transfers from parents $(\partial T/\partial y_c < 0)$, because both the parents' and child's consumption must benefit from the increase in family income that arises from higher child's income, and the only way that parents can increase their consumption in this situation is to reduce transfers.

A sharper distinction between exchange and altruistic motives for transfers can be obtained by following Cox (1987) in modeling both possible motives for transfers in a single framework, with parents' dominating the bargaining arrangement. As in Chapter 3, the outcome can be described in relation to the utility possibility frontier expressed in terms of the "private" utilities U^p and U^c, as illustrated in Figure 9.2.

Each point on the frontier satisfies condition (9.15) and the frontier's position depends on $y_p + y_c$ and the "private" utility function parameters. The child's participation constraint is given by the horizontal line at U_0^c, where $U_0^c = U^c(y_c, 0)$ The feasible allocations lie along the utility possibility frontier above this horizontal line. The parents' "social" preferences $W(U^p, U^c)$ are best achieved at the tangency of the highest indifference curve $W(U^p, U^c) = $ constant and the utility possibility frontier, provided the tangency is above the participation constraint, as illustrated in Figure 9.2. At such a tangency point, (9.14a) and (9.14b) are satisfied with $\mu = W_c/W_p$. In this case, transfers are determined by altruistic motives.

If, however, the parents' social preferences are not "sufficiently altruistic" in the sense that the tangency point would occur below the horizontal line given by the participation constraint, then the best possible outcome occurs at the intersection of the participation constraint and the utility possibility frontier. In this case, transfers are governed by exchange motives. That is, parents must compensate their child by sufficient transfers so that he(she) achieves the level of utility that would be achieved

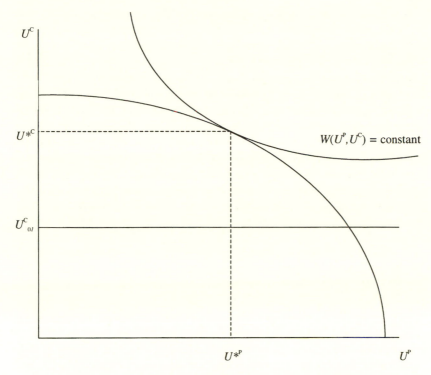

Figure 9.2 Transfers determined by altruistic motives.

outside the transfer-service arrangement. We now consider the comparative static results in this situation.

Letting λ be the Lagrange multiplier associated with the child's participation constraint, the first-order conditions when it is binding are

$$W_p U_x^p = (W_c + \lambda) U_x^c \tag{9.20a}$$

where $\lambda > 0$

$$W_p U_S^p = -(W_c + \lambda) U_S^c \tag{9.20b}$$

These two conditions imply the efficiency condition (9.15). It is plausible to interpret the price of child services as $p = -(U_S^c/U_x^c)$, because if child services could be purchased on the market at price p, then parents would equate (U_S^p/U_x^p) to p, as in condition (9.15).

In contrast to the case in which the child' participation constraint is not binding, conditions (9.20a) and (9.20b) indicate that transfers no longer equate the marginal utilities of the parents and the child viewed from the parents' perspective; that is, $W_p U_x^p > W_c U_x^c$ and $W_p U_S^p > -W_c U_S^c$. Let $\theta = (W_c + \lambda)/W_p$. Then

$$\frac{\partial T}{\partial y_c} = \frac{\theta U_{xx}^c (U_S^c)^2 - U_S^c U_x^c U_{xS}^c + [\theta U_{xS}^c U_S^c - (\theta U_{SS}^c + U_{SS}^p) U_x^c](U_{x0}^c - U_x^c)}{H}$$

(9.21)

where U_{x0}^c is the child's marginal utility of consumption evaluated at the participation constraint (i.e. when $U^c = U^c(y_c, 0)$) and $H > 0$ by the second-order conditions for a constrained maximum.[1] Because of diminishing marginal utility, the marginal utility of consumption when transfers are received is less than when they are not (i.e. $U_{x0}^c > U_x^c$), and also $U_{SS}^j < 0$, $U_{xx}^j < 0$, $j = \text{p, c}$. Thus, from (9.21), there is the possibility that higher child income increases transfers from parents. The first two terms, which are negative if $U_{xS}^c \leq 0$, reflect the fact that a higher child's income increases joint income, which increases the parents' consumption. Also,

$$\frac{\partial T}{\partial y_p} = -\frac{(U_{xx}^p)(U_S^c)^2}{H}$$

(9.22)

$$\frac{\partial S}{\partial y_c} = \frac{-\theta U_x^c U_S^c U_{xx}^c + U_{xS}^c (U_x^c)^2 + [\theta U_{xS}^c U_x^c - (\theta U_{xx}^c + U_{xx}^p) U_S^c](U_{x0}^c - U_x^c)}{H}$$

(9.23)

$$\frac{\partial S}{\partial y_p} = \frac{U_{xx}^p U_S^c U_x^c}{H}$$

(9.24)

These conditions indicate that higher parents' income always increases transfers to their child and services from the child ((9.22) and (9.24)). Equation (9.23) indicates that, in the case in which the child's preferences are additively separable ($U_{xS}^c = 0$), a higher child's income unambiguously reduces child services.

Note that, with θ replacing μ, the quantities in the numerator multiplying $U_{x0}^c - U_x^c$ in (9.21) and (9.23) are the same as those multiplying $\partial \mu / \partial y_c$ in (9.16) and (9.18), respectively. This is to be expected because this restricted model is a special case of the general cooperative framework in which the allocations depend on bargaining power. Thus, part of the impact of the child's income when there is a binding participation constraint is interpretable as a bargaining effect. While the parents have all of the bargaining power in this restricted model, the child may be able to extract more transfers from the parents when his(her) income increases because the utility that he(she) requires to participate in the transfer arrangement increases with his(her) income. Indeed, with the parents having all the bargaining power, he(she) always receives his(her) utility at the "threat point" associated with the participation constraint.

The comparative static results when the child's participation constraint is binding can be illustrated in Figure 9.3. For given joint income, a higher

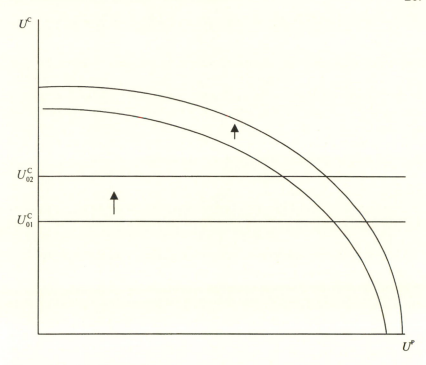

Figure 9.3 Binding participation constraint: impact of higher child's income.

child's income shifts the participation constraint in Figure 9.3 upwards. The parents must compensate the child by more in order to achieve the same level of child services. Thus, transfers *increase* with the child's share of joint income. For given parents' income, a higher child's income shifts the utility possibility frontier outward and the participation constraint upwards. Transfers from the parents could increase or decrease, as (9.21) indicates.[2] Finally, higher parents' income shifts the utility possibility frontier outwards, thereby increasing transfers and child services.

It is possible to give a more explicit exchange interpretation to these results by expressing transfers as the product of the price of child services and their quantity; that is, $T = pS$, and so $S(\partial p/\partial y_j) = \partial T/\partial y_j - p\partial S/\partial y_j$, $j = p, c$. Using the expressions in (9.21)–(9.24) and the definition $p = -(U_S^c/U_x^c)$, and assuming additive separability of preferences, we find that the parents' income does not affect the price of child services ($\partial p/\partial y_p = 0$). Thus, higher parents' income raises transfers to their child entirely because the demand for child services increases with parents' income.

The following equation shows that a higher income for the child increases the implicit price of child services:

$$S\left(\frac{\partial p}{\partial y_c}\right) = \frac{(\theta U_{xx}^c + U_{xx}^p)(U_S^c)p - (\theta U_{SS}^c + U_{SS}^p)U_x^c(U_{x0}^c - U_x^c)}{H} \quad (9.25)$$

The child requires a larger compensation to produce a given level of services because his(her) marginal utility of consumption is lower when his(her) income is higher. We have seen above that with additive separability, child services decline with a higher child's income. The net effect on transfers is unclear. The change in transfers in response to a higher child's income clearly depends on both supply side effects on price and demand side responses. When market substitutes for child services are poor, we would expect parents' demand to be relatively insensitive to price, and so an upward shift in the child's supply curve when his(her) income increases will raise the implicit price proportionately more than the fall in the quantity of child services demanded, thereby increasing transfers.

There is a sharper distinction between exchange and altruistic motives in this restricted model because only one of the motives is effective at the margin. If the child's participation constraint is binding, then the exchange motive determines transfers in the way just described in relation to (9.21)–(9.24). If it is not binding, then the altruistic motive determines transfers in the way indicated by Becker (1981), with the comparative static results being those in (9.16)–(9.19) with $\partial \mu / \partial y_j = 0$, $j = $ p, c. Thus, if the parents always make the child service decision (the "dominant parents assumption"), higher child's income reduces transfers from parents when altruistic motives rule the transfer decision, but it can increase transfers when exchange motives rule. This allows an empirical test for the dominance of the two motives.

In his empirical analysis using US data, Cox (1987) finds that the amount of transfers received increases with the recipient's income among families receiving transfers. This is not consistent with purely altruistic motives for transfers. It is, however, consistent with a more general cooperative framework in which the recipient's income increases their bargaining power, with one particular instance of this being dominant altruistic parents making the child service and transfer decisions in the face of a binding child's participation constraint.

A similar outcome arises in the analysis of bequests by Bernheim et al. (1985). In their model, parents threaten their child with disinheritance if he(she) does not provide his(her) parents with a particular level of child service ("attention") in exchange for a bequest. The levels of service and bequest come from maximizing the parents' utility subject to the utility level that the child would achieve if he did not receive a bequest, which is increasing in his own income. That is, the child's participation constraint is binding, and at the margin bequests are used to purchase child services, with parents obtaining the entire surplus generated by the transaction between parents and child (as in the model above). The threat to disinherit must, however, be credible, and because parents are assumed to care about their child's welfare (their preferences are altruistic), it is less likely to be so if the parents have only one child. With two or more children, the threat is more likely to be credible because the parents are assumed to care for all of their children, thereby reducing the incentive to renege on the promise to disinherit children who do not comply and to redistribute the estate amongst the other children. Furthermore, such reneging entails breaking a promise to their children, which parents may be hesitant to do.

In line with their theoretical model, Bernheim et al. (1985) find that services provided by their children, measured by frequency of visits and telephone calls, increase with the level of bequeathable wealth in multi-child families, but not in single-child families. Furthermore, services do not increase with non-bequeathable wealth (social security and pension annuities).

9.3 RELAXING LIQUIDITY CONSTRAINTS THROUGH FAMILY TRANSFERS

In contrast to the first section, in which there was no capital market, here we consider an asymmetric situation in which parents have access to a capital market, but their adult children are not able to borrow against their future income. This can arise because young adults have not yet established their reputations with lenders. Even though many are a good credit risk in the sense that they will repay their loans, financial intermediaries may not lend to them because they do not know this. The parents of these young adults have, however, an informational advantage on other lenders. They have better information about whether their child will default on a loan. To keep things simple, we assume that a young adult will repay his(her) loan and that his(her) parents know this, but banks do not.

As in the previous section, we assume that the parents' social preferences $W[U^p, U^c]$ are weakly separable, where $U^j = U^j_1(x_{j1}) + U^j_2(x_{j2})/(1 + \rho)$, $j = \mathrm{p,c}$, U^j_t is the private utility index in the period t, x_{jt} is consumption in period t and ρ is the subjective rate of time preference, which is assumed to be the same for parent and child for simplicity. Because the parents have access to a capital market in which the market rate of interest is r, but the child does not, the budget constraints are

$$x_{p1} + T_1 + \frac{x_{p2} + T_2}{1 + r} = y_{p1} + \frac{y_{p2}}{1 + r} = Y_p \qquad (9.26a)$$

$$x_{ct} = y_{ct} + T_t, \qquad t = 1, 2 \qquad (9.26b)$$

where y_{jt} are the earnings of agent j in period t ($j = \text{p}, \text{c}$; $t = 1, 2$) and T_t are net transfers from parent to child in period t. In the spirit of the liquidity constraint problem, $y_{c1} < y_{c2}$, and so any family lending arrangement should have $T_1 > 0$ and $T_2 < 0$. Because the child must be willing to participate in any lending arrangement with his parents, there is again a participation constraint:

$$U_1^c(y_{c1} + T_1) + \frac{U_2^c(y_{c2} + T_2)}{1 + \rho} \geq U_x^c(y_1^c) + \frac{U_2^c(y_{c2})}{1 + \rho} \qquad (9.27)$$

Again, the socially efficient allocation will be found amongst those that are efficient in terms of private preferences, and we can characterize the efficient outcome arising from cooperative behaviour by maximizing $U^p + \mu U^c$ subject to constraints (9.26a), (9.26b) and (9.27), where μ is a Lagrange multiplier that weights child's utility relative to parents and reflects bargaining and/or altruistic behaviour. Rather than undertake the detailed comparative static analysis in the general cooperative case, as was done in the previous section, the discussion focuses on the particular case in which parents have all the bargaining power and the child's participation constraint (9.27) is binding. This is the case first discussed by Cox (1990), and it provides more information about the nature of the intra-family lending arrangement. Thus, again the situation is depicted in Figure 9.2, with the position of the utility possibility frontier being determined by $Y_p + Y_c$, where $Y_c = y_{c1} + y_{c2}/(1 + r)$, which is the child's wealth evaluated at the market interest rate. If the parents are not sufficiently altruistic, the lending arrangement provides a distribution of utilities given by the intersection of the utility possibility frontier, which depicts all efficient allocations, and the child's participation constraint.

Let $\mu = W_c/W_p$. Then the first-order conditions in addition to the participation constraint itself are

$$U_1^{p'} = (\mu + \lambda)U_1^{c'} \qquad (9.28a)$$

$$\frac{U_2^{p'}}{U_1^{p'}} = \frac{1 + \rho}{1 + r} \qquad (9.28b)$$

$$\frac{U_1^{p'}}{1 + r} = \frac{(\mu + \lambda)U_2^{c'}}{1 + \rho} \qquad (9.28c)$$

where $U_t^{j'} = \partial U_t^j/\partial x_{jt}$ and λ is the Lagrange multiplier associated with the binding participation constraint ($\lambda > 0$). These conditions imply that

$$\frac{U_2^{p'}}{U_1^{p'}} = \frac{1 + \rho}{1 + r} = \frac{U_2^{c'}}{U_1^{c'}} \qquad (9.29)$$

This is the condition for the efficient inter-temporal allocation of resources, as we would expect from Figure 9.2. The same condition holds when the participation constraint is not binding ($\lambda = 0$), but the first-order conditions indicate that when the participation constraint is binding, $U_t^{p\prime} > \mu U_t^{c\prime}, t = 1, 2$. That is, parental transfers are not sufficient to generate proportionality between the parents' and the child's marginal utility of consumption in each period.

Parents transfer resources in the first period when

$$U_1^{c\prime}(y_{c1}) > \frac{(1 + r)U_2^{c\prime}(y_{c2})}{1 + \rho} \tag{9.30}$$

This means that transfers are determined by the demand for loans in the first period, and condition (9.30) is more likely to be satisfied the larger is y_{c2} relative to y_{c1}. The level of parental wealth Y_p does not affect the chances of condition (9.30) being satisfied. Given that transfers are being made,

$$\frac{\partial T_1}{\partial y_{c1}} = \{U_1^{c\prime\prime}(U_2^{c\prime})^2 + U_1^{c\prime}U_2^{c\prime\prime}[U_1^{c\prime}(y_{c1} + T_1) - U_1^{c\prime}(y_1^c)](1 + \rho)\}\left(\frac{B}{A}\right) \tag{9.31}$$

where $U_t^{c\prime\prime} = \partial^2 U_t^c/\partial x_{ct}^2$ and $U_t^{c\prime}$ and $U_t^{c\prime\prime}$ are evaluated at $x_{ct} = y_{ct} + T_t$ ($t = 1, 2$), while $U_t^{c\prime}(y_{ct})$ is evaluated at $x_{ct} = y_{ct}$. Also, $B = [U_1^{c\prime\prime}/(1 + r)^2 + U_2^{c\prime\prime}/(1 + \rho)](\mu + \lambda)/(1 + \rho)^2 < 0$ and $A < 0$ by the second-order conditions. Because of diminishing marginal utility, it is also the case that $U_1^{c\prime}(y_{c1} + T_1) < U_1^{c\prime}(y_{c1})$, and so the first term in (9.31) is negative while the second is positive. On the one hand, higher first period income for the child raises the family wealth (evaluated at the market rate of interest). The parents wish to share in this higher family wealth in terms of higher first period consumption (i.e. make smaller transfers to their child). But, on the other hand, it increases the bargaining power of the child because his(her) utility outside the family lending arrangement increases, and this improves the terms of the family loan from the child's point of view (see the example below). In terms of Figure 9.3, the utility possibility frontier shifts out at the same time that the participation constraint shifts up. The net effect on first period transfers can be positive, but it would have to be negative if the participation constraint were not binding. In the illustration in Figure 9.3, the net effect is a small increase in transfers.

Holding first period income constant, an increase in second period income raises the child's wealth Y_c by $dy_{c2}/(1 + r)$, and so higher child's wealth, or "permanent income", has the following effect on first period transfers:

$$\frac{\partial T_1}{\partial Y_c} = (1 + r)U_1^{c\prime}U_2^{c\prime\prime}[-U_2^{c\prime}(y_{c2})]\left(\frac{B}{A}\right) > 0 \tag{9.32}$$

Thus, higher child wealth or permanent income increases first period transfers. Higher parental wealth has no impact on the amount of transfers (i.e. $\partial T_1 / \partial Y_p = 0$).

In contrast, when the participation constraint is not binding, parents transfer resources in the first period when $\mu U_1^{c\prime}(y_{c1}) > U_1^{p\prime}$ ($T_1 = 0$). Whether this condition is satisfied depends on y_{c1} and Y_p, with a transfer being more likely when the child's income is lower and the parents' wealth is higher. The existence of a first period transfer does *not* depend on the child's income in the second period, or on his(her) wealth (Y_c) given first period income. Furthermore, given that first period transfers are made, it is easily shown that $\partial T_1 / \partial Y_p > 0$, $\partial T_1 / \partial y_{c1} < 0$ and, given y_{c1}, $\partial T_1 / \partial Y_c = \partial T_1 / \partial Y_p$.[3] These contrasts suggest tests between transfers motivated by a family lending arrangement and those motivated by altruism, to which we return below.

A simple example illustrates how the family lending arrangement works. Let $U_t^j = \ln(x_{jt})$, $j = p, c$; $t = 1, 2$, and let $\rho = r$. With these preferences, the optimal time pattern of consumption is $x_{j1} = x_{j2}$ ($j = p, c$), and since $y_{c1} < y_{c2}$, the child wishes to borrow in the first period. Total family consumption in each period is given by $x_{p1} + x_{c1} = (1 + r)(Y_p + Y_c)/(2 + r)$, and how it is divided depends on condition (9.28a). Letting $\theta = \mu + \lambda$, this condition implies that $x_{p1} = (1 + r)(Y_p + Y_c)/(2 + r)(1 + \theta)$ and $x_{c1} = \theta(1 + r)(Y_p + Y_c)/(2 + r)(1 + \theta)$. It is as if the child were given $\theta(Y_p + Y_c)/(1 + \theta)$ of family wealth and was able to borrow at the market rate of interest. The value of θ is determined by the child's participation constraint (9.27), which implies that θ satisfies

$$\ln\left[\frac{\theta}{1 + \theta}\right] = \ln(y_{c1}) + \frac{\ln(y_{c2})}{1 + r} - \ln(Y_p + Y_c) \qquad (9.33)$$

From (9.33), it is clear that θ is increasing in child's income in each period.

The transfers in each period are, of course, given by $T_t = x_{ct} - y_{ct}$, $t = 1, 2$. The present value of these transfers evaluated at the market rate of interest is $T_1 + T_2/(1 + r) = \theta(Y_p + Y_c)/(1 + \theta) - Y_c = (2 + r)$ $(x_{p1}^0 - x_{p1})/(1 + r)$, where x_{p1}^0 is the parents' first period consumption if they did not participate in the lending arrangement. Because the parents obtain all of the efficiency gains from the lending arrangement (so $x_{p1}^0 < x_{p1}$), this present value must be less than zero.[4] This implies that the child borrows from his(her) parents at an interest rate that exceeds the market rate. The amount by which it exceeds the market rate declines as θ increases; that is, it declines as the child's income, and therefore bargaining power, increases.

Empirical analysis by Cox (1990) supports a model in which the bargaining power of the child, as indicated by his(her) income, affects transfers from parents because of liquidity constraints. He finds that the probability of receiving a transfer is *inversely* related to the child's current income and *directly* related to his(her) permanent income. The significant positive effect of permanent income is not consistent with transfers being motivated by purely altruistic reasons. While not statistically significant at conventional levels, the positive effects of both current and permanent income of the child on transfer *amounts* are consistent with a family lending arrangement in which the terms of the loan depend on the child's bargaining power. In particular, the positive impact of current income is not consistent with transfers being motivated by altruism alone. As Cox does not have a good measure of parents' permanent income, it is not possible to test the different predictions of its impact in the two situations.

9.4 MARKET INCENTIVES AND TRANSFERS

Here we consider the interaction between transfers from parents to their children and the labour market effort of children (e.g. their labour supply). A child's earnings are determined in part by the effort that he(she) expends, but also by luck. His(her) effort may not, however, be observed by his(her) parents (i.e. it is private information), and we shall assume that it is not. Following Chami (1998), the analysis also incorporates the idea that while parents want to help their children financially when they need it, they also want them to behave responsibly. In the model, this idea takes the form of assuming that parents' welfare depends directly on the labour market effort exerted by the child as well as indirectly through the income he(she) earns and the disutility that effort causes him(her); that is, effort is a "merit good" for the parents.

In order to incorporate luck and unobserved effort by the child into the model, we assume that there are two possible outcomes for the child's income, high (y_H) and low (y_L), with the probability of low income being given by $P(e)$, where e is the effort exerted by the child and $dP(e)/de = P'(e) < 0$. That is, the child can increase the probability of a good earnings outcome by exerting more effort, but cannot ensure it. We allow for the possibility that the parents' transfer to their child may vary with their child's realized income (T_j, $j = L, H$). The child's utility is given by the additively separable function $U^c = V(x_c) - v(e)$, where x_c is the child's consumption, $V'(x_c) = dV/dx_c > 0$ and $v'(e) = dv/de > 0$, reflecting the disutility of effort.

The discussion of "lazy rotten kids" in Chapter 3 indicated that the parents are better off if they pre-commit to a transfer, rather than "having the last word", in the sense of making their transfer after the child's effort has been expended and earnings realized. This is also true in the model analyzed here (Chami 1996, 1998), and so we assume that the parents precommit to a transfer scheme of T_L and T_H. Thus, we first determine how the child would respond to the transfers, and then solve for the parents' optimal level of transfers given the child's response rule.

It is assumed that the child chooses effort to maximize his expected utility, which is given by $P(e)V(y_L + T_L) + [1 - P(e)]V(y_H + T_H) - v(e)$. This implies that

$$P'(e)(V_L - V_H) = v'(e) \tag{9.34}$$

where $V_j = V(y_j + T_j)$, $j = L, H$. As $P'(e) < 0$ and $v'(e) > 0$, condition (9.34) indicates that $V_L < V_H$. In words, the expected utility gain from increasing effort (through higher earnings) is equal to the disutility of additional effort. Totally differentiating this first-order condition, we obtain

$$\frac{\partial e}{\partial T_L} = -\frac{[P'(e)V_L']}{D} < 0 \tag{9.35}$$

$$\frac{\partial e}{\partial T_H} = \frac{[P'(e)V_H']}{D} > 0 \tag{9.36}$$

where $V_j' = dV(y_j + T_j)/d(y_j + T_j)$, $j = L, H$, and $D = P''(e)(V_L - V_H) - v''(e) < 0$ by the second-order condition. Thus, a higher transfer when low income is realized reduces effort while a higher transfer when high income occurs increases effort. Because $V_L < V_H$, diminishing marginal utility implies $V_L' > V_H'$, and from (9.35) and (9.36), this implies that $|\partial e/\partial T_L| > \partial e/\partial T_H$, and as $\partial e/\partial T_j = \partial e/\partial y_j$, $j = L, H$, an equal increase in earnings in both states $(dy = dy_L = dy_H)$ produces a reduction in effort $(\partial e/\partial y < 0)$.

This analysis indicates that the child's effort can be expressed as a function of income in the two states: $e = e(y_L + T_L, y_H + T_H)$. Assuming for simplicity that the parents have only one child, the parents take the child's effort response function as a constraint in their expected utility maximization problem. The parents' preferences are given by the additively separable utility function $U^P = U(x_P) + w(e) + \beta[V(y_j + T_j) - v(e)]$, where $x_p = y_P - T_j$ is parents' own consumption, $w(e)$ reflects the parents' concern that the child acts responsibly $(w'(e) \geq 0)$ and β reflects the parents' degree of altruism $(\beta \geq 0)$. This is a special case of the parents' "social" preferences $W[U^P, U^c]$ used above, where $\beta = W_c/W_p$. Parents are assumed to choose transfers in the two states to maximize their expected utility subject to the child's effort response function $e = e(y_L + T_L, y_H + T_H)$, and this implies that

$$[P'(e)(U_L - U_H) + w'(e)]\left(\frac{\partial e}{\partial T_L}\right) = P(e)[U_L' - \beta V_L'] \tag{9.37}$$

$$[P'(e)(U_L - U_H) + w'(e)]\left(\frac{\partial e}{\partial T_H}\right) = [1 - P(e)][U'_H - \beta V'_H] \quad (9.38)$$

where $U_j = U(y_P - T_j)$, $j = L, H$, and $U_j' = dU(y_P - T_j)/d(y_P - T_j)$. Chami (1998) refers to parents for whom $w'(e) > 0$ and $\beta > 0$ as "altruistic principals", because their preferences have attributes of both pure altruism and the pure principal–agent problem in which the parents desire to elicit appropriate effort.

The effort level that solves (9.34), which is reflected in the child's effort response function, is not the efficient level of effort that would emerge if the parents and child cooperated and effort was observed. The efficient level would satisfy

$$P'(e)[\lambda(V_L - V_H) + (U_L - U_H)] + w'(e) = v'(e) \quad (9.39)$$

where λ is the weight given to the child's utility (i.e. the Lagrange multiplier on child's expected utility when maximizing EU^P subject to $EU^c \geq U^{c*}$, where E is the expectations operator). Comparison with (9.39) indicates that condition (9.34) does not incorporate the parents' preferences in the determination of the effort level, thereby leading to inefficient levels of effort. This reflects the parents' lack of information about their child's effort and the difference in preferences between them.[5] Unable to observe effort, the parents rely on observed earnings as a signal of the child's effort.[6]

The left-hand sides of conditions (9.37) and (9.38) indicate the net impact on parents' welfare from the change in the child's labour market effort encouraged by a higher transfer in the particular income state. The right-hand sides indicate the net impact on the parents' welfare from the changes in the parents' and child's consumption as a result of the transfer. The parents must balance their desire to shield their child from labour market risk (because of their altruism) with their desire to induce higher effort from their child. Even when parents do not care directly about their child's effort, so that $w'(e) = 0$, the left-hand sides of (9.37) and (9.38) are generally non-zero.

Let us consider this *pure altruism* case (i.e. $\beta > 0$ and $w'(e) = 0$) in more detail. It must be the case that $T_L > T_H$. To show this, suppose instead that $T_L < T_H$. Then $U_L > U_H$, which implies that $U_L' < U_H'$ and $P'(e)(U_L - U_H) < 0$. From (9.35) and (9.37), $U_L' > \beta V_L'$, while from (9.36) and (9.38), $U_H' < \beta V_H'$. But from the child's first-order condition (9.34), $V_L < V_H$, and so $V_H' < V_L'$. It follows that $U_H' < \beta V_H' < \beta V_L' < U_L'$, which implies that $U_H' < U_L'$, which contradicts the assumption that $T_L < T_H$. Thus, $T_L > T_H$. With this pattern of transfers, $U_L < U_H$, and so the left-hand side of (9.37) is negative while the left-hand side of (9.38) is positive. It follows that $U_L' < \beta V_L'$ and $U_H' > \beta V_H'$.

Thus, even when the parents are pure altruists, they do not equate their marginal utility of consumption with the weighted value of their child's marginal utility of consumption, despite the fact that they may make transfers in both income states. This contrasts with, for example, (9.14a), and it reflects the imperfect information about effort available to the parents. If the child's effort did not affect the likelihood of each outcome (i.e. $P'(e) = 0$ as well as $w'(e) = 0$), then they would equate these weighted marginal utilities. They would also do so if they could observe effort, in which case they would contract for effort and transfers directly (i.e. they would offer their child a "package" of e, T_L and T_H), and so transfers do not provide disincentives for effort.[7] In these situations, the parents can make transfers at the margin to compensate for labour market risk without having to worry about their disincentive effects on effort.

Now consider the other extreme case. Suppose that $w'(e) > 0$ but $\beta = 0$. Proof by contradiction in the same manner as above for the pure altruism case shows that in this case $T_L < T_H$. Furthermore, with $T_L < T_H$, $U_L > U_H$. From (9.38), the fact that $[1 - P(e)]U_H' > 0$ implies that $P'(e)(U_L - U_H) + w'(e) > 0$, which entails that $[P'(e)(U_L - U_H) + w'(e)](\partial e/\partial T_L) < 0 < P(e)U_L'$. From (9.37), this implies that $T_L = 0$. Thus, in the absence of altruistic motives, the parents would only provide a transfer when income is observed to be high, because this provides an incentive for high effort.

An altruistic principal, for whom both motives are operative, may provide $T_L > T_H$ or $T_L < T_H$, depending on the relative strength of the two motives. Empirical results, such as those in Cox (1987), which show transfers increasing with the child's income could reflect the dominance of the incentive motive over the altruistic one, although both motives are operating. Conversely, even if transfers are found to decline with higher child's income, it would not imply that *only* altruistic motives are operative at the margin, but rather that they dominate incentive motives.

If the government were to step in and offer state benefits to those who experience a low-income outcome (say, through unemployment insurance or an income support program), this would affect the family transfer scheme of an altruistic principal. The benefits would raise y_L, and a comparative static analysis applied to (9.37) and (9.38) indicates that transfers from parents in the low-income state (T_L) are reduced *dollar-for-dollar* to offset the increase in state benefits. Transfers in the high-income state (T_H) are unchanged.

This chapter has shown how parents' selfish behaviour can give rise to transfers between generations, either in the form of a "family capital market", or of exchanges for services that do not have substitutes in the market, or as incentives to encourage children to "act responsibly" by exerting appropriate effort from the parents' point of view. The next chapter considers how transfer motives, either selfish or altruistic, may affect household formation decisions.

Notes

1. In particular, $H = 2\theta U_S^c U_x^c U_{xS}^c - (\theta U_{SS}^c + U_{SS}^p)(U_x^c)^2 - (\theta U_{xx}^c + U_{xx}^p)(U_S^c)^2 > 0$.

2. If the new intersection in Figure 9.3 had occurred at higher value of U^p, then we could infer that transfers are smaller, because we know that S declines when the child's income increases.

3. As suggested in the Section 3.2, parents who are an effective altruist with respect to their children are able to relax the borrowing constraint faced by their adult children through inter vivos transfers.

4. The parents' welfare gain is $(2 + r)\ln[(Y_p + Y_c)/(1 + \theta)Y_p]/(1 + r)$.

5. If parents' and their child's preferences were the same (i.e. $V(x_c) = U(x_p)$ and $w(e) = -v(e)$) and $\lambda = 1$, then (9.34) would be equivalent to (9.39).

6. Note that in the case of "lazy rotten kids" in Chapter 3, child's earnings are a perfect predictor of child's effort. Thus, transfers do not need to be conditional on earnings' outcomes.

7. Altruistic parents would maximize their utility, implying that (9.39) is satisfied and that $P(e)[U_L' - \beta V_L'] = 0$ and $[1 - P(e)][U_H' - \beta V_H'] = 0$. In contrast to the previous two sections, the child's participation constraint would never be binding. Because of his aversion to risk and his parents' transfers in at least one of the states, it is always worthwhile to participate in the transfer scheme rather than remain on his(her) own.

CHAPTER TEN

Household Formation

THE ANALYSES in Chapters 2–8 were concerned with nuclear families and their formation and dissolution. This chapter addresses the issue of when adult children leave their parental home for reasons other than marriage, and when parents may live with their middle-aged children (three-generation households). It focuses on the former, because the analytical framework is basically the same for both issues. Sharing housing and other consumer durable goods is an implicit transfer that can fully or partially substitute for financial transfers motivated by either exchange or altruistic motives. Thus, the transfer motives studied in the previous chapter may lie behind household formation decisions. But in this chapter we focus on the public good nature of housing and other durable goods shared in a household as a key factor in household formation decisions.

10.1 SELFISH PARENTS

For simplicity, a one-child family is assumed. Let $U^P(x_p, h_p, i)$ and $U^C(x_c, h_c, i)$ be the parents' and child's "private" utility indices, where $i = r, a$, with "r" indicating a child's residence with parents and with "a" indicating that they live apart; and h_j and x_j are their respective consumption of housing and other goods. Housing is assumed to be a pure public good for residents of the house; that is, housing services per person are not affected by household size. Some "impurity" in this public good would not affect the predictions of the model. Note that the living arrangement may have a direct effect on utility separate from housing and other consumption in that arrangement, which may reflect tastes for privacy or independence. As a child who becomes an adult starts out in the parental home, there is likely to be asymmetry in bargaining power between them. If the parents are selfish, they can use their bargaining power to extract the child's gain from the joint consumption economies that arise when they live together. In particular, selfish parents would choose h_p and demand payments from their child, R, to maximize $U^P(x_p, h_p, r)$ subject to (a) $x_p = y_p + R - ph_p$, (b) $x_c = y_c - R$ and (c) $U^C(x_c, h_p, r) = V^a(y_c, p)$, where y_j indicate the parents' and child's incomes ($j = p, c$), p is the relative price of housing and $V^a(y_c, p)$ is the child's indirect utility function if he(she) lives apart from the parents.

That is, the parents choose the household's joint housing consumption and charge their child rental payments (R) so that the child is just willing to participate in this co-residence arrangement. In addition to the participation constraint (c), the first-order conditions for the parents' choice problem are

$$U_b^P + \lambda U_b^C = p U_x^P \tag{10.1a}$$

$$U_x^P = \lambda U_x^C \tag{10.1b}$$

where $U_b^C = \partial U^C / \partial h_p$, $U_x^C = \partial U^C / \partial x_c$, etc. and λ is the Lagrange multiplier associated with the participation constraint. These two conditions imply the efficiency condition for provision of the household public good, housing:

$$\frac{U_b^P}{U_x^P} + \frac{U_b^C}{U_x^C} = p \tag{10.2}$$

Assuming separable utility for simplicity, from the first-order conditions, we can derive that

$$\frac{\partial R}{\partial y_c} = \frac{\{-\lambda U_{xx}^C (U_b^C)^2 + V_y^a B\}}{D} \tag{10.3}$$

where $U_{xx}^C = \partial U_x^C / \partial x_c$, etc., $V_y^a = \partial V^a / \partial y_c$ and $B = U_x^C (U_{bb}^P + \lambda U_{bb}^C) + p U_{xx}^P (p U_x^C - U_b^C)$. Because of diminishing marginal utility and because $p U_x^C - U_b^C > 0$ by the first-order conditions (see the efficiency condition (10.2)), $B < 0$, while $D > 0$ by the second-order conditions. The first term in curly brackets in (10.3) is positive, and it arises because a higher child's income raises joint family income $(y_p + y_c)$, and therefore the demand for housing and other goods, thereby tending to increase transfers from the child to her parents. The second term is negative, reflecting the fact that higher child's income increases her utility when living apart, and therefore her bargaining power, thereby tending to reduce transfers to her parents. The net effect is unclear. This can be illustrated with Figure 10.1, which is similar to Figure 9.3.

The first term in (10.3) reflects the outward movement of the utility possibility frontier, the position of which depends on the joint income of the child and parents $(y_p + y_c)$, with the parents sharing in the additional resources in terms of higher consumption of housing and other goods, obtained through higher transfers from their child. The second term reflects the upward shift of the participation constraint, which tends to reduce transfers to parents.

The effect of parents' income on transfers to them and on housing demand is

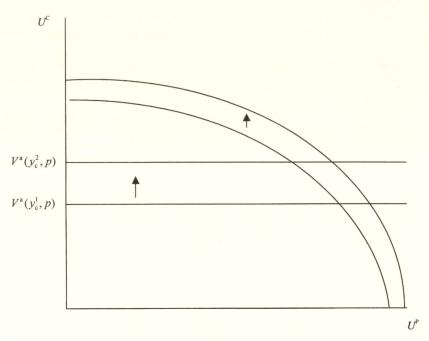

Figure 10.1 Impact of higher child's income on child's rental payments.

$$\frac{\partial R}{\partial y_p} = \frac{U_{xx}^P U_h^C (U_h^C - pU_x^C)}{D} > 0 \qquad (10.4a)$$

$$\frac{\partial h_p}{\partial y_p} = \frac{U_{xx}^P U_x^C (U_h^C - pU_x^C)}{D} > 0 \qquad (10.4b)$$

Thus, higher parents' income increases rental transfers to them from their child and housing consumption. Note that higher parents' income only shifts the utility possibility frontier outward, and so its effect is unambiguous. How much the parents can charge their child will also depend on the child's taste for independence or privacy, with a stronger taste for living apart reducing the rental payments that the parents can extract, because it increases the child's utility when living apart from his(her) parents.

As the following shows, a higher child's income has an ambiguous effect on the amount of housing chosen by the parents:

$$\frac{\partial h_p}{\partial y_c} = \frac{\{-\lambda U_{xx}^C U_h^C U_x^C + V_y^a C\}}{D} \qquad (10.5)$$

where $C = U_{xx}^P(pU_x^C - U_h^C) - \lambda U_{xx}^C U_h^C$, which is ambiguous in sign. The first term in curly brackets in (10.5) is positive, reflecting a higher demand for housing with higher income for the child (an outward shift of the utility possibility frontier). The second term reflects a bargaining effect, but its direction depends on the parents' preferences relative to those of their child.

The parents are effectively letting their child share their house in return for a transfer, and so they also make the decision about whether they and their child should live together. This decision will also depend on the parents' taste for privacy or independence, which has some probability distribution in the population. Let W^r represent the parents' utility when they live with their child and W^a their utility when they live apart, and so they live together if $W^r \geq W^a$. Because $\partial W^a/\partial y_c = 0$, how their child's income affects their decision about whether to live with their child depends on $\partial W^r/\partial y_c$, which can be expressed as

$$\frac{\partial W^r}{\partial y_c} = U_x^P\left(\frac{\partial R}{\partial y_c}\right) + (U_h^P - pU_x^P)\left(\frac{\partial h_p}{\partial y_c}\right) \tag{10.6}$$

Using (10.2), (10.3) and (10.5), we derive

$$\frac{\partial W^r}{\partial y_c} = V_y^a \frac{U_x^P(B - pC) + (U_h^P C)}{D} \tag{10.7}$$

Equation (10.7) indicates that the impact of a higher child's income on the parents' utility when they live with their child reflects changes in his(her) bargaining power with higher income. The sign of $\partial W^r/\partial y_c$ is ambiguous, because, while $B - pC$ is easily shown to be negative, C may be positive.[1] If $C > 0$, which ensures that the parents' housing consumption increases with the child's income (see (10.5)), it is *possible* that a higher child's income could *increase* the chances that the parents and child live together. If however $C \leq 0$, higher child's income certainly decreases these chances.

The impact of parents' income on utility when living together with their child is derived from $\partial W^r/\partial y_p = U_x^P(1 + \partial R/\partial y_p) + (U_h^P - pU_x^P)$ $(\partial h_p/\partial y_p)$. Using (10.2), (10.4a) and (10.4b), we obtain $\partial W^r/\partial y_p = U_x^{Pr}$, where U_x^{Pi} indicates the parents' marginal utility of consumption in residence state i, and analogously, $\partial W^a/\partial y_p = U_x^{Pa}$. Because their consumption is higher when living together with their child, $U_x^{Pr} < U_x^{Pa}$, and so $\partial W^r/\partial y_p < \partial W^a/\partial y_p$. This implies that the chances of living apart increase with higher parents' income; that is, if parents have tastes favouring privacy, they can better afford to give up the joint consumption economies available from co-residence for privacy when they are richer.

Using the same methods, we obtain the impact of the price of housing on parents' utility when living with their child:

$$\frac{\partial W^r}{\partial p} = -h_p^r U_x^{Pr} + V_p^a \frac{\{U_x^P(B - pC) + (U_h^P C)\}}{D} \tag{10.8}$$

where h_p^r is the quantity of housing consumed when parents and child live together. Because a higher price of housing reduces the child's utility when living apart, $V_p^a < 0$, but the impact of the child's lower bargaining power is unclear because, as discussed in relation to (10.7), the sign of the quantity in curly brackets is ambiguous. Also, $\partial W^a/\partial p = -h_p^a U_x^{Pa}$. While $U_x^{Pa} > U_x^{Pr}$ for the reasons given above, it is also the case that $h_p^r > h_p^a$, and so for this reason as well, the sign of $\partial W^r/\partial p - \partial W^a/\partial p$ is not clear. Thus, the impact of the price of housing on the chances that the parents and child live together in this model could be in either direction.

Below we will contrast the predictions of the "selfish parents" model with those of a model in which parents are altruistic toward their children, which indicates that, under plausible conditions, a higher child's income reduces the chances that the parents live with their child, while higher parents' income increases them. The different prediction of the impact of parents' income suggests a way of distinguishing empirically between the two models, and an observation of a positive impact of child's income on the chances of co-residence would only be consistent with the "selfish parent" model. Before discussing this alternative model, we consider the a priori plausibility of the selfish parent model as a depiction of co-residence decisions.

The model predicts that children living with their parents make transfers to their parents when living together; for example, payments for "room and board". Casual observation suggests that such payments are relatively rare, or just token amounts, and it also suggests that payments are more likely to occur in families in which parents are poorer. But the model predicts that larger payments should be made to richer parents (see (10.4a)). This raises doubts about the model.

As in the previous chapter, we can relax the assumption about the parents having all of the bargaining power in the context of the general cooperative framework. But this would still entail transfers from the child to parents when they live together and parents are selfish, and the qualitative predictions would be similar to those above. Rather than pursue this more general formulation, we contrast the selfish parents model with one in which parents have altruistic preferences and have all of the bargaining power.

10.2 ALTRUISTIC PARENTS

It is now assumed that, as in Chapters 3 and 9, the parents' utility is a function of the utility of their child as well as their own consumption of housing and other goods. Housing is again a local public good for a household. Let the parents' welfare function, or "social preferences" again take the "Bergson–Samuelson", or "caring" form: $W = W[U^P(x_p, h_p, i), U^C(x_c, h_c, i)]$, $i = r, a$.

Similar to Section 9.4, it is efficient for parents to pre-commit to a transfer scheme in which transfers differ between the two living arrangements. We first determine how the child would respond to the transfers, and then solve for the parents' optimal levels of transfers in each living arrangement given the child's response rule. Taking parental transfers in the co-residence and living apart states as given, as well as his(her) income and the price of housing, the child chooses whether to live with parents or not to maximize his(her) utility. This gives the child's choices conditional on the amount of financial transfers from parents in each living arrangement. The parents choose financial transfers, their own consumption of housing and other goods to maximize their welfare subject to: (i) $y_p = x_p + ph_p + T_i$, (ii) $y_c + T_i = x_c + \delta_i ph_c$, (iii) $T_i \geq 0$, and (iv) the child's transfer response rule, where y_p is parental income, y_c is the child's income, p is the relative price of housing, T_i is financial transfers from parents to child in the ith living arrangement, and $\delta_r = 0$, $\delta_a = 1$.

As expected from the results in Chapter 3, whether or not financial transfers are made in each state depends upon parental income relative to child's income (y_p/y_c). This can be seen more clearly if particular preferences are assumed. Let $W = x_p^\beta h_p^\phi (x_c^\alpha h_c^{1-\alpha})^\gamma$, where the γ parameter indicates the degree of altruism $(0 < \gamma < 1)$ and $\beta + \phi + \gamma = 1$; that is, Cobb–Douglas utility similar to that assumed in previous chapters is used to illustrate the transfer rules. When parents and their adult child live together, parents make financial transfers according to the following rule:

$$T_r = \alpha\gamma y_p - (1 - \alpha\gamma)y_c \qquad (10.9)$$

and so financial transfers are made when $y_c/(y_p + y_c) < \alpha\gamma$. When parents and child live apart, the financial transfer rule is

$$T_a = \gamma y_p - (1 - \gamma)y_c \qquad (10.10)$$

implying that transfers are made when $y_c/(y_p + y_c) < \gamma$. Clearly, higher parental income and lower child's income increase the probability that financial transfers are given in either state, and also increase the amount of transfer given.

It is interesting to compare financial transfers in the two types of living arrangement. From expressions (10.9) and (10.10), it follows that

$$T_a - T_r = (1 - \alpha)\gamma(y_p + y_c) = p(h_p^r - h_p^a) > 0 \qquad (10.11)$$

where h_p^r and h_p^a indicate parents' housing consumption when parent and child live together and apart, respectively. Thus, if financial transfers are made in both situations, financial transfers are smaller when the parents and child are co-residing than when they are living apart, and they indeed are lower by the amount of additional parental housing expenditure when co-residing. This difference arises because transfers are made through the joint consumption of the public good (housing) when they live together. This is a cheaper way to make transfers, and financial transfers are lowered during co-residence to reflect exactly these joint consumption economies. Financial transfers are only used during co-residence when there is no longer scope to make transfers efficiently through the public good.

Indeed, comparison of the conditions for making financial transfers in the two living arrangements indicates a clear ordering with respect to the child's share of total family income:

(a) when $y_c/(y_p + y_c) < \alpha\gamma$, financial transfers are made in both situations ($T_r > 0$ and $T_a > 0$);

(b) when $\alpha\gamma \leq y_c/(y_p + y_c) < \gamma$, no financial transfers are made when they live together, but they are made when they live apart ($T_r = 0$ and $T_a > 0$); and

(c) when $y_c/(y_p + y_c) \geq \gamma$, no financial transfers are made in either living arrangement ($T_r = 0$ and $T_a = 0$).

"Effective transfers" when the parents and child live together could be defined as $ph_p^r + T_r$, and when transfers are made in both living arrangements, these exceed T_a by $\phi(y_p + y_c) = ph_p^a$. Thus, as we expect, more transfers are made by altruistic parents in a situation in which it is cheaper to do so, and effective transfers are larger by the amount of housing consumption that the parents would have chosen if living on their own, again reflecting the joint consumption economies available when living together.

In general, when y_p/y_c is large enough, financial transfers are made in both states; when y_p/y_c is in an intermediate range, no financial transfers are made during co-residence, but they are made when the child lives apart; and when y_p/y_c is sufficiently low, no financial transfers are made in either state. The co-residence/living apart decision is effectively made by the parents if they would make financial transfers to the child when he(she) lives apart; they "dictate" the co-residence decision by manipulating the level of transfers to the child. There may be, however, a binding child participation constraint: parents may have to provide a sufficiently high level of transfers in their chosen state in order to make their choice acceptable to their child.

For instance, if the child has a strong taste for privacy but the parents' optimum is co-residence, parents would need to provide a sufficiently high level of financial transfers when living together to give the child the same level of utility as he(she) could achieve living apart. As the analysis in the first section and the preceding chapter would suggest, the impact of the child's income on transfers when this participation constraint is binding has a "bargaining component"; for instance, with separable preferences, $\partial T_r/\partial y_c = \{\lambda U_{xx}^C(U_h^C)^2 + (U_x^{Cr} - U_x^{Ca})B\}/D$, where B was defined in the preceding section, U_x^{Ci} is the child's marginal utility of consumption in living arrangement i, and $D > 0$. Because $U_x^{Cr} < U_x^{Ca}$ (due to transfers from parents and joint consumption economies when co-residing) and $B < 0$, the second term in the curly brackets is positive, while the first term is negative. That is, altruistic parents would usually reduce transfers to their child when the child's income increases, but that reduction is at least partially offset when the participation constraint is binding because the child demands higher transfers to live with his(her) parents. Similarly, if the child wished to live with his(her) parents, but the parents wanted him(her) to live apart, they would increase transfers to induce him(her) to live apart. When this participation constraint is binding, a higher child's income would reduce parents' transfers to their child when they live apart (at least for separable preferences), because lower transfers are needed to "bribe" him(her) to live apart when his(her) income is higher. From here forward, we ignore the boundary situations in which the participation constraint is binding.

If parents are too poor (relative to the child) to make financial transfers, then they have no way to control the household living arrangement decision of their child. But as they care about the child's utility, whatever choice maximizes the child's utility also maximizes their utility, and so it continues to be the case that they live together if and only if the parents' utility when they live together exceeds their utility when living apart. Initially, we focus on this last case, in which no financial transfers are made in either state ($T_a = T_r = 0$).

10.2.1 No Financial Transfers from Parents

The child's utility when living apart is given by the indirect utility function $V^a(p, y_c) = V^a$, and his(her) utility when living with parents is given by the direct utility function $U^C(y_c, h_p, r) = V^r$. Using the first-order conditions in each living arrangement, it then follows that

$$\frac{\partial V^r}{\partial p} - \frac{\partial V^a}{\partial p} = U_x^{Ca} h_c^a - \varepsilon_{hp} U_h^{Cr}\left(\frac{h_p^r}{p}\right) \tag{10.12}$$

$$\frac{\partial V^r}{\partial y_c} - \frac{\partial V^a}{\partial y_c} = U_x^{Cr} - U_x^{Ca} \tag{10.13}$$

$$\frac{\partial V^{\mathrm{r}}}{\partial y_{\mathrm{p}}} - \frac{\partial V^{\mathrm{a}}}{\partial y_{\mathrm{p}}} = U_h^{\mathrm{Cr}}\left(\frac{\partial h_{\mathrm{p}}^{\mathrm{r}}}{\partial y_{\mathrm{p}}}\right) \tag{10.14}$$

where ε_{hp} is the absolute value of the price elasticity of parents' demand for housing ($\varepsilon_{hp} > 0$).

When living with his(her) parents, the child can spend his(her) entire income on consumption, while he(she) must spend some of it on housing if he(she) lives apart from his(her) parents. Thus, $x_c^{\mathrm{r}} > x_c^{\mathrm{a}}$, and so $U_x^{\mathrm{Cr}} < U_x^{\mathrm{Ca}}$, which, from (10.13), indicates that $\partial V^{\mathrm{r}}/\partial y_c < \partial V^{\mathrm{a}}/\partial y_c$. The higher the child's income, the better he(she) can afford to purchase his(her) own housing, and the higher the chances of living apart from his(her) parents (given some random variation in tastes for living apart). As housing is a normal good, (10.14) implies that $\partial V^{\mathrm{r}}/\partial y_{\mathrm{p}} > \partial V^{\mathrm{a}}/\partial y_{\mathrm{p}}$. The higher the parents' income, the more attractive is living with parents to him(her) because the parents' housing consumption, which he(she) consumes jointly, is higher. In the case of the Cobb–Douglas preferences used for illustration above, it is more convenient to express the differences in utility between the two living arrangements in terms of proportionate differences, which indicate that $\partial \ln(V^{\mathrm{r}})/\partial \ln(y_c) - \partial \ln(V^{\mathrm{a}})/\partial \ln(y_c) = -(1 - \alpha)$ and $\partial \ln(V^{\mathrm{r}})/\partial \ln(y_{\mathrm{p}}) - \partial \ln(V^{\mathrm{a}})/\partial \ln(y_{\mathrm{p}}) = (1 - \alpha)$.

From (10.12), the sign of $\partial V^{\mathrm{r}}/\partial p - \partial V^{\mathrm{a}}/\partial p$ is ambiguous. In particular, it depends on the price elasticity of parents' housing demand, ε_{hp}. Clearly, when $\varepsilon_{hp} = 0$, $\partial V^{\mathrm{r}}/\partial p > \partial V^{\mathrm{a}}/\partial p$, and a higher price of housing increases the chances of parents and child living together. But as ε_{hp} increases, $\partial V^{\mathrm{r}}/\partial p - \partial V^{\mathrm{a}}/\partial p$ becomes smaller and eventually turns negative. In other words, there is a critical value for ε_{hp} which makes $\partial V^{\mathrm{r}}/\partial p = \partial V^{\mathrm{a}}/\partial p$. This critical value is given by

$$\varepsilon_{hp}^{\mathrm{c}} = \frac{[U_x^{\mathrm{Ca}}\, p h_c^{\mathrm{a}}]}{(U_h^{\mathrm{Cr}} h_{\mathrm{p}}^{\mathrm{r}})} \tag{10.15}$$

When ε_{hp} is larger than $\varepsilon_{hp}^{\mathrm{c}}$, a higher price of housing increases utility living apart more than utility living with parents, thereby increasing the probability of living apart from parents. In the case of constant elasticity of substitution (CES) preferences for the child, this critical value is unity. Thus, with the Cobb–Douglas preferences used in the illustration above, which imply a unitary price elasticity of housing demand, the price of housing does not affect the co-residence decision.

Thus, the model predicts that the impact of the price of housing on the probability of living apart is intimately related to the price elasticity of parents' housing demand. When it is less than a critical value (e.g. unity in the case of CES preferences), a higher price of housing reduces the probability that the young adult lives apart from his(her) parents, but the opposite is true if the price elasticity of housing demand is above the critical value. These predictions reflect the fact that a higher housing price reduces the child's utility in the parental home as well as when he(she) lives away from home. If parents did not adjust their housing consumption (zero price elasticity of housing demand), then a young adult's housing and utility in the parental household would not change, while his(her) utility when living apart would fall; thus, the probability of living apart would fall. When the parents' housing response is relatively small (inelastic housing demand), this fall in the probability continues to hold. If, however, parents' housing response is relatively elastic, a higher housing price entails that the young adult's utility falls more in the parental household than when living apart as a consequence of the large decline in housing available when living with parents. Evidence of inelastic housing demand in Britain (Ermisch 1996) suggests a negative impact of the price of housing on the probability of living apart.

It may seem plausible that an increase over time in the price of housing would have little effect on parents' housing, because of transaction and moving costs. But if, as is the case in cross-section studies, the impact of the price of housing on young people's living arrangements is identified from spatial differences in the price of housing, it is more plausible to assume that parents' housing demand has adjusted to differences in housing prices. In this case, the housing demand elasticity need not be small, and its size is linked to the effect of the price of housing on whether young people live with their parents or not.

10.2.2 Parents Make Financial Transfers in at Least One Living Arrangement

The predictions regarding the effects of parents' and child's income on the co-residence decision do not follow from (10.13) and (10.14) when there are financial transfers from parents to children, because the amount of these transfers responds to changes in parents' and child's income. These effects must be derived from the parents' point of view, as they effectively make the co-residence decision when they make financial transfers.

We now consider parents who are not as poor relative to their child as those described in the previous section, but who are not affluent enough to make financial transfers when they live together. They would, however, make financial transfers if their child lives apart from them (case (b) in the example above). In this case, the parents' indirect utility function when living apart from their child is given by $W^a(y_p + y_c, p)$, because housing and other consumption of both parents and child depend only on the relative price of housing and the *joint income* of parents and child, $y_p + y_c$, as in most models involving an altruistic agent making transfers. When living together, the parents' indirect utility function is given by

$W^r(y_p, p, y_c)$, because joint housing consumption and the parents' other consumption depends on parental income and the relative price of housing while the child's other consumption equals his(her) income. Then

$$\frac{\partial W^r}{\partial y_c} - \frac{\partial W^a}{\partial y_c} = W_C^r U_x^{Cr} - W_C^a U_x^{Ca} \tag{10.16}$$

$$\frac{\partial W^r}{\partial y_p} - \frac{\partial W^a}{\partial y_p} = W_P^r U_x^{Pr} - W_P^a U_x^{Pa} \tag{10.17}$$

where $W_j^i = (\partial W^i / \partial U^j)$, $i = r, a$; $j = C, P$.

The sign of (10.16) depends on the difference between the consumption (x_j) of the child when living with parents and that when living apart from them, and the sign of (10.17) depends on this consumption difference for the parents. When living together without financial transfers, the first-order conditions are given by $U_h^P / U_x^P + \mu U_h^C / U_x^P = p$ and $U_x^P > \mu U_x^C$, where $\mu = W_C^r / W_P^r$. Comparison with (10.2) indicates that parents do not choose the efficient level of housing in this situation. The inefficiency arises because the amount of implicit, indivisible transfer through shared housing exceeds the amount of the total transfer the parents' wish to make, but they cannot elicit transfers from their child to reduce their net transfer. This tends to produce less consumption by the parents than when living apart from their child ($x_p^r < x_p^a$) and more consumption by the child ($x_c^r > x_c^a$). This suggests a tendency for $W_C^r U_x^{Cr} < W_C^a U_x^{Ca}$ and $W_P^r U_x^{Pr} > W_P^a U_x^{Pa}$, and so, from (10.16) and (10.17), a higher child's income tends to reduce the chances that the parents and child live together while higher parents' income tends to increase them. These predictions are qualitatively similar to the situation in which parents do not make financial transfers in either living arrangement.

These tendencies are confirmed in the example of Cobb–Douglas preferences assumed above ($W = x_p^\beta h_p^\phi (x_c^\alpha h_c^{1-\alpha})^\gamma$), where the γ parameter indicates the degree of altruism ($0 < \gamma < 1$ and $\beta + \phi + \gamma = 1$). Expressed in terms of proportionate differences in utility in the two living arrangements, the expressions analogous to (10.16) and (10.17) are

$$\frac{\partial \ln(W^r)}{\partial \ln(y_c)} - \frac{\partial \ln(W^a)}{\partial \ln(y_c)} = \left[\gamma\alpha - \frac{y_c}{y_p + y_c} \right] \tag{10.16CD}$$

$$\frac{\partial \ln(W^r)}{\partial \ln(y_p)} - \frac{\partial \ln(W^a)}{\partial \ln(y_p)} = \left[\frac{y_c}{y_p + y_c} - \gamma\alpha \right] \tag{10.17CD}$$

It was shown above that financial transfers will only be zero when parents and child live together but positive when they live apart (i.e. case (b) above pertains) if $\alpha\gamma \leq y_c/(y_p + y_c) < \gamma$. This implies that higher child's income increases the chances of living apart while higher parental income reduces them, and these income effects will be larger the more that $y_c/(y_p + y_c)$ exceeds $\gamma\alpha$. It also implies that the responsiveness of living arrangement decisions to child's and parents' income are larger when no financial transfers are given in either living arrangement (i.e. case (c) above pertains) than when financial transfers are given when they live apart. For instance, with these Cobb–Douglas preferences, the effect of parents' income on the proportionate difference in *parents'* utility between co-residence and living apart when no financial transfers are given when they live apart is $\gamma(1 - \alpha)$, which exceeds its value of $[y_c/(y_p + y_c) - \gamma\alpha]$ when $T_a > 0$, because $y_c/(y_p + y_c) < \gamma$. An analogous statement applies to the effect of child's income on the proportionate difference in parents' utility. This is very plausible because the ability to make changes in financial transfers when such transfers are being made reduces the need to change the living arrangement in response to changes in parents' or child's income.

Note that the effects of parental income and child's income tend to be larger when the degree of altruism γ is smaller, both because $y_c/(y_p + y_c) - \gamma\alpha$ is larger when $T_a > 0$ and because it is more likely that $T_a = 0$. Similarly, these income effects are larger when the share of child's income spent on housing is larger (i.e. α is smaller).

The impact of the relative price of housing on the co-residence decision when parents do not make financial transfers when living together with their child, but do so when living apart is

$$\frac{\partial W^r}{\partial p} - \frac{\partial W^a}{\partial p} = W_P^a h_p^a U_x^{Pa} + W_C^a h_c^a U_x^{Ca} - W_P^r h_p^r U_x^{Pr} \qquad (10.18)$$

The sign of this expression is again ambiguous. With Cobb–Douglas preferences, $\partial\ln(W^r)/\partial\ln(p) - \partial\ln(W^a)/\partial\ln(p)$ is zero, and so the price of housing does not affect the odds of living apart relative to living together. In part this ambiguity arises because the amount of the financial transfer depends on the relative price of housing, but the direction of the impact is ambiguous. In the Cobb–Douglas case, financial transfers are independent of the price of housing.

Finally, parents who are very rich relative to their child (y_p/y_c is sufficiently high) want to provide a large amount of support to their child. Thus, they want their child to live with them because this is a cheaper way to make transfers, owing to joint consumption economies from housing. Such very wealthy parents also make financial transfers when there is no longer scope to make transfers efficiently through the public good (case (a) above). Together the parents and child have the same resources and face the same prices as when living apart, but they can consume housing jointly. Thus, unless parents or child have a strong taste for privacy, they must be better off living together. The effects of incomes and the price of housing take the same form as in (10.16)–(10.18), but the pattern of the amounts of housing and other consumption by child and parents in the two living arrangements is not clear for preferences in general. In the case of Cobb–Douglas preferences, $x_p^r = x_p^a$ and $x_c^r = x_c^a$, and $h_p^r = h_c^a + h_p^a$. It follows, therefore, from (10.16)–(10.18) that the difference between utility in the two living arrangements is independent of the price of housing and parents' and child's income. In general, with the balance of advantage so strongly in favour of living together, changes in parents' and child's income are not likely to affect the co-residence decision for these rich families.

10.2.3 Empirical Implications

In this theoretical framework, young adults live apart from their parents when their utility living apart exceeds the utility they receive in the parental home. Young people will, of course, differ in their tastes regarding living with their parents. After assuming some distribution for a random variable representing these tastes, the comparative static results of the previous sections yield predictions about differences in the probability that the child lives apart from the parents. An immediate implication is that measures of *both* parents' and child's income should be included in any empirical model, as well as a measure of housing price. The analysis of this section suggests that parental income should have a negative effect on the probability that the child lives apart, while child's income should have a positive effect on this probability. When parents do not make financial transfers, higher parental income increases the chances of co-residence because it increases the amount of (joint) housing consumption in the parental home relative to that when living apart. Without transfers, higher child's income means that he(she) can more easily afford to purchase his(her) own housing. If financial transfers are made when living apart, but not when living together, higher parental income increases the chances of co-residence because parents would like to provide more help to their child when their income is higher and it is cheaper to do so when living together because of the public good aspect of housing. Conversely, when the child's income is higher, parents choose to provide less help to their child, thereby reducing the advantages of co-residence for providing support.

As noted in the previous section, the prediction of the impact of parents' income in this model differs in direction from that in the selfish parents' model, in which higher parents' income increases the probability of living apart. Furthermore, a finding that higher child's income reduces the probability of living apart would only be consistent with the selfish parents' model.

We could make inferences about the impacts of the price of housing and young adults' incomes on living arrangements on the basis of cross-section variation in living arrangements, as in Börsch-Supan (1986), Ermisch and Overton (1985), and Haurin et al. (1993, 1994). One disadvantage of this approach is that information about parental income is usually not available for young adults not living with their parents, but the theory suggests that it is important for young people's household membership decisions. This disadvantage could be overcome with appropriate panel data, as in Rosenzweig and Wolpin (1993, 1994).

The analysis of British panel data (Ermisch 1999) indicates that higher child's income increases the probability of living apart, while higher parents' income has the opposite effect. The latter result is not consistent with the model with selfish parents, and both results support altruistic behaviour on the part of parents. In addition, a higher housing price discourages leaving the parental home, particularly to form partnerships, and it encourages returns to it. For the reasons given above, this behaviour is consistent with price-inelastic housing demand.

10.3 ALTRUISTIC PARENTS' SUPPORT FOR YOUNG PEOPLE'S HUMAN CAPITAL INVESTMENT

The model studied in the previous section can be readily extended to improve our understanding of the interaction among young people's human capital investment, labour market luck and financial transfers from parents and their living arrangements. In the years when children are deciding whether or not to leave their parental home they are also likely to be making large investments in their human capital, both in formal education or in their jobs, and they are likely to find it difficult to borrow against their future income. In order to highlight the interaction of these decisions and constraints with those of co-residence and financial transfers from parents, the model above is reformulated as a simple, two-period dynamic model. As in Section 9.3, it is assumed that parents can borrow and lend at a given interest rate, but children face a binding borrowing constraint in the period in which they are making human capital investments (the first period of the model).[2] It is also assumed that there are no financial transfers in the second period and the parents and child do not live together, which is plausible because an offspring's income is likely to be high enough in the second period to preclude these. This simplifies the exposition, and it is also consistent with the British empirical evidence, which shows that the proportion of young adults not in full-time education who receive transfers is very small, particularly among those aged 24 or older. Labour supply decisions other than those associated with human capital investment are also ignored in this model.

The child's preferences are represented by the intertemporal separable utility function $U^c(x_{c1}, h_{c1}, i) + R^c U^c(x_{c2}, h_{c2}, a)$, where $R^c = 1/(1 + \rho_c)$ is the discount factor, with ρ_c being the child's rate of time preference; x_{ct} and h_{ct} are his other and housing consumption in period t ($t = 1, 2$); $U^c(x_{ct}, h_{ct}, i)$ is his period-specific utility function, and i indicates whether the parent and child live together ($i = r$) or live apart ($i = a$) in the first period. The young adult offspring chooses human capital investment in the first period and housing and other consumption in each period to maximize his(her) utility subject to

$$y + T_i = x_{c1} + ks + \delta^i p h_{c1} \qquad (10.19a)$$

$$y_2(s) = x_{c2} + p h_{c2} \qquad (10.19b)$$

where y can be interpreted as "potential earnings" (i.e. what earnings would be if there were no human capital investment, or a "basic earning capacity", which varies with individual ability); s is the child's human capital investment and k is its cost per unit; T_i ($i = r, a$) are financial transfers from the parents to the child; $y_2(s)$ is second period earnings; p is the price of housing in terms of other consumption (assumed constant over time); and $\delta^i = 1$ if $i = a$, with $\delta^i = 0$ if $i = r$.

Intertemporal separability means that there are *conditional* demand functions for housing and other consumption in each period, which condition on human capital investment, s. That is, the effects of the cost of human capital investment (k), on these demands operate only through net income in each period, $y + T_i - ks$ and $y_2(s)$. Human capital investment is the only way the child can transfer income through time. The demands for x_{c1} and h_{c1} are functions of $y + T_i - ks$, p and the living arrangement in the first period ($i = a, r$), and the demands for x_{c2} and h_{c2} are functions of s and p. Thus, the child has a conditional indirect utility function $V_i^c = V^c(s, y + T_i - ks, p, i)$, for the ith living arrangement.

As in the previous section, the parents are assumed to have caring preferences, represented by the utility function $W[U^P(x_{p1}, h_{p1}, i) + R^P U^P(x_{p2}, h_{p2}, a), V^c(s, y + T_i - ks, p_h, i)]$, where $R^P = 1/(1 + \rho_p)$ is the parents' discount factor; and h_{pt} and x_{pt} are parental housing and other consumption, respectively. As before, preferences concerning privacy may lead to differences in utility by living arrangement, even when housing and other consumption are the same in both states.

Parents choose transfers to their child and their own housing and other consumption in each period to maximize their utility subject to the following wealth constraint: $M = x_{p1} + p_h h_{p1} + (x_{p2} + p_h h_{p2})/(1 + \theta) + T_i$ ($i = r, a$), $T_i \geq 0$, where M is parental wealth and θ is the interest rate.

The separability of $W( )$ means that we can derive *conditional* demand and financial transfer functions, such as

$$T_i = T(s, M, y - ks, p, r, \rho_p, \rho_c, i) \qquad (10.20)$$

and there is a conditional indirect utility function for the parents:

$$W_i^p = W^{p^*}(s, M, y - ks, p, r, \rho_p, \rho_c, i) \qquad (10.21)$$

As in the previous section, when the parents are making financial transfers in at least one of the living arrangements, the parents are also effectively making the living arrangement choice. Thus, the decision involves a comparison of parents' utility in the two living arrangements. The parents and adult child live together in the first period if and only if $W_r^p > W_a^p$. When parents are too poor to make financial transfers, they have no way to control the household living arrangement decision of their child. But as they care about the child's utility, it continues to be the case that they live together if and only if $W_r^p > W_a^p$.

The comparative static results are similar to those in the static model in the previous section. There are again three transfer regimes that depend on parents' wealth relative to their child's net earnings in the first period $(M/(y - ks))$. In this model, the motive for transfers of either type (co-residence or financial) is purely to smooth consumption. The model predicts a tendency for young adults making larger human capital investments (higher s) to live with their parents. Also, those with higher basic earning capacity or better labour market luck (y), or with poorer parents (lower M) are more likely to live away from their parental home.

The analysis here, which conditions on s, does not address the choice of human capital investment per se. It is consistent with the child achieving efficient investment through transfers from his parents, but it is also consistent with the non-cooperative game proposed by Rosenzweig and Wolpin (1993). In their analysis, parents decide on the level of transfers and on their living arrangement conditional on the human capital investment decision of their adult child, while the child takes into account the parents' *transfer rule* when making his(her) investment decision. Thus, the young adult "moves first" in their model, in the sense that parents respond to the human capital investment of their child and can only influence it by the *transfer rule* (i.e. (10.20)).

In some countries, like Britain, certain forms of human capital investment, such as university education, dictate moving away from home. Thus, young people making very heavy investments in human capital through university education are often forced by institutional constraints to live apart from parents. In terms of the model, human capital investment above some level can only be carried out when living apart from parents. This dictates the living arrangement decision, but financial transfers from parents can respond according to (10.20), which implies that the probability of a financial transfer should be larger for university students making this large human capital investment.

Rosenzweig and Wolpin's (1993) empirical analysis shows that young men with lower earnings or higher tuition costs are more likely to live with their parents and also more likely to receive a financial transfer if living apart. Given earnings, tuition costs and schooling level, young men enrolled in college were more likely to live with their parents, or to receive a transfer if they lived apart. But those making large human capital investments outside the educational system, as indicated by low earnings relative to their educational attainment, were less likely to live with their parents and less likely to receive a transfer, presumably because the parents anticipate future income gains from these investments. Thus, parents appear to play a large role in helping their young adult children avoid large consumption losses while they are making human capital investments, as the simple model above suggested.

10.4 AN EXCHANGE MODEL OF CO-RESIDENCE

This model is similar to the one analyzed in Section 9.3. Parents are not effective altruists, but they are assumed to cooperate with their child and may make financial transfers to their children in the form of loans, which are repaid later. Following Cox (1990), it is assumed that the parents know that their child will honour his(her) commitments and repay parental loans, but financial intermediaries do not. Children have access to the "family capital market" in which parents make loans at or above the market rate of interest faced by the parents, with the terms of the loan being the outcome of bargaining between the parents and their child.

The adult child wishes to choose human capital investment, housing and other consumption in each period to maximize $U_1^c(x_{c1}, h_{c1}, i) + R^c U_2^c(x_{c2}, h_{c2}, a)$, $i = r, a$, subject to a number of constraints, which vary according to whether the child lives with his(her) parents in the first period or not. Note that he(she) is assumed to live apart from his(her) parents in the second period. This is a relatively conventional inter-temporal investment–consumption problem. With $\delta^i = 1$ if $i = a$ and $\delta^i = 0$ if $i = r$, the constraints are: (a) $y + L = x_{c1} + ks + \delta^i ph_{c1}$; (b) $h_{c1} = h_{p1}$ if $\delta^i = 0$; and (c) $y_2(s) = x_{c2} + ph_{c2} + (1 + r_c)L$, where L is the loan from the parents and r_c is the interest charged by the parents.

The optimal amount of human capital investment in this model is independent of living arrangements and consumption decisions in each period. Young adults choose human capital investment, s, to satisfy $dy_2(s)/ds = k(1 + r_c)$. This equation determines the optimal value s^*, from which we can derive the optimal amounts of housing and other consumption in each period for each of the two living arrangements. The child borrows from his(her) parents if and only if $U_{1x}^c(y - ks^* - \delta^i ph_{c1}, h_{c1}, i) > R^c(1 + r_c)U_{2x}^c(y_2(s^*) - ph_{c2}^*, h_{c2}^*, a)$ where $U_{tx}^c = \partial U_t^c/\partial x_{ct}$, $t = 1, 2$. The amount of the parental loan must satisfy $U_{1x}^{ci} = R^c(1 + r_c)U_{2x}^{ci}$, where i indicates the living arrangement in the first period. It is determined by the earnings and consumption profiles implied by s^* and the child's preferences, particularly R^c. As higher s^* raises future earnings and lowers current net earnings, higher human capital investment increases the chances that the child borrows from his(her) parents in each living arrangement. For given human capital investment, higher current earning capacity reduces the likelihood of a parental loan.

Because the child must pay for his(her) own housing if living apart in the first period, but not if living with parents, $U_{1x}^c(y - ks^*, h_{p1}, r) < U_{1x}^c(y - ks^* - ph_{c1}, h_{c1}, a)$, while $U_{2x}^{cr} = U_{2x}^{ca}$. Thus, if a loan would be taken out if parents and child live together, it also would be taken out if they live apart. Also, if no loan would be taken if living apart, then there would also be no loan if living together. Young people with low basic earning capacity and/or high levels of human capital investment would borrow from their parents in both living arrangements, while those with more "moderate" levels of y or s^* would only borrow when living apart from their parents. Finally, young adults with high y or low s^* would not borrow in either living arrangement.

It is assumed that parents' preferences are such that their altruism "outweighs" their taste for privacy in the sense that they are happy to have their child live with them. Then adult children choose whether to live with their parents or not. Among those with "moderate" levels of y or s^*, who would only borrow when living apart from their parents, we obtain the following impacts on the difference in the child's utility between the two living arrangements:

$$\frac{\partial V_c^r}{\partial M} - \frac{\partial V_c^a}{\partial M} = U_{1h}^{cr}\left(\frac{\partial h_p^r}{\partial M}\right) > 0 \qquad (10.22)$$

$$\frac{\partial V_c^r}{\partial y} - \frac{\partial V_c^a}{\partial y} = U_{1x}^{cr} - U_{1x}^{ca} < 0 \qquad (10.23)$$

because $x_{c1}^r > x_{c1}^a$,

$$\frac{\partial V_c^r}{\partial s^*} - \frac{\partial V_c^a}{\partial s^*} = 0 \qquad (10.24)$$

Equation (10.24) follows because $\partial V_c^i/\partial s^* = -kU_{1x}^{ci} + R^c U_{2x}^{ci}[dy_2(s)/ds] = 0$, $i = r, a$, from the first-order conditions. Higher parental wealth increases the chances of living together (10.22), because it increases the amount of (shared) housing consumption when doing so, but higher child earning capacity in the first period reduces the likelihood of co-residence (10.23). The prediction that the amount of human capital investment does not affect the choice of living arrangement differs from that of the altruistic model in the previous section. Thus, the estimated impact of the child's human capital investment on the probability of living with parents offers a way to discriminate between the two models. The significant impacts of human capital investment variables on the probability of co-residence found by Rosenzweig and Wolpin (1993) is evidence against the pure exchange model of living arrangement decisions presented in this section.

The discussion above indicated that higher human capital investment and lower basic earning capacity should increase the chances of taking out a loan from the parents. But the model predicts that, as in the model of Section 9.3, parental wealth should not affect the likelihood of a parental loan (i.e. loans are demand-determined), in contrast to the altruistic model of the previous section, in which the chances of a parental transfer to children increase with parental wealth. Unfortunately, it is not difficult to find reasons why parental wealth might affect the likelihood of a parental loan in a somewhat more general model. For instance, some parents may be liquidity constrained, and the chances of this being the case decline with parental wealth. Secondly, if lending to a child is riskier than other lending, then declining absolute risk aversion with higher wealth would lead to more lending to children among wealthier parents.

10.5 THREE-GENERATION HOUSEHOLDS

It is possible to use these same models to analyze whether middle-aged people live with their own parents. One obvious way to formulate the problem is to reverse the roles of parent and child in the analysis above. Analogous to Section 10.1, a middle-aged child may be selfish and have all of the bargaining power. The child would demand transfers from his parent(s) when they live together. A higher parent's pension income could either increase or decrease the chances that the parent chooses to live with their child, depending on the child's and parent's preferences (see (10.7)). The chances of living together decrease with higher child's income, because, if the child has tastes favouring privacy, he(she) can better afford to give up the joint consumption economies available from co-residence for privacy when he(she) is richer.

Alternatively, while there is likely to be mutual altruism (see Chapter 3), as indeed could be the case between parents and young adult offspring, only one of the generations can be an effective altruist. In the context of middle-aged children and their elderly parents, it is plausible to assume that the middle-aged children are more likely to be the effective altruist because their income is large relative to their elderly parents, particularly when the parent is a widow. The analysis in Section 10.2 then predicts that larger pension incomes would reduce the probability that an elderly mother lives with her children, while a higher child's income would increase this probability. Because the discrepancy between the income of elderly parents and their middle-aged children is probably smaller than between middle-aged parents and their young adult child, it is less likely that a middle-aged child is an effective altruist (in terms of financial transfers) toward his(her) elderly parent.

NOTES

1. $B - pC = U_x^C(U_{bb}^P + \lambda U_{bb}^C) + \lambda p U_{xx}^C U_b^C < 0$, because of diminishing marginal utility.

2. The assumption about parents' ability to borrow and lend is consistent with the results of the econometric analyses by Rosenzweig and Wolpin (1993, 1994).

CHAPTER ELEVEN

Social Interaction

AN INDIVIDUAL'S preferences, and therefore behaviour, may depend on what others in society are perceived to be doing. This may take the form of "learning" or "social influence". Certain decisions, particularly concerning the use of new technology, such as modern contraception, are subject to substantial uncertainty. Learning about other people's experiences through social interaction may reduce this uncertainty and make it more likely that a person adopts a new technology. Social influence captures the possibility that a person's preferences may be altered by those with whom the person interacts. For instance, the behaviour of others may affect childbearing outside marriage because of social stigma associated with non-marital births when they are rare and its erosion as more childbearing is outside marriage. Cohabitation without legal marriage may be another type of behaviour that is influenced by what other people are doing. Initially, the chapter focuses on models of social influence, but we return later to social learning in the context of adopting modern methods of contraception. To be more concrete, the decision of whether or not to have a child outside marriage is used to illustrate a generic social interaction model. It is mentioned frequently that out-of-wedlock childbearing is one of the phenomena that social interaction models help us understand, particularly its dynamics and spatial patterns (e.g. see Crane 1991; Durlauf and Young 2001; Glaeser and Scheinkman 2001).

11.1 A GENERIC SOCIAL INTERACTION MODEL

In the model of non-marital childbearing presented in Chapter 7, a woman who meets a man whom she rejects as a husband, or who rejects her as a wife, faces a decision about whether or not to have a child with this man. She is more likely to have a child on her own the higher is her utility per period as a single mother (relative to remaining single and childless), and the less that having a child slows down her subsequent search for a husband. Social influence is likely to affect the former. Using this model as our foundation, a linear approximation to a woman's expected discounted utility if she has a child outside marriage is expressed as $V_1 = \alpha_1 + \beta_1[P^e(x) - \delta] + z'\eta_1 + \xi_1$ while her utility if she remains single and childless is given by $V_0 = \alpha_0 + \beta_0[P^e(x) - \delta] + z'\eta_0 + \xi_0$. The *expected* proportion of women in a woman's "reference group" x(e.g. nationality, religious or ethnic group) who have their first birth outside marriage when a couple does not agree to marry is denoted as $P^e(x)$. Observable individual attributes (e.g. educational attainment, wages, non-labour income), denoted as z, may affect utility in these two states, and ξ_1 and ξ_0 are unobserved woman-specific variables, which reflect her preferences and other unobservable influences on the utility from each choice. For instance, ξ_1 may also reflect attributes of the potential father. The other Greek letters represent parameters. For instance, the α_j parameters may reflect state benefits to single mothers (in which case $\alpha_1 > \alpha_0$), the cost and availability of abortion, and other economic influences on all women facing the decision of whether to have a child outside marriage or not.

Social, or "normative", influences on utility are indicated by the terms $\beta_1(P^e(x) - \delta)$ and $\beta_0(P^e(x) - \delta)$, with $\beta_0 \leq 0 < \beta_1$. The parameter δ is a threshold parameter, such that when $P^e(x) < \delta$, the expected level of non-marital fertility in a woman's reference group exerts a negative influence on utility from single motherhood and a positive influence on utility from remaining single and childless. The opposite is the case when $P^e(x) > \delta$. A value of $P^e(x)$ below δ could reflect "social stigma". Thus, the utility associated with non-marital childbearing is larger, and the utility associated with remaining childless is lower, when more women in her reference group become mothers outside marriage.

Among pairs of the opposite sex who meet while searching for a spouse and do not agree to marry, the woman chooses to become a mother outside marriage if and only if $V_1 > V_0$; that is, when $\xi = \xi_1 - \xi_0 > -\{\alpha + \beta[P^e(x) - \delta] + z'\eta\}$, where $\alpha = \alpha_1 - \alpha_0$, $\beta = \beta_1 - \beta_0$ and $\eta = \eta_1 - \eta_0$. Social influence exists when $\beta > 0$. The taste and father-attributes variable ξ is assumed to have some random, symmetric (about the origin) distribution in the reference group population, and so the probability that a woman with reference group x becomes a single mother when the pair do not agree to marry, denoted as $P(x)$, is given by the probability that ξ is less than $\alpha + \beta[P^e(x) - \delta] + z'\eta$, or

$$P(x) = H[\alpha + \beta(P^e(x) - \delta) + z'\eta] \tag{11.1}$$

where $H[\ ]$ is a specified continuous, strictly increasing distribution function, such as the logistic distribution.[1]

A *social equilibrium* occurs when people's expectations are consistent with the average proportion in the reference group who become single mothers when a couple does not marry; that is, when the actual proportion in the reference group is equal to the expected proportion. The actual proportion in the reference group who become single mothers is given by

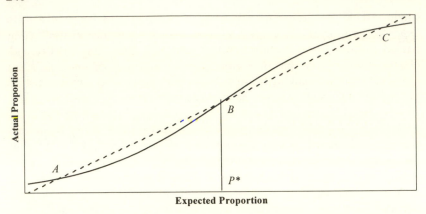

Figure 11.1 Equilibrium proportions becoming a single mother, "large" beta.

$$P(x) = \int H[\alpha + \beta(P^e(x) - \delta) + z'\eta]dP(z \mid x) \qquad (11.2)$$

where $P(z \mid x)$ is the distribution of z in the reference group defined by x. In *equilibrium*, people's expectations are consistent with the mathematical expectation in (11.2); that is, $P^e(x) = P(x)$.

The non-linear curves in Figures 11.1 and 11.2 plot the relationship between actual and expected proportions becoming single mothers (i.e. (11.2)) for two values of β, and the 45-degree line represents the condition that $P^e(x) = P(x)$.[2] At the points at which the curve intersects the line, actual and expected proportions are equal; thus these are social equilibria. These figures illustrate Manski's (1993) demonstration that

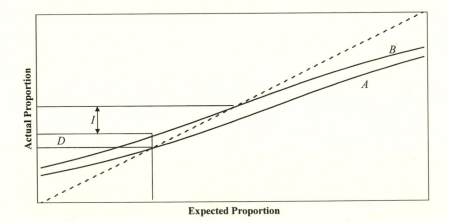

Figure 11.2 Equilibrium proportions becoming a single mother, "moderate" beta.

this model is "coherent", in the sense of there being a solution to the 'social equilibrium' equation that arises from substituting $P(x)$ for $P^e(x)$ in (11.2), and that, with $\beta > 0$, there is the possibility of more than one social equilibrium for given values of the parameters and given the distribution of z in the reference group.

Consider the case in which $H[\cdot]$ is the logistic distribution function and $\alpha + z'\eta$ is distributed symmetrically about the origin. If $\beta < 4$, there is a unique social equilibrium (see curve A or B in Figure 11.2). If, however, $\beta > 4$, then there are at least three social equilibria (see Figure 11.1). The intuition behind why this critical value happens to be 4 in the case of the logistic distribution can be explained using Figure 11.1.[3] Note that in order to obtain the three equilibria in Figure 11.1 it must be the case that in the neighbourhood of equilibrium B, at which $P(x) = 0.5$, $\partial P(x)/\partial P^e(x) > 1$. With the logistic distribution, $\partial P(x)/\partial P^e(x) = \beta P(x)[1 - P(x)]$, and so around equilibrium B, $\partial P(x)/\partial P^e(x) = 0.25\beta$. Thus, $\partial P(x)/\partial P^e(x) > 1$ in the neighbourhood of B requires $\beta > 4$. It should be noted, however, that $\beta > 4$ is not a sufficient condition for multiple equilibria. If, for example, the distribution of observable attributes (z) is sufficiently skewed toward people who favour (are against) childbearing outside marriage, or the symmetry is not around the origin, there can be one high-level (low-level) equilibrium. These possibilities are illustrated by curve A in Figure 11.3 and curve B in Figure 11.4.

Given its frequent use in empirical analysis, the logistic distribution is convenient for illustrating the implications of a social interaction model. But these are similar for any relationship between actual and expected proportions that exhibits the S-shape illustrated in Figure 11.1 for sufficiently strong social interaction effects (i.e. a large enough value of β). In

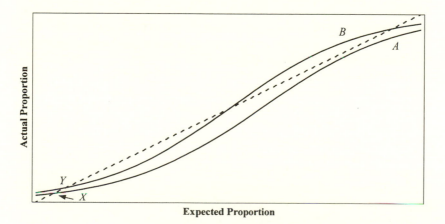

Figure 11.3 Equilibrium proportions becoming a single mother, "large" beta.

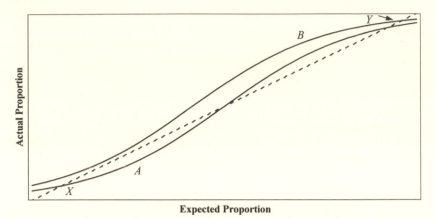

Figure 11.4   Equilibrium proportions becoming a single mother, "large" beta.

this case, multiple equilibria emerge. If we make some plausible assumptions about dynamics we can characterize an equilibrium like *B* in Figure 11.1 as unstable.

In the spirit of Schelling (1978), assume the following dynamics. A birth cohort of young women base their expectations on the behaviour of the preceding birth cohort. Starting at any value of the expected proportion above the one corresponding to equilibrium *B* in Figure 11.1, denoted as *P**, the proportion who become single mothers in the current cohort will exceed their expectations, which increases the expected proportion in the succeeding cohort. Some people with attributes who would not have had a child outside marriage at a lower expected proportion becoming single mothers now have a child rather than remain single and childless. This behaviour raises the proportion becoming single mothers and increases the expected value for the next cohort and so forth until the society converges to a "pervasive non-marital childbearing" equilibrium at point *C*.

Conversely, starting at values of the expected proportion below *P**, the current cohort will be disappointed because the proportion of them becoming single mothers will be less than they expected, and so the succeeding cohort has lower expectations. People who would have become a single mothers if more of their peers did, will not do so, leading to lower expectations for the next cohort and so on, ultimately producing a "rare non-marital childbearing" equilibrium at *A*. With these dynamics, the equilibrium at *B* is clearly unstable, and so there are only two stable equilibrium candidates. Initial expectations can, therefore, be important in determining the proportion who become single mothers when people respond sufficiently to what others are doing. In this sense, "history matters" for the selection of the low-level or high-level equilibrium. Furthermore, *temporary* changes in the socio-economic environment that alter non-marital childbearing behaviour and/or expectations can produce dramatic changes in the proportion who become single mothers, by causing a move from a type-*A* equilibrium to a type-*C* equilibrium. For example, some temporary development that encouraged women to expect that the proportion becoming single mothers would be above P^* in Figure 11.1 would produce a *permanent* dramatic increase in the proportion.

Figure 11.2 illustrates two situations in which social interaction effects are present, but smaller in size than in Figure 11.1. In each there is a unique stable equilibrium to which a society converges no matter what the initial expectations are. The two situations differ in the level of α, or alternatively in the distribution of observable attributes (z). Curve *A* corresponds to a situation in which either α is lower than in the situation corresponding to curve *B*, or these attributes are skewed toward types of women who are against childbearing outside marriage, while curve *B* represents a situation in which these attributes are distributed symmetrically about the origin.[4] If social influence is relatively strong, but not large enough to produce multiple equilibria, small changes in the socioeconomic environment, such as higher state benefits for single mothers (leading to a larger α), can produce large changes in the proportion becoming single mothers. There is a "multiplier effect" of such changes in the "fundamental" determinants of differences in utility between the two actions. This is illustrated in Figure 11.2. Suppose the initial situation is represented by curve *A*, but now the distribution of attributes in the reference group changes in favour of non-marital childbearing, or α increases, such that curve *B* is now the relevant one. The direct effect of this change is denoted by the distance *D* in Figure 11.2. It raises the proportion becoming a single mother by about 6 percentage points. The indirect effect of the change is denoted by the distance *I* in Figure 11.2, which raises the proportion by an additional 15 percentage points. The latter effect arises because the expected proportion of women who become single mothers increases, thereby eroding social stigma.

The *social multiplier* is the ratio of the total effect on the proportion becoming a single mother to the direct effect; that is $(D + I)/D$. In other words, each person's actions change not only because of the direct change in some fundamental determinant but also because of the change in the behaviour of their peers.[5] If this social multiplier is large, populations with slightly different distributions of attributes or parameters could exhibit very different proportions of women who become single mothers. It may indeed be impossible to distinguish empirically between a large social multiplier and multiple social equilibria. The social multiplier will be larger when social influence (β) is larger, because larger β produces a steeper relationship between the actual proportion who become single mothers and the expected proportion in the relevant range of $P^e(x)$ (i.e. $\partial P(x)/\partial P^e(x)$ is larger).

When social influences are much larger (e.g. $\beta > 4$ with the logistic distribution), but the distribution of observable attributes are skewed toward women who are against childbearing outside marriage, there would again be a unique low-level equilibrium such as that corresponding to curve A in Figure 11.3. A shift in the distribution of attributes favourable to non-marital childbearing could then produce a situation of multiple equilibria like that corresponding to curve B Figure 11.3. There would only be a small increase in the equilibrium proportion of women becoming single mothers as a consequence of the distributional shift (from point X to Y), because the stronger social influence corresponding to the large value of β would dampen the response to the shift. Women in the reference group would be stuck at the low-level equilibrium because of the effect of social stigma.

Now suppose again that social influences are large ($\beta > 4$ in the logistic case), and that there are two stable equilibria, as in Figure 11.1. This situation is reproduced as curve A in Figure 11.4. Suppose that for historical reasons, the initial equilibrium corresponding to this situation is the low-level one at point X. A sufficient increase in α, say because of an increase in state benefits to single mothers, would make curve B in Figure 11.4 the relevant relationship between expected and actual proportions becoming a single mother, and the equilibrium proportion would jump dramatically to that corresponding to point Y in Figure 11.4.[6] Thus, a moderate change in a fundamental determinant of the utility of single motherhood can produce an enormous change in the proportion of women becoming a single mother when faced with the decision (because they either reject a man as a husband or are rejected by him). Such is the potential power of social interaction effects.

Figure 11.5 shows how the percentage of births that are outside marriage has changed between 1975 and 1997 in a number of European countries. What is apparent in all of them is the dramatic change in this percentage over a couple of decades. It is difficult to believe that the fundamental determinants of the decision to become a single mother have changed by these orders of magnitude. The large observed changes in the percentage of births that are non-marital may reflect small changes in these determinants, the effects of which are magnified by social interaction effects.

Glaeser and Scheinkman (2001) present another way of measuring social interaction effects. While it is beyond the scope of this chapter to provide the details, they show that the fundamental social interaction

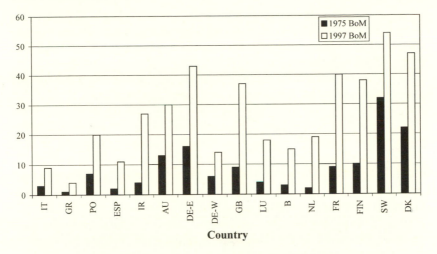

Figure 11.5 Percentage of births outside marriage.

parameter (comparable to β above) is related to the difference between the variance of the behavioural variable calculated from aggregate data (between American cities in their analysis) and its variance calculated at the individual level (within cities). If a woman's behaviour is affected by the behaviour of her neighbours, then the variance from aggregate data should substantially exceed the individual level variance. They apply their methods to the share of families that are headed by a woman, which is strongly related to childbearing outside marriage (although it is also affected by divorce). They find evidence of large social interaction effects on female headship. Crane (1991) also provides evidence of neighbourhood social influences on teenage childbearing, which is usually outside marriage. Thus, there is evidence to support the social influences on nonmarital fertility suggested by the theoretical model outlined above.

11.2 SOCIAL INTERACTION AND RISE IN COHABITING UNIONS

Social interaction effects may also explain the clustering of European countries in terms of a cross-section snapshot of the prevalence of cohabiting unions in 1996, shown in Figure 11.6.[7]

The countries fall into three broad groups in terms of the percentage of women aged 25–29 who live in a cohabiting union. The lowest are Italy, Greece, Portugal, Spain and Ireland, shown in the bottom left-hand corner (all below 5% cohabiting). In the top right-hand corner are France, Finland, Sweden and Denmark (all above 25%). The remaining countries of the European Union are in the middle. Such clustering is

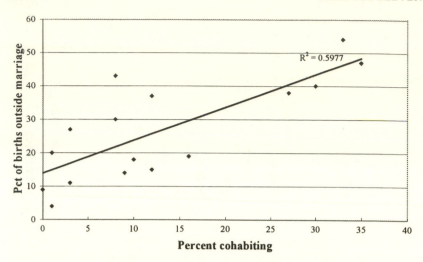

Figure 11.6 Percentage of births outside marriage (1997) and percentage of women aged 25–29 cohabiting (1996) in 16 European countries.

consistent with a social interaction model with multiple equilibria. The dramatic increase in the proportion of British young people cohabiting in their first partnership over one generation, from one-third to four-fifths, is also consistent with large social interaction effects, either producing multiple equilibria or a large social multiplier.

Great Britain may provide an example of the process through which social interaction helped produce a large rise in pre-marital cohabitation. There have been important changes in young people's education that may have been a driving force for change in patterns of first partnership in Britain. For instance, one-third of 18-year-olds were in full-time education in 1992, compared with 15% in 1979. The dramatic shift toward cohabiting unions may be a consequence of the trend in higher education, which was magnified by the erosion of social stigma, as outlined in the previous section.

Bagnoli and Bergstrom (1993) argue that young men who expect to prosper in later life will postpone marriage until their success becomes evident to potential marriage partners. Those who do not expect their economic status to advance much will seek to marry at a relatively young age. The careers of those who obtain university degrees take longer to develop and their earnings peak later in their life. Thus, as more young men went on to higher education, the proportion of young men who think it is worth waiting to signal their better economic status is likely to have increased.

The increasing proportion of young women obtaining university degrees are likely to be less willing to accept the traditional marital division of labour and have stronger lifetime attachment to paid employment. Thus, they may also wish to signal their economic status. In any case, because of assortative mating, they wish to marry men with degrees. Even if they were as willing to make long-term commitments at each age as in the past, they would not find men who wished to do so, for the reasons given above.

Beyond a certain age, young people may nevertheless prefer to have a live-in partner, and cohabiting unions cater for this preference while allowing them to postpone making a long-term commitment. Thus, higher educational achievement encourages young people to enter live-in partnerships later and to cohabit when they do. The observation of short spells of cohabiting unions before either dissolving the union or marrying their partner is consistent with the argument that they are used while waiting to signal economic success and as a learning experience before stronger commitments are made. The social interaction model outlined above could explain why cohabitation spread so rapidly in response to these stronger incentives to cohabit before marriage, even if these were confined to university graduates.

British evidence suggests that, as the arguments above predict, university graduates used to be more likely to cohabit in their first partnership, but this is no longer the case as cohabiting in one's first partnership has become widespread, arguably through social interaction effects. Ermisch and Francesconi (2000c) found that there was a social class gradient in the odds of cohabitation relative to marriage among people born during 1950–1962, rising with father's job status, but this has disappeared. For the 1950–1962 cohort, compared to all occupations other than professional or managerial, the odds of cohabiting relative to marrying are 2.8 (2.6) times higher for women (men) having a father in a professional job and are 30% (50%) higher for women (men) whose father was in a managerial job, but these differentials disappear for the those born during 1963–1976. These are, of course, the social groups who were responsible for a large proportion of university entrants among those born in the 1950s. The results are consistent with social interaction effects spreading cohabitation widely from university graduates, who always had an incentive to cohabit before marrying, to a large proportion of the population.

Ermisch (2003) shows that in Britain a higher incidence of cohabitation in first partnerships is strongly associated with the rise in childbearing outside marriage. Cross-national correlation also supports such an association. The percentage of women aged 25–29 who lived in a cohabiting union is plotted in Figure 11.6 against each country's percentage of all births outside marriage in 1997. The correlation coefficient between these two variables is 0.77, and Figure 11.6 displays the linear regression line. Among women aged 20–24, the correlation coefficient is the same.

This suggests that the expansion of higher education acting in conjunction with social interaction effects may also lie behind the large increase in childbearing outside marriage in Britain. In order for this argument to be correct it is not necessary to show that university graduates were themselves having children in cohabiting unions to a significant degree. They were the pioneers of cohabiting unions, but social interaction effects spread them widely throughout society, to people who would have stronger incentives to have children within such unions (see Chapter 7).

11.3 SOCIAL LEARNING OR SOCIAL INFLUENCE?

Social interaction may also account for the fact that the classic fertility transitions in Europe (from high to low fertility) during the nineteenth and early twentieth centuries appear to have occurred too quickly once they started and under too wide a range of social and economic conditions to be consistent with their being driven entirely by socio-economic change (Kohler 2001). Similar remarks apply to fertility transitions in contemporary developing countries. As we have seen in the first section of the chapter, small changes in fundamental socio-economic determinants of behaviour can, however, produce large and rapid changes in behaviour when strong social interaction effects operate. Thus, the social interaction model may also explain large and rapid fertility decline in one country or region while there is little change in another, which is similar in terms of socio-economic conditions.

The previous two sections have focused on social influence as the explanation for a positive value of the social interaction coefficient β. But, as noted at the beginning of the chapter, social interaction may also arise because of learning when a decision is subject to substantial uncertainty. An example of this, which we pursue in this section, is the adoption of modern methods of contraception in a situation in which such methods are novel. Following Kohler (2001, Chapter 3), we adapt the model of the previous section in a way that allows a distinction between social influence and learning and use an empirical study that employs this framework to estimate the key parameters of this model (Kohler et al. 2001).

The first section emphasized how social networks constrain behaviour, but they also provide opportunities for the exchange of information. Suppose a woman has four "network partners" with whom she exchanges information about family planning. At one extreme, none of these network partners interact with one another; their only link is secondary in that each of them interacts with this particular woman. At the other extreme, they may all interact with each other so that all six possible links between these four partners exist. *Network density* is the concept that describes the connected-ness of the network partners, and it is defined as the proportion of all possible social links that exist in the network. In our example network of four partners, it is the number of actual links divided by six. The maximum network density is unity, and a very sparse network has a density of zero. As discussed more fully in Kohler (2001, Chapter 3), a sparse network is most efficient for obtaining information, because, in our example, four different sources of information are tapped by social interaction. Denser networks are less efficient for obtaining information because the partners already share most of the information available to them and there is little advantage in terms of additional information from maintaining contacts with all four partners. By integrating a woman into a larger group, dense networks are more likely to constrain a woman's ability to deviate from prevailing behaviour; that is, they exert a stronger normative influence than sparse networks. A woman's only alternative to agreeing with other members of this group may be to leave the group. In sum, the sparse network is either equivalent to the dense network in terms of information gathering or more effective, while social influence is stronger in dense networks than sparse ones because of the indirect links through other network partners in dense networks.

Information on the density of social networks can be used to distinguish between the dominance of social influence or social learning on behaviour. If learning dominates, then both dense and sparse networks containing a larger proportion of women using modern contraceptive methods should increase the chances that a woman will adopt these methods. Because sparse networks are more efficient sources of information, the impact of density on these chances is either zero or negative. If social influence dominates, then the proportion of women in a woman's social network using modern methods would have a weak effect on her adoption of these methods in sparse networks, but a strong effect in dense networks. That is, the impact of the proportion increases with the density of the network.

To embed these ideas in the generic social interaction model of the first section, let $\beta = \beta_0 + \beta_1 D$, where D is network density defined above. Now let V_1 be the utility from using modern methods of contraception and V_0 be the utility from using traditional methods, and $P^e(x)$ is the proportion using modern methods in the woman's social network x. Then, the difference in utilities is given by $\alpha + \beta_0(P^e(x) - \delta) + \beta_1(P^e(x) - \delta)D + z'\eta + \xi$, and the probability that an individual woman uses modern methods is

$$P(x) = H[\alpha - \delta\beta_0 + \beta_0 P^e(x) - \beta_1 \delta D + \beta_1 D P^e(x) + z'\eta] \qquad (11.3)$$

If ξ has a logistic distribution, then with data on the density of social networks and the use of modern methods of contraception within these networks, we can estimate the following logistic regression model:

$$P(x) = H[\gamma_0 + \gamma_1 P^e(x) + \gamma_2 D + \gamma_3 D P^e(x) + z'\eta] \qquad (11.4)$$

where $\gamma_0 = \alpha - \delta\beta_0$, $\gamma_1 = \beta_0$, $\gamma_2 = -\beta_1\delta$, and $\gamma_3 = \beta_1$. This is a straight-forward "logit" model with an interaction between density and the proportion in the network using modern methods. From these relationships, it is clear that from the estimates of (11.4) we can estimate some of the funda-mental parameters of the model in (11.3). In particular, $\delta = -\gamma_2/\gamma_3$, $\beta_0 = \gamma_1$ and $\beta_1 = \gamma_3$. Kohler et al. (2001) provide estimates of the γ_j parameters from evidence from South Nyanza District of Kenya during the mid-1990s that differ by region. For one group of regions (OKW), their estimates imply that $\beta_0 = -1.71$, $\beta_1 = 3.89$ and $\delta = 0.71$, while for the other region (Obisa), $\beta_0 = 4.50$, $\beta_1 = -2.81$ and $\delta = -0.12$. These results indicate that social influence is the dominant aspect of social networks in the OKW region, because the impact of the proportion of women in the social network who have ever used family planning on a woman's probability of adopting family planning increases with the density of the network. The fact that in Obisa the impact of the proportion declines with density indicates that social learning dominates in this region.

What do these parameter estimates imply about the strength of the social interaction effect and the possibility of multiple equilibria? The estimated size of the effect, $\beta = \beta_0 + \beta_1 D$, clearly depends on the density of the social network. For most women in the sample, the density of their network varies from one-half to unity (only 11% have network densities less than one-half), and the mean density is relatively high (about 0.8). Thus, it appears that social interaction effects are not sufficiently high to produce multiple equilibria, but they are large enough to suggest large multiplier effects.

The estimate of the threshold parameter, δ, for the OKW region ($\delta = 0.71$) indicates that when the proportion of women in the social network who have ever used family planning is less than 0.71, social influence constrains the use of modern contraception (i.e. it supports the status quo). But when this proportion exceeds 0.71, social influence accelerates the use of modern contraceptives. In the Obisa region, this threshold parameter is indeed negative. Thus, a higher proportion in the network using modern methods always increases the probability that an individual woman uses them.

Kohler et al. (2001) argue that the greater prevalence of market activities in the Obisa region may explain why social learning is the dominant form of the social interaction effect there. Further empirical analysis indicates that a higher proportion of women in a village who sell goods at a market reduces the threshold parameter (δ), which suggests that social learning is a more important channel through which social interaction operates in villages with high market activities. The empirical estimates also indicate that more market activity is associated with larger social interaction effects (β) for sparse networks, while for dense networks market activity has little impact on the size of social effects, presumably because market activity facilitates information diffusion but not normative influences. The estimates imply that more market activity shifts the parameters δ and β toward social learning effects and away from social influence effects. These results suggest that market development over time may produce a dominance of social learning over social influence, thereby increasing diffusion of modern contraceptive methods and lowering fertility.

11.4 MARKETS AND MULTIPLIERS

So far we have discussed social interaction and social multipliers operating through preferences, often called non-market interactions. Social multipliers and multiple equilibria can also arise through market interactions. The discussion in this section considers briefly some examples of interaction through marriage markets. Of course, all markets represent a form of social interaction. Higher demand for a good by person A increases its price, thereby reducing the consumption of person B. This negative interaction lies at the core of economics. Here we are concerned with positive social interaction mediated by the marriage market.

As mentioned often in earlier chapters, sharing public goods are one source of the gain from marriage. Changes in emotional feelings toward one another may, however, motivate a couple to contemplate dissolving their marriage. But divorce brings costs, because finding another partner involves time and effort, and there is a risk of remaining single and not enjoying the joint consumption economies of marriage. The expected gain from divorce depends, therefore, on the prospects of remarriage. These prospects depend on the decisions of others to divorce and remarry. If many couples are expected to divorce, then the prospects of remarriage are high because there are more people in the remarriage market. Divorce is then less costly and each particular couple is more likely to decide to divorce. If instead the divorce rate is expected to be low, then divorce is more costly and is less likely to occur. Thus, there is the possibility of multiple equilibria because of this self-fulfilling nature of divorce expectations. That is, either a high-divorce or a low-divorce equilibrium may be supported with the same set of fundamental factors affecting divorce decisions. Chiappori and Weiss (2000) analyse a model that addresses this issue.

Even if there is a unique equilibrium, exogenous factors that influence divorce, such as welfare payments to single mothers, are subject to a social multiplier effect. By improving remarriage prospects for all divorcees (i.e. reducing the cost of divorce), an increase in the divorce rate generated by a small change in its fundamental determinants can give rise to a large change in the divorce rate. Furthermore, because people do not take into account that one's own divorce increases the remarriage chances of all other divorcees, the marriage market produces too few divorces. That is, there is a search externality that produces inefficiency.

Goldin and Katz (2000) provide an important example of how social interaction through the marriage market magnified the impact of the contraceptive pill on women's career decisions. In the absence of reliable contraception, women undertaking lengthy professional education would have to incur the cost of sexual abstinence or the risk of pregnancy. By increasing the ease and reliability of contraception, women could make this investment at a much lower cost, thereby encouraging more of them to enter professional careers.

The pill also had an indirect, social multiplier effect. Women undertaking lengthy education generally delay marriage. If in the interim other women marry, career women are likely to have to settle for a poorer match at the end of their training because the pool of eligible bachelors is smaller. By reducing the penalty of delaying marriage (sexual abstinence or pregnancy risk), the pill encouraged all women and men to delay marriage to a time when their tastes and character were better formed, thereby allowing them to make a better match. This created a better ("thicker") marriage market for career women, thereby reducing the cost of delaying marriage while undertaking their professional studies and encouraging them to pursue a career. Goldin and Katz (2000) present an impressive array of evidence supporting this argument.

Much of this book has focused on decisions at the individual level and the impacts of prices and resources on them. This final chapter has indicated that there are often important feedback effects of the choices of one's peers on one's own choices. This has been a growing area of research in recent years.

NOTES

1. If we assume the extreme value distribution for ξ_1 and ξ_0, then ξ is distributed according to a logistic distribution.

2. Figure 11.1 assumes that $H[\cdot]$ is the logistic distribution function and that $\alpha + z'\eta$ takes on three values, -0.5, 0 and 0.5, which are distributed symmetrically about the origin (with probabilities 0.25, 0.5 and 0.25), and that $\beta = 6$. Curve B in Figure 11.2 makes the same assumptions except that $\beta = 3$.

3. For a more formal demonstration of the circumstances in which multiple equilibria arise in the logistic model, see Brock and Durlauf (2000).

4. Curve A in Figure 11.2 assumes that $H[\cdot]$ is the logistic distribution function and that $\alpha + z'\eta$ takes on three values, -0.8, -0.3 and 0.2, which occur with probabilities 0.25, 0.5 and 0.25, and that $\beta = 3$. The previous footnote stated the assumptions for curve B.

5. It can be thought of as the ratio of the per capita response of the entire peer group to a change in an attribute (e.g. education) or a parameter (e.g. cost of contraception) that affects the entire peer group to the response of an individual to that same attribute or parameter that affects only that person (e.g. see Glaeser and Scheinkman 2001).

6. For curve B of Figure 11.4, α is raised by 0.5, so that $\alpha + z'\eta$ takes on three values, 0, 0.5 and 1, which are distributed symmetrically about 0.5 (with probabilities 0.25, 0.5 and 0.25).

7. While there may be under-reporting of cohabiting unions in the 1996 Eurobarometer Survey from which these data are derived, the relative position of different countries is probably accurate (Kiernan 1999).

Bibliography

Aiyagari, S.R., J. Greenwood and N. Guner. 2000. On the state of the union. *Journal of Political Economy* 108: 213–244.

Altonji, J.G., F. Hayashi and L.J. Kotlikoff. 1992. Is the extended family altruistically linked? Direct tests using micro data. *American Economic Review* 82: 1177–1198.

Bagnoli, M. and T. Bergstrom. 1993. Courtship as a waiting game. *Journal of Political Economy* 101: 185–202.

Becker, G.S. 1960. An economic analysis of fertility. In *Demographic and Economic Change in Developed Countries*, 209–231. Princeton, NJ: National Bureau of Economic Research.

———. 1965. A theory of the allocation of time. *Economic Journal* 75: 493–517.

———. 1981. *A Treatise on the Family*. Cambridge, MA: Harvard University Press.

Becker, G.S. and H.G. Lewis. 1973. On the interaction between the quantity and quality of children. *Journal of Political Economy* 81: S279–S288.

Becker, G.S. and N. Tomes. 1986. Human capital and the rise and fall of families. *Journal of Labor Economics* 4: S1–S39.

Behrman, J.R. and A.B. Deolalikar. 1989. The intrahousehold demand for nutrients in rural south India: individual estimates, fixed effects, and permanent income. *Journal of Human Resources* 25: 665–696.

Behrman, J.R., R. Pollak and P. Taubman. 1982. Parental preferences and provision for progeny. *Journal of Political Economy* 90: 52–73.

Behrman, J.R., M.R. Rosenzweig and P. Taubman. 1994. Endowments and the allocation of schooling in the family and in the marriage market: the twins experiment. *Journal of Political Economy* 102: 1131–1174.

Behrman, J.R., A.D. Foster, M.R. Rosenzweig and P. Vashishtha. 1999. Women's schooling, home teaching and economic growth. *Journal of Political Economy* 107: 682–714.

Bergstrom, T.C. 1989. A fresh look at the rotten kid theorem—and other household mysteries. *Journal of Political Economy* 97: 1138–1159.

———. 1996. Economics in a family way. *Journal of Economic Literature* 34: 1903–1934.

Bergstrom, T.C. and R.C. Cornes. 1981. Gorman and Musgrave are dual: an andipodean theorem on public goods. *Economic Letters* 7: 371–378.

Bergstrom, T.C., L. Blume and H. Varian. 1986. On the private provision of public goods. *Journal of Public Economics* 29: 25–49.

Bernheim, B.D., A. Schleifer and L.H. Summers. 1985. The strategic bequest motive. *Journal of Political Economy* 93: 1045–1076.

Binmore, K.G. 1985. Bargaining and coalitions. In *Game-Theoretic Models of Bargaining*, ed. A. Roth, 259–304. Cambridge: Cambridge University Press.

Böheim, R. and J.F. Ermisch. 2001. Partnership dissolution in the UK—the role of economic circumstances. *Oxford Bulletin of Economics and Statistics* 63: 197–208.

Börsch-Supan, A. 1986. Household formation, housing prices, and public policy. *Journal of Public Economics* 30: 145–164.

Bourguignon, F. 1999. The cost of children: may the collective approach to household behavior help? *Journal of Population Economics* 12: 503–521.

Brien, M., L. Lillard and L. Waite. 1999. Inter-related family building behaviors: cohabitation, marriage, and nonmarital conception. *Demography* 36: 535–551.

Brock, W. and S. Durlauf. 2000. Interactions-based models. In *Handbook of Econometrics*, Vol. 5, ed. J. Heckman and E. Leamer, 3297–3380. Amsterdam: North-Holland.

Browning, M. and P.-A. Chiappori. 1998. Efficient intra-household allocations: a general characterization and empirical tests. *Econometrica* 66: 1241–1278.

Browning, M. and V. Lechene. 2001. Caring and sharing: tests between alternative models of intra-household allocation. Institute of Economics Discussion Paper No. 01-07, University of Copenhagen.

Browning, M., F. Bourguignon, P.-A. Chiappori and V. Lechene. 1994. Income and outcomes: a structural model of intrahousehold allocation. *Journal of Political Economy* 102: 1067–1096.

Bruce, N. and M. Waldman. 1990. The rotten-kid theorem meets the Samaritan's dilemma. *Quarterly Journal of Economics* 105: 155–166.

Buchanan, J. 1975. The Samaritan's dilemma. In *Altruism, Morality and Economic Theory*, ed. E.S. Phelps. New York: Russell Sage Foundation.

Burdett, K. and M.G. Coles. 1997. Marriage and class. *Quarterly Journal of Economics* 112: 141–168.

_____. 1999. Long-term partnership formation: marriage and employment. *The Economic Journal* 109: F307–F334.

Burdett, K. and J.F. Ermisch. 2002. Single mothers. Working Paper Institute for Social and Economic Research Working Papers. Paper 2002-30, Colchester: University of Essex.

Chami, R. 1996. King Lear's dilemma: precommitment versus the last word. *Economics Letters* 52: 171–176.

_____. 1998. Private income transfers and market incentives. *Economica* 65: 461–478.

Chiappori, P.-A. 1992. Collective labor supply and welfare. *Journal of Political Economy* 100: 437–467.

Chiappori, P.-A. and Y. Weiss. 2000. Marriage contracts and divorce: an equilibrium analysis. Mimeo. Chicago, IL: University of Chicago.

Chiappori, P.-A., B. Fortin and G. Lacroix. 2002. Household labor supply, sharing rule and the marriage market. *Journal of Political Economy* in press.

Cigno, A. 1991. *Economics of the Family*. Oxford: Oxford University Press.

_____. 1998. Fertility decisions when infant survival is endogenous. *Journal of Population Economics* 11: 21–28.

Cigno, A. and F. Rosati. 1992. The effects of financial markets and social security on saving and fertility behaviour in Italy. *Journal of Population Economics* 5: 319–344.

Clark, S. 1999. Law, property and marital dissolution. *Economic Journal* 109: C41–C54.

Cox, D. 1987. Motives for private income transfers. *Journal of Political Economy* 95: 508–546.

_____. 1990. Intergenerational transfers and liquidity constraints. *Quarterly Journal of Economics* 105: 187–217.

Cox, D. and F. Raines. 1985. Interfamily transfers and income redistribution. In *Horizontal Equity, Uncertainty and Measures of Well-Being*, ed. M. David and T. Smeeding, 393–421. Chicago, IL: University of Chicago Press (for National Bureau of Economic Research).

Crane, J. 1991. The epidemic theory of ghettos and neighborhood effects on dropping out and teenage childbearing. *American Journal of Sociology* 96: 1226–1259.

Dasgupta, P. 1988. Trust as a commodity. In *Trust: Making and Breaking Cooperative Relations*, ed. D. Gambetta, 49–72. Oxford: Basil Blackwell.

Del Boca, D. and C. Flinn. 1994. Expenditure decisions of divorced mothers and income composition. *Journal of Human Resources* 29: 742–761.

_____. 1995. Rationalizing child support decisions. *American Economic Review* 85: 1241–1262.

Duncan, G.J. and S. Hoffman. 1985. A reconsideration of the economic consequences of marital dissolution. *Demography* 22: 485–497.

_____. 1988. What *are* the economic consequences of divorce? *Demography* 25: 641–645.

Durlauf, S.N. and H.P. Young. 2001. The new social economics. In *Social Dynamics*, ed. S.N. Durlauf and H.P. Young. London: MIT Press.

Ermisch, J.F. 1988. Econometric analysis of birth rate dynamics in Britain. *Journal of Human Resources* 23: 563–576.

_____. 1989. Purchased child care, optimal family size and mother's employment. *Journal of Population Economics* 2: 79–102.

_____. 1996. The demand for housing in Britain and population ageing: microeconometric evidence. *Economica* 63: 383–404.

_____. 1999. Prices, parents and young people's household formation. *Journal of Urban Economics* 45: 47–71.

_____. 2001. Cohabitation and childbearing outside marriage in Britain. In *Out of Wedlock*, ed. L. Wu and B. Wolfe, 109–139. New York: Russell Sage Foundation.

_____. 2003. The puzzling rise in childbearing outside marriage. In *Sociology's Contribution to Understanding British Society*, ed. D. Gallie, J.F. Ermisch and A. Heath. Oxford: Oxford University Press.

Ermisch, J.F. and M. Francesconi. 2000a. Educational choice, families and young people's earnings. *Journal of Human Resources* 35: 143–176.

_____. 2000b. Cohabitation in Great Britain: not for long, but here to stay. *Journal of the Royal Statistical Society, Series A* 163: 153–171.

_____. 2000c. Patterns of household and family formation. In *Seven Years in the Lives of British Families*, ed. R. Berthoud and J. Gershuny, 21–34. Bristol: The Policy Press.

_____. 2001a. Family matters: impacts of family background on educational attainments. *Economica* 68: 137–156.

_____. 2001b. Family structure and children's achievements. *Journal of Population Economics* 14: 249–270.

Ermisch, J.F. and E. Overton. 1985. Minimal household units: a new approach to the analysis of household formation. *Population Studies* 39: 33–54.

Ermisch, J.F. and R.E. Wright. 1991. Welfare benefits and lone parents' employment in Great Britain. *Journal of Human Resources* 26: 424–456.

Flinn, C. 2000. Modes of interaction between divorced parents. *International Economic Review* 41: 544–578.

Fortin, B. and G. Lacroix. 1997. A test of the unitary and collective models of household labour supply. *Economic Journal* 107: 933–955.

Friedberg, L. 1998. Did unilateral divorce raise divorce rates? Evidence from panel data. *American Economic Review* 88: 608–627.

Garen, J. 1984. The returns to schooling: a selectivity bias approach with a continuous choice variable. *Econometrica* 52:1199–1218.

Glaeser, E.L. and J.A. Scheinkman. 2001. Measuring social interactions. In *Social Dynamics*, ed. S.N. Durlauf and H.P. Young, 83–131. London: MIT Press.

Goldin, C. and L.F. Katz. 2000. The power of the pill: oral contraceptives and women's career and marriage decisions. Cambridge, MA: National Bureau of Economic Research Working Paper 7527.

Haurin, D.R., P.H. Hendershott and D. Kim. 1993. The impact of real rents and wages on household formation. *Review of Economics and Statistics* 75: 284–293.

_____. 1994. Housing decisions of American youth. *Journal of Urban Economics* 35: 28–44.

Heckman, J.J. 1979. Sample selection bias as specification error. *Econometrica* 47: 153–162.

Heckman, J.J. and R.J. Willis. 1976. Estimation of a stochastic model of reproduction: an econometric approach. In *Household Production and Consumption*, ed. N. Terleckyj. New York: Columbia University Press.

Hotz, V.J., J. Klerman and R.J. Willis. 1997. The economics of fertility in developed countries. In *Handbook of Population and Family Economics*, ed. M.R. Rosenzweig and O. Stark, 75–347. Amsterdam: Elsevier.

Jarvis, S. and S.P. Jenkins. 1999. Marital splits and income changes: evidence from the British Household Panel Survey. *Population Studies* 53: 237–254.

Jürges, H. 2000. Of rotten kids and Rawlsian parents: the optimal timing of intergenerational transfers. *Journal of Population Economics* 13: 147–158.

Kiernan, K. 1999. Cohabitation in Western Europe. *Population Trends* 96: 25–32.

Kohler, H.-P. 2001. *Fertility and Social Interaction*. Oxford: Oxford University Press.

Kohler, H.-P., J.R. Behrman and S.C. Watkins. 2001. The density of social networks and fertility decisions: evidence from the South Nyanza District, Kenya. *Demography* 38: 43–58.

Konrad, K. and K.E. Lommerud. 1995. Family policy with non-cooperative families. *Scandinavian Journal of Economics* 97: 581–601.

Koopmans, T.C. and M. Beckman. 1957. Assignment problems and the location of economic activities. *Econometrica* 25: 53–76.

Kotlikoff, L.J. and L.H. Summers. 1981. The role of intergenerational transfers in aggregate capital accumulation. *Journal of Political Economy* 89: 706–732.

Lam, D. 1988. Marriage markets and assortative mating with household public goods. *Journal of Human Resources* 23: 462–487.

Laslet, P. 1980. Introduction: comparing illegitimacy over time and between cultures. In *Bastardy and Its Comparative History*, ed. P. Laslet, K. Oosterveen and R. Smith. London: Edward Arnold.

Lichter, D.L. and D.R. Graefe. 2001. Find a mate? The marital and cohabitation histories of unwed mothers. In *Out of Wedlock*, ed. L. Wu and B. Wolfe, 317–343. New York: Russell Sage Foundation.

Lillard, L.A. and L.J. Waite. 1993. A joint model of childbearing and marital disruption. *Demography* 30: 653–681.

Lindbeck, A. and J.W. Weibull. 1988. Altruism and time consistency: the economics of fait accompli. *Journal of Political Economy* 96: 1165–1182.

Lundberg, S. 1988. Labor supply of husbands and wives: a simultaneous equations approach. *Review of Economics and Statistics* 70: 224–235.

Lundberg, S. and R. Pollack. 1993. Separate spheres bargaining and the marriage market. *Journal of Political Economy* 101: 988–1010.

——. 2001. Efficiency in marriage. Cambridge, MA: National Bureau of Economic Research Working Paper 8642.

Lundberg, S., R. Pollack and T. Wales. 1997. Do husbands and wives pool their resources? *Journal of Human Resources* 32: 461–480.

Manser, M. and M. Brown. 1980. Marriage and household decision-making: a bargaining analysis *International Economic Review* 21: 31–44.

Manski, C. 1993. Identification of endogenous social effects: the reflection problem. *Review of Economic Studies* 60: 531–542.

McElroy, M.B. 1990. The empirical content of Nash-bargained household behavior. *Journal of Human Resources* 25: 559–583.

McElroy, M.B. and M.J. Horney. 1981. Nash-bargained household decisions: toward a generalization of the theory of demand. *International Economic Review* 22: 333–349.

Mincer, J. 1963. Market prices, opportunity costs and income effects. In *Measurement in Economics: Studies in Mathematical Economics in Honor of Yehuda Grunfeld*, ed. C.F. Christ, M. Friedman, L.A. Goodman et al., 67–82. Stanford, CA: Stanford University Press.

Mnookin, R.H. and L. Kornhauser. 1979. Bargaining in the shadow of the law. *Yale Law Journal* 88: 950–997.

Moffitt, R. 1984. Optimal life-cycle profiles of fertility and labor supply. *Research in Population Economics* 5: 29–50.

——. 2001. Policy interventions, low-level equilibria, and social interactions. In *Social Dynamics*, ed. S.N. Durlauf and H.P. Young. London: MIT Press.

Nash, J.F. 1950a. The bargaining problem. *Econometrica* 18: 155–162.

——. 1950b. Equilibrium points in *n*-person games. *Proceedings of the National Academy of Sciences USA* 36: 48–49.

Olsen, R.J. and G. Farkas. 1990. The effect of economic opportunity and family background on adolescent cohabitation and childbearing among low-income blacks. *Journal of Labor Economics* 8: 341–362.

Oosterveen, K., R.M. Smith and S. Stewart. 1980. Family reconstitution and the study of bastardy: evidence from certain English parishes. In *Bastardy and Its Comparative History*, ed. P. Laslet, K. Oosterveen and R. Smith. London: Edward Arnold.

Peters, H.E. 1986. Marriage and divorce: informational constraints and private contracting. *American Economic Review* 76: 437–454.

Rao, V. 1993. The rising price of husbands: a hedonic analysis of dowry increases in rural India. *Journal of Political Economy* 101: 666–677.

Rosenzweig, M.R. 1988. Risk, implicit contracts and the family in rural areas of low-income countries. *Economic Journal* 98: 1148–1170.

_____. 1990. Population growth and human capital investments: theory and evidence. *Journal of Political Economy* 98: S38–S70.

_____. 1993. Women, insurance capital, and economic development in rural India. *Journal of Human Resources* 28: 735–758.

Rosenzweig, M.R. and T.P. Schultz. 1985. The demand for and supply of births: fertility and its life cycle consequences. *American Economic Review* 75: 992–1015.

_____. 1987. Fertility and investments in human capital: estimates of the consequence of imperfect fertility control in Malaysia. *Journal of Econometrics* 36: 163–184.

Rosenzweig, M.R. and O. Stark. 1989. Consumption smoothing, migration, and marriage: evidence from India. *Journal of Political Economy* 97: 905–926.

Rosenzweig, M.R. and K. Wolpin. 1980. Testing the quantity–quality model of fertility: the use of twins as a natural experiment. *Econometrica* 48: 227–240.

_____. 1993. Intergenerational support and the life cycle: incomes of young men and their parents: human capital investments, coresidence, and intergenerational transfers. *Journal of Labor Economics* 11: 84–112.

_____. 1994. Parental and public transfers to young women and their children. *American Economic Review* 84: 1195–1212.

_____. 1995. Sisters, siblings, and mothers: the effect of teen-age childbearing on birth outcomes in a dynamic family context. *Econometrica* 63: 303–326.

Rubinstein, A. 1982. Perfect equilibrium in a bargaining model. *Econometrica* 50: 97–109.

Sah, R. 1991. The effect of child mortality changes on fertility choice and parental welfare. *Journal of Political Economy* 99: 582–606.

Sahib, P.R. and X. Gu. 2002. "Living in sin" and marriage: a matching model. *Journal of Population Economics* 15: 261–282.

Samuelson, P.A. 1954. The pure theory of public expenditure. *Review of Economics and Statistics* 36: 387–389.

_____. 1956. Social indifference curves. *Quarterly Journal of Economics* 70: 1–22.

Schelling, T.C. 1960. *The Strategy of Conflict*. Cambridge, MA: Harvard University Press.

_____. 1978. *Micromotives and Macrobehavior*. New York: W.W. Norton.

Schultz, T.P. 1997. Demand for children in low income countries. In *Handbook of Population and Family Economics*, ed. M.R. Rosenzweig and O. Stark, 349–430. Amsterdam: Elsevier.

Smith, C. 2002. The Child Support Payment Behaviour of Noncustodial Fathers, and the Impact of Child Support Payments on the Behaviour of UK Lone Mothers: Econometric Analyses. Ph.D. Thesis, University of Essex.

Smout, C. 1980. Aspects of sexual behaviour in nineteenth century Scotland. In *Bastardy and Its Comparative History*, ed. P. Laslet, K. Oosterveen and R. Smith. London: Edward Arnold.

Upchurch, D., L.A. Lillard and C.W.A. Panis. 2001. The impact of nonmarital childbearing on subsequent marital formation and dissolution. In *Out of Wedlock*, ed. L. Wu and B. Wolfe, 344–380. New York: Russell Sage Foundation.

Warr, P. 1982. Pareto optimal redistribution and private charity. *Journal of Public Economics* 19: 131–138.

Weiss, Y. 1997. The formation and dissolution of families: Why marry? Who marries whom? And what happens upon divorce? In *Handbook of Population and Family Economics*, ed. M.R. Rosenzweig and O. Stark, 82–123. Amsterdam: Elsevier.

Weiss, Y. and R.J. Willis. 1985. Children as collective goods and divorce settlements. *Journal of Labor Economics* 3: 268–292.

_____. 1993. Transfers among divorced couples: evidence and interpretation. *Journal of Labor Economics* 11: 629–679.

_____. 1997. Match quality, new information, and marital dissolution. *Journal of Labor Economics* 15: S293–S329.

Willis, R.J. 1973. A new approach to the economic theory of fertility behavior. *Journal of Political Economy* 81: S14–S64.

_____. 1999. A theory of out-of-wedlock childbearing. *Journal of Political Economy* 107: S33–S64.

Wilson, W.J. 1987. *The Truly Disadvantaged*. Chicago, IL: University of Chicago Press.

Wolpin, K. 1984. An estimable dynamic stochastic model of fertility and child mortality. *Journal of Political Economy* 92: 852–874.

Wrightson, K. 1980. The nadir of English illegitimacy in the seventeenth century. In *Bastardy and its Comparative History*, ed. P. Laslett, K. Oosterveen and R. Smith, 176–191. London: Edward Arnold.

Zhang, J. and W. Chan. 1999. Dowry and wife's welfare: a theoretical and empirical analysis. *Journal of Political Economy* 107: 786–808.

Index